The Norton Sampler

Second Edition

The Norton Sampler

Short Essays for Composition

Second Edition

Thomas Cooley

The Ohio State University

W · W · NORTON & COMPANY

New York · London

W. W. Norton & Company, Inc., 500 Fifth Avenue, New York, N.Y. 10110
W. W. Norton & Company Ltd., 37 Great Russell Street, London WC1B 3NU

ISBN 0 393 95179 0

1 2 3 4 5 6 7 8 9 0

Contents

Exposition

2. Essays That Classify and Divide

3. Essays That Analyze a Process

Preface

In its first edition, the *Sampler* was subjected to a rigorous trial by examination that the editor is gratified to have passed. The book was adopted at nearly six hundred schools, and one hundred teachers graciously responded to a detailed questionnaire supplied by the publisher. Those responses, along with my own experience of the last three years discovering which essays work best in the classroom, have guided me in the revisions for the second edition.

They have been extensive. Fifteen of the old essays have been replaced with twenty new ones. The chapters on "Persuasion and Argumentation," especially, have been augmented. As before, my first concern has been to find well-written essays that illustrate standard rhetorical strategies and that appeal to students with diverse backgrounds and interests. In this edition, I have sought to broaden that appeal even further by supplying essays covering a still wider range of human experience. Thus there are more contributions by women, on both feminist and non-feminist topics, and more minority voices. The changes bring the total to forty-seven essays, *all* of which are complete.

It was Edgar Allan Poe who said that a long poem does not exist. As editor of these short readings for composition, I have kept in mind the unity of effect that Poe taught us to value. Most of the essays in this collection, therefore, are only two to four pages long, and even the longest can be easily read at a single sitting.

It is misleading to talk about unity, I believe, however, when one is dealing with a fragment. How do we tell our students about beginnings, middles, and ends or about an author's shapely rhetoric when the shape is actually an editor's? (I have found that even "classics" such as Alexander Petrunkevitch's "The Spider and the Wasp" are routinely reprinted with amputations.) It is the

rhetoric of the short piece that our students are learning in beginning composition classes, and such pieces have their own unique
rules of order. Thus I have taken pains to gather complete essays
or, in a few cases (indicated in the headnotes), complete *chapters*
of books.

The organization of the *Sampler* remains the same, and it still
represents but one way of proceeding, hardly the only way. The
first chapter provides sample paragraphs for teachers who like to
discuss the parts of an essay before examining the kinds, and it
also demonstrates the basic technique of explaining by examples.
Of the traditional modes of discourse that organize the rest of the
volume, narration comes first because these are personal narratives
and many teachers may want to have students tell about their own
lives in their first complete essays.

The next six chapters, the bulk of the book, illustrate strategies
of exposition and can be taken up in any order, though here the
plan has been to build from the simple (as I perceive it) to the
more complex. For example: Chapter 5 ("Essays That Define")
presents extended definitions that draw upon the techniques of
classification and analysis discussed earlier.

Description is treated in a single chapter (Chapter 8) because
this mode is seldom isolated from the others in practice; the
teacher who requires more examples will find them throughout
the collection. Chapters 9 and 10 are devoted to persuasion and
argumentation, and they observe the classical division of persuasion into *logos, pathos,* and *ethos* (although I have not burdened
the student with these terms). Some teachers will want to start
here.

The questions after each selection are intended to help students
understand what they are reading and especially to aid them in
analyzing standard rhetorical strategies and techniques. The comparative questions—which invite students to make connections
between essays—are an innovation; and so is the inclusion of
student essays in full parity with those of the professionals. The
"Essays for Further Reading" are more complicated, and generally
longer, than the rest; but they too have been selected from a wide
range of subjects. The editor has, therefore, resisted the temptation to make them exclusively—or even largely—"literary."

Many people have helped in the preparation of this second edition of the *Sampler,* and it is a pleasure to name them here: Kim
Diane Gainer, Sheila P. Cooley, John Lauritsen, Paula Thompson,
and members of the staff at W. W. Norton—especially Nancy

Palmquist and my fine editor and friend Barry Wade—have devoted many hours to this book. The following colleagues, students, and friends at Ohio State have also been most helpful with the new edition: William Allen, Richard D. Altick, Daniel R. Barnes, Madeline Barnes, Gail Burke, Katherine Burkman, Ellen Carter, Edward P. J. Corbett, William Ellis, Ronald Fortune, David O. Frantz, Paul Fullmer, John B. Gabel, James Griffith, Katharine Hoch, Julian H. Markels, Betty Milum, Richard Milum, Patrick Moore, Mildred Munday, Frank O'Hare, W. N. Protheroe, Barbara Rigney, David Robinson, Joan Samuelson, Arnold Shapiro, Frances Shapiro, Pamela Transue, Charles Wheeler, and Christian K. Zacher.

For the criticism and encouragement that guided me in the initial stages of writing, I wish to thank the following at other places: Judith Barnet, Cape Cod Community College; Richard Benston, Bakersfield College; Harry Brent, Rutgers University—Camden College of Arts and Sciences; Lois Bueler, Winona State University; Larry Carver, the University of Texas at Austin; John Cope, Western State College of Colorado; Charles B. Dodson, University of North Carolina at Wilmington; Betty Flowers, the University of Texas at Austin; Ramsey Fowler, Memphis State University; Barbara Goff, Rutgers University—Cook College; David Goslee, the University of Tennessee; William Gracie, Miami University; Joan Hartman, the College of Staten Island; Robert W. Hill, Clemson University; John Huxhold, Meramec Community College; Bernetta Jackson, Washington University; H. Gerald Joiner, Clayton Junior College; Russ Larson, Eastern Michigan University; Kristin Lauer, Fordham University; James MacKillop, Onondaga Community College; Catharine McCue, Framingham State College; John Mellon, University of Illinois at Chicago Circle; Tom Miles, West Virginia University; Robin Mitchell, Marquette University; James Murphy, California State University—Hayward; Elizabeth Penfield, University of New Orleans; Richard Poulsen, Brigham Young University; Kenn Sherwood Roe, Shasta College; Charles Schuster, the University of Iowa; Jayana Sheth, Baruch College; Susan Shreve, George Mason University; Lynne Shuster, Erie Community College; Donald Smith, University of New Haven; Tori Haring Smith, University of Illinois at Urbana-Champaign; Craig Snow, the University of Arizona; William Tucker, the University of North Carolina at Greensboro; John L. Vifian, Central Washington State College; and J. Peter Williams, County College of Morris.

The Norton Sampler

Second Edition

Introduction

Suppose that you went on a strenuous camping trip in the mountains, while all your friends decided to relax at the seashore. Suppose, also, that you got bored after two days without company and that you composed a letter inviting your best friend to forsake the surf and join you on the rocks. Your letter might contain the following elements:

— the story of your time on the road, your arrival in camp, and the events of the first two days, including an account of the skunk that got into your provisions;
— directions for getting there and a list of equipment, food, and clothes to bring;
— a description of your campsite, the yellow tent, the beautiful blue valley in the distance, and the crystal lake nearby;
— all the reasons why your friend should join you and why the mountains are preferable to the shore.

The four parts of your letter would conform to the four traditional MODES [1] (or "means") of writing: NARRATION, EXPOSITION, DESCRIPTION, and PERSUASION. The first part would be in the narrative mode. Narration is writing that tells a story; it records events, actions, adventures. It tells, in short, what happened. The part of your letter that gives directions is exposition. This is informative writing, or writing that explains. In this book, exposition receives more attention than the other modes because it is the one you are likely to use most often in the years to come. Examinations, term papers, insurance claims, job and graduate school applications, sales reports, almost every scrap of practical

---

[1] Terms printed in all capitals are defined in the Glossary.

prose you write over a lifetime, including your last will and testament, will demand expository skills.

The third part of your letter, of course, is description. This is the mode that captures how a person, thing, place, or idea looks, feels, sounds, or otherwise impresses the senses or the mind. The last part of your letter, the part designed to convince your friend to join you, is in the persuasive mode. Persuasion is writing that seeks assent, conveys advice, or moves the reader to action. In a sense, all writing is persuasion because the writer must convince the reader that what he or she says deserves to be heeded.

As our hypothetical letter to a friend suggests, the four modes of writing seldom appear in "pure" states. An accomplished writer is not likely to say, "Well I shall produce an expository definition today." The mode (or means) that a writer chooses will vary with his or her purpose (as in our letter). A writer may set out to define something and end up describing it or telling the story of its invention. Writers often mix the modes in actual practice, and you will find more than one essay in this collection that could be placed under a different heading.

Nevertheless, a single mode often dominates the others in any given essay. Furthermore, composing themes that largely narrate, explain, describe, or persuade is a valuable exercise toward learning to write well; and so is concentrating on a single strategy within a mode. A good piece of exposition, for example, may follow several methods of development; but before learning to combine, say, PROCESS ANALYSIS with DEFINITION it is useful to study each of these strategies independently. Therefore, the modes and strategies of writing have been separated in this book.

The narrative mode is exemplified in Chapter 1 ("Essays in the First Person Singular"). The next six chapters (2–7) give examples of the common strategies of exposition: CLASSIFICATION, PROCESS ANALYSIS, CAUSE AND EFFECT, DEFINITION, COMPARISON AND CONTRAST, METAPHOR AND ANALOGY. Chapter 8 ("Essays That Appeal to the Senses") is a collection of descriptive writing. Chapter 9 ("Essays That Appeal to Reason") and Chapter 10 ("Essays That Appeal to Emotion and Ethics") present examples of the different strategies of persuasion. At the end of the book you will find a collection of "Essays for Further Reading."

No one expects you to imitate word for word these highly finished productions of professional writers (though you may well emulate some of the student writing included here). But you can analyze standard rhetorical devices and techniques and so learn to use them in your own writing.

By RHETORIC, as the term will be applied in these pages, we mean "the art of using language effectively"—both in writing and in reading. A skilled writer is usually a skilled reader, in fact. The patterns of words on the written page (and of the sounds those words stand for) lodge themselves in the reader's head. When the writer puts pen to paper, therefore, he or she has a store of patterns to impose upon his or her own black marks. A writer learns some patterns of language by hearing them used orally. But others—such as the printed alphabet—can only be learned by reading.

The purpose of this collection of readings, then, is that set forth by Mark Twain in "The Art of Authorship." Attempting to analyze his own methods of composition, Twain found that "whenever we read a sentence and like it, we unconsciously store it away in our model-chamber; and it goes with a myriad of its fellows to the building, brick, by brick, of the eventual edifice which we call our style. And let us guess that whenever we run across other forms— bricks—whose color, or some other defect, offends us, we unconsciously reject these, and so one never finds them in our edifice."

This is a book of prose forms. Each essay offers proven rhetorical designs that you can store away in your "model-chamber," ready at hand whenever you have a verbal edifice to construct. Such a collection provides this further advantage over reading at random: the defective bricks have already been discarded for you.

Paragraphs
for Analysis

Beginning with Chapter 1, this book presents entire essays.
Since an essay, like a stereo system, is made up of integrated
components, however, you may want to start with the following model paragraphs, included here for two purposes.
First, they illustrate the standard ways in which paragraphs
function and develop. We begin with an introductory paragraph from the opening of an essay that appears complete
in a later chapter. It is followed by a TRANSITION [1] paragraph
and a concluding paragraph; but the "parent" essays are not
included, so you will have to surmise what has gone before
or after. The last four selections, each lifted from the main
body of its parent essay, illustrate various methods of paragraph development. They are arranged in order of increasing
complexity.

The second purpose of these sample paragraphs is to show
how good writers use specific examples to help explain their
ideas. When John McPhee says that the history of Florida
is measured in freezes, he backs up this claim by citing the
good people of Keystone City during the Great Freeze of
1895. When William Allen defines "style" by telling how
he combed his hair in high school, this concrete example
gives us a tight grip on a slippery subject. Selected for their
use of lively examples like these, the following paragraphs
isolate, for careful study, a basic strategy of informative and
persuasive writing that you will encounter in almost every
essay in this book.

The traditional definition of a paragraph is a group of

---

[1] Terms printed in all capitals are defined in the Glossary.

related sentences on the same topic. This definition suggests two important facts about paragraphs in general. One is that paragraphs build up by a process of addition. A paragraph combines two or more statements into a unit of thought. That unit is the sum of its parts, for no single part carries the entire meaning of the paragraph in all its complexity.

The other fundamental aspect of paragraphs is suggested by that word related in our definition. The sentences in a paragraph must stand in some recognizable relation to one another. If you combine the last sentence of each chapter in this book and, after indenting, run them all together on the same page, you will assemble only a cluster of unrelated sentences, hardly a paragraph. A good paragraph develops a topic in some systematic way. It can unfold in chronological order (as in NARRATIVE writing). It can develop spatially (as in DESCRIPTION), ranging over an object from left to right, top to bottom, front to back. Or, in EXPOSITORY writing, a paragraph can progress from step to step of a logical ARGUMENT, by assertion and example, COMPARISON AND CONTRAST, CAUSE AND EFFECT, statement and restatement.

The movement of a paragraph depends upon what it says. However, that movement can be traced through grammatical clues. These are often connecting words like and, but, although, therefore, on the other hand, moreover, now, consequently, and for example. But they may also be verbs (or other parts of speech): conclude, infer, imply, disagree. Such words glance backward to statements that the writer has entertained for a moment and forward to statements that complete, qualify, or deny what has gone before. In the following paragraphs, look for grammatical clues that can help you analyze how each paragraph is organized. An understanding of the basic principles of paragraph structure is a big step toward writing well-organized paragraphs of your own.

Alexander Petrunkevitch
Intelligence vs. Instinct

Alexander Petrunkevitch (1875–1964) was a Yale professor of zoology and one of the world's leading experts on spiders. "Intelligence vs. Instinct" (editor's title) is a paragraph from his essay, "The Spider and the Wasp," reprinted in its entirety and with more information about the author in Chapter 3 ("Essays That Analyze a Process"). This model introductory paragraph comes near the beginning of its parent essay and sets up much of what follows. Notice that it makes a clear general statement of the author's subject but only hints at details. The author is showing his hand and then taking it up again, ready to play his cards one by one. The study questions following this and each selection in these pages should help you to understand not only what an author is saying but how it is said.

In the feeding and safeguarding of their progeny the insects and spiders exhibit some interesting analogies to reasoning and some crass examples of blind instinct. The case I propose to describe here is that of the tarantula spiders and their arch-enemy, the digger wasps of the genus Pepsis. It is a classic example of what looks like intelligence pitted against instinct—a strange situation in which the victim, though fully able to defend itself, submits unwittingly to its destruction.

QUESTIONS

Understanding

1. Why do the wasps and spiders that Petrunkevitch is going to discuss fight each other?
2. What *human* qualities does their combat display?

Strategies and Structure

1. You cannot be sure until you have seen this paragraph in the context of its parent essay, but which sentence appears to be the TOPIC SENTENCE (the one that states the author's main subject most precisely)?
2. Is the author's main topic developed fully here or merely stated for future development? Explain your answer.
3. From this paragraph, we know that the loser in the combat between wasp and spider is destroyed, but we do not know which insect is the victim. Why might the author not want to tell us in an introductory paragraph like this one?

4. What aspect of the "case" of spider and wasp is likely to receive most of the author's attention in the essay to come? How does this paragraph anticipate that interest?

Words and Figures of Speech

1. Consult your dictionary for the definition of *progeny* if you do not already know the word.
2. What is an ANALOGY?

Comparing

1. When you read "The Spider and the Wasp" in Chapter 3 (or you may want to take a peek now), see if your answers to the "Strategies and Structure" questions were reasonably accurate.

Discussion and Writing Topics

1. Write a paragraph describing an insect or animal doing something that seems to exhibit human intelligence. For example: a raccoon opening a garbage can.

Shana Alexander

Fashions in Funerals

Born in New York City in 1925, Shana Alexander is a journalist and broadcaster. Since attending Vassar College, she has worked as an editor for Harper's Bazaar, Flair, Life, McCall's, Newsweek, and other publications. As a radio and television commentator for CBS News, she has appeared on "Spectrum" and "60 Minutes." Her books include The Feminine Eye (1970) and Talking Woman (1976), the source of the following passage. It is a TRANSITION paragraph from an essay comparing the funeral customs of cannibals with those in Nashville, Tennessee, home of the high-rise mausoleum and drive-in funeral. With the aid of the study questions, see if you can read Alexander's clues to what comes before and after.

When word of the feast reached civilization, the authorities concluded that on this occasion justice had literally been served, and perhaps a bit too swiftly, so they hauled the seven cannibals into court, where a wise Australian judge dismissed all the charges, and acquitted the seven men. "The funerary customs of the people of Papua and New Guinea," he explained, "have been, and in many cases remain, bizarre in the extreme."

QUESTIONS

Understanding

1. Why does the Australian judge dismiss the charges against the cannibals?
2. What is Shana Alexander's opinion of the judge's decision?

Strategies and Structure

1. What incident has Alexander probably just described in the essay from which this transition paragraph is taken? Point out the clues by which she suggests what has gone before.
2. You cannot tell from this paragraph that the author will later discuss funeral customs in Nashville, but the paragraph does anticipate a comparison between the customs of "civilized" society and those of primitive society. How? By what signals does it alert us to such a comparison?
3. Do you think the author of this paragraph will go on to write an essay that shows the superiority of modern civilization over primitive "savagery" or one that shows such terms to be relative, open to judgment? Explain your answer by referring to specific words and phrases in the paragraph.

Words and Figures of Speech

1. What are the CONNOTATIONS of *bizarre*?
2. Explain the pun in Alexander's first sentence.

Comparing

1. How does the TONE of this paragraph differ from Petrunkevitch's tone in the preceding paragraph?

Discussion and Writing Topics

1. Write a paragraph explaining a funeral custom you consider bizarre and pointing forward or backward to an example of its observance that you do not actually describe.

Roger Angell
Time Out

A native of New York City and graduate of Harvard (A.B., 1942), Roger Angell has been a sportswriter and editor for The New Yorker since 1956. Author of The Stone Arbor and Other Stories (1960) and A Day in the Life of Roger Angell (1970), a collection of humorous sketches, he has also written The Summer Game (1972), a book on baseball and the American mind. "Time Out" (editor's title) appears at the end of The Summer Game. It is a model concluding paragraph that recalls and rounds out what has gone before. Again, look for the signals that help us identify its context.

The last dimension is time. Within the ballpark, time moves differently, marked by no clock except the events of the game. This is the unique, unchangeable feature of baseball, and perhaps explains why this sport, for all the enormous changes it has undergone in the past decade or two, remains somehow rustic, unviolent, and introspective. Baseball's time is seamless and invisible, a bubble within which players move at exactly the same pace and rhythms as all their predecessors. This is the way the game was played in our youth and in our fathers' youth, and even back then—back in the country days—there must have been the same feeling that time could be stopped. Since baseball time is measured only in outs, all you have to do is succeed utterly; keep hitting, keep the rally alive, and you have defeated time. You remain forever young. Sitting in the stands, we sense this, if only dimly. The players below us—Mays, DiMaggio, Ruth, Snodgrass—swim and blur in memory, the ball floats over to Terry Turner, and the end of this game may never come.

QUESTIONS

Understanding

1. What is unique about the rules of baseball as Angell describes it? How does baseball differ from football and basketball in this regard?

2. Willie Mays entered the major leagues in 1951; Joseph Paul DiMaggio in 1936; George Herman Ruth in 1914; Fred Carlisle (Snow) Snodgrass in 1908; and Terence Lamont ("Cotton Top") Turner in 1901. Why do you think Angell's paragraph goes backward in time like this?

3. Where does "this game" in the final sentence take place? What implications does such a game hold for the individual baseball fan?

Strategies and Structure

1. What has Angell been discussing prior to these closing remarks? How does he let us know?

2. How does Angell create a sense of an ending in this concluding paragraph? Point to specific words and phrases that suggest finality.

3. What is the effect of Angell's referring to the reader as "you" in the closing sentences of the paragraph?

Words and Figures of Speech

1. What are the CONNOTATIONS of *rustic* (sentence 3)? How does Angell's use of this word help to define *country* two sentences earlier?

2. Why is *floats* (last sentence) appropriate in its context? What other verbs in the sentence does it resemble?

3. Because it is unbroken, Angell likens baseball's time to a "bubble"; what else does this ANALOGY suggest?

Comparing

1. When you read E. B. White's "Once More to the Lake" ("Essays for Further Reading"), compare his treatment of time with Angell's.

Discussion and Writing Topics

1. If successful batting stops time by (theoretically) prolonging a baseball game forever, what is the *pitcher's* role with regard to time? Write a paragraph describing that role.

2. What is the spectator's role at a baseball or football game? Are the players the fans' heroes or their scapegoats?

3. Unlike baseball as Angell describes it, professional football is neither "unviolent" nor "introspective." What does the tremendous popularity of football say about the changes in American culture since "the country days"?

Magda Denes
In an Abortion Hospital

Magda Denes is a clinical psychologist in private practice in New York City. At Yeshiva University (Ph.D., 1961) and New York University, she received training in Gestalt therapy, group therapy, and psychoanalysis. The mother of two children, she has also had first-hand experience with abortion. "In an Abortion Hospital" (editor's title) is from the preface of her recent book, In Necessity and Sorrow: Life and Death in an Abortion Hospital *(1976). The paragraph is structured by placing its component sentences "in parallel" with one another, a basic form of paragraph development.*

In some ways I am an exceptionally privileged woman of thirty-seven. I am in the room of a private, legal abortion hospital, where a surgeon, a friend of many years, is waiting for me in the operating room. I am only five weeks pregnant. Last week I walked out of another hospital, unaborted, because I had suddenly changed my mind. I have a husband who cares for me. He yells because my indecisiveness makes him anxious, but basically he has permitted the final choice to rest in my hands: "It would be very tough, especially for you, and it is absolutely insane, but yes, we could have another baby." I have a mother who cares. I have two young sons, whose small faces are the most moving arguments I have against going through with this abortion. I have a doctorate in psychology, which, among other advantages, assures me of the professional courtesy of special passes in hospitals, passes that at this moment enable my husband and my mother to stand in my room at a nonvisiting hour and yell at each other over my head while I sob.

QUESTIONS

Understanding

1. Why is the woman described in this paragraph stalling? What is her state of mind?
2. What clues does Denes give to suggest that the woman will not go through with the abortion on the occasion reported here?
3. What is the significance of the patient's having a doctorate in psychology? In what ways are her "privileges" irrelevant?

Strategies and Structure

1. The basic strategy of this paragraph is simple addition; it gives all ideas roughly equal weight by giving them parallel form. Point out (or underline) every use of "I am" or "I have" in the paragraph.
2. In which two sentences does Denes *not* follow this basic sentence pattern?
3. How does she vary the basic pattern (while still maintaining it) in the second and last sentences of the paragraph?
4. Given that the patient here is badly upset, why might Denes choose to relate her thoughts in a seemingly simple order?
5. How does the way the author organizes this paragraph show that she was in a different state of mind when she wrote it than when she was in the hospital?
6. Why is *sob* placed at the end of this paragraph? How would our response to the whole paragraph be different if this one word were placed, say, at the beginning?

Words and Figures of Speech

1. Why is the clinical term *unaborted* more appropriate here than words like *unsullied* or *undefiled*?

2. We are told that the faces of the author's two children are "moving arguments" against abortion. Faces are not literally arguments, but how might they inspire this METAPHOR?

Comparing

1. What fundamental difference do you see between the organization of this paragraph and that of the next one, by Jacob Bronowski?

Discussion and Writing Topics

1. Do you consider abortion an open or closed issue? If you think abortion is permissible under certain circumstances, what are they?
2. Why is the age of a fetus an important consideration in legal, religious, and personal debates about abortion? Should it be?
3. Feminists argue that a woman's body is hers to control. How does the abortion issue enter into this argument?

Jacob Bronowski

The Process of Learning

Polish-born Jacob Bronowski (1908–1974) was trained as a mathematician at Cambridge University. He taught at Oxford and other British universities, and in 1964 became resident fellow and trustee of the Salk Institute for Biological Studies in California. Interested throughout his life in the relation between the arts and science, he was a playwright, a radio commentator, an expert on the poet William Blake, and the author of many books, including Science and Human Values *(1958);* Insight *(1964); and* The Identity of Man *(1965). The following paragraph (with editor's title) is from* The Common Sense of Science *(1951); it demonstrates another basic form of paragraph development.*

The process of learning is essential to our lives. All higher animals seek it deliberately. They are inquisitive and they experiment. An experiment is a sort of harmless trial run of some action which we shall have to make in the real world; and this, whether it is made in the laboratory by scientists or by fox-cubs outside their earth. The scientist experiments and the cub plays; both are learning to correct their errors of judgement in a setting in which errors are not fatal. Perhaps this is what gives them both their air of happiness and freedom in these activities.

QUESTIONS

Understanding

1. What is an experiment as defined by Bronowski?
2. How do experiments, according to him, contribute to the process of learning?

Strategies and Structure

1. What is the TOPIC SENTENCE of this paragraph?
2. Do the other sentences in the paragraph repeat the idea of the topic sentence or narrow it down? Explain your answer.
3. Point out individual words that help to tie one of Bronowski's sentences to another because they appear in both sentences. How does Bronowski differ from Denes (preceding paragraph) in the use of this device of organization?
4. Given the flow of Bronowski's ideas from one sentence to another, why could he *not* have adopted the parallel form of the paragraph by Denes?

Words and Figures of Speech

1. Look up the root meaning of *experiment* in your dictionary. How does it fit the learning process that Bronowski describes?

Comparing

1. What does the structure of this paragraph have in common with the paragraph by Magda Denes? In what sense do both proceed by addition?
2. How do the "units" that Bronowski is adding together differ from those in Denes's paragraph?

Discussion and Writing Topics

1. Bronowski explains how men and animals test their judgment. How do they show their mutual "inquisitiveness" or curiosity?

John McPhee

Orange Freeze

Born in 1931, John McPhee is a native of Princeton, New Jersey, and a graduate of Princeton University, where he sometimes teaches creative writing. Most of the time, however, he is a magazine staff writer and editor for, among others, The New Yorker, Time, Holiday, National Geographic, and Playboy. Known for his precise style and wide range of interests, he has written a number of books, including A Sense of Where You Are (1965); The Pine Barrens (1968); The Crofter and the Laird (1969); The Deltoid Pumpkin Seed (1973, a study of experimental aircraft); The Survival of the Bark Canoe (1975); and Coming into the Country (1978). "Orange Freeze" (editor's title) appeared in Oranges (1967). This paragraph has a more complex organization than the two preceeding paragraphs because it combines the methods of both.

The history of Florida is measured in freezes. Severe ones, for example, occurred in 1747, 1766, and 1774. The freeze of February, 1835, was probably the worst one in the state's history. But, because more growers were affected, the Great Freeze of 1895 seems to enjoy the same sort of status in Florida that the Blizzard of '88 once held in the North. Temperatures on the Ridge on February 8, 1895, went into the teens for much of the night. It is said that some orange growers, on being told what was happening out in the groves, got up from their dinner tables and left the state. In the morning, it was apparent that the Florida citrus industry had been virtually wiped out. The groves around Keystone City, in Polk County, however, went through the freeze of 1895 without damage. Slightly higher than anything around it and studded with sizable lakes, Keystone City became famous, and people from all over the Ridge came to marvel at this Garden

of Eden in the middle of the new wasteland. The citizens of
Keystone City changed the name of their town to Frostproof.

QUESTIONS

Understanding

1. Who (besides McPhee) measures the history of Florida in
   freezes? Why?
2. Why does McPhee mention the lakes around Keystone City?
3. What does their choice of a new name tell you about the citizens
   of that town?

Strategies and Structure

1. What is McPhee's TOPIC SENTENCE? How many examples does he
   give in support of it?
2. Point out the three sentences by which McPhee narrows down his
   initial idea (as Bronowski does in "The Process of Learning").
3. How do these three sentences stand in relation to *each other*? Are
   they on a par in meaning and in form (as in the paragraph by
   Magda Denes on abortion) or are some more narrow than others?
   Explain your answer.
4. What proposition, or statement, do sentences 5–7 illustrate?
5. Are the last three complete sentences of this paragraph "in parallel" (as in the Denes paragraph) or "in sequence" (as in the
   Bronowski paragraph)? Explain your answer.
6. How has McPhee shifted his focus by the end of this selection?
   From what to what? Is this a legitimate maneuver? Why or why
   not?

Words and Figures of Speech

1. How does McPhee's calling Keystone City a "Garden of Eden"
   contribute to the sense of the miraculous in the town's escape
   from the great freeze?

Comparing

1. How is McPhee's use of history and the past different from Roger
   Angell's in "Time Out"?

Discussion and Writing Topics

1. How did your hometown or county get its name? Is there an interesting history behind that name or the name of any other town in which you have lived?

William Allen

Haircut

> A native of Texas, William Allen is a writer, teacher, and holder
> of the world's record for stationary broom-balancing. (His essay
> "Toward an Understanding of Accidental Knots" is reprinted in
> Chapter 4 along with more biographical information about Allen.)
> "Haircut" (editor's title) is from the book, Starkweather (1976);
> it recalls the author's coming-of-age in the 1950s. Here is another
> example of the "mixed" paragraph development that places some
> sentences "in parallel" and others "in sequence." Most paragraphs,
> in fact, combine these two basic forms of organization.

My teen-age days were more style than substance. My friends and I realized at an early age the power and status of having an automobile, and I worked hard and saved my money to buy one. Within weeks after I got my 1953 Ford, it was shaved hood and deck, lowered in back, had pinstripes, twin glass-pack mufflers, skirts, Oldsmobile taillights, and a rolled and pleated interior. It was one of the better-looking cars in South Oak Cliff and, by doing things like occasionally skipping school and racking my pipes outside the classroom windows, I built an identity around it. Just as my car looked good but wasn't "hot," I spent more of my energy trying to look cool rather than being tough. We were all fanatics about our hair, working on it in the school restrooms until our arms grew weak. I plastered mine with Brylcreem and combed it in a weird, complicated style that Charlie [1] himself often wore. I can't tell you where the aesthetic sense came from

---

[1] Charles Starkweather, executed 12:04 A.M., June 25, 1959, for the murder of ten Nebraskans in eight days.

that developed that hairdo, but it was absolute and I was in ac-
cord with it. Using my comb and both hands, I would work till
I was ready to collapse—then finally it would be just right, a work
of art. During those days I walked around like I had a book on
my head, and was a master at avoiding areas likely to generate
sudden gusts of wind.

QUESTIONS

Understanding

1. What distinction can you make between a hairdo and hair? How
   might this distinction help you define the concept of style?
2. What does it mean to say that something has more style than
   substance?
3. Why does Allen end with a reference to the wind?

Strategies and Structure

1. This paragraph develops its topic by use of examples. What is
   Allen's TOPIC SENTENCE, and what are the two chief examples he
   uses to illustrate it?
2. Which sentence provides a TRANSITION from one example to the
   other?
3. Are the sentences explaining the first example arranged "in
   parallel" or "in sequence"?
4. How are the sentences arranged that explain the second example?
5. If you were breaking up Allen's paragraph into two paragraphs,
   where would you divide it? Would this division be an improvement? Why or why not?

Words and Figures of Speech

1. What does *style* mean when applied to writing?
2. What is an "aesthetic" sense? Look the word up in your dictionary. How is it different from *ascetic*?

Comparing

1. Both "Haircut" and "In an Abortion Hospital" incorporate ele-

ments of personal NARRATIVE (the kind of writing you will study in Chapter 1). Point out some of the narrative aspects of the two.

Discussion and Writing Topics

1. How was style achieved and measured in your high school?
2. What happened to those who could not keep up with the styles for lack of money or "coolness"?
3. Can you recall classmates who had substance that outweighed style? What were they like? (For an essay on this subject, see Ellen Willis's "Memoirs of a Non-Prom Queen" in Chapter 4.)
4. Do you find any evidence to suggest that the automobile is declining as a status symbol in America? What others seem to be going strong?

Narration

1

Essays in the First Person Singular

NARRATION [1] *is the story-telling mode of writing; it recounts actions and events; it answers the question, "What happened?" The essays in this chapter are written in the narrative mode. They are personal narratives in which each author records experiences from his or her private life.*

One reason for beginning with personal narratives is suggested by Henry David Thoreau's famous opening words in Walden:

In most books, the *I*, or first person, is omitted; in this it will be retained; that, in respect to egotism, is the main difference. We commonly do not remember that it is, after all, always the first person that is speaking. I should not talk so much about myself if there were anybody else whom I knew as well. . . . Moreover, I, on my side, require of every writer, first or last, a simple and sincere account of his own life. . . .

The common feature of these openly autobiographical selections is the controlling presence of a distinct personality— like yours. You may not think that you know yourself well, but whom do you know better?

Another reason for beginning with personal narratives is that essays have always been personal. Our modern word essay *comes from the French* essayer, *meaning "to try." An essay is your personal trial or attempt to grapple with a subject or problem. Yours and nobody else's. Another person addressing the same subject would necessarily speak in a different voice from a different perspective. Because they*

---

[1] Terms printed in all capitals are defined in the Glossary.

invited readers to listen in (like informal guests in the writer's living room), these modest attempts at self-expression became known as "personal" or "familiar" essays.

Any writer who gives an account of his or her own experiences must understand the difference between events and the telling of events. Think of actions as sounds for a moment—the sounds of a college band playing the national anthem. When the band strikes up "Oh, say can you see," your ear hears trombones, trumpets, and drums all in a single harmonious strain. If you were to look at the written parts of the different instruments in their music-holders, however, you would have to separate them. You might follow a single bar of trombone music, then race over to the trumpet section, then back to the drums. But you would be alternating between parts, as the readers of a book must do when his or her eyes move from left to right and down the printed page. Events in real life often occur simultaneously; in a written narrative, they must be printed in sequence.

The sequence of events in a narrative is called the PLOT; unlike random events in real life, the plot of a narrative must be controlled and directed by the narrator. So must the POINT OF VIEW. Point of view is the vantage from which a narrative is told. It is not a difficult concept to master if you think of the difference between watching a football game in the stadium and watching it on television. The camera controls your point of view on the screen; you see only what the camera focuses upon. In the stands, however, you are free to scan the entire field, to watch the quarterback or the line, to concentrate on the cheerleaders. Your point of view is determined by your eyes alone; your vantage is a high place above the total action.

In narration, point of view is controlled in part by the grammatical PERSON in which an author chooses to write. Many narratives are told "in the third person" or "from the third-person point of view." For example, you might write: "The tornado hit while George was playing cards; he had just drawn a third ace, but when he plunked it down, the table was gone." Here the narrator and George are different persons; the narrator does not say how George felt inside at the crucial moment; the story is told after the fact and from the outside (of George). The essays in this chapter are "first-person" narratives, the point of view you would adopt in an autobiography or an account of your adventures during the first day of your college career. Here the "I" is an actor in each drama, and we see the world of the narrative through the narrator's eyes.

Authors of narrative essays in the first person have great freedom: they may record their personal thoughts on anything that has happened to them. As attested by master essayist E. B. White (whose "Once More to the Lake" appears at the end of this volume), "There is one thing the essayist cannot do, though—he cannot indulge himself in deceit or in concealment, for he will be found out in no time." Modern readers of essays, like Thoreau, require a "simple and sincere account"—the sincerity that comes of personal integrity and the simplicity that comes from discipline. The essayist may wander at will, but may not ramble. He or she may be relaxed, even self-indulgent. But if the reader can not follow along because the essayist writes obscurely or is dishonest, their partnership will be disbanded. And this is what a personal essay amounts to, finally—a friendly partnership between reader and author.

Loren Eiseley

The Angry Winter

Born in Lincoln, Nebraska, in 1907, Loren Eiseley was a distinguished anthropologist and sociologist. After graduate work at the University of Pennsylvania, he taught there for twelve years before becoming Franklin Professor of Anthropology and History of Science in 1961. The recipient of more than a dozen honorary degrees from universities throughout the U.S. and Canada, he also taught at the University of Kansas, Oberlin College, Columbia, Berkeley, and Harvard. Eiseley's major works include The Immense Journey (1957); Darwin's Century (1958); The Firmament of Time (1960); The Mind as Nature (1962); and The Invisible Pyramid (1970). The following personal narrative is the complete Part 1, Chapter 5, of The Unexpected Universe (1969). It recalls a deep winter's conflict between the author and his dog. The volume bears the following dedication: "To Wolf, who sleeps forever with an ice age bone across his heart, the last gift of one who loved him."

A time comes when creatures whose destinies have crossed 1
somewhere in the remote past are forced to appraise each
other as though they were total strangers. I had been huddled
beside the fire one winter night, with the wind prowling outside and shaking the windows. The big shepherd dog on the
hearth before me occasionally glanced up affectionately,
sighed, and slept. I was working, actually, amidst the debris
of a far greater winter. On my desk lay the lance point of ice
age hunters and the heavy leg bone of a fossil bison. No remnants of flesh attached to these relics. The deed lay more than
ten thousand years remote. It was represented here by naked
flint and by bone so mineralized it rang when struck. As I

worked in my little circle of light, I absently laid the bone beside me on the floor. The hour had crept toward midnight. A grating noise, a heavy rasping of big teeth diverted me. I looked down.

The dog had risen. That rock-hard fragment of a vanished beast   2
was in his jaws and he was mouthing it with a fierce intensity I had never seen exhibited by him before.

"Wolf," I exclaimed, and stretched out my hand. The dog   3
backed up but did not yield. A low and steady rumbling began to rise in his chest, something out of a long-gone midnight. There was nothing in that bone to taste, but ancient shapes were moving in his mind and determining his utterance. Only fools gave up bones. He was warning me.

"Wolf," I chided again.   4

As I advanced, his teeth showed and his mouth wrinkled to   5
strike. The rumbling rose to a direct snarl. His flat head swayed low and wickedly as a reptile's above the floor. I was the most loved object in his universe, but the past was fully alive in him now. Its shadows were whispering in his mind. I knew he was not bluffing. If I made another step he would strike.

Yet his eyes were strained and desperate. "Do not," something   6
pleaded in the back of them, some affectionate thing that had followed at my heel all the days of his mortal life, "do not force me. I am what I am and cannot be otherwise because of the shadows. Do not reach out. You are a man, and my very god. I love you, but do not put out your hand. It is midnight. We are in another time, in the snow."

"The *other* time," the steady rumbling continued while I   7
paused, "the other time in the snow, the big, the final, the terrible snow, when the shape of this thing I hold spelled life. I will not give it up. I cannot. The shadows will not permit me. Do not put out your hand."

I stood silent, looking into his eyes, and heard his whisper   8
through. Slowly I drew back in understanding. The snarl diminished, ceased. As I retreated, the bone slumped to the floor. He placed a paw upon it, warningly.

And were there no shadows in my own mind, I wondered. Had   9
I not for a moment, in the grip of that savage utterance, been about to respond, to hurl myself upon him over an invisible haunch ten thousand years removed? Even to me the shadows had whispered—to me, the scholar in his study.

"Wolf," I said, but this time, holding a familiar leash, I spoke   10
from the door indifferently. "A walk in the snow." Instantly from
his eyes that other visitant receded. The bone was left lying. He
came eagerly to my side, accepting the leash and taking it in his
mouth as always.

A blizzard was raging when we went out, but he paid no heed.   11
On his thick fur the driving snow was soon clinging heavily. He
frolicked a little—though usually he was a grave dog—making up
to me for something still receding in his mind. I felt the snow-
flakes fall upon my face, and stood thinking of another time, and
another time still, until I was moving from midnight to midnight
under ever more remote and vaster snows. Wolf came to my side
with a little whimper. It was he who was civilized now. "Come
back to the fire," he nudged gently, "or you will be lost." Automatically I took the leash he offered. He led me safely home and
into the house.

"We have been very far away," I told him solemnly. "I think   12
there is something in us that we had both better try to forget."
Sprawled on the rug, Wolf made no response except to thump his
tail feebly out of courtesy. Already he was mostly asleep and
dreaming. By the movement of his feet I could see he was running
far upon some errand in which I played no part.

Softly I picked up his bone—our bone, rather—and replaced it   13
high on a shelf in my cabinet. As I snapped off the light the white
glow from the window seemed to augment itself and shine with a
deep, glacial blue. As far as I could see, nothing moved in the
long aisles of my neighbor's woods. There was no visible track,
and certainly no sound from the living. The snow continued to
fall steadily, but the wind, and the shadows it had brought, had
vanished.

QUESTIONS

Understanding

1. Who are the "creatures" of Eiseley's first sentence?
2. What "other time" is he talking about in paragraphs 6 and 7?
   Why was the "terrible" snow also "final" (par. 7)?
3. Apparently the dog in Eiseley's narrative is not hungry, because

he goes to sleep easily after playing. Why, then, does he snarl over a fossilized bone that he could not eat even if he wanted to?

4. What is it that both dog and man should try to forget in paragraph 12?

Strategies and Structure

1. The dog's resistance to the man (pars. 5–8) is one of the two principal actions in Eiseley's narrative. What is the other? Where is it narrated?

2. In Eiseley's little drama, setting and lighting effects are very important. What are the chief *places* of his narrative, and how do they serve him? How do the desklamp and the powerful "white glow" of the snow contribute to the real conflict of the drama?

3. Where does that drama actually take place?

4. What is the function of the leash in paragraph 11?

5. How is the man who tells this story different from the man it is told about?

6. As the narrator, Eiseley has the difficult task of portraying the thoughts of an animal. How does he solve this difficulty?

7. Why does Eiseley end by referring to his neighbor's woods and the vanished shadows?

Words and Figures of Speech

1. Why is "Wolf" an appropriate name for the dog in Eiseley's narrative?

2. There are literal shadows on the snow outside the scholar's window, but what are the "shadows" that flit through his mind and the mind of the dog?

3. Why might Eiseley picture himself as "huddled" by the fire while the wind is "prowling" outside (par. 1)? How does this METAPHOR fit in with the rest of the narrative?

4. What are the CONNOTATIONS of "glacial" in paragraph 13? Why do you suppose Eiseley chose this word instead of "diamond" or "ice" blue?

5. He does not use the word, but how might *instinct* be applied in a discussion of Eiseley's narrative?

6. Consult your dictionary for the meanings of any of the following words that are not familiar to you: *destiny* (par. 1), *appraise* (1), *debris* (1), *chide* (4), *visitant* (10), *augment* (13).

Comparing

1. Eiseley's personal narrative tells a story, but it also explains one cause of human (and animal) aggression. When you study CAUSE AND EFFECT essays in Chapter 4, compare Eiseley's analysis of aggressive behavior with Paul Colinvaux's in "Why Japan Bombed Pearl Harbor." Do they confirm or contradict one another?
2. When Eiseley's dog threatens to spring, which does he resemble more closely, the spider or the wasp in Alexander Petrunkevitch's essay on those two creatures in Chapter 3?

Discussion and Writing Topics

1. Tell the story of an occasion on which you almost "lost your head." Recount the events leading up to the incident in such a way as to suggest *why* you acted as you did.
2. It was once thought that criminals were throwbacks to man's animalistic ancestors. What do you think of this explanation for criminal behavior? Do you suppose Eiseley would accept it? Why or why not?
3. What is the "collective unconscious" posited by some modern psychologists?
4. What is a cultural anthropologist? What does he or she study?

David Dubber

Crossing the Bar on a Fiberglas Pole

David Dubber was a freshman at Indiana University when he wrote this account of breaking a collegiate pole-vaulting record. He graduated in 1967 with a B.S. in business, and now lives with his family in Evansville, Indiana. A professional writer in the public relations and advertising division of a large pharmaceutical company, Dubber recently began working on "an American fictional novel."

A one hundred foot asphalt runway leads to a metal shoot and metal standards and a crossbar. Behind the shoot rises a pile of foam rubber scraps. This is the pole vaulting field at the 1963 S. I. A. C. (Southern Indiana Athletic Conference) Track and Field Meet. The stands are filled.

The meet is over but the crowd has stayed to watch the finish of the pole-vaulting event. There are two television cameras trying to squeeze in just one more Double Cola commercial before swinging back to tape the last of the vaulting event. The crossbar has been raised to thirteen feet, six inches, nearly a foot higher than the old, long-standing record. It is my job—it seems my duty since I have kept the crowd—to gather my strength into one single attempt to propel my body up and over that crossbar with the aid of my fiberglas pole. Many times lately I have heard people debating whether or not the pliable fiberglas pole should be allowed in competition. People say that one has only to "hang on to the thing and it will throw you to any desired height."

These recollections bring me much bitterness as I stand

before my trial. I am developing a fatalistic attitude toward this towering height and wish I had never come out for track, or at least I wish I had never heard of this silly "bending" pole. But it is too late to untwine this tightly woven cord; the crowd is waiting. I completely dismiss distracting thoughts and put all my powers, mental and physical, into this one leap.

Mentally I run through the particulars of the vault. I have   4
counted my steps down to the tape mark on the runway where my left foot is to hit the runway for the last time. I must remember to keep my body loose to conserve strength. I must also remember to strike my left foot on the mark hard enough to give me a four-foot jump on the pole before switching my balance and strength to my hands; otherwise I will not get off the ground. It must be a quick and trained reflex that is well routed in the grooves of my mind.

Now the crowd is dead silent. I count ten as I leave the world—   5
seeing only the runway and crossbar directly ahead, believing only that I will succeed in clearing the bar, hearing only the beating of my own heart. Slowly I begin an easy jog down the runway as the pole I cling to bounces slightly in front of me in a syncopation of my steps. Gradually my speed picks up until my body attains a swift glide. The tip of the pole descends as I approach the shoot. Although my main concern is making good contact between the end of my pole and the shoot, I am also watching the tape marking. After a few years practice, a vaulter learns to compensate for any misjudgment the last few strides before he reaches the shoot. Through some inexplicable mechanism the vaulter's sub-conscious tells his body how much to shorten or lengthen the stride in order to hit the take-off mark. Just as the tip of my pole touches the backstop of the shoot, I push the pole straight forward and with one final bound I smack the pavement with the ball of my left foot and straighten my half bent left leg with a great thrust to give me my height on the pole.

All my weight shifts to my hands, and as the angle of the pole   6
increases toward the vertical, my body climbs to about three-fourths the height of the crossbar. As I come up I throw my head back toward the ground causing my hips to sweep upward until my feet pass through my line of vision and on, one foot further, so that I am now completely upside down. The pole bends suddenly to about four feet from the ground, and my body, remaining

in the inverted position, falls rapidly with it. In my upside down position, all the stress is put on the abdominal area of the body. The tension wrenches the stomach and the intestines. The pole now stops its bend and starts to reflex back up to a straight position, but my body is still falling straight down. At this moment the strain multiplies as my body is brought to an abrupt stop and then starts back in the opposite direction. The inverted position must be maintained. Unbelievable pressure is put on the abdominal area. My hands and fingers clench the pole like wrenches. Just as the deep-sea pole comes alive in the hands of a fisherman when he has hooked a fighting sailfish, this pole strains to pull away from me as it jiggles violently from side to side. I feel I can't hold on any longer. In my fury to keep from losing the pole I wish the people who had said one merely has to "hang on" to the fiberglas pole for the ride could take my place now and try "hanging on" to this monster. I feel the muscle fibers along my stomach straining to the point of popping, and my numb fingers seem to be slipping off the rising pole; but suddenly, my body ceases to resist and rises upward toward the stars.

I am amazed to realize that I am still on the pole. My body 7 writhes slowly to the left, and my feet come up to the crossbar. My body continues turning as the bar passes under my shins, knees, and thighs, and my body stops in a half-twist as the crossbar stands directly under my waist. At this point I lock my arms in a half-bent position, the pole begins its final slight bend. My waist is approximately three feet higher than my hands and well above the crossbar. The slight bend of the pole lowers my body four to six inches. I keep my arms locked in bent position as again the pressure mounts on my tight, quivering stomach muscles. As the pole becomes a straight line, I straighten my arms out keeping my head forward and down, my body arched into a parabola around the crossbar. I stiffen my arms, and the fingertips, tired and pained, become the only things supporting my weight on the pole. I push off with my stiff fingertips, pulling my elbows up, back, and over; I throw my head back as my weak fingers barely clear the bar. I let go of all tension and let my body fall easily, down, and backward—sinking into the soft white mass, seeing only the dark blue sky. Wait! Not only the dark blue sky, but also a crossbar lying across the tops of two standards up there in the heavens, quivering a bit perhaps, but not falling, not in a thousand years. The hundred or so people who have gathered around the pit rush to pick me up as the masses in the stands exhale a roar. I look back at the pole lying over there alone, still, and I know what a marvelous monster it is to ride.

QUESTIONS

Understanding

1. Dubber's job is to clear the bar at a record height. Why is it also his "duty" (par. 2)?

2. As the pole launches him upward, Dubber wishes that critics of the fiberglas pole could take his place. Why? What does he want them to find out?

3. Dubber is writing about a single event and a relatively unfamiliar sport, but what does his narrative suggest about competition in general?

Strategies and Structure

1. Why does Dubber keep referring to the fiberglas pole? Besides narrating the story of how he broke the record, what *argument* is he developing? What is the counterargument of his opponents?

2. What is the effect of the last sentence in paragraph 1? What difference would it have made if Dubber had written instead, "The stands *were* filled"?

3. If the opening paragraphs of this essay create suspense, does the last paragraph continue the suspense or resolve it? Explain your answer.

4. Dubber mentions the crowd at the beginning and end of his narrative. What happens to the crowd in between? Why?

5. To read the last three paragraphs of this essay takes much longer than an actual pole vault. Dubber could not possibly have formulated all these sensations while he broke the record. Does this mean his account is "untrue"? Why or why not?

Words and Figures of Speech

1. PERSONIFICATION is the device of conferring life on inanimate

objects. Where does Dubber use this figure of speech? Why does he use it?

2. When Dubber starts to "leave the world" (par. 5), he is taking off from the physical earth. In what other sense can these words be understood?

3. If you find anything awkward in the following phrases, suggest ways of changing them: "untwine this tightly woven cord" (par. 3); "abdominal area of the body" (6); "marvelous monster" (7).

Comparing

1. In Chapter 3, you will encounter essays that analyze processes. What process is Dubber explaining as he tells his story? When you read Ruth Rudner's "Body Surfing" (Chapter 3), ask yourself what attitude toward her sport Rudner's surfer shares with Dubber's pole-vaulter.

Discussion and Writing Topics

1. Has any experience in sports—a tournament competition, a particularly smooth dive, a lucky hook shot—made you understand for a moment how a champion athlete feels? Tell the story of that experience. Try to convey its sensations and the glimpse of mastery that it gave you.

2. Narrate your triumph in a board game (like Monopoly or chess) as if it required all the stamina, skill, and split-second timing of a field sport. Be as dramatic as you please.

3. Do you consider competition to be healthy? Why or why not? To what extent is it avoidable in life?

Joyce Maynard

Four Generations

Born in 1953, Joyce Maynard grew up in Durham, New Hampshire, where her father taught at the university. Maynard thus spent her adolescence in the 1960s, only she saw it as a time with no place for youth; at nineteen, while a sophomore at Yale, Maynard published her first book, Looking Backward: A Chronicle of Growing Up Old in the Sixties (1973). Since then, Maynard has produced the daughter so proudly displayed in "Four Generations" and a novel called Baby Love (1981). Published in 1979, the following personal narrative tells the story of another daughter's belated visit to the bedside of a dying grandparent.

My mother called last week to tell me that my grandmother is dying. She has refused an operation that would postpone, but not prevent, her death from pancreatic cancer. She can't eat, she has been hemorrhaging, and she has severe jaundice. "I always prided myself on being different," she told my mother. "Now I *am* different. I'm yellow." 1

My mother, teling me this news, began to cry. So I became the mother for a moment, reminding her, reasonably, that my grandmother is eighty-seven, she's had a full life, she has all her faculties, and no one who knows her could wish that she live long enough to lose them. Lately my mother has been finding notes in my grandmother's drawers at the nursing home, reminding her, "Joyce's husband's name is Steve. Their daughter is Audrey." In the last few years she hadn't had the strength to cook or garden, and she's begun to say she's had enough of living. 2

My grandmother was born in Russia, in 1892—the oldest 3

daughter in a large and prosperous Jewish family. But the prosperity didn't last. She tells stories of the pogroms and the cossacks who raped her when she was twelve. Soon after that, her family emigrated to Canada, where she met my grandfather.

Their children were the center of their life. The story I loved 4 best, as a child, was of my grandfather opening every box of Cracker Jack in the general store he ran, in search of the particular tin toy my mothed coveted. Though they never had much money, my grandmother saw to it that her daughter had elocution lessons and piano lessons, and assured her that she would go to college.

But while she was at college, my mother met my father, who 5 was blue-eyed and blond-haired and not Jewish. When my father sent love letters to my mother, my grandmother would open and hide them, and when my mother told her parents she was going to marry this man, my grandmother said if that happened, it would kill her.

Not likely, of course. My grandmother is a woman who used to 6 crack Brazil nuts open with her teeth, a woman who once lifted a car off the ground, when there was an accident and it had to be moved. She has been representing her death as imminent ever since I've known her—twenty-five years—and has discussed, at length, the distribution of her possessions and her lamb coat. Every time we said goodbye, after our annual visit to Winnipeg, she'd weep and say she'd never see us again. But in the meantime, while every other relative of her generation, and a good many of the younger ones, has died (nursed usually by her), she has kept making knishes, shopping for bargains, tending the healthiest plants I've ever seen.

After my grandfather died, my grandmother lived, more than 7 ever, through her children. When she came to visit, I would hide my diary. She couldn't understand any desire for privacy. She couldn't bear it if my mother left the house without her.

This possessiveness is what made my mother furious (and then 8 guilt-ridden that she felt that way, when of course she owed so much to her mother). So I harbored the resentment that my mother—the dutiful daughter—would not allow herself. I—who had always performed specially well for my grandmother, danced and sung for her, presented her with kisses and good report cards —stopped writing to her, ceased to visit.

But when I heard that she was dying, I realized I wanted to go to   9
Winnipeg to see her one more time. Mostly to make my mother
happy, I told myself (certain patterns being hard to break). But
also, I was offering up one more particularly fine accomplishment:
my own dark-eyed, dark-skinned, dark-haired daughter, whom my
grandmother had never met.

I put on my daughter's best dress for our visit to Winnipeg, the   10
way the best dresses were always put on me, and I filled my
pockets with animal crackers, in case Audrey started to cry. I
scrubbed her face mercilessly. On the elevator going up to her
room, I realized how much I was sweating.

Grandma was lying flat with an IV tube in her arm and her eyes   11
shut, but she opened them when I leaned over to kiss her. "It's
Fredelle's daughter, Joyce," I yelled, because she doesn't hear well
anymore, but I could see that no explanation was necessary. "You
came," she said. "You brought the baby."

Audrey is just one, but she has seen enough of the world to   12
know that people in beds are not meant to be so still and yellow,
and she looked frightened. I had never wanted, more, for her to
smile.

Then Grandma waved at her—the same kind of slow, finger-   13
flexing wave a baby makes—and Audrey waved back. I spread her
toys out on my grandmother's bed and sat her down. There she
stayed, most of the afternoon, playing and humming and sipping
on her bottle, taking a nap at one point, leaning against my grandmother's leg. When I cranked her Snoopy guitar, Audrey stood up
on the bed and danced. Grandma wouldn't talk much anymore,
though every once in a while she would say how sorry she was that
she wasn't having a better day. "I'm not always like this," she
said.

Mostly she just watched Audrey. Sometimes Audrey would get   14
off the bed, inspect the get-well cards, totter down the hall. "Where
is she?" Grandma kept asking. "Who's looking after her?" I had
the feeling, even then, that if I'd said, "Audrey's lighting matches,"
Grandma would have shot up to rescue her.

We were flying home that night, and I had dreaded telling her,   15
remembering all those other tearful partings. But in the end, I was
the one who cried. She had said she was ready to die. But as I
leaned over to stroke her forehead, what she said was, "I wish I
had your hair" and "I wish I was well."

On the plane flying home, with Audrey in my arms, I thought 16
about mothers and daughters, and the four generations of the family that I know most intimately. Every one of those mothers loves
and needs her daughter more than her daughter will love or need
her some day, and we are, each of us, the only person on earth
who is quite so consumingly interested in our child.

Sometimes I kiss and hug Audrey so much she starts crying— 17
which is, in effect, what my grandmother was doing to my mother,
all her life. And what makes my mother grieve right now, I think,
is not simply that her mother will die in a day or two, but that,
once her mother dies, there will never again be someone to love
her in quite such an unreserved, unquestioning way. No one else
who believes that, fifty years ago, she could have put Shirley Temple out of a job, no one else who remembers the moment of her
birth. She will only be a mother, then, not a daughter anymore.

Audrey and I have stopped over for a night in Toronto, where 18
my mother lives. Tomorrow she will go to a safe-deposit box at the
bank and take out the receipt for my grandmother's burial plot.
Then she will fly back to Winnipeg, where, for the first time in
anybody's memory, there was waist-high snow on April Fool's
Day. But tonight she is feeding me, as she always does when I
come, and I am eating more than I do anywhere else. I admire the
wedding china (once my grandmother's) that my mother has set
on the table. She says (the way Grandma used to say to her, of the
lamb coat), "Some day it will be yours."

QUESTIONS

Understanding

1. Who are the representatives of the four generations cited in Maynard's title? What do they have in common physically?
2. Why had Maynard stopped writing and visiting her Canadian
   grandmother before the last visit described here? Why does she go
   back to see the dying woman?
3. What does her treatment of Maynard's baby reveal about the
   grandmother? What does Maynard's presenting the baby as a
   proud "accomplishment" (par. 9) reveal about *her*?

4. How does Maynard treat her daughter when they are alone together?

5. With her own daughter, is Maynard breaking the generational pattern that has characterized her family for so long, or is she repeating it? Explain your answer.

6. Who seems to be more concerned with death here, the dying grandmother or the granddaughter? Why do you say so?

7. In Maynard's narrative, how does the grandmother's long-standing attitude toward her children and grandchildren resemble her attitude toward life when she is dying?

Strategies and Structure

1. Roughly how many years does Maynard's narrative span in all? Where does she mention the earliest years?

2. Most of Maynard's narrative tells what happened in the past, though not necessarily the distant past. After comparing the verb TENSES in paragraph 18 with those in paragraph 13, explain whether Maynard's visit to her dying grandmother is an event of the present or the past time of the narrative.

3. What events are taking place in the present time of Maynard's narrative?

4. "Four Generations" is both an account of events over time and a meditation upon their meaning. Point out passages in which Maynard comments directly on the meaning of events. How else does she give her narrative a sense of meditation or reflection?

5. By what carefully selected specific details does Maynard give us a picture of her grandmother in paragraphs 5 and 6? What physical characteristics and qualities of temperament do these details reveal? How does Maynard begin to characterize her grandmother in the very first paragraph of this essay?

6. By what specific details in paragraphs 13–15 does Maynard reveal the grandmother's state of mind in the presence of death? The granddaughter's?

7. How would you describe the *pace* of Maynard's narration in paragraphs 7–12? How does the length of the paragraphs here compare with that of other paragraphs in the narrative?

8. Why do you think Maynard breaks the text of her essay after paragraphs 3 and 15? Why do you suppose she puts the third paragraph, about her grandmother's distant past, before the break rather than after?

9. What is the effect of ending this narrative by referring to the wedding china (par. 18)?

Words and Figures of Speech

1. In paragraph 9, Maynard presents her daughter to her grandmother as an "accomplishment." Which single word in paragraph 8 names the quality in the grandmother that encourages "accomplishments" in her offspring?
2. What are the CONNOTATIONS of *consumingly* in paragraph 16? How does Maynard's treatment of her own daughter in paragraph 17 justify the use of this strong word?
3. Explain the difference in DENOTATION between *emigrated* (par. 3) and *immigrated*.
4. What is the effect of Maynard's choice of the word "reasonably" in paragraph 2?
5. Why does Maynard refer to "pogroms" in paragraph 3 instead of "persecution" or "discrimination"?
6. Consult your dictionary for any of these words that you don't know: *pancreatic* (par. 1), *hemorrhaging* (par. 1), *jaundice* (par. 1), *cossacks* (par. 3), *coveted* (par. 4), *elocution* (par. 4), *imminent* (par. 6), and *knishes* (par. 6).
7. What is the difference in meaning between *imminent* (par. 6) and *eminent*?

Comparing

1. Compare and contrast Maynard's treatment of the generations and the idea of family continuity with Alex Haley's treatment of the same themes in the next essay in this chapter.
2. How does Maynard's account of handing down a tradition from mother to daughter *contrast* with E. B. White's account of a father and son in "Once More to the Lake" ("Essays for Further Reading")?

Discussion and Writing Topics

1. Do you think Maynard was justified in not writing or visiting her grandmother when she was well? Why or why not?

2. Write an essay that gives an account of your own last visit with a relative or friend.

3. Write an essay about your family that tells about events and gestures (at a family reunion, perhaps) that show a family resemblance in spirit or behavior across several generations.

Alex Haley

My Furthest-Back Person— "The African"

When Alex Haley's Roots was published in 1976, it created a
literary stir; and when the film version appeared soon after on
national television, this account of seven generations of an Afro-
American family became part of the American consciousness. A
native of Tennessee, Haley joined the U.S. Coast Guard in 1939
after briefly attending a North Carolina teachers' college. He
taught himself to write at sea, and later the Coast Guard created
the rating "journalist" expressly for him. When Haley retired
from the service in 1959, he began writing for men's adventure
magazines and then for Reader's Digest. One of his Playboy interviews led to his co-authoring The Autobiography of Malcolm X
in 1965. Then began the years of intensive genealogical research
that Haley recalls in "My Furthest-Back-Person—'The African.'"
This is not so much the family story of a descendant of African
slaves as it is the narrative of his personal quest for that story.

My Grandma Cynthia Murray Palmer lived in Henning,   1
Tenn. (pop. 500), about 50 miles north of Memphis. Each
summer as I grew up there, we would be visited by several
women relatives who were mostly around Grandma's age,
such as my Great Aunt Liz Murray who taught in Oklahoma,
and Great Aunt Till Merriwether from Jackson, Tenn., or
their considerably younger niece, Cousin Georgia Anderson
from Kansas City, Kan., and some others. Always after the
supper dishes had been washed, they would go out to take seats
and talk in the rocking chairs on the front porch, and I would

scrunch down, listening, behind Grandma's squeaky chair, with the dusk deepening into the night and the lightning bugs flicking on and off above the now shadowy honeysuckles. Most often they talked about our family—the story had been passed down for generations—until the whistling blur of lights of the southbound Panama Limited train *whooshing* through Henning at 9:05 P.M. signaled our bedtime.

So much of their talking of people, places and events I didn't   2
understand: For instance, what was an "Ol' Massa," an "Ol' Missus" or a "plantation"? But early I gathered that white folks had done lots of bad thing to our folks, though I couldn't figure out why. I guessed that all they talked about had happened a long time ago, as now or then Grandma or another, speaking of some-one in the past, would excitedly thrust a finger toward me, exclaim-ing, "Wasn't big as *this* young 'un!" And it would astound me that anyone as old and gray-haired as they could relate to my age. But in time my head began both a recording and picturing of the more graphic scenes they would describe, just as I also visualized David killing Goliath with his slingshot, Old Pharaoh's army drowning, Noah and his ark, Jesus feeding that big multitude with nothing but five loaves and two fishes, and other wonders that I heard in my Sunday school lessons at our New Hope Methodist Church.

The furthest-back person Grandma and the others talked of—   3
always in tones of awe, I noticed—they would call "The African." They said that some ship brought him to a place that they pro-nounced " 'Naplis." They said that then some "Mas' John Waller" bought him for his plantation in "Spotsylvania County, Va." This African kept on escaping, the fourth time trying to kill the "hate-ful po' cracker" slave-catcher, who gave him the punishment choice of castration or of losing one foot. This African took a foot being chopped off with an ax against a tree stump, they said, and he was about to die. But his life was saved by "Mas' John's" brother—"Mas' William Waller," a doctor, who was so furious about what had happened that he bought the African for himself and gave him the name "Toby."

Crippling about, working in "Mas' William's" house and yard,   4
the African in time met and mated with "the big house cook named Bell," and there was born a girl named Kizzy. As she grew up her African daddy often showed her different kinds of things,

telling her what they were in his native tongue. Pointing at a banjo, for example, the African uttered, "*ko*"; or pointing at a river near the plantation, he would say, "*Kamby Bolong.*" Many of his strange words started with a "*k*" sound, and the little, growing Kizzy learned gradually that they identified different things.

When addressed by other slaves as "Toby," the master's name for him, the African said angrily that his name was "*Kin-tay.*" And as he gradually learned English, he told young Kizzy some things about himself—for instance, that he was not far from his village, chopping wood to make himself a drum, when four men had surprised, overwhelmed, and kidnaped him. **5**

So Kizzy's head held much about her African daddy when at age 16 she was sold away onto a much smaller plantation in North Carolina. Her new "Mas' Tom Lea" fathered her first child, a boy she named George. And Kizzy told her boy all about his African grandfather. George grew up to be such a gamecock fighter that he was called "Chicken George," and people would come from all over and "bet big money" on his cockfights. He mated with Matilda, another of Lea's slaves; they had seven children, and he told them the stories and strange sounds of their African great-grandfather. And one of those children, Tom, became a blacksmith who was bought away by a "Mas' Murray" for his tobacco plantation in Alamance County, N.C. **6**

Tom mated there with Irene, a weaver on the plantation. She also bore seven children, and Tom now told them all about their African great-great-grandfather, the faithfully passed-down knowledge of his sounds and stories having become by now the family's prideful treasure. **7**

The youngest of that second set of seven children was a girl, Cynthia, who became my maternal Grandma (which today I can only see as fated). Anyway, all of this is how I was growing up in Henning at Grandma's, listening from behind her rocking chair as she and the other visiting old women talked of that African (never then comprehended as *my* great-great-great-great-grandfather) who said his name was "*Kin-tay*," and said "*ko*" for banjo, "*Kamby Bolong*" for river, and a jumble of other "*k*"-beginning sounds that Grandma privately muttered, most often while making beds or cooking, and who also said that near his village he was kidnaped while chopping wood to make himself a drum. **8**

The story had become nearly as fixed in my head as in Grand- **9** ma's by the time Dad and Mama moved me and my two younger brothers, George and Julius, away from Henning to be with them at the small black agricultural and mechanical college in Normal, Ala., where Dad taught.

To compress my next 25 years: When I was 17 Dad let me   10
enlist as a mess boy in the U.S. Coast Guard. I became a ship's cook out in the South Pacific during World War II, and at night down by my bunk I began trying to write sea adventure stories, mailing them off to magazines and collecting rejection slips for eight years before some editors began purchasing and publishing occasional stories. By 1949 the Coast Guard had made me its first "journalist"; finally with 20 years' service, I retired at the age of 37, determined to make a full time career of writing. I wrote mostly magazine articles; my first book was "The Autobiography of Malcolm X."

Then one Saturday in 1965 I happened to be walking past the   11
National Archives building in Washington. Across the interim years I had thought of Grandma's old stories—otherwise I can't think what diverted me up the Archives' steps. And when a main reading room desk attendant asked if he could help me, I wouldn't have dreamed of admitting to him some curiosity hanging on from boyhood about my slave forebears. I kind of mumbled that I was interested in census records of Alamance County, North Carolina, just after the Civil War.

The microfilm rolls were delivered, and I turned them through   12
the machine with a building sense of intrigue, viewing in different census takers' penmanship an endless parade of names. After about a dozen microfilmed rolls, I was beginning to tire, when in utter astonishment I looked upon the names of Grandma's parents: Tom Murray, Irene Murray . . . older sisters of Grandma's as well—every one of them a name that I'd heard countless times on her front porch.

It wasn't that I hadn't believed Grandma. You just *didn't* not   13
believe my Grandma. It was simply so uncanny actually seeing those names in print and in official U.S. Government records.

During the next several months I was back in Washington   14
whenever possible, in the Archives, the Library of Congress, the Daughters of the American Revolution Library. (Whenever black attendants understood the idea of my search, documents I requested reached me with miraculous speed.) In one source or

another during 1966 I was able to document at least the highlights of the cherished family story. I would have given anything to have told Grandma, but, sadly, in 1949 she had gone. So I went and told the only survivor of those Henning front-porch storytellers: Cousin Georgia Anderson, now in her 80's in Kansas City, Kan. Wrinkled, bent, not well herself, she was so overjoyed, repeating to me the old stories and sounds; they were like Henning echoes: "Yeah, boy, that African say his name was '*Kin-tay*'; he say the banjo was '*ko*,' an' the river '*Kamby-Bolong*,' an' he was off choppin' some wood to make his drum when they grabbed 'im!" Cousin Georgia grew so excited we had to stop her, calm her down, "You go' head, boy! Your grandma an' all of 'em—they up there watching what you do!"

That week I flew to London on a magazine assignment. Since by now I was steeped in the old, in the past, scarcely a tour guide missed me—I was awed at so many historical places and treasures I'd heard of and read of. I came upon the Rosetta stone [1] in the British Museum, marveling anew at how Jean Champollion, the French archaeologist, had miraculously deciphered its ancient demotic and hieroglyphic texts . . .

The thrill of that just kept hanging around in my head. I was on a jet returning to New York when a thought hit me. Those strange, unknown-tongue sounds, always part of our family's old story . . . they were obviously bits of our original African "*Kin-tay*'s*" native tongue. What specific tongue? Could I somehow find out?

Back in New York, I began making visits to the United Nations Headquarters lobby; it wasn't hard to spot Africans. I'd stop any I could, asking if my bits of phonetic sounds held any meaning for them. A couple of dozen Africans quickly listened, and took off—understandably dubious about some Tennessean's accent alleging "African" sounds.

My research assistant, George Sims (we grew up together in Henning), brought me some names of ranking scholars of African linguistics. One was particularly intriguing: A Belgian- and English-educated Dr. Jan Vansina; he had spent his early career living in West African villages, studying and tape-recording count-

15

16

17

18

---

[1] Ancient Egyptian stone tablet. The French archaeologist Champollion (1790–1832) used it to decipher hieroglyphic writing.

less oral histories that were narrated by certain very old African men; he had written a standard textbook, "The Oral Tradition."

So I flew to the University of Wisconsin to see Dr. Vansina. In [19] his living room I told him every bit of the family story in the fullest detail that I could remember it. Then, intensely, he queried me about the story's relay across the generations, about the gibberish of *"k"* sounds Grandma had fiercely muttered to herself while doing her housework, with my brothers and me giggling beyond her hearing at what we had dubbed "Grandma's noises."

Dr. Vansina, his manner very serious, finally said, "These sounds [20] your family has kept sound very probably of the tongue called 'Mandinka.'"

I'd never heard of any "Mandinka." Grandma just told of the [21] African saying *"ko"* for banjo, or *"Kamby Bolong"* for a Virginia river.

Among Mandinka stringed instruments, Dr. Vansina said, one [22] of the oldest was the *"kora."*

"Bolong," he said, was clearly Mandinka for "river." Preceded [23] by *"Kamby,"* it very likely meant "Gambia River."

Dr. Vansina telephoned an eminent Africanist colleague, Dr. [24] Philip Curtin. He said that the phonetic *"Kin-tay"* was correctly spelled *"Kinte,"* a very old clan that had originated in Old Mali. The Kinte men traditionally were blacksmiths, and the women were potters and weavers.

I knew I must get to the Gambia River. [25]

The first native Gambian I could locate in the U.S. was named [26] Ebou Manga, then a junior attending Hamilton College in upstate Clinton, N.Y. He and I flew to Dakar, Senegal, then took a smaller plane to Yundum Airport, and rode in a van to Gambia's capital, Bathurst. Ebou and his father assembled eight Gambia government officials. I told them Grandma's stories, every detail I could remember, as they listened intently, then reacted. " 'Kamby Bolong' of course is Gambia River!" I heard. "But more clue is your forefather's saying his name was 'Kinte.' " Then they told me something I would never even have fantasized—that in places in the back country lived very old men, commonly called *griots*, who could tell centuries of the histories of certain very old family clans. As for *Kintes*, they pointed out to me on a map some family villages, Kinte-Kundah, and Kinte-Kundah Janneh-Ya, for instance.

The Gambian officials said they would try to help me. I re- [27]

turned to New York dazed. It is embarrassing to me now, but despite Grandma's stories, I'd never been concerned much with Africa, and I had the routine images of African people living mostly in exotic jungles. But a compulsion now laid hold of me to learn all I could, and I began devouring books about Africa, especially about the slave trade. Then one Thursday's mail contained a letter from one of the Gambian officials, inviting me to return there.

Monday I was back in Bathurst. It galvanized me when the officials said that a *griot* had been located who told the *Kinte* clan history—his name was Kebba Kanga Fofana. To reach him, I discovered, required a modified safari: renting a launch to get upriver, two land vehicles to carry supplies by a roundabout land route, and employing finally 14 people, including three interpreters and four musicians, since a *griot* would not speak the revered clan histories without background music.   28

The boat Baddibu vibrated upriver, with me acutely tense: Were these Africans maybe viewing me as but another of the pith-helmets? After about two hours, we put in at James Island, for me to see the ruins of the once British-operated James Fort. Here two centuries of slave ships had loaded thousands of cargoes of Gambian tribespeople. The crumbling stones, the deeply oxidized swivel cannon, even some remnant links of chain seemed all but impossible to believe. Then we continued upriver to the left-bank village of Albreda, and there put ashore to continue on foot to Juffure, village of the *griot*. Once more we stopped, for me to see *toubob kolong*, "the white man's well," now almost filled in, in a swampy area with abundant, tall, saw-toothed grass. It was dug two centuries ago to "17 men's height deep" to insure survival drinking water for long-driven, famishing coffles of slaves.   29

Walking on, I kept wishing that Grandma could hear how her stories had led me to the *"Kamby Bolong."* (Our surviving story-teller Cousin Georgia died in a Kansas City hospital during this same morning, I would learn later.) Finally, Juffure village's playing children, sighting us, flashed an alert. The 70-odd people came rushing from their circular, thatch-roofed, mud-walled huts, with goats bounding up and about, and parrots squawking from up in the palms. I sensed him in advance somehow, the small man amid them, wearing a pillbox cap and an off-white robe—the *griot*. Then the interpreters went to him, as the villagers thronged around me.   30

And it hit me like a gale wind: every one of them, the whole ³¹ crowd, was *jet black*. An enormous sense of guilt swept me—a sense of being some kind of hybrid . . . a sense of being impure among the pure. It was an awful sensation.

The old *griot* stepped away from my interpreters and the crowd ³² quickly swarmed around him—all of them buzzing. An interpreter named A. B. C. Salla came to me; he whispered: "Why they stare at you so, they have never seen here a black American." And that hit me: I was symbolizing for them twenty-five millions of us they had never seen. What did they think of me—of us?

Then abruptly the old *griot* was briskly walking toward me. His ³³ eyes boring into mine, he spoke in Mandinka, as if instinctively I should understand—and A. B. C. Salla translated:

"Yes . . . we have been told by the forefathers . . . that many ³⁴ of us from this place are in exile . . . in that place called America . . . and in other places."

I suppose I physically wavered, and they thought it was the ³⁵ heat; rustling whispers went through the crowd, and a man brought me a low stool. Now the whispering hushed—the musicians had softly begun playing *kora* and *balafon,* and a canvas sling lawn seat was taken by the *griot,* Kebba Kanga Fofana, aged 73 "rains" (one rainy season each year). He seemed to gather himself into a physical rigidity, and he began speaking the *Kinte* clan's ancestral oral history; it came rolling from his mouth across the next hours . . . 17th-and 18th-century *Kinte* lineage details, predominantly what men took wives; the children they "begot," in the order of their births; those children's mates and children.

Events frequently were dated by some proximate singular physi- ³⁶ cal occurrence. It was as if some ancient scroll were printed indelibly within the *griot's* brain. Each few sentences or so, he would pause for an interpreter's translation to me. I distill here the essence:

The *Kinte* clan began in Old Mali,[2] the men generally black- ³⁷ smiths ". . . who conquered fire," and the women potters and

[2] Haley's branch of the clan apparently moved from mid-western Africa northward into present-day Morocco and Algeria, then southward again into the Senegal region. The ancient names "Mali" and "Mauretania" were revived by modern West African states that gained independence from France in 1960.

weavers. One large branch of the clan moved to Mauretania from where one son of the clan, Kairaba Kunta Kinte, a Moslem Marabout holy man, entered Gambia. He lived first in the village of Pakali N'Ding; he moved next to Jiffarong village; ". . . and then he came here, into our own village of Juffure."

In Juffure, Kairaba Kunta Kinte took his first wife, ". . . a Mandinka maiden, whose name was Sireng. By her, he begot two sons, whose names were Janneh and Saloum. Then he got a second wife, Yaisa. By her, he begot a son, Omoro." [38]

The three sons became men in Juffure. Janneh and Saloum went off and found a new village, Kinte-Kundah Janneh-Ya. "And then Omoro, the younger son, when he had 30 rains, took as a wife a maiden, Binta Kebba. [39]

"And by her, he begot four sons—Kunta, Lamin, Suwadu, and Madi . . ." [40]

Sometimes, a "begotten," after his naming, would be accompanied by some later-occurring detail, perhaps as ". . . in time of big water buffalo." Having named those four sons, now the *griot* stated such a detail. [41]

"About the time the king's soldiers came, the eldest of these four sons, Kunta, when he had about 16 rains, went away from this village, to chop wood to make a drum . . . and he was never seen again . . ." [42]

Goose-pimples the size of lemons seemed to pop all over me. In my knapsack were my cumulative notebooks, the first of them including how in my boyhood, my Grandma, Cousin Georgia and the others told of the African *"Kin-tay"* who always said he was kidnaped near his village—while chopping wood to make a drum . . . [43]

I showed the interpreter, he showed and told the *griot*, who excitedly told the people; they grew very agitated. Abruptly then they formed a human ring, encircling me, dancing and chanting. Perhaps a dozen of the women carrying their infant babies rushed in toward me, thrusting the infants into my arms—conveying, I would later learn, "the laying on of hands . . . through this flesh which is us, we are you, and you are us." The men hurried me into their mosque, their Arabic praying later being translated outside: "Thanks be to Allah for returning the long lost from among us." Direct descendants of Kunta Kinte's blood brothers were hastened, some of them from nearby villages, for a family portrait to be [44] taken with me, surrounded by actual ancestral sixth cousins. More symbolic acts filled the remaining day.

When they would let me leave, for some reason I wanted to go   45
away over the African land. Dazed, silent in the bumping Land Rover, I heard the cutting staccato of talking drums. Then when we sighted the next village, its people came thronging to meet us. They were all—little naked ones to wizened elders—waving, beaming, amid a cacophony of crying out; and then my ears identified their words: "*Meester Kinte! Meester Kinte!*"

Let me tell you something: I am a man. But I remember the   46
sob surging up from my feet, flinging up my hands before my face and bawling as I had not done since I was a baby . . . the jet-black Africans were jostling, staring . . . I didn't care, with the feelings surging. If you really knew the odyssey of us millions of black Americans, if you really knew how we came in the seeds of our forefathers, captured, driven, beaten, inspected, bought, branded, chained in foul ships, if you really knew, you needed weeping . . .

Back home, I knew that what I must write, really, was our black   47
saga, where any individual's past is the essence of the millions'. Now flat broke, I went to some editors I knew, describing the Gambian miracle, and my desire to pursue the research; Doubleday contracted to publish, and Reader's Digest to condense the projected book; then I had advances to travel further.

What ship brought Kinte to Grandma's " 'Naplis" (Annapolis,   48
Md., obviously)? The old *griot's* time reference to "king's soldiers" sent me flying to London. Feverish searching at last identified, in British Parliament records, "Colonel O'Hare's Forces," dispatched in mid-1767 to protect the then British-held James Fort whose ruins I'd visited. So Kunta Kinte was down in some ship probably sailing later that summer from the Gambia River to Annapolis.

Now I feel it was fated that I had taught myself to write in the   49
U.S. Coast Guard. For the sea dramas I had concentrated on had given me years of experience searching among yellowing old U.S. maritime records. So now in English 18th Century marine records I finally tracked ships reporting themselves in and out of the Commandant of the Gambia River's James Fort. And then early one afternoon I found that a Lord Ligonier under a Captain Thomas Davies had sailed on the Sabbath of July 5, 1767. Her cargo: 3,265 elephants' teeth, 3,700 pounds of beeswax, 800 pounds of cotton,

32 ounces of Gambian gold, and 140 slaves; her destination: "Annapolis."

That night I recrossed the Atlantic. In the Library of Congress 50
the Lord Ligonier's arrival was one brief line in "Shipping In The Port Of Annapolis—1748–1775." I located the author, Vaughan W. Brown, in his Baltimore brokerage office. He drove to Historic Annapolis, the city's historical society, and found me further documentation of her arrival on Sept. 29, 1767. (Exactly two centuries later, Sept. 29, 1967, standing, staring seaward from an Annapolis pier, again I knew tears.) More help came in the Maryland Hall of Records. Archivist Phebe Jacobsen found the Lord Ligonier's arriving customs declaration listing, "98 Negroes"—so in her 86-day crossing, 42 Gambians had died, one among the survivors being 16-year-old Kunta Kinte. Then the microfilmed Oct. 1, 1767, Maryland Gazette contained, on page two, an announcement to prospective buyers from the ship's agents, Daniel of St. Thos. Jenifer and John Ridout (the Governor's secretary): "from the River GAMBIA, in AFRICA . . . a cargo of choice, healthy SLAVES . . ."

QUESTIONS

Understanding

1. This essay tells the story of three different kinds of quests. One is a writer's search for material; another is his quest for bits and pieces of personal family history. What is the third? Point out specific paragraphs (for example, par. 46) that contribute to this part of the story.

2. Which of the three kinds of searches in Haley's essay do you consider most important? Why?

3. Why is Haley struck with the color of the Gambians in paragraph 31?

4. What is the significance of the laying-on-of-hands ceremony in paragraph 44?

5. What message does Haley's personal narrative hold for others who might search the distant past for their roots?

Strategies and Structure

1. Through roughly how many years of his life does Haley's narrative carry us? Why does he start with his childhood instead of some later stage; when he retired from the Coast Guard, for example?

2. As Haley's life moves forward in time, his search moves deeper into the past. Where do the two time dimensions of the narrative come together? How does Haley create the impression of relentless pursuit, of past and present inevitably meeting?

3. How do Haley's various accounts of the front-porch storytellers anticipate his account of the *griot* he meets in Gambia. How does the boy's reaction to the family story condition *our* reaction to the *griot's* words in paragraphs 34–42?

4. Haley could have told us from the beginning who the African was and where he came from. Why does he choose *not* to do this in retelling the story? What effect does he achieve by withholding such information?

5. How is the *language* of Haley's own account of his search different from the language of both the Africans and his relatives in America? What two different kinds of historical evidence does Haley's historian offer us?

6. Why does Haley so often *repeat* the elements of the family legend, the fact that the African was captured while making a drum, for instance?

7. Describe the effect of Haley's "Let me tell you something" at the beginning of paragraph 46.

8. Why do you think Haley omitted paragraph 31 in a version of this essay that appeared in *Reader's Digest*, a magazine intended for a vast general audience?

9. Haley ends his narrative by quoting an advertisement in the *Maryland Gazette* of October 1767. Is this an effective ending to his story? Why or why not?

Words and Figures of Speech

1. What are the implications of the words *roots*? Why is the METAPHOR appropriate to the kind of search that Haley is conducting?

2. What is the effect when Haley's history switches from the word *mated* (as in pars. 6 and 7) to *begot* (in pars. 35, 38, 40, 41)?
3. What is an *odyssey* (par. 46)? Explain the literary ALLUSION implied by the word. Why is the term appropriate to Haley's story?
4. Who are the "pith-helmets" in paragraph 29? What FIGURE OF SPEECH does the term exemplify?
5. Consult your dictionary for the precise meanings of any of the following words you are not sure of: *graphic* (par. 2), *archives* (11), *uncanny* (13), *phonetic* (17), *linguistics* (18), *gibberish* (19), *eminent* (24), *galvanized* (28), *coffles* (29), *proximate* (36), *indelibly* (36), *staccato* (45), *wizened* (45), *cacophony* (45), *saga* (47).

Comparing

1. Both Haley's essay and Loren Eiseley's "The Angry Winter" (at the beginning of this chapter) tell the story of a thoughtful man's return to the past. How do the two narratives *differ* in this regard?

Discussion and Writing Topics

1. Tell the story that emerges from any legends of your own family that you can recall.
2. Relate any events in your family history that have a general social significance. Try to do so without losing their personal flavor.
3. After the publication of *Roots* in book form, a British reporter alleged that Haley's *griot* knew in advance what Haley wanted to hear and stretched the facts to please him. Would Haley's entire search be invalidated if it should turn out that the griot's Kinte was not the same African his aunts talked about? Why or why not?
4. How exclusively "black" do you find Haley's essay to be? Explain your answer.

WRITING TOPICS for Chapter One
Essays in the First Person Singular

1. Write an autobiography in which you give a chronological account of the formative events of your life.

2. Which aspects of college have you found most different from high school? Which have you found especially shocking or liberating? Tell the story of your adjustment to a new environment.

3. Have you had a religious or intellectual experience that has *changed* your life? Try to recapture it.

4. Do you have a special skill or talent (like David Dubber's)? Relate how it has served you in past challenges or emergencies.

5. Recount your reaction to the news of a relative's or close friend's death.

6. Describe your reaction to one of the following: an athletic event; an election or political rally; a meeting with a famous person; an impressive building or natural scene; an accident.

7. Recall a childhood journey that you find unusually memorable. Organize your account around the stages of the journey.

8. From your own perspective, tell the story of a family reunion you have attended. Pay special attention to the oldest family members.

9. How do you expect to act at the tenth anniversary of your high school graduating class? The twentieth? Describe the scene.

Exposition

2

Essays That
Classify and Divide

When we divide a group of similar objects, we separate
them from one another. For example, a physiologist divides
human beings according to body types: mesomorph (muscular and bony), ectomorph (skinny), and endomorph (soft
and fleshy). When we CLASSIFY [1] an object, we place it
within a group of similar objects. The zoologist puts a
monkey and a man in the order Primates because both mammals have nails and opposable thumbs. A librarian classifies
Mark Twain's Adventures of Huckleberry Finn along with
Herman Melville's Moby-Dick because both are works of
prose fiction by nineteenth-century American authors.
Shakespeare's Macbeth would go into a different class, however, because its distinguishing features are different. The
technical definition of a class is a group with the same
distinguishing features.

The simplest classification systems divide things into
those that exhibit a set of distinguishing features and those
that do not. A doctor conducting genetic research among
identical male twins would divide the human race first into
Males and Females; then he would subdivide the Males into
Twins and Non-Twins; and finally he would subdivide the
Twins into the categories, Identical and Nonidentical.

The doctor's simple system has limited uses, but it re-
sembles even the most complicated systems in one respect.
The categories do not overlap. They are mutually exclusive.
A classification system is useless if it "cross-ranks" items.
Suppose, for example, that we classified all birds according to

---

[1] Terms printed in all capitals are defined in the Glossary.

the following categories: *Flightless, Nocturnal, Flat-billed, Web-Footed*. Our system might work well enough for owls (nocturnal), but where would a duck (flat-billed, web-footed) fit? Or a penguin (flightless, web-footed)? A system of classifying birds must have one and only one pigeonhole for pigeons. Otherwise it makes a distinction that does not distinguish, a flaw as serious as failing to make a distinction that really does exist. Our faulty system would not differentiate between a penguin and an ostrich since both are flightless, but a naturalist would see a big difference between the two.

The distinguishing features of a class must set its members apart from those of other classes or subclasses. How the features of a given class are defined, however, will vary with who is doing the classifying and for what purpose. A teacher divides a group of thirty students according to scholarship: types A, B, C, D, and F. A basketball coach would divide the same group of students into forwards, guards, and centers. The director of a student drama group would have an entirely different set of criteria. All three sets are valid for the purposes they are intended to serve. And classification must serve some larger purpose, or it becomes an empty game.

When you write a classification theme, keep your purpose firmly in mind. Are you classifying teachers in order to decide what a good teacher is? To demonstrate that different kinds of teachers can be equally instructive? To explain why some teachers fail? Return often to your reasons and conclusions, for classification is a method of organization that should propose as well as arrange.

The following paragraph from an essay on lightning by Richard Orville goes well beyond merely dividing its subject into three categories:

> There are several types of lightning named according to where the discharge takes place. Among them are intracloud lightning, by far the most common type, in which the flash occurs within the thundercloud; air-discharge lightning, in which the flash occurs between the cloud and the surrounding air; and cloud-to-ground lightning, in which the discharge takes place between the cloud and the ground.

This short paragraph names the types of lightning. But it also suggests a basis for defining all three types ("according to where the discharge takes place"); it defines them on that basis; it tells us that intracloud lightning is the commonest type; and it sets up all that follows.

In the next paragraphs of his essay, Orville explains what causes the three kinds of lightning; how much electrical power they generate; how scientists study them, and where such familiar names as "forked, streak, heat, hot, cold, ribbon, and bead" lightning fit into these categories. After discussing the related topic of thunder, Orville ends by explaining why we need to know as much as possible about his subject. The final sentence of his essay reads: "In the end, we hope that our effort will bring the goal of lightning prediction, and perhaps limited control, within the realm of applied technology."

The author of our example has taken the trouble to study lightning, classify it, and explain his system to us because human life and property may depend upon such efforts in the future. You may not be writing about life-and-death matters, but your theme should explain why a particular system of classification is valid, what we can learn from it, and what good that knowledge can do.

Noel Perrin
The Grades of Maple Syrup

*Born in New York City in 1927, Noel Perrin teaches English at
Dartmouth College. A veteran of the Korean War who received
the Bronze Star, he is also a "sometime farmer" in Thetford
Center, Vermont. Devoted to his avocation, Perrin has become a
guide to the rural life for city folk and other amateurs. A
contributor to Vermont Life, Country Journal, and The New
Yorker, he writes about such subjects as making butter, "sugaring,"
buying a chain saw or a pickup truck, and finding the perfect
fence post. He has also written books on censorship in England and
on Japanese warfare. "The Grades of Maple Syrup" is reprinted
from First Person Rural (1978), a collection of essays that Perrin
soon followed with the sequel, Second Person Rural (1980). In
the following essay, Perrin, alias Jonathan Corncob, engages in the
simple classification of a down-home commodity.*

Maple syrup comes in three grades. In New York State [1]
they are called Light Amber, Medium Amber, and Dark
Amber. In Vermont they are called Fancy, A, and B. I am
speaking, of course, of pure maple syrup: The well-known
'blends' that are sold in supermarkets (at the moment most
of them contain 3% maple syrup) come in one grade only,
called Mediocre.

Of the two systems, Vermont's is clearly better. When you [2]
know that the syrup you're about to buy has been classified
Medium Amber, you don't know much. You might as well
grade meat Pink, Dark Pink, and Red. But even Vermont's
system no longer serves the consumer well, though it once did.
To understand why, you need to know a little of the history
of maple marketing.

A hundred years ago, most Vermont farms produced only maple   3
sugar, and no syrup whatsoever. Syrup would have been too hard
to ship. Tin cans had been only quite recently perfected by the
brothers Appert in France and were expensive. Plastic jugs didn't
exist. The common shipping container in Vermont was a barrel,
keg, or box made of wood—and maple sugar left the farm chiefly in
wooden boxes. I know a man in East Corinth whose grandfather
made his living producing boxes for farmers to ship their butter
and maple sugar off to market in. He produces boxes still—but now
they are hat boxes and miniature trunks to give little girls to pack
doll clothes in.

Furthermore, a hundred years ago maple sugar was not a luxury   4
item. It was competitive in price with cane sugar. Cane sugar in
the 1870s sold for about 7¢ a pound, and maple sugar sold for an
average of 9¢ a pound—a farmer in Cabot sold four tons of it for
that price in 1878. Occasionally maple sugar even undersold cane;
another Cabot farmer sold all of his last-run sugar at 6¢ a pound
that year.

Maple sugar was also used competitively with cane. That is, the   5
buyer expected to use it as a general sweetening agent—in his
coffee, with strawberries and cream, in cake recipes, and so on.
For this reason it was sold almost entirely in bulk, just as cane
sugar is now. A young sugarmaker in northern Vermont was saying something revolutionary when he wrote in 1886, 'I have
learned that small packages generally sell the best, those containing from ten to 30 pounds finding the quickest market.' Think
what the large packages must have been like. By contrast, a small
package of maple sugar in 1978 is likely to be four ounces, and a
large one half a pound.

So much was maple sugar considered a general sweetening agent   6
that a certain number of Vermont chauvinists (they have existed
in all ages) felt that none of that Cuban of Louisiana cane stuff
need be tolerated at all. A fellow in Bakersfield said flatly in 1876,
'There ought not to be a pound of foreign sugar brought into the
State.'

Now we come to the point. If maple sugar is competitive with   7
cane, and if it's used as a general sweetener, the last thing you
want is for it to have a lot of maple flavor. You just want it to be
sweet. Maple-flavored coffee *may* be good, but it's not what most
coffee drinkers are after.

And, in fact, this is what Vermont producers (and also New   8
York producers, and the early Wisconsin producers, etc.) were
trying to make: colorless and hence flavorless maple sugar. That
is, the very fanciest Fancy Grade.

'There is no good reason why we cannot make the Maple   9
equally white and pure as the West Indies,' one of the big producers in South Reading said in 1878. A somewhat more realistic
farmer in Waitsfield didn't think he could boil his sap down to a
sugar without *any* flavor or tint–but he thought it was a goal one
should approach as closely as possible. Speaking of his own maple
sugar, he wrote, 'Like the human race it is of all shades of color,
and I think this is one of the cases in which prejudice against color
is justifiable. We have all seen maple sugar that was nearly as
white as loaf sugar, and I suppose all would be glad to make it.'
All would be glad to make it because the housewife in Boston or
New York would pay the highest price for it.

Here is the origin of the Fancy, A, B grading system, and also of   10
the Light Amber, Medium Amber, Dark Amber. Fancy means
palest and mildest flavored–what you make at the beginning of
each season. A means somewhat darker and more flavor. B means
still darker and still more flavor. (Ungraded or C is, of course,
darker yet–and really dark C is usually too strong to use by itself
with any pleasure. That's why so much of it winds up in supermarket blends.)

This system made perfect sense in 1878. In 1978, when virtu-   11
ally all maple syrup and sugar is sold *because* of its flavor, it
makes very little sense. I won't say it makes no sense at all, because the differences between the three grades are not simply matters of intensity. To most palates, the pale Fancy grade has a
subtlety and delicacy that B completely lacks. To most palates, B
has a kind of full-bodied quality, a robustness, sort of like a Burgundy wine, that Fancy completely lacks. A is a brilliant compro-
mise, subtle but sturdy.

Nevertheless, to use a scale on which palest is always best seems   12
to me silly. Here are three kinds of maple syrup, each a good thing
in its own right. I myself prefer Fancy on plain raised doughnuts at
a sugar-on-snow supper, A on vanilla ice cream and on waffles, B
on pancakes–though I also like to switch them around occasionally. But the casual buyer, seeing all three kinds together, figures
that A must be an inferior version of Fancy, and B an inferior

version of A. Whereas if you kept the same divisions, but called the three grades Mild, Medium, and Strong, the casual buyer would know what he was getting.

On the other hand, maybe after a hundred years the tradition is [13] too engrained, and the present grading system cannot be changed. After all, we still call ourselves sugarmakers, and groves of maples sugar orchards, and the buildings that house our evaporators sugarhouses, when for three-quarters of a century we have been syrupmakers tapping our syrupbushes and boiling down the sap in our syruphouses. In that case, it seems to me that maple syrup cans should at least carry an explanation of what Fancy, A, and B mean.

Too many people are missing a treat, not putting some wonder- [14] ful dark rich B on their pancakes from time to time.

QUESTIONS

Understanding

1. Why does Perrin prefer Vermont's system of grading maple syrup to New York's? What single example does he use to show the defects of the New York system?

2. What is wrong today with even Vermont's system, according to Perrin? How has the consumer's view of maple syrup changed over the years?

3. What is the relationship between color and flavor in maple sugar, according to Perrin's history of its competition with cane sugar?

4. How did Vermont producers of maple sugar define their "Fancy" grade a hundred years ago?

5. What system of grading does Perrin propose to replace the old one? How would it be an improvement?

6. Why does Perrin refuse to divide modern *blends* of maple syrup into more than one grade?

Strategies and Structure

1. Division and classification are closely related mental operations: we *divide* a whole category (wine) into subcategories (red, pink,

white); we *classify* a given sample (a glass of wine from Burgundy) by placing it into the category or subcategory (full-bodied red) to which it belongs. Which operation is Perrin primarily engaged in here? Explain your answer.

2. In paragraphs 3–7 (a third of his entire essay), Perrin is neither classifying nor dividing. What is he doing instead? Would the essay have been better or worse without this section? Why?

3. In which paragraph does Perrin most fully define the features that distinguish each class of maple sugar or syrup? What verb does he repeatedly use to introduce them?

4. In paragraph 7, Perrin uses the TRANSITION sentence, "Now we come to the point." How effective do you find this direct statement? How often does he use such transitions in this short essay? Should he do so more often? Less often?

5. Why do you think Perrin's conclusion (par. 14) is so much shorter than the preceding paragraph? How does it resemble his introduction (par. 1) in TONE?

6. How does Perrin create a sense of the past in paragraphs 4, 5, 6, and 9? Why do you think he mentions (par. 3) the man, living now, who makes miniature boxes and trunks?

Words and Figures of Speech

1. The author of "The Grades of Maple Syrup" seems fond of names. Point out several examples of his use of New England place names. What sort of flavor do they lend to his homely subject?

2. Perrin says Vermont farmers still call themselves "sugarmakers" and use the terms "sugar orchards" and "sugarhouses" (par. 13). What names should they use instead for strict accuracy?

3. Why do you think Perrin points out that the old names for syrup manufacture are still in use? Why might names, particularly place names, tend to change more slowly than other terms?

4. Who was Nicolas Chauvin? (If he is not in your dictionary, try the biographical dictionaries in the reference section of your school library.) Why has Chauvin's name given us the modern word *chauvinist* (par. 6)?

5. The word *mediocre* (par. 1) has an interesting ETYMOLOGY. Its Latin roots mean "half-way up a mountain." Why is this an appropriate word history for the name of the class that Perrin humor-

ously proposes for all supermarket blends of maple syrup? (Why does Perrin capitalize the word, by the way?)

6. What is the common alternate spelling of *syrup*?

Comparing

1. In "The Grades of Maple Syrup," Perrin is dividing his subject (maple syrup) into sub-classes. How does this operation compare with Susan Allen Toth's treatment of her subject (movie dates) in "Cinematypes" later in this chapter? Is she basically *dividing* (separating items of a class into sub-classes) or *classifying* (putting separate items into a class by themselves)?

Discussion and Writing Topics

1. How many different kinds of sugar are in common use today? (Check the shelves of your local supermarket for help here.) Devise a system for classifying them—by color, flavor, source, or some other means—and explain your system.

2. How might your basic categories for classifying sugar be further broken down into sub-categories, or grades?

3. Some record stores, especially the chains, have elaborate classification systems for their wares ("Blue Grass," "Rhythm and Blues," "Show Tunes," and so forth). Visit one and make a list of their different classifications for records. How would you define the kind of music that goes into each of several representative categories?

Deairich Hunter
Ducks vs. Hard Rocks

*Deairich Hunter, fifteen years old, is a high school junior in
Wilmington, Delaware, where he writes a column for The Eye,
a student news magazine. For four months, Hunter lived in
Brooklyn and attended the predominantly black, inner-city school
he describes in "Ducks vs. Hard Rocks." Hunter was a duck, one
who escaped by returning to his old school in a less fierce
environment. Hunter stayed long enough in the ghetto, however,
to learn the basic categories into which he and his classmates fell—
in New York and other densely urban centers. This essay by a
student is about trying to stay out of the "hard rocks" category
long enough to grow up and still remember.*

Although the chaos and viciousness of the Miami riot hap-   1
pened months ago, the chaos and viciousness of daily life for
many inner-city black people goes on and on. It doesn't seem
to matter where you are, though some places are worse than
others. A few months ago I left my school in Wilmington,
Delaware, moved to Brooklyn, New York, and really began to
understand.

After you stay in certain parts of New York for awhile, that   2
chaos and viciousness gets inside of you. You get used to seeing
the younger guys flashing pistols and the older ones shooting
them. It's not unusual to be walking down the street or
through the park and see somebody being beaten or held up.
It's no big deal if someone you know is arrested and beat up
by the cops.

In my four months in Brooklyn I was mugged three times.   3

Although such events may seem extraordinary to you, they   4

68

are just a part of life in almost any minority neighborhood. It seems like everybody knows how to use some kind of weapon, whether it's a pair of nun-chucks (two round sticks attached by a chain) or an ice pick. As long as it will do the job, you can use it.

In Brooklyn you fall into one of two categories when you start   5
growing up. The names for the categories may be different in other cities, but the categories are the same. First, there's the minority of the minority, the "ducks," or suckers. These are the kids who go to school every day. They even want to go to college. Imagine that! School after high school! They don't smoke cheeb (marijuana) and they get zooted (intoxicated) after only one can of beer. They're wasting their lives waiting for a dream that won't come true.

The ducks are usually the ones getting beat up on by the ma-   6
jority group—the "hard rocks." If you're a real hard rock you have no worries, no cares. Getting high is as easy as breathing. You just rip off some duck. You don't bother going to school; it's not necessary. You just live with your mom until you get a job—that should be any time a job comes looking for you. Why should you bother to go look for it? Even your parents can't find work.

I guess the barrier between the ducks and the hard rocks is the   7
barrier of despair. The ducks still have hope, while the hard rocks are frustrated. They're caught in the deadly, dead-end environment and can't see a way out. Life becomes the fast life—or incredibly boring—and death becomes the death that you see and get used to every day. They don't want to hear any more promises. They believe that's just the white man's way of keeping them under control.

Hard rocks do what they want to do when they want to do it.   8
When a hard rock goes to prison it builds up his reputation. He develops a bravado that's like a long, sad joke. But it's all lies and excuses. It's a hustle to keep ahead of the fact that he's going nowhere.

Actually, there is one more category, but this group is not really 9
looked upon as human. They're the junkies. They all hang together, but they don't actually have any friends. Everybody in the neighborhood knows that a drug addict would cut his own throat if he could get a fix for it. So everybody knows junkies will stab you in the back for a dollar.

A guy often becomes a junkie when he tries to get through the   10
despair barrier and reach the other side alone. Let's say a hard
rock wants to change, to better himself, so he goes back to school.
His friends feel he's deserting them, so they desert him first. The
ducks are scared of him and won't accept him. Now this hard rock
is alone. If he keeps going to school, somebody who is after him
out of spite or revenge will probably catch him and work him over.
The hard rock has no way to get back. His way of life is over; he
loses his friends' respect, becoming more and more of an outcast.
Then he may turn to drugs.

I guess the best way to help the hard rocks is to help the ducks.   11
If the hard rocks see the good guy making it, maybe they will
change. If they see the ducks, the ones who try, succeed, it might
bring them around. The ducks are really the only ones who might
be able to change the situation.

The problem with most ducks is that after years of effort they   12
develop a negative attitude, too. If they succeed, they know they've
got it made. Each one can say he did it by himself and for himself.
No one helped him and he owes nobody anything, so he says, "Let
the hard rocks and the junkies stay where they are"—the old every-
man-for-himself routine.

What the ducks must be made to realize is that it was this same   13
attitude that made the hard rocks so hard. They developed a sense
of kill or be killed, abuse or be abused, take it or get taken.

The hard rocks want revenge. They want revenge because they   14
don't have any hope of changing their situation. Their teachers
don't offer it, their parents have lost theirs, and their grandparents
died with a heartful of hope but nothing to show for it.

Maybe the only people left with hope are the only people who   15
can make a difference—teens like me. We, the ducks, must learn
to care. As a fifteen-year-old, I'm not sure I can handle all that.
Just growing up seems hard enough.

QUESTIONS

Understanding

1. Who or what is Hunter classifying in this essay?
2. What is a "duck" as Hunter defines one? A "hard rock"?

3. What is the third category in Hunter's classification system?
4. On whom does the main hope for the future of all three groups depend, according to Hunter? Why them and not the other groups?
5. To which category does Hunter himself belong?

Strategies and Structure

1. This is an essay in classification, but it also sets forth a "thesis," or proposition supported by persuasive argument. Where does Hunter set forth his thesis? What is it?
2. Why do you think Hunter waits until after he has classified his subject to make his plea instead of doing so beforehand?
3. In what sense is Hunter's essay itself evidence in support of his thesis about the need for caring? In which paragraph does he suggest that the responsibility of saving the others may be too great for even the most compassionate of ducks?
4. The minority that Hunter is classifying would understand his categories but might not appreciate the part of his essay that makes a plea to do away with these very categories. To whom does Hunter address this plea? Who is his intended audience here?
5. "Ducks vs. Hard Rocks" sounds like the title of an essay in comparison and contrast (Chapter 6). Why is this nevertheless an essay in classification rather than comparison?

Words and Figures of Speech

1. What is "bravado" (par. 7)? How is it different from courage?
2. How effective do you find the SIMILE in which Hunter compares the bravado of the hard rocks to "a long, sad joke" (par. 7)?
3. Hunter's use of such SLANG words as *ducks, hard rocks, nun-chucks* (par. 3), *cheeb* (par. 4), and *zooted* (par. 4) shows that he knows the "lingo" of his environment. How does this knowledge of language help establish his authority as our interpreter, despite his tender age? Interpreter of what?
4. Hunter's TONE when he defines ducks (par. 5) is heavily sarcastic. (See SATIRE in the glossary.) Read this paragraph out loud to yourself in the tone of voice you think Hunter intended. By the use of what punctuation mark does the author signal the tone of this passage for us?
5. Why do you suppose the hard rocks call a duck a duck?

Comparing

1. Classification often serves a larger purpose than mere sorting and placing. Compare Hunter's essay with the essay (immediately preceding) by Noel Perrin. Which essay in classification seems to have a larger purpose? Is the other, therefore, trivial or simply different? Explain your answer.

Discussion and Writing Topics

1. Does it matter that Hunter is only fifteen years old? Does this knowledge undermine or support his authority here? Would he be more or less compassionate, do you think, if he were much older? If he had stayed in Brooklyn?

2. Are Hunter's categories of inner-city types accurate, in your opinion? Does he leave out any sub-groups you can think of?

3. How would you sub-divide a racial or regional group (Oriental or Indian Americans, inner-city students, rural blacks or whites, "wasps") of whom you have first-hand experience? Write a classification essay about that group.

Susan Allen Toth

Cinematypes

*A native of Iowa, Susan Allen Toth went to school at Smith
College, Berkeley, and the University of Minnesota (Ph.D., 1969).
She is now a professor of English at Macalester College in St.
Paul, where she has done research and teaching in American
local-color fiction, women's studies, and geography in literature.
Her short stories and interviews have appeared in* Redbook *and*
Ms., *and her* Blooming: A Small-Town Girlhood *appeared in 1981.
"Cinematypes" was first printed in* Harper's *(May, 1980) with the
subtitle, "Going to the Movies." It classifies films, but Toth's
wistful essay in classification is mainly about other types, one of
whom was born in 1940 and has been going to the movies (the
same ones) almost ever since.*

Aaron takes me only to art films. That's what I call them,   1
anyway: strange movies with vague poetic images I don't
always understand, long dreamy movies about a distant
Technicolor past, even longer black-and-white movies about
the general meaninglessness of life. We do not go unless at
least one reputable critic has found the cinematography
superb. We went to *The Devil's Eye*,[1] and Aaron turned to
me in the middle and said, "My God, this is *funny*." I do not
think he was pleased.

When Aaron and I go to the movies, we drive our cars   2
separately and meet by the box office. Inside the theater he
sits tentatively in his seat, ready to move if he can't see well,
poised to leave if the film is disappointing. He leans away from
me, careful not to touch the bare flesh of his arm against the
bare flesh of mine. Sometimes he leans so far I am afraid he
may be touching the woman on his other side. If the movie

[1] 1960 satiric comedy by Swedish director Ingmar Bergman, generally
known for the starkness and seriousness of his films.

73

is very good, he leans forward, too, peering between the heads of the couple in front of us. The light from the screen bounces off his glasses; he gleams with intensity, sitting there on the edge of his seat, watching the screen. Once I tapped him on the arm so I could whisper a comment in his ear. He jumped.

After *Belle de Jour*[2] Aaron said he wanted to ask me if he could   3
stay overnight. "But I can't," he shook his head mournfully before I had a chance to answer, "because I know I never sleep well in strange beds." Then he apologized for asking. "It's just that after a film like that," he said, "I feel the need to assert myself."

Pete takes me only to movies that he thinks have redeeming   4
social value. He doesn't call them "films." They tend to be about poverty, war, injustice, political corruption, struggling unions in the 1930s, and the military-industrial complex. Pete doesn't like propaganda movies, though, and he doesn't like to be too de-pressed, either. We stayed away from *The Sorrow and the Pity*;[3] it would be, he said, just too much. Besides, he assured me, things are never that hopeless. So most of the movies we see are made in Hollywood. Because they are always topical, these movies offer what Pete calls "food for thought." When we saw *Coming Home*, Pete's jaw set so firmly with the first half-hour that I knew we would end up at Poppin' Fresh Pies afterward.

When Pete and I go to the movies, we take turns driving so no   5
one owes anyone else anything. We leave the car far from the theater so we don't have to pay for a parking space. If it's raining or snowing, Pete offers to let me off at the door, but I can tell he'll feel better if I go with him while he finds a spot, so we share the walk too. Inside the theater Pete will hold my hand when I get scared if I ask him. He puts my hand firmly on his knee and covers it completely with his own hand. His knee never twitches. After a while, when the scary part is past, he loosens his hand slightly and I know that is a signal to take mine away. He sits companionably close, letting his jacket just touch my sweater, but he does not infringe. He thinks I ought to know he is there if I need him.

---

[2] Sensual 1967 movie by Spanish director Luis Buñuel, in which the glamorous actress Catherine Deneuve plays the role of a prostitute.

[3] 1972 documentary by Marcel Ophuls about France during the Nazi occupa-tion. *Coming Home*, below: 1978 film of a wounded Vietnam veteran re-turning home.

One night, after *The China Syndrome*,[4] I asked Pete if he 6
wouldn't like to stay for a second drink, even though it was past
midnight. He thought a while about that, considering my offer
from all possible angles, but finally he said no. Relationships
today, he said, have a tendency to move too quickly.

Sam likes movies that are entertaining. By that he means movies 7
that Will Jones in the *Minneapolis Tribune* loved and either *Time*
or *Newsweek* rather liked; also movies that do not have sappy love
stories, are not musicals, do not have subtitles, and will not force
him to think. He does not go to movies to think. He liked *California Suite* and *The Seduction of Joe Tynan*,[5] though the plots,
he said, could have been zippier. He saw it all coming too far in
advance, and that took the fun out. He doesn't like to know what
is going to happen. "I just want my brain to be tickled," he says. It
is very hard for me to pick out movies for Sam.

When Sam takes me to the movies, he pays for everything. He 8
thinks that's what a man ought to do. But I buy my own popcorn,
because he doesn't approve of it; the grease might smear his flannel slacks. Inside the theater, Sam makes himself comfortable. He
takes off his jacket, puts one arm around me, and all during the
movie he plays with my hand, stroking my palm, beating a small
tattoo on my wrist. Although he watches the movie intently, his
body operates on instinct. Once I inclined my head and kissed him
lightly just behind his ear. He beat a faster tattoo on my wrist,
quick and musical, but he didn't look away from the screen.

When Sam takes me home from the movies, he stands outside 9
my door and kisses me long and hard. He would like to come in,
he says regretfully, but his steady girlfriend in Duluth wouldn't like
it. When the *Tribune* gives a movie four stars, he has to save it to
see with her. Otherwise her feelings might be hurt.

I go to some movies by myself. On rainy Sunday afternoons I 10
often sneak into a revival house or a college auditorium for old
Technicolor musicals, *Kiss Me Kate, Seven Brides for Seven
Brothers, Calamity Jane*, even, once, *The Sound of Music*. Wearing saggy jeans so I can prop my feet on the seat in front, I sit

---

[4] 1979 movie warning against the dangers of nuclear power plants.
[5] Popular 1979 movies, both starring Alan Alda among others.

toward the rear where no one can see me. I eat large handfuls of popcorn with double butter. Once the movie starts, I feel completely at home. Howard Keel and I are old friends; I grin back at him on the screen. I know the sound tracks by heart. Sometimes when I get really carried away I hum along with Kathryn Grayson, remembering how I once thought I would fill out a formal like that. I am rather glad now I never did. Skirts whirl, feet tap, acrobatic young men perform impossible feats, and then the camera dissolves into a dream sequence I know I can comfortably follow. It is not, thank God, Bergman.

If I can't find an old musical, I settle for Hepburn and Tracy, vintage Grant or Gable, on adventurous days Claudette Colbert or James Stewart. Before I buy my ticket I make sure it will all end happily. If necessary, I ask the girl at the box office. I have never seen *Stella Dallas* or *Intermezzo*.[6] Over the years I have developed other peccadilloes: I will, for example, see anything that is redeemed by Thelma Ritter. At the end of *Daddy Long Legs* I wait happily for the scene when Fred Clark, no longer angry, at last pours Thelma a convivial drink. They smile at each other, I smile at them, I feel they are smiling at me. In the movies I go to by myself, the men and women always like each other.

11

QUESTIONS

Understanding

1. Toth is classifying not movies, but what or whom exactly?
2. Toth names representatives of three types. Which one would you characterize as a protective companion? Which one seems most intense? Which represents the provincial, boy-next-door type?
3. Who represents the fourth type in Toth's classification system? How would you characterize this person?
4. What kind of movie does Toth herself prefer? What does she think of the kinds of movies her male friends take her to?
5. How strong are the personal attachments between Toth and her dates? How do they end differently from the movies she likes to see?

---

[6] Two 1930s tearjerkers.

6. Why do Toth's friends only take her to the kinds of movies *they* like? What does this habit reveal about them?

Strategies and Structure

1. Toth describes her relationship with Aaron in three paragraphs. The first tells the kind of movie he prefers; the second describes how he behaves toward her when they go to the movies; the third describes "afterwards." To what extent does this pattern hold for the next two "cinematypes" she describes?

2. Toth devotes one paragraph to her kind of movie and a second paragraph to how she behaves when she goes to the movie alone. Why doesn't she include a third paragraph at the end?

3. Toth is sensitive to "signals" (par. 5). What signal do the characters give each other in her favorite movies but not in real life?

4. Who drives when Toth goes or is taken to the movies? How do these details about transportation help characterize her companions and her relationships with them? Point out other similar concrete details (such as the references to popcorn) by which Toth deftly pictures her types.

5. Toth says Pete will hold her hand "when I get scared if I ask him" (par. 5). What role is she playing here? Where else in the essay does she seem to act the same way?

6. Films project images by bathing them in an intense light that seems to flicker as the frames shift. What influence of cinematic technique upon Toth's presentation of her types can you detect in paragraphs 2, 5, and 8?

Words and Figures of Speech

1. With both Aaron and Pete, Toth "goes" to the movies. What verb does she use with Sam? Why the shift?

2. Given the personality she assumes here, why does Toth call what she sees "movies" instead of "films"? What are the differences in the CONNOTATIONS of the two terms?

3. What is an "art" film (par. 1)?

4. What does his use of the CLICHÉ "food for thought" (par. 4) reveal about Pete?

5. "Cinematography" (par. 1) is the technical name for the visual art of film making. How does Toth's use of such terms suggest another image of her besides the one she displays at the movies?

6. Consult your dictionary if you are ill at ease with any of the following: *tentatively* (par. 2), *propaganda* (par. 4), *topical* (par. 4), *companionably* (par. 5), *infringe* (par. 5), *tattoo* (par. 8), *peccadilloes* (par. 11), and *convivial* (par. 11).

Comparing

1. Compare and contrast the personality of the author of "Cinematypes" with that of the author of "Memoirs of a Non-Prom Queen," in the next chapter. Which one seems more sure of herself, and why do you say so?
2. How do both Toth and Joyce Maynard ("Four Generations," Chapter 1) give the impression of being *detached* from their subjects?

Discussion and Writing Topics

1. Movies, especially those made in Hollywood, are said to appeal to the American public as a form of wish fulfillment, of dreams-come-true. How does Toth's experience at the movies support or go against this observation? Your own experience?
2. In what ways, if any, do you find the "rules" of dates and dating to impose role-playing and "typing" upon the participants?
3. Classify dates you have had by type. Describe each type as vividly as you can by citing specific details, including bits of conversation, that dramatize the relationships. Be as objective or peevishly personal as you like.

Isaac Asimov

What Do You Call
a Platypus?

Isaac Asimov was born in Petrovichi, Russia, in 1920, entered the
United States at age three, and became a naturalized citizen in
1928. After attending undergraduate and graduate school at
Columbia (Ph.D. in chemistry, 1948), he began teaching bio-
chemistry at the Boston University School of Medicine. His more
than two hundred books deal with an astounding range of subjects:
bio-chemistry, the human body, ecology, mathematics, physics,
astronomy, genetics, history, the Bible, and Shakespeare—to name
only a few. Asimov's first real acclaim came with a short story,
"Nightfall," in 1941; he continues to be best known, perhaps, for
his science fiction, including I, Robot (1950); the "Foundation"
trilogy (1951–53); and The Caves of Steel (1954). More recently,
he has published Opus 200 (1979), In Joy Still Felt (1980), and
In the Beginning (1981), an examination of the creation story.
"What Do You Call a Platypus?" is an essay on taxonomy, the
science of classification, that shows both the limitations of that
science and how it can provide new knowledge of the world.

In 1800, a stuffed animal arrived in England from the newly   1
discovered continent of Australia.

The continent had already been the source of plants and   2
animals never seen before—but this one was ridiculous. It was
nearly two feet long, and had a dense coating of hair. It also
had a flat rubbery bill, webbed feet, a broad flat tail, and a
spur on each hind ankle that was clearly intended to secrete
poison. What's more, under the tail was a single opening.

Zoologists stared at the thing in disbelief. Hair like a mam-   3
mal! Bill and feet like an aquatic bird! Poison spurs like a
snake! A single opening in the rear as though it laid eggs!

There was an explosion of anger. The thing was a hoax. Some 4
unfunny jokester in Australia, taking advantage of the distance
and strangeness of the continent, had stitched together parts of
widely different creatures and was intent on making fools of innocent zoologists in England.

Yet the skin seemed to hang together. There were no signs of 5
artificial joining. Was it or was it not a hoax? And if it wasn't a
hoax, was it a mammal with reptilian characteristics, or a reptile
with mammalian characteristics, or was it partly bird, or *what?*

The discussion went on heatedly for decades. Even the name 6
emphasized the ways in which it didn't seem like a mammal
despite its hair. One early name was *Platypus anatinus* which is
Graeco-Latin [1] for "Flat-foot, ducklike." Unfortunately, the term,
platypus, had already been applied to a type of beetle and there
must be no duplication in scientific names. It therefore received
another name, *Ornithorhynchus paradoxus*, which means "Bird-
beak, paradoxical."

Slowly, however, zoologists had to fall into line and admit that 7
the creature was real and not a hoax, however upsetting it might
be to zoological notions. For one thing, there were increasingly
reliable reports from people in Australia who caught glimpses of
the creature alive. The *paradoxus* was dropped and the scientific
name is now *Ornithorhynchus anatinus.*

To the general public, however, it is the "duckbill platypus," 8
or even just the duckbill, the queerest mammal (assuming it is a
mammal) in the world.

When specimens were received in such condition as to make it 9
possible to study the internal organs, it appeared that the heart
was just like those of mammals and not at all like those of reptiles.
The egg-forming machinery in the female, however, was not at all
like those of mammals, but like those of birds or reptiles. It
seemed really and truly to be an egg-layer.

It wasn't till 1884, however, that the actual eggs laid by a crea- 10
ture with hair were found. Such creatures included not only the
platypus, but another Australian species, the spiny anteater. That
was worth an excited announcement. A group of British scientists
were meeting in Montreal at the time, and the egg-discoverer, W.
H. Caldwell, sent them a cable to announce the finding.

[1] Combination of Greek and Latin; many scientific names put Latin endings
on Greek roots.

It wasn't till the twentieth century that the intimate life of the 11 duckbill came to be known. It is an aquatic animal, living in Australian fresh water at a wide variety of temperatures—from tropical streams at sea level to cold lakes at an elevation of a mile.

The duckbill is well adapted to its aquatic life, with its dense 12 fur, its flat tail, and its webbed feet. Its bill has nothing really in common with that of the duck, however. The nostrils are differently located and the platypus bill is different in structure, rubbery rather than duckishly horny. It serves the same function as the duck's bill, however, so it has been shaped similarly by the pressures of natural selection.

The water in which the duckbill lives is invariably muddy at the 13 bottom and it is in this mud that the duckbill roots for its food supply. The bill, ridged with horny plates, is used as a sieve, dredging about sensitively in the mud, filtering out the shrimps, earthworms, tadpoles and other small creatures that serve it as food.

When the time comes for the female platypus to produce 14 young, she builds a special burrow, which she lines with grass and carefully plugs. She then lays two eggs, each about three quarters of an inch in diameter and surrounded by a translucent, horny shell.

These the mother platypus places between her tail and abdo- 15 men and curls up about them. It takes two weeks for the young to hatch out. The new-born duckbills have teeth and very short bills, so that they are much less "birdlike" than the adults. They feed on milk. The mother has no nipples, but milk oozes out of pore openings in the abdomen and the young lick the area and are nourished in this way. As they grow, the bills become larger and the teeth fall out.

Yet despite everything zoologists learned about the duckbills, 16 they never seemed entirely certain as to where to place them in the table of animal classification. On the whole, the decision was made because of hair and milk. In all the world, only mammals have true hair and only mammals produce true milk. The duckbill and spiny anteater have hair and produce milk, so they have been classified as mammals.

Just the same, they are placed in a very special position. All the 17 mammals are divided into two subclasses. In one of these subclasses ("Prototheria" or "first-beasts")are the duckbill and five species of the spiny anteater. In the other ("Theria" or just "beast") are all the other 4,231 known species of mammals.

But all this is the result of judging only living species of mammals. Suppose we could study extinct species as well. Would that help us decide on the place of the platypus? Would it cause us to confirm our decision—or change it? [18]

Fossil remnants exist of mammals and reptiles of the far past, but these remnants are almost entirely of bones and teeth. Bones and teeth give us interesting information but they can't tell us everything. [19]

For instance, is there any way of telling, from bones and teeth alone, whether an extinct creature is a reptile or a mammal? [20]

Well, all living reptiles have legs splayed out so that the upper part above the knee is horizontal (assuming they have legs at all). All mammals, on the other hand, have legs that are vertical all the way down. Again, reptiles have teeth that all look more or less alike, while mammals have teeth that have different shapes, with sharp incisors in front, flat molars in back, and conical incisors and premolars in between. [21]

As it happens, there are certain extinct creatures, to which have been given the name "therapsids," which have their leg bones vertical and their teeth differentiated just as in the case of mammals. —And yet they are considered reptiles and not mammals. Why? Because there is another bony difference to be considered. [22]

In living mammals, the lower jaw contains a single bone; in reptiles, it is made up of a number of bones. The therapsid lower jaw is made up of seven bones and because of that those creatures are classified as reptiles. And yet in the therapsid lower jaw, the one bone making up the central portion of the lower jaw is by far the largest. The other six bones, three on each side, are crowded into the rear angle of the jaw. [23]

There seems no question, then, that if the therapsids are reptiles they are nevertheless well along the pathway towards mammals. [24]

But how far along the pathway are they? For instance, did they have hair? It might seem that it would be impossible to tell whether an extinct animal had hair or not just from the bones, but let's see— [25]

Hair is an insulating device. It keeps body heat from being lost too rapidly. Reptiles keep their body temperature at about that of the outside environment. They don't have to be concerned over loss of heat and hair would be of no use to them. [26]

Mammals, however, maintain their internal temperature at 27 nearly 100° F. regardless of the outside temperature; they are "warm-blooded." This gives them the great advantage of remaining agile and active in cold weather, when the chilled reptile is sluggish. But then the mammal must prevent heat loss by means of a hairy covering. (Birds, which also are warm-blooded, use feathers as an insulating device.)

With that in mind, let's consider the bones. In reptiles, the 28 nostrils open into the mouth just behind the teeth. This means that reptiles can only breathe with their mouths empty. When they are biting or chewing, breathing must stop. This doesn't bother a reptile much, for it can suspend its need for oxygen for considerable periods.

Mammals, however, must use oxygen in their tissues constantly, 29 in order to keep the chemical reactions going that serve to keep their body temperature high. The oxygen supply must not be cut off for more than very short intervals. Consequently mammals have developed a bony palate, a roof to the mouth. When they breathe, air is led above the mouth to the throat. This means they can continue breathing while they bite and chew. It is only when they are actually in the act of swallowing that the breath is cut off and this is only a matter of a couple of seconds at a time.

The later therapsid species had, as it happened, a palate. If they 30 had a palate, it seems a fair deduction that they needed an uninterrupted supply of oxygen that makes it look as though they were warm-blooded. And if they were warm-blooded, then very likely they had hair, too.

The conclusion, drawn from the bones alone, would seem to be 31 that some of the later therapsids had hair, even though, judging by their jawbones, they were still reptiles.

The thought of hairy reptiles is astonishing. But that is only 32 because the accident of evolution seems to have wiped out the intermediate forms. The only therapsids alive seem to be those that have developed *all* the mammalian characteristics, so that we call them mammals. The only reptiles alive are those that developed *none* of the mammalian characteristics.

Those therapsids that developed some but not others seem to 33 be extinct.

Only the duckbill and the spiny anteater remain near the border 34 line. They have developed the hair and the milk and the single-boned lower jaw and the four-chambered heart, but not the nipples or the ability to bring forth live young.

For all we know, some of the extinct therapsids, while still having their many-boned lower jaw (which is why we call them reptiles instead of mammals), may have developed even beyond the duckbill in other ways. Perhaps some late therapsids had nipples and brought forth living young. We can't tell from the bones alone. 35

If we had a complete record of the therapsids, flesh and blood, as well as teeth and bone, we might decide that the duckbill was on the therapsid side of the line and not on the mammalian side. —Or are there any other pieces of evidence that can be brought into play? 36

An American zoologist, Giles T. MacIntyre, of Queens College, has taken up the matter of the trigeminal nerve, which leads from the jaw muscles to the brain. 37

In all reptiles, without exception, the trigeminal nerve passes through the skull at a point that lies between two of the bones making up the skull. In all mammals that bring forth living young, without exception, the nerve actually passes *through* a particular skull bone. 38

Suppose we ignore all the matter of hair and milk and eggs, and just consider the trigeminal nerve. In the duckbill, does the nerve pass through a bone, or between two bones? It has seemed in the past that the nerve passed through a bone and that put the duckbill on the mammalian side of the dividing line. 39

Not so, says MacIntyre. The study of the trigeminal nerve was made in adult duckbills, where the skull bones are fused together and the boundaries are hard to make out. In young duckbills, the skull bones are more clearly separated and in them it can be seen, MacIntyre says, that the trigeminal nerve goes between two bones. 40

In that case, there is a new respect in which the duckbill falls on the reptilian side of the line and MacIntyre thinks it ought not to be considered a mammal, but as a surviving species of the otherwise long-extinct therapsid line. 41

And so, a hundred seventy years after zoologists began to puzzle out the queer mixture of characteristics that go to make up the duckbill platypus—there is still argument as to what to call it. 42

Is the duckbill platypus a mammal? A reptile? Or just a duckbill platypus? 43

QUESTIONS

Understanding

1. What are the chief distinguishing features of mammals as reported by Asimov? Of reptiles?
2. Which mammalian features does the platypus lack? Which reptilian characteristics does it possess?
3. How does the example of the platypus show the limitations of the zoological CLASSIFICATION system?
4. What new evidence does Asimov cite for reclassifying the platypus? How convincing do you find it? Why?

Strategies and Structure

1. Why do you think Asimov begins his case for reclassifying the platypus by recounting the confused history of how the animal got its name?
2. Why does it matter what we *call* a platypus? For what ultimate purpose is Asimov concerned with the creature's name?
3. Why does Asimov refer to extinct creatures beginning with paragraph 18? What is the function of the therapsids (par. 22) in his line of reasoning?
4. This essay in reclassification ends with three alternatives (par. 43). Why three instead of just two?
5. The logic of paragraph 32 depends upon an unstated assumption about the order of evolution. Which does Asimov assume came first, reptiles or mammals? How does this assumption influence his entire ARGUMENT? Is the assumption valid?

Words and Figures of Speech

1. Why was "paradoxical" (par. 6) an appropriate part of the platypus's name? How does it differ in precise usage from "ambiguous" and "ambivalent"?
2. Asimov refers to the "egg-forming machinery" (par. 9) of the female platypus. How technical is this term? What does it suggest about the audience for whom Asimov intends this essay?
3. What is meant by "the pressures of natural selection" (par. 12)?

4. Asimov's essay is an exercise in "taxonomy," although he does not use the word. What does it mean according to your dictionary?

Comparing

1. Asimov's essay has some features of a logical argument of the sort you will encounter in Chapter 9. What is he attempting to prove or disprove? When you read William Buckley's "Capital Punishment" (Chapter 9), *contrast* the kind of evidence presented in his logical argument with that presented in Asimov's.

Discussion and Writing Topics

1. What would *you* call a platypus? Why?
2. Explain why a whale is classified as a mammal instead of a fish.
3. A classification system provides a means of arranging information about the known world. Using Asimov's train of thought or some other example, explain how classification systems also help us gain *new* knowledge.

W R I T I N G   T O P I C S   for Chapter Two
Essays That Classify and Divide

Write an essay on one of the following subjects that uses classification or division as its organizing principle. Remember that a good classification essay not only assigns members to a class but also gives interesting reasons for the divisions it makes and draws interesting conclusions about its subject:

1. Your teachers in high school or college

2. Blind dates

3. Drugs and drug-abusers

4. Moral codes

5. Fraternities or sororities

6. Neighborhoods, high schools, or churches in your hometown

7. Landlords in the campus area

8. Fast-food restaurants

9. Food in the dining facilities on your campus

10. Attitudes toward getting a college education

11. Cameras, bicycles, or motorcycles

12. Modern families

13. Movies you have seen in the last year

14. Television soap operas

15. Styles of rock, folk, country and western, or classical music

16. Ways of seeing (for the first time) a city, museum, or foreign country

17. Ways of reacting to personal disappointment or tragedy

18. Life-styles among people under thirty

3

Essays That
Analyze a Process

Analysis breaks its object into components. It differs from
CLASSIFICATION [1] by attending to a particular member of a
class rather than the class in general. When we classify an
artichoke, for example, we put it in the category of "thistle-
like plants." When we analyze an artichoke, we pull apart
an individual specimen and note that it is made up of layer
upon layer of fibrous green scales. If we analyze the growth
of an artichoke from a seed, we are analyzing a process
(which tends to be in motion) rather than an object (which
tends to be stable). Most how-to-do-it essays analyze processes, as do most accounts of how something works (a
typewriter, a city transit system, gravity). The selections in
this chapter are essays in PROCESS ANALYSIS.

In the following analysis, John McPhee tells how orange
juice concentrate is made from fresh oranges:

As the fruit starts to move along a concentrate plant's assembly
line, it is first culled. In what some citrus people remember as
"the old fresh-fruit days," before the Second World War,
about forty per cent of all oranges grown in Florida were
eliminated at packinghouses and dumped in fields. Florida milk
tasted like orangeade. Now, with the exception of split and
rotten fruit, all of Florida's orange crop is used. Moving up a
conveyer belt, oranges are scrubbed with detergent before they
roll on into juicing machines. There are several kinds of juicing
machines, and they are something to see. One is called the
Brown Seven Hundred. Seven hundred oranges a minute go into
it and are split and reamed on the same kind of rosettes that

[1] Terms printed in all capitals are defined in the Glossary.

are in the centers of ordinary kitchen reamers. The rinds that come pelting out the bottom are integral halves, just like the rinds of oranges squeezed in a kitchen. Another machine is the Food Machinery Corporation's FMC In-line Extractor. It has a shining row of aluminum teeth. When an orange tumbles in, the upper jaw comes crunching down on it while at the same time the orange is penetrated from below by a perforated steel tube. As the jaws crush the outside, the juice goes through the perforations in the tube and down into the plumbing of the concentrate plant. All in a second, the juice has been removed and the rind has been crushed and shredded beyond recognition.

From either machine, the juice flows on into a thing called the finisher, where seeds, rag, and pulp are removed. The finisher has a big stainless-steel screw that steadily drives the juice through a fine-mesh screen. From the finisher, it flows on into holding tanks. . . .

The first thing to notice about this analysis is that it combines several processes into one. McPhee describes the journey of fresh oranges from the time they enter the conveyor belt until the juice reaches the holding tanks. But because all companies do not use the same machines, he must digress to explain the differences between the Brown Seven Hundred and the In-line Extractor. The discussion returns from its divergent branches in the beginning of the second paragraph, "From either machine. . . ." McPhee picks up the flow so smoothly that we hardly notice any interruption; but, like many accounts of a complex process, his is a composite. The author has reduced the complexities to their elements and takes care of inconsistencies in brief asides to the reader. (The business of extracting "chilled juice" from fresh oranges is so different from making concentrate that McPhee has to describe it in a separate segment of his account.)

One aside in our example, however, has little to do with the process of making orange concentrate. This is the author's reference to the days before World War II when all Florida milk tasted like orangeade. To keep our interest, McPhee is laying out many things at once, including the changing history of Florida's citrus industry. Process analysis often draws upon other strategies of EXPOSITION and upon the other MODES OF DISCOURSE. When McPhee switches from what happened in "the old fresh-fruit days" to what happens "now," he slips into NARRATION. Process analysis might even be regarded as a specialized form of narration that tells what happens from one stage of a process to another. But the ultimate purpose of process analysis is to explain how rather than to tell what. And although process analysis often describes the parts of an operation, it focuses upon their function rather than their appearance (the business of DESCRIPTION).

Perhaps the most important lesson to be learned from McPhee's analysis is that he divides the process of making concentrate into stages: (1) culling, (2) scrubbing, (3) extracting, (4) straining, (5) storing. When you begin an essay in process analysis, make a list of the stages of the operation you are describing or the directions you are giving. Once you have a rough list of stages, make sure that they are separate and distinct. (McPhee does not isolate the movement of oranges up the conveyor belt as a stage because the conveyor is involved in more than one stage of the process of making concentrate.) When you are satisfied that none of the items on your list repeat others and that you have omitted no essential items, you are ready to decide upon the order in which your steps will be presented to the reader.

The usual order of a process analysis is chronological, beginning with the earliest stage of the process and ending with the last or with the finished product. If you are describing a cyclical rather than a linear process, however, you will have to break into the cycle at an arbitrary point, proceed through the cycle, and return to your starting place. For example, you might describe the circulation of the blood by starting as it leaves the heart, tracing it through the arteries and vessels, and concluding as it flows back into the heart. If the order of the process you are describing is controlled by a piece of mechanism, let that mechanism work for you. The first part of McPhee's analysis is organized as much by that conveyor belt as by time. Whatever order you choose, do not digress from it so long that the reader loses the sequence. Sequence is the backbone of process analysis, and it must be flexible yet strong.

Ruth Rudner

Body Surfing

An outdoor enthusiast, Ruth Rudner has "always preferred
mountains to schools," although she attended several, including
Antioch College, Columbia School of General Studies, and the
University of Vienna. In 1963 she went to live in the Alps and
wrote about skiing, hiking, climbing, "being" in the Alps.
Returning to America, she began to explore and write about the
Rockies, Sierras, and Appalachians. Rudner now lives in New York
City but continues to meditate on other "wild places of the world
and especially Tibet." She is the author of Wandering: A Walker's
Guide to the Mountain Trails of Europe (1972), Huts and Hikes
in the Dolomites (1974), and Off and Walking: A Hiker's Guide
to American Places (1977). "Body Surfing" is a chapter from
Forgotten Pleasures (1978), Rudner's guide for the "seasonal
adventurer." It explains how to turn yourself into a human
surfboard.

There is hardly a pleasure more elemental than body surfing.   1
For a willingness to be carried by the sea you get your own
personal chance to emerge from it. It seems downright primordial . . . the beginning of life.

Body surfing is simply making a surfboard out of your body   2
to ride the crest of a wave as it breaks and rolls onto the sand.
You must catch the wave at just the right moment for a real
ride. If you are too early the wave breaks over you, or just
behind you and then all you get is a shove and a dousing. If
you are too late you are *in* the crest just after it releases itself
and its power, and you get left behind while it rolls on to the
shore without you.

The right moment is the whole thing. It is a moment most   3 apt to happen in the Pacific where the waves are big, slow, power-ful and even. They are easy to predict since they come in a regular series. But other seas will do, if the Pacific isn't immediately available.

Stand, or tread water, until you see the right wave far out, 4 gathering momentum. Then position yourself—swim farther out or farther in if necessary—so that you are ready to plunge toward shore in the trough created in front of the cresting wave. Once you are in the trough, swim as hard as you can. Ideally, you will be sucked down into the trough. Suddenly the cresting water above you lifts you, holds you, shoots you forward. At this moment, arch, point your body with your arms like tensed wings down at your sides, flat and bulletlike. You become a missile projected by the churning, breaking wave. If it works, if you are *in*, if you *catch* the wave, you become a part of it, the forward part of the cresting wave, like the prow of a boat made somehow of churning foam, and you can ride all the way home to the sand, and come home *into* the sand like a wedge, grinding into the shore like the wave itself.

The ultimate ride sends you all the way up onto the beach, 5 stinging from the grinding into the sand, dazed perhaps—for the space of a wave or two.

The perfect catch, the ultimate ride, the pure moment of release, 6 of flying—it's to feel at one with the wave, in it, of it, connected to its rhythm, yet *using* its power, its locomotion, to give you the ride.

A lot of time is spent waiting for the right wave, making false 7 starts, getting half-rides, bad rides, so-so rides. These are the ones that leave you bobbing somewhere just off shore, or the ones in which the wave chops at another wave and you get battered in between. These, of course, are part of it, part of the fun, but not the experience you dream of, that you're willing to spend an hour shivering and treading water for.

Atlantic body surfing is less dependable and less exciting— 8 unless it's a wild surf and you really like being tossed and battered and turned upside down. Usually it's too mild for long, rushing, rolling rides, or too wild for anything but a series of dunkings.

Even so, wherever you find a wave, try it. All of it can be good 9 practice for that day when you will get to the ultimate Pacific wave.

Q U E S T I O N S

Understanding

1. What is the fundamental appeal of body surfing, according to Rudner?
2. What is the trickiest and most critical step in achieving the perfect ride?
3. Why does Rudner find body surfing less satisfying in the Atlantic than in the Pacific? Why should we try it anyway, no matter where?

Strategies and Structure

1. Rudner's essay defines the sport of body surfing before explaining how to engage in it. Which paragraph sets forth the formal definition?
2. Which single paragraph contains an entire mini-analysis of the whole process of body surfing?
3. Into how many steps does Rudner divide that process? What are they?
4. In which paragraph does the author describe the ideal product or result of the process she is analyzing?
5. How do paragraphs 7–9 (about false starts and faulty conditions) relate to Rudner's earlier discussion of "the ultimate ride" (par. 5)? Would the essay be better or worse without these paragraphs? Why?
6. Which sentence in paragraph 4 captures with its repetitions the rhythms of riding a big wave?

Words and Figures of Speech

1. In what double sense is Rudner using the word *elemental* in paragraph 1?
2. Both *primordial* (par. 1) and *elemental* mean "basic" or "primary." What is the *difference* in meaning between the two words? Between *primordial* and *ultimate* (par. 5)?
3. In a single paragraph (par. 4), Rudner compares the hurling surfer to a bird, a bullet, a missile, the prow of a boat, and a wedge. Is

this a "mixed" METAPHOR or a series of individual metaphors? Explain your answer. How effective do you find the comparisons?

Comparing

1. Rudner thinks of body surfing as one of life's "forgotten pleasures," along with skating on a woodland pond and cross-country skiing. How does her attitude toward her subject resemble Noel Perrin's in "The Grades of Maple Syrup" (Chapter 2)? Which writer nevertheless seems more tranquil when discussing his or her simple pleasure?
2. Rudner analyzes the process of body surfing before specifying its ultimate endproduct in paragraphs 5 and 6. In "The Spider and the Wasp" (the last essay in this chapter), the endproduct is a food supply for the wasp's young, and Alexander Petrunkevitch analyzes the process of gathering that food. How does the order of presenting process and product compare in the two essays?

Discussion and Writing Topics

1. Write a process analysis in which you explain how to use and care for a surfboard, how to do the crawl or other swimming stroke (don't forget the breathing), how to skin dive with scuba gear, or how to catch salt-water crabs.
2. Explain how to indulge in any simple forgotten pleasure (like berry picking or riding the subway or bus all afternoon) that you can recall from your childhood.

Katie Kelley

Garbage

*Katie Kelly, a free-lance writer, lives in New York City, but her
hometown is Albion (Boone Co.), Nebraska (population: 2010),
to which she returns once a year or so. A former contributing
editor of* Time *and an editor and contributor to women's magazines, she is the author of* The Wonderful World of Women's
Wear Daily *(1972) and* My Prime Time: Confessions of a T.V.
Watcher *(1980). The following essay is Kelly's analysis of how
New York City processes its enormous flow of garbage. Soon after
writing this piece for the* Saturday Review, *she published a book-
length investigation of the same subject,* Garbage: The History
and Future of Garbage in America *(1973).*

New Yorkers are a provincial lot. They wear their city's   1
accomplishments like blue ribbons. To anyone who will listen
they boast of leading the world in everything from Mafia
murders to porno moviehouses. They can also boast that their
city produces more garbage than any other city in the world.
In fact, it produces more than many countries.

In its 1970–71 garbage season—a boffo season if there ever   2
was one—New York City produced an average of 28,900 tons
per day, as against a mere 4,800 tons per day for Los Angeles
and a paltry 2,000 tons per day for San Francisco. But it is not
only in quantity that New York excels. Fully 20 per cent of
the city's garbage consists of quality paper: canceled checks,
rough drafts of Broadway hits, executive memos, IBM punch
cards, and so on. On Mondays alone seven million pounds of
the Sunday *New York Times* are donated to New York garbage cans.

Then there's the packaging. According to the city's flam-   3

boyant environmental protection administrator, Jerome Kretchmer, in the rest of the country packaging accounts for under 20 per
cent of the total garbage; in New York, for 40 per cent. Much of
this whopping total consists of flip tops, snack paks, variety packs,
plastic cases, bottles, tin cans, and other containers. Another big
chunk is aluminum. If the aluminum that New Yorkers throw out
every day were converted into Reynolds Wrap, it would make a
sheet more than 7,500 miles long—roughly the distance from New
York to Samoa.

The remaining 40 per cent of Fun City's garbage consists of   4
such mundane leavings as egg shells, coffee grounds, wilted lettuce
leaves, and pot scrapings, together with such odds and ends as tex-
tile scraps, tires, wood, glass, plastics, etc. (The 73,000 cars abandoned on New York City streets last year constitute a separate class
of garbage. Though some find their way to the dump, most of
these wrecks are bought up by scrap dealers.)

If New York produces more garbage than any other city in the   5
world, it stands to reason that the cost of getting rid of it must be
correspondingly prodigious. It is. Last year the bill for pickup,
processing, and delivery came to $176,246,604. Though one would
expect innovation from the undisputed leader in the field of garbage, New York is forced to dispose of its trash in ways familiar to
every small town in the country: It burns the stuff in incinerators—
about 30 per cent of New York City garbage is incinerated—and/or
buries it in landfills.

The largest of the city's seven incinerators, the Brooklyn incin-   6
erator is a yellow-brick building with high walls, few windows, and
two 200-foot-tall smoke stacks, one of which is equipped with an
electrostatic precipitator to reduce pollution. (Although a cut
above the average in cleanliness, New York's incinerator stacks still
spew thousands of pounds of soot over the city every day.) Garbage trucks parade up to the Brooklyn plant, dumping their loads
into a pit capable of holding 12,500 tons of garbage. A crane
moves back and forth over this pit, periodically clanking down to
gouge out a one-ton bite. The crane then drops the garbage onto
conveyor belts, which in turn feed it into the incinerator ovens.

Measuring thirty by seven by two hundred feet, each of the   7
Brooklyn incinerator's four ovens is capable of burning up ten tons
of garbage an hour at temperatures averaging 1,600° to 1,800° F.
The towering stacks create such an upward draft that, upon look-

ing into one of the iron grates, I felt as if, if I didn't hold on, I would be sucked into that fiery furnace.

After the garbage has been burned, the cooled residue is dumped   8
onto barges, which are towed off by tugboats to one of five landfill sites around the city. The largest of these is the 3,000-acre Fresh Kills site on Staten Island.

Fresh Kills, which daily receives about 11,000 tons of garbage,   9
is a strange place. Much of this former swampland resembles the ash heaps of *The Great Gatsby*.[1] Vast, forlorn, endless. A vision of death. In the foreground, a discarded funeral wreath. A doll with outstretched arms. A man's black sock. A nylon stocking. And, beyond, refrigerators, toilets, bathtubs, stoves.

Yet Fresh Kills is also—in places and in its own way—unexpect-   10
edly beautiful. Thousands of gulls wheel in the air. Banking sharply, they dip down one by one to settle in for a good feast. In areas where the garbage is fresh, there is an overpowering stench, but where it is older, its blanket of earth is covered with grass, bushes, shrubs, trees. Summertime in Fresh Kills is a time of flowers and birdsong. A volunteer vegetable garden flourishes in the landfill. Here, in the world's largest compost heap, the seeds and sprouts of kitchen scraps thrive. Come fall, offices all around New York's City Hall are decorated with gourds and pumpkins harvested at Fresh Kills. In the fall, too, quail and pheasants scurry through Fresh Kills' underbrush, creating a problem for the Department of Sanitation: Hunters try to poach on this municipal game preserve.

"Fresh Kills turns me on," Jerome Kretchmer said a few days   11
after my visit to the site. Recently, he went on, he had taken his seven-year-old daughter's class out to Fresh Kills for a field trip. Even the sight of the barges heading off for the landfill sites excited him: "You can stand on the shore on Monday morning and watch the barges going out. And you know what went on in New York City over the weekend. There are fetuses and dead cats. Packages, boxes, cartons from fancy stores, dress scraps. Wow, man! Whatever went on in the city is going out to Fresh Kills. You can see it all. What we used. What we wasted."

Opened in 1948, Fresh Kills is already almost full to the brim,   12

[1] Novel by F. Scott Fitzgerald published in 1925; it compares modern life to a wasteland of ashes near a Long Island railroad track.

for New York City, like every other city in this country, has more garbage than it can cope with. The city is, in fact, due to run out of landfill space—preferably swampland or a sandpit or gulley—in 1985. The solution: Pile it higher. But even here there are limits. As one city official put it: "We have to leave some room between the sea gulls and the planes."

"It sure has changed out here," one worker, who has been at 13 Fresh Kills for years, told me. "Why, there used to be fresh natural springs over there." He gestured out over the hundreds of acres of garbage. Natural crab beds once flourished in the area. Now they, too, are gone, buried under tons of garbage.

QUESTIONS

Understanding

1. In what two ways does New York City's garbage differ from that of other cities? What about the process of handling that garbage? How different is *it*?

2. Why does Fresh Kills "turn on" (par. 11) Administrator Kretchmer? What story does he read in the city's garbage?

3. New York's great garbage dump is a place of death for Kelly (par. 9). What other associations does it hold for her? In which direction does the last paragraph (13) tip the balance?

Strategies and Structure

1. Kelly divides the process of handling New York's garbage into three main stages. If the first is collection, what are the other two? Where are they explained?

2. To which stage does Kelly pay least attention? Should she have paid more? Why or why not?

3. Abandoned cars are a substantial form of garbage that Kelly leaves out of her process analysis. Why does she do so?

4. Point out specific details (for example, the money figures in paragraph 5) by which Kelly establishes her authority as an expert in the "field" she is explaining to us.

5. What is the purpose of the last sentence in paragraph 7?

6. What is the role of environmental protectionist Kretchmer in Kelly's essay?
7. How effective do you find the example of the giant aluminum roll in paragraph 3? Explain your answer.
8. What is the effect of including "fetuses" in the list of items in paragraph 11? How interesting do you find most of the "catalogues" of garbage in Kelly's essay?

Words and Figures of Speech

1. "Fresh Kills" may sound like a well-chosen name for a garbage graveyard, but in American place-names "Kill" has nothing to do with death. What geographical meaning does the word have, according to your dictionary?
2. Describe the TONE of Kelly's essay as set by SLANG words like *boffo* (par. 2) and *Fun City* (4).
3. Look up any of the following words you do not already know: *provincial* (par. 1), *paltry* (2), *flamboyant* (3), *mundane* (4), *prodigious* (5), and *innovation* (6).

Comparing

1. What hints of a PERSUASIVE ARGUMENT about ecology can you find in Kelly's PROCESS ANALYSIS? How does the evidence set forth in her essay confirm Paul Colinvaux's "ecological thesis"—that human culture is altered by changes in population and living habits—in "Why Japan Bombed Pearl Harbor" (Chapter 4)?
2. How does Kelly's reporter resemble Susan Allen Toth's female movie-goer in "Cinematypes" (Chapter 2)?

Discussion and Writing Topics

1. How does your hometown or city dispose of its garbage? Of cars abandoned on the streets? Explain either process step by step.
2. Some cities (Cleveland, Ohio, for example) are experimenting with garbage as a source of fuel. Conceive and analyze such an ideal recycling process.

3. Cities in many parts of the U.S. must cope with the problem of snow removal in winter. How well does your town handle the job? What steps are taken after a snowfall? What additional steps would you recommend to the mayor?

4. A town's history may often be read in its refuse. Describe a dump you have visited as the end product of some sequence of human events.

John Fischer

Barbed Wire

John Fischer (1910–1978) grew up in the Panhandle section of
Texas and Oklahoma, the region he describes in From the High
Plains (1978) and that he revisits in the following essay. A
graduate of the University of Oklahoma, Fischer later received
several honorary degrees and taught as a Regent's Professor at the
University of California. His other books include The Stupidity
Problem (1964), Six in the Easy Chair (1973), and Vital Signs,
U.S.A. (1975). "Barbed Wire," subtitled "And the Art of Stringing
It," explains how to make a fence the way Fischer's grandfather
used to—for posterity, including the young grandson who learned
other virtues besides stringing a wire taut. This somewhat more
complicated essay in process analysis appeared in Harper's, a
magazine Fischer edited for fifteen years.

If you grew up in a city, it is possible that you have never had ₁
occasion to look closely at a barbed wire fence. In that case, it
might be fun to try to invent it, in imagination, for yourself.
It sounds easy. You only have to set two posts in the ground
and string between them wires, fitted with barbs at about six-
inch intervals. The problem is to fix the barbs so firmly that a
heavy animal brushing against the fence will not break them
off, or slide them along the wire. If they slide, you will soon
have all the barbs shoved up against one post or the other,
with a naked wire in between. Another problem is to figure
out a way to make your wire cheaply and fast—that is, with
machinery requiring a minimum of hand labor.

You might think of soldering on the barbs, but that quickly ₂
turns out to be a poor idea. The soldered joint is inherently

weak, and since each one has to be made by hand, the process would be prohibitively expensive. Another possibility is to take a ribbon of steel about one inch wide, cut zigzags along one side to form sharp points, and then twist the ribbon as you string it. This, too, has been tried and found impractical. The ribbon can be rolled, and cut by machinery, but it is too heavy to handle easily, uses too much expensive steel per foot, and is too weak to resist the impact of a charging bull. Another abortive scheme involved spiked spools strung on a wire.

According to the Bivins Museum in Tascosa, Texas, 401 patents for barbed wire have been recorded, and more than 1,600 variants have been catalogued. Out of all these attempts, only two proved successful. Both were patented at nearly the same time by two neighbors in De Kalb County, Illinois: Joseph F. Glidden and Jacob Haish. Whether they got their ideas independently, and who got his first, are questions that have provoked much expensive litigation. Their concepts were quite similar. Each involved clasping barbs around a wire at appropriate intervals—and then twisting that wire together with another one, so that the barbs are tightly gripped between the two. The only essential difference, to the eye of anyone but a patent lawyer, was in slightly variant methods of clasping the barb.

Whether or not Glidden was the original inventor, he certainly was the more successful businessman. He made his first wire in 1873, forming the barbs with a converted coffee grinder and twisting the twin wires in his barn with a hand-cranked grindstone. He sold his first wire, and took out his patent, in 1874. That same year he formed a partnership with a neighbor, I. L. Ellwood, and built a factory in De Kalb. Before the end of the next year, their factory was turning out five tons of wire a day, using improved, steam-operated machinery. In 1876 Glidden sold a half interest in his invention to the Washburn and Moen Manufacturing Company of Worcester, Massachusetts, which had been supplying him with plain wire; in payment he got $60,000, plus a royalty of 25 cents for every hundredweight of barbed wire sold.[1]

---

[1] Washburn and Moen eventually merged with the American Steel and Wire Company, a subsidiary of U.S. Steel. American Steel and Wire's museum in Worcester is the prime source of information about barbed wire. [Fischer's note.]

How profitable this deal proved to be can be glimpsed from the ⁵ following figures. In his first year of manufacture, Glidden sold 10,000 pounds of wire. Two years later, Washburn and Moen sold 2.8 million pounds. Within the next five years, sales mounted to more than 80 million pounds a year—yielding Glidden an income of more than $200,000 annually, the equivalent of at least $1 million today, and that was before the era of income taxes. The manufacturers' profits amounted to many times that.

Much of his wire was being shipped to Texas. Glidden and his ⁶ money followed it, leaving a permanent impress on the settlement of the High Plains and especially on its main city, Amarillo. There I came across his traces nearly sixty years later.

But in the meantime I had a chance to become well acquainted ⁷ with his product. When I was eleven years old, my grandfather John Fischer taught me how to string wire during a summer I spent on his homestead near Apache, Oklahoma. To my eyes he seemed a very old man, but he was still wiry, lean, hard-muscled, and accustomed to working from sunup till long after dark.

Like inventing barbed wire, stringing it is a more complex busi- ⁸ ness than you might think. First you find your posts. My grand-father insisted that they be either cedar, locust, or bois d'arc, also known as Osage orange. These woods will last in the ground for many years, while cottonwood or pine will rot quickly unless creo-soted—and we had no creosote in those days. Some he cut himself along a little creek that ran across one corner of his 160-acre farm; others he bought or bartered from neighbors. Each post had to be exactly six feet long.

When the posts were all collected, with a mule team and wagon, ⁹ he stacked them near the edge of the pasture he planned to fence, and then marked his line. This he did with a borrowed surveyor's transit, a handful of stakes, and a few rolls of binder twine. At thirty-foot intervals he scratched a mark on the hard prairie soil to indicate where he wanted each post to go. One of my jobs was to make a hole in the ground with a crowbar at each mark, and fill it with water from a five-gallon, galvanized-iron milk can, thus soft-ening the earth for my grandfather, who followed me with his post-hole digger.

The first post set, to a depth of precisely two feet, was of course ¹⁰ at a corner of the tract he was going to enclose. It had to be braced in both directions of the future fence lines. For braces he used two other posts planted diagonally in the earth with their feet anchored against heavy stones; their top ends he sawed at the proper angle and fastened to the corner post with tenpenny nails. Then we set about the weary labor of digging holes and setting intermediate posts until we came to the place he had marked for his next corner. We had to do only three sides of the forty-acre pasture, because the fourth side abutted a field enclosed years earlier; but at that, the post-setting took us the best part of two weeks.

Then we drove the wagon into Apache to get a load of wire. It came on big wooden spools, so heavy that the hardware dealer had to help us load them. Grandfather let me drive back, a proud and nervous assignment for me, although the mules—named Pete and Repeat—were gentle enough. 11

At the rear end of the wagon bed he rigged a pole, crosswise, to serve as a spindle on which a spool of wire could be mounted and easily unwound. We drove the wagon close to a corner post, twisted the end of the wire around it one foot above the ground, and stapled it fast. Next we drove along the line of posts for about 200 yards, unreeling wire on the ground behind us. There Grandpa stopped, unhitched the team, blocked three wheels of the wagon with rocks, and jacked up the fourth wheel, the rear one next to the fence line. He cut the wire and twisted the loose end around the axle of a jacked-up wheel, fastening it to a spoke for additional security. By turning the wheel, we wound the wire around the axle until it was taut. (There were patent wire-stretchers, but Grandpa did not own one. The wheel-stretching method worked just as well, and saved money.) After he had lashed the wheel to maintain the tension, we went back down the line and stapled the wire to each post. Then we repeated the process, time after time, until we had the pasture enclosed with a standard fence of four strands, spaced a foot apart. We finished up by making a wire gate at the corner nearest the house. 12

Three tips for fence-stringers: 13

—Wear the heaviest leather gauntlets you can find. Even so, you are bound to get your hands and arms torn, so carry some iodine and bandages with you.

—Staple the wire on the side of the posts facing into the pasture. When a heavy animal runs into the fence, he will press the wire against the posts, not the staples. If the wire were on the other side, the staples might pop out.

—Hang the expense, and use two staples for each fastening of the wire. One of them might someday rust or work loose.

I haven't seen that fence in decades, but my brother told me a   14
few years ago that it was still standing and tight. Probably it is the most nearly permanent thing I have ever worked on. Certainly its useful life has been far longer than that of any article or book I have written.

QUESTIONS

Understanding

1. How did the successful inventors of barbed wire solve the thorny problem of fixing the barbs so they would not slide?
2. Why was so much of the first barbed wire shipped to Texas and Oklahoma instead of, say, Massachusetts (where it was made) and other older, northern states?
3. John Fischer's essay begins by addressing itself to city dwellers. Why is his subject of interest to anybody but ranchers and farmers?
4. Barbed wire is an American invention. In what sense is the story (pars. 3–6) of Joseph L. Glidden, its co-inventor and best promoter, a typically American story?
5. As Fischer portrays him here, what was his Oklahoma grandfather like?
6. Besides the art of stringing wire, what other lessons did the boy in this essay learn from the experience of helping his grandfather that summer near Apache, Oklahoma? What virtues does the grandfather appear to uphold in the last paragraph?

Strategies and Structure

1. Depending on how you count, Fischer divides the process of making a barbed wire fence into about eight steps. Starting from scratch, what is the original step as introduced in paragraph 1 and discussed in the following several paragraphs?
2. Paragraph 8 gives a collective name to all the other steps of making a fence the Fischer way. What is this entire stage called? By which

TRANSITIONAL phrase does the author link this one with the stage he has been describing earlier?

3. The first step in the second stage of building a barbed wire fence is finding the posts (par. 8). The next is marking where they are to be placed (par. 9). What is the next step, described in paragraphs 9 and 10?

4. Into what three subordinate steps 'does Fischer divide this final endeavor with the bare posts? Which one is the boy's responsibility?

5. What subsequent step (or steps) in the fencing process is identified in paragraph 11? Paragraph 12? Paragraph 13? Which step most clearly shows the grandfather's ingenuity, by the way?

6. To be recognizable as such, the "steps" in a process analysis must come in sequence without overlapping too much. Why do you think Fischer puts his three "tips" on fence making (par. 13) in a category by themselves?

7. Paragraph 7 serves to join Fischer's account of how barbed wire is made with his explanation of how it is used to make a sturdy fence. How successful do you find this paragraph as a link between the two main strands of the essay?

8. How does the invitation to invent barbed wire "in imagination" (par. 1) broaden the appeal of this essay? How do the figures in paragraph 5 have the same effect? What sole reward does Fischer promise us in paragraph 1 for attending to his analysis.

9. Of the common modes of writing besides EXPOSITION—PERSUASION, DESCRIPTION, and NARRATION—which dominates paragraph 7? Point out other passages in the same mode throughout Fischer's essay. How do they contribute to his explanation of a process?

Words and Figures of Speech

1. Fischer writes about the "art" of stringing wire. He is so exacting and precise when analyzing the process, why do you suppose he calls it an art rather than a science?

2. What is the difference between a "homestead" (par. 7), like the one Fischer worked on as a boy, and a "farm"?

3. One meaning of *traces* (par. 6) is the harnesses by which draft animals (like Pete and Re-pete) drag their burdens along. What other specialized meaning of the word is intended here? How are the two meanings related?

4. As a METAPHOR from hunting, why is "came across his traces" (par. 6) appropriate here when applied to an inventor?

5. Why do you think Fischer uses the second PERSON pronoun *you* in paragraph 1 instead of simply referring to "city dwellers" or "urbanites" in the third person (*"they"*)?

6. "Hang the expense," says Fischer (par. 13) of the extravagance of using two staples instead of one at each fastening of the wire. Why is the CLICHÉ justified here?

7. What does Fischer mean by the phrase "useful life" in paragraph 14? What does it suggest about his idea of the nature and purpose of "art"? Why might he use such HYPERBOLE when referring to his writing?

Comparing

1. For Fischer, the taut barbed wire fencing of his grandfather's day represented some of the strengths and hardships of American prairie life. How do they contrast with the qualities of American life in the sunbelt today as evoked by Frank Trippett's "The Great American Cooling Machine" in the next chapter?

2. Both Fischer's essay on barbed wire and Noel Perrin's essay on maple syrup (Chapter 2) analyze homely subjects into their parts. Why is Fischer's essay, by comparison, best understood as a process analysis rather than an essay in classification?

Discussion and Writing Topics

1. Reconstruct the invention and explain the application of some common, useful device such as the ice-cream churn (hand-cranked variety), the lightning rod, free-standing woodstove, or hay baler.

2. Explain how to do something practical (bake bread, build a fire, shoe a horse) that you learned from a grandparent or other older person. Focus on the steps and stages that you were taught to follow, but try also to give a sense of the person and the learning experience itself.

Alexander Petrunkevitch
The Spider and the Wasp

Alexander Petrunkevitch (1875–1964), a native of Russia who come to the United States in his late twenties, was a world-renowned zoologist. After lecturing briefly at Harvard, he taught at Indiana University and then Yale for many years. Author of learned books on insects and a treatise in German on free will, he also translated poems by Byron (into Russian) and Pushkin (from Russian into English). Beginning in 1911, with an index to the species in Central and South America, Petrunkevitch devoted more than fifty years to the study of spiders. (His second book on amber spiders appeared in the year of his death.) "The Spider and the Wasp," which analyzes a natural process of life-out-of-death, is a product of that life-long fascination.

To hold its own in the struggle for existence, every species of [1] animal must have a regular source of food, and if it happens to live on other animals, its survival may be very delicately balanced. The hunter cannot exist without the hunted; if the latter should perish from the earth, the former would, too. When the hunted also prey on some of the hunters, the matter may become complicated.

This is nowhere better illustrated than in the insect world. [2] Think of the complexity of a situation such as the following: There is a certain wasp, *Pimpla inquisitor*, whose larvae feed on the larvae of the tussock moth. *Pimpla* larvae in turn serve as food for the larvae of a second wasp, and the latter in their turn nourish still a third wasp. What subtle balance between fertility and mortality must exist in the case of each of these four species to prevent the extinction of all of them!

An excess of mortality over fertility in a single member of the group would ultimately wipe out all four.

This is not a unique case. The two great orders of insects, Hymenoptera and Diptera, are full of such examples of interrelationship. And the spiders (which are not insects but members of a separate order of arthropods) also are killers and victims of insects.   3

The picture is complicated by the fact that those species which are carnivorous in the larval stage have to be provided with animal food by a vegetarian mother. The survival of the young depends on the mother's correct choice of a food which she does not eat herself.   4

In the feeding and safeguarding of their progeny the insects and spiders exhibit some interesting analogies to reasoning and some crass examples of blind instinct. The case I propose to describe here is that of the tarantula spiders and their arch-enemy, the digger wasps of the genus Pepsis. It is a classic example of what looks like intelligence pitted against instinct—a strange situation in which the victim, though fully able to defend itself, submits unwittingly to its destruction.   5

Most tarantulas live in the Tropics, but several species occur in the temperate zone and a few are common in the southern U.S. Some varieties are large and have powerful fangs with which they can inflict a deep wound. These formidable looking spiders do not, however, attack man; you can hold one in your hand, if you are gentle, without being bitten. Their bite is dangerous only to insects and small mammals such as mice; for a man it is no worse than a hornet's sting.   6

Tarantulas customarily live in deep cylindrical burrows, from which they emerge at dusk and into which they retire at dawn. Mature males wander about after dark in search of females and occasionally stray into houses. After mating, the male dies in a few weeks, but a female lives much longer and can mate several years in succession. In a Paris museum is a tropical specimen which is said to have been living in captivity for 25 years.   7

A fertilized female tarantula lays from 200 to 400 eggs at a time; thus it is possible for a single tarantula to produce several thousand young. She takes no care of them beyond weaving a cocoon of silk to enclose the eggs. After they hatch, the young walk away, find convenient places in which to dig their burrows and spend the   8 rest of their lives in solitude. Tarantulas feed mostly on insects and millepedes. Once their appetite is appeased, they digest the food for several days before eating again. Their sight is poor, being limited to sensing a change in the intensity of light and to the perception of moving objects. They apparently have little or no sense of hearing, for a hungry tarantula will pay no attention to a loudly chirping cricket placed in its cage unless the insect happens to touch one of its legs.

But all spiders, and especially hairy ones, have an extremely   9
delicate sense of touch. Laboratory experiments prove that tarantulas can distinguish three types of touch: pressure against the body wall, stroking of the body hair and riffling of certain very fine hairs on the legs called trichobothria. Pressure against the body, by a finger or the end of a pencil, causes the tarantula to move off slowly for a short distance. The touch excites no defensive response unless the approach is from above where the spider can see the motion, in which case it rises on its hind legs, lifts its front legs, opens its fangs and holds this threatening posture as long as the object continues to move. When the motion stops, the spider drops back to the ground, remains quiet for a few seconds and then moves slowly away.

The entire body of a tarantula, especially its legs, is thickly   10
clothed with hair. Some of it is short and woolly, some long and stiff. Touching this body hair produces one of two distinct reactions. When the spider is hungry, it responds with an immediate and swift attack. At the touch of a cricket's antennae the tarantula seizes the insect so swiftly that a motion picture taken at the rate of 64 frames per second shows only the result and not the process of capture. But when the spider is not hungry, the stimulation of its hairs merely causes it to shake the touched limb. An insect can walk under its hairy belly unharmed.

The trichobothria, very fine hairs growing from disklike mem-   11
branes on the legs, were once thought to be the spider's hearing organs, but we now know that they have nothing to do with sound. They are sensitive only to air movement. A light breeze makes them vibrate slowly without disturbing the common hair. When one blows gently on the trichobothria, the tarantula reacts with a quick jerk of its four front legs. If the front and hind legs are stimulated at the same time, the spider makes a sudden jump. This reaction is quite independent of the state of its appetite.

These three tactile responses—to pressure on the body wall, to [12] moving of the common hair and to flexing of the trichobothria— are so different from one another that there is no possibility of confusing them. They serve the tarantula adequately for most of its needs and enable it to avoid most annoyances and dangers. But they fail the spider completely when it meets its deadly enemy, the digger wasp Pepsis.

These solitary wasps are beautiful and formidable creatures. [13] Most species are either a deep shiny blue all over, or deep blue with rusty wings. The largest have a wing span of about four inches. They live on nectar. When excited, they give off a pungent odor—a warning that they are ready to attack. The sting is much worse than that of a bee or common wasp, and the pain and swelling last longer. In the adult stage the wasp lives only a few months. The female produces but a few eggs, one at a time at intervals of two or three days. For each egg the mother must provide one adult tarantula, alive but paralyzed. The tarantula must be of the correct species to nourish the larva. The mother wasp attaches the egg to the paralyzed spider's abdomen. Upon hatching from the egg, the larva is many hundreds of times smaller than its living but helpless victim. It eats no other food and drinks no water. By the time it has finished its single gargantuan meal and become ready for wasphood, nothing remains of the tarantula but its indigestible chitinous skeleton.

The mother wasp goes tarantula-hunting when the egg in her [14] ovary is almost ready to be laid. Flying low over the ground late on a sunny afternoon, the wasp looks for its victim or for the mouth of a tarantula burrow, a round hole edged by a bit of silk. The sex of the spider makes no difference, but the mother is highly discriminating as to species. Each species of Pepsis requires a certain species of tarantula, and the wasp will not attack the wrong species. In a cage with a tarantula which is not its normal prey the wasp avoids the spider, and is usually killed by it in the night.

Yet when a wasp finds the correct species, it is the other way [15] about. To identify the species the wasp apparently must explore the spider with her antennae. The tarantula shows an amazing tolerance to this exploration. The wasp crawls under it and walks over it without evoking any hostile response. The molestation is so great and so persistent that the tarantula often rises on all eight legs, as if it were on stilts. It may stand this way for several minutes. Meanwhile the wasp, having satisfied itself that the victim is of the right species, moves off a few inches to dig the spider's grave. Working vigorously with legs and jaws, it excavates a hole 8 to 10 inches deep with a diameter slightly larger than the spider's girth. Now and again the wasp pops out of the hole to make sure that the spider is still there.

When the grave is finished, the wasp returns to the tarantula   16
to complete her ghastly enterprise. First she feels it all over once more with her antennae. Then her behavior becomes more aggressive. She bends her abdomen, protruding her sting, and searches for the soft membrane at the point where the spider's leg joins its body—the only spot where she can penetrate the horny skeleton. From time to time, as the exasperated spider slowly shifts ground, the wasp turns on her back and slides along with the aid of her wings, trying to get under the tarantula for a shot at the vital spot. During all this maneuvering, which can last for several minutes, the tarantula makes no move to save itself. Finally the wasp corners it against some obstruction and grasps one of its legs in her powerful jaws. Now at last the harassed spider tries a desperate but vain defense. The two contestants roll over and over on the ground. It is a terrifying sight and the outcome is always the same. The wasp finally manages to thrust her sting into the soft spot and holds it there for a few seconds while she pumps in the poison. Almost immediately the tarantula falls paralyzed on its back. Its legs stop twitching; its heart stops beating. Yet it is not dead, as is shown by the fact that if taken from the wasp it can be restored to some sensitivity by being kept in a moist chamber for several months.

After paralyzing the tarantula, the wasp cleans herself by drag-   17
ging her body along the ground and rubbing her feet, sucks the drop of blood oozing from the wound in the spider's abdomen, then grabs a leg of the flabby, helpless animal in her jaws and drags it down to the bottom of the grave. She stays there for many minutes, sometimes for several hours, and what she does all that time in the dark we do not know. Eventually she lays her egg and attaches it to the side of the spider's abdomen with a sticky secretion. Then she emerges, fills the grave with soil carried bit by bit in

her jaws, and finally tramples the ground all around to hide any trace of the grave from prowlers. Then she flies away, leaving her descendant safely started in life.

In all this the behavior of the wasp evidently is qualitatively dif-   18
ferent from that of the spider. The wasp acts like an intelligent animal. This is not to say that instinct plays no part or that she reasons as man does. But her actions are to the point; they are not automatic and can be modified to fit the situation. We do not know for certain how she identifies the tarantula—probably it is by some olfactory or chemo-tactile sense—but she does it purposefully and does not blindly tackle a wrong species.

On the other hand, the tarantula's behavior shows only confu-   19
sion. Evidently the wasp's pawing gives it no pleasure, for it tries to move away. That the wasp is not simulating sexual stimulation is certain, because male and female tarantulas react in the same way to its advances. That the spider is not anesthetized by some odorless secretion is easily shown by blowing lightly at the tarantula and making it jump suddenly. What, then, makes the tarantula behave as stupidly as it does?

No clear, simple answer is available. Possibly the stimulation by   20
the wasp's antennae is masked by a heavier pressure on the spider's body, so that it reacts as when prodded by a pencil. But the explanation may be much more complex. Initiative in attack is not in the nature of tarantulas; most species fight only when cornered so that escape is impossible. Their inherited patterns of behavior apparently prompt them to avoid problems rather than attack them. For example, spiders always weave their webs in three dimensions, and when a spider finds that there is insufficient space to attach certain threads in the third dimension, it leaves the place and seeks another, instead of finishing the web in a single plane. This urge to escape seems to arise under all circumstances, in all phases of life and to take the place of reasoning. For a spider to change the pattern of its web is as impossible as for an inexperienced man to build a bridge across a chasm obstructing his way.

In a way the instinctive urge to escape is not only easier but   21
more efficient than reasoning. The tarantula does exactly what is most efficient in all cases except in an encounter with a ruthless and determined attacker dependent for the existence of her own species on killing as many tarantulas as she can lay eggs. Perhaps

in this case the spider follows its usual pattern of trying to escape, instead of seizing and killing the wasp, because it is not aware of its danger. In any case, the survival of the tarantula species as a whole is protected by the fact that the spider is much more fertile than the wasp.

QUESTIONS

Understanding

1. In which paragraph does Petrunkevitch announce his main topic? When does he actually begin to discuss it? How do the wasp larvae of paragraph 2 anticipate his main "case"?

2. If the digger wasp's favorite kind of tarantula always loses the deadly struggle between them, why does that species not disappear?

3. What might happen to the digger wasp if it were a more prolific breeder? What delicate natural balance do spider and wasp together illustrate?

4. What opposing kinds of behavior do spider and wasp respectively represent?

5. The first half of paragraph 8 is a miniature process analysis. What process does it analyze?

Strategies and Structure

1. Petrunkevitch begins his process analysis with its end result and then returns to the first step, the wasp's hunt for her prey. What is that end result? In which paragraph is it explained?

2. Point out the six stages—from hunting to burying—into which Petrunkevitch analyzes the wasp's conquest of the spider.

3. Petrunkevitch enlarges the combat between spider and wasp to human scale by calling the wasp "her" and by referring to the wasp as the spider's "arch-enemy" (par. 5). Point out other similar techniques by which he minimizes the difference in scale between our world and the world of the insects.

4. Petrunkevitch's process analysis incorporates elements of the COMPARISON AND CONTRAST essay (Chapter 6). Does his compari-

son alternate point by point between spider and wasp, or does he concentrate on one for a while and then concentrate on the other? Explain your answer by referring to several specific passages.

5. Paragraph 12 is a TRANSITION paragraph. Which sentences look backward? Which look forward?

6. Which sentence in paragraph 19 sets up the remainder of the essay?

7. How does paragraph 4 fit in with the rest of Petrunkevitch's essay?

Words and Figures of Speech

1. Such words as *Hymenoptera, Diptera, arthropods,* and *trichobothria* (pars. 3, 9, 11) show that Petrunkevitch, a distinguished zoologist, was comfortable with the technical vocabulary of science; but this essay is sprinkled with nontechnical terms as well, for example: *wasphood* (par. 13), *pops out of the hole* (15), *shot* (16), *prowlers* (17). Give several other examples of your own.

2. From the range of Petrunkevitch's DICTION, what conclusions can you draw about the make-up of the readership of *Scientific American,* the magazine in which this essay appeared?

3. Consult your dictionary for the exact meanings of any of the following words you cannot define precisely: *subtle* (par. 2), *carnivorous* (4), *progeny* (5), *formidable* (6, 13), *appeased* (8), *tactile* (12), *pungent* (13), *gargantuan* (13), *chitinous* (13), *molestation* (15), *exasperated* (16), *secretion* (17, 19), *qualitatively* (18), *instinct* (5, 18), *olfactory* (18), *simulating* (18), *anesthetized* (19).

Comparing

1. According to "The Spider and the Wasp," Loren Eiseley's "The Angry Winter" (Chapter 1), and Carl Sagan's "The Quest for Extraterrestrial Intelligence" ("Essays for Further Reading"), how do all creatures acquire their distinctive patterns of intelligence and instinct?

2. In its treatment of the relationship between the human world and the insect world, how does the scale of Petrunkevitch's essay resemble that of Annie Dillard's "Transfiguration" (Chapter 7)?

Discussion and Writing Topics

1. Describe the process by which an insect or animal that you have observed feeds its young and starts them off in life.
2. Analyze the stages of maturation that bring a human being to adulthood.
3. Develop a parallel between two insects and two people (or types of people) with whom you are familiar.
4. Do you have a pet that has shown signs of true intelligence over and beyond mere instinct? Describe his or her behavior.

WRITING TOPICS for Chapter Three
Essays That Analyze a Process

Write an essay analyzing one of the following processes or giving directions for one of the following operations:

1. How to play chess

2. How to change a tire

3. How to install an electric circuit in a house

4. How to make wine, beer, or mead

5. How to milk a cow

6. How to keep bees

7. How to thread and operate a sewing machine

8. How to make butter

9. How a piano works

10. How a solar heating system works

11. How to conserve energy in a house

12. How to install and operate a CB radio

13. How to meet a girl or guy

14. How to make a good (or bad) impression on your boyfriend's or girlfriend's parents

15. How to excel in school

16. How to take and develop photographs

17. How iron ore is made into steel

18. How a fuel injection system (or carburetor) works

19. How an internal combustion engine works

20. How to sail a boat

21. How to buy a used car

22. How to buy a horse or other livestock

23. How to buy stocks, bonds, or other securities

24. How to beat inflation in small ways

25. How to get rich

4
Essays That Analyze Cause and Effect

PROCESS ANALYSIS [1] *(Chapter 3) is concerned with sequence in time and space. Sequence is one kind of relationship among objects and events; another is causation. When we confuse the two, we are reasoning as Mark Twain's hero does in* Adventures of Huckleberry Finn. *Alone in the woods one night, Huck sees an evil omen:*

Pretty soon a spider went crawling up my shoulder, and I flipped it off and it lit in the candle; and before I could budge it was all shriveled up. I didn't need anybody to tell me that that was an awful bad sign and would fetch me some bad luck, so I was scared and most shook the clothes off of me. I got up and turned around in my tracks three times and crossed my breast every time; and then I tied up a little lock of my hair to keep witches away. But I hadn't no confidence.

Huck is right to be scared; all sorts of misadventures are going to befall him and Jim in Mark Twain's masterpiece. But Huck commits the blunder of thinking that because the misadventures follow the burning of the spider, they were necessarily caused by it: he confuses mere sequence with causation. This mistake in logic is commonly known as the post hoc, ergo propter hoc *fallacy—Latin for "after this, therefore because of this."*

Huck Finn does not realize that two conditions have to be met to prove causation:

B can not have happened without A;
Whenever A happens, B must happen.

---

[1] Terms printed in all capitals are defined in the Glossary.

The chemist who observes again and again that a flammable substance burns (B) only when combined with oxygen (A) and that it always burns when so combined, may infer that oxidation causes combustion. The chemist has discovered in oxygen the "immediate" cause of combustion. The flame necessary to set off the reaction and the chemist himself, who lights the match, are "ultimate" causes.

Often the ultimate causes of an event are more important than the immediate causes, especially when we are dealing with psychological and social rather than purely physical factors. Let us raise the following question about a college freshman: Why does Mary smoke? Depending upon whom we asked, we might get responses like these:

Mary: "I smoke because I need something to do with my hands."
Mary's boyfriend: "Mary smokes because she thinks it looks sophisticated."
Medical doctor: "Because Mary has developed a physical addiction to tobacco."
Psychologist: "Because of peer pressure."
Sociologist: "Because 30 percent of all female Americans under 20 years of age now smoke. Mary is part of a trend."
Advertiser: "Because she's come a long way, baby."

Each of these explanations tells only part of the story. For a full answer to our question about why Mary smokes, we must take all of these answers together. Together they form what is known as the "complex" cause of Mary's behavior.

Most essays in CAUSE AND EFFECT that you will be asked to read or to write will examine the complex cause of an event or phenomenon. There are two reasons for addressing all the contributing causes. The first is to avoid over-simplification. Interesting questions are usually complex, and complex questions probably have complex answers. The second reason is to anticipate objections that might be raised against your argument.

Often a clever writer will run through several causes to show that he or she knows the ground before making a special case for one or two. When a clergyman asked journalist Lincoln Steffens to name the ultimate cause of corruption in city government, Steffens replied with the following analysis:

> Most people, you know, say it was Adam. But Adam, you remember, he said that it was Eve, the woman; she did it. And Eve said no, no, it wasn't she; it was the serpent. And that's where you clergy have stuck ever since. You blame the serpent, Satan. Now I come and I am trying to show you that it was, it is, the apple.

Steffens was giving an original answer to the old question of original sin. Man's fallen state, he said, is due not to innate depravity but to economic conditions.

When explaining causes, be as specific as you can without over-simplifying. When explaining effects, be even more specific. Here is your chance to display the telling fact or colorful detail that can save your essay from the ho-hum response. Consider this explanation of the effects of smoking written by England's King James I (of the King James Bible). His Counter-Blaste to Tobacco (1604) found smoking to be

> A custom lothsome to the eye, hatefull to the Nose, harmefull to the braine, dangerous to the Lungs, and in the blacke stinking fume thereof, neerest resembling the horrible Stigian smoke of the pit that is bottomelesse.

In a more recent essay on the evils of tobacco, Erik Eckholm strikes a grimmer note. "But the most potentially tragic victims of cigarettes," he writes, "are the infants of mothers who smoke. They are more likely than the babies of nonsmoking mothers to be born underweight and thus to encounter death or disease at birth or during the initial months of life."

In singling out the effects of smoking upon unwitting infants, Eckholm has chosen an example that might be just powerful enough to convince some smokers to quit. Your examples need not be so grim, but they must be specific to be powerful. And they must be selected with the interests of your audience in mind. Eckholm is addressing the young women who are smoking more today than ever before. When writing for a middle-aged audience, he points out that smoking causes cancer and heart disease at a rate

70 percent higher among pack-a-day men and women than among nonsmokers.

Your audience must be taken into account because writing a cause and effect analysis is much like constructing a persuasive argument. It is a form of reasoning that carries the reader step by step through a "proof." Your analysis may be instructive, amusing, or startling; but first it must be logical.

Frank Trippett

The Great American Cooling Machine

Frank Trippett is a reporter, photographer, and newspaper editor.
He was born in Columbus, Mississippi, in 1926. After World War
II, he worked briefly in Meridian, Mississippi, before moving to
Virginia and then Florida, where he was a bureau chief for the
St. Petersburg Times. In the sixties, Trippett served as an associate
editor of Newsweek and senior editor of Look. Since 1971 he has
been a free-lance writer, author of The First Horsemen (1974)
and Child Ellen (1975). "The Great American Cooling Machine"
first appeared in Time; it analyzes some of the chilling effects of
air conditioning on American society and character.

"The greatest contribution to civilization in this century   1
may well be air conditioning—and America leads the way."
So wrote British Scholar-Politician S.F. Markham 32 years
ago when a modern cooling system was still an exotic luxury.
In a century that has yielded such treasures as the electric knife,
spray-on deodorant and disposable diapers, anybody might
question whether air conditioning is the supreme gift. There
is not a whiff of doubt, however, that America is far out front
in its use. As a matter of lopsided fact, the U.S. today, with a
mere 5% of the population, consumes as much man-made
coolness as the whole rest of the world put together.

Just as amazing is the speed with which this situation came   2
to be. Air conditioning began to spread in industries as a
production aid during World War II. Yet only a generation
ago a chilled sanctuary during summer's stewing heat was a
happy frill that ordinary people sampled only in movie houses.
Today most Americans tend to take air conditioning for

granted in homes, offices, factories, stores, theaters, shops, studios, schools, hotels and restaurants. They travel in chilled buses, trains, planes and private cars. Sporting events once associated with open sky and fresh air are increasingly boxed in and air cooled. Skiing still takes place outdoors, but such attractions as tennis, rodeos, football and, alas, even baseball are now often staged in synthetic climates like those of Houston's Astrodome and New Orleans' Superdome. A great many of the country's farming tractors are now, yup, air-conditioned.

It is thus no exaggeration to say that Americans have taken to   3
mechanical cooling avidly and greedily. Many have become all but addicted, refusing to go places that are not air-conditioned. In Atlanta, shoppers in Lenox Square so resented having to endure natural heat while walking outdoors from chilled store to chilled store that the mall management enclosed and air-conditioned the whole sprawling shebang. The widespread whining about Washington's raising of thermostats to a mandatory 78°F suggests that people no longer think of interior coolness as an amenity but consider it a necessity, almost a birthright, like suffrage. The existence of such a view was proved last month when a number of federal judges, sitting too high and mighty to suffer 78°, defied and denounced the Government's energy-saving order to cut back on cooling. Significantly, there was no popular outrage at this judicial insolence; many citizens probably wished that they could be so highhanded.

Everybody by now is aware that the cost of the American way is   4
enormous, that air conditioning is an energy glutton. It uses some 9% of all electricity produced. Such an extravagance merely to provide comfort is peculiarly American and strikingly at odds with all the recent rhetoric about national sacrifice in a period of menacing energy shortages. Other modern industrial nations such as Japan, Germany and France have managed all along to thrive with mere fractions of the man-made coolness used in the U.S., and precious little of that in private dwellings. Here, so profligate has its use become that the air conditioner is almost as glaring a symptom as the automobile of the national tendency to overindulge in every technical possibility, to use every convenience to such excess that the country looks downright coddled.

But not everybody is aware that high cost and easy comfort are   5
merely two of the effects of the vast cooling of America. In fact,

air conditioning has substantially altered the country's character and folkways. With the dog days at hand and the thermostats ostensibly up, it is a good time to begin taking stock of what air conditioning has done besides lower the indoor temperature.

Many of its byproducts are so conspicuous that they are scarcely noticed. To begin with, air conditioning transformed the face of urban America by making possible those glassy, boxy, sealed-in skyscrapers on which the once humane geometries of places like San Francisco, Boston and Manhattan have been impaled. It has been indispensable, no less, to the functioning of sensitive advanced computers, whose high operating temperatures require that they be constantly cooled. Thus, in a very real way, air conditioning has made possible the ascendancy of computerized civilization. Its cooling protection has given rise not only to moon landings, space shuttles and Skylabs but to the depersonalized punch-cardification of society that regularly gets people hot under the collar even in swelter-proof environments. It has also reshaped the national economy and redistributed political power simply by encouraging the burgeoning of the sultry southerly swatch of the country, profoundly influencing major migration trends of people and industry. Sunbelt cities like Phoenix, Atlanta, Dallas and Houston (where shivering indoor frigidity became a mark of status) could never have mushroomed so prosperously without air conditioning; some communities—Las Vegas in the Nevada desert and Lake Havasu City on the Arizona-California border—would shrivel and die overnight if it were turned off.

It has, as well, seduced families into retreating into houses with closed doors and shut windows, reducing the commonalty of neighborhood life and all but obsoleting the front-porch society whose open casual folkways were an appealing hallmark of a sweatier America. Is it really surprising that the public's often noted withdrawal into self-pursuit and privatism has coincided with the epic spread of air conditioning? Though science has little studied how habitual air conditioning affects mind or body, some medical experts suggest that, like other technical avoidance of natural swings in climate, air conditioning may take a toll on the human capacity to adapt to stress. If so, air conditioning is only like many other greatly useful technical developments that liberate man from nature by increasing his productivity and power in some ways—while subtly weakening him in others.

Neither scholars nor pop sociologists have really got around to   8
charting and diagnosing all the changes brought about by air conditioning. Professional observers have for years been preoccupied
with the social implications of the automobile and television. Mere
glancing analysis suggests that the car and TV, in their most deci-
sive influences on American habits, have been powerfully aided
and abetted by air conditioning. The car may have created all
those shopping centers in the boondocks, but only air conditioning
has made them attractive to mass clienteles. Similarly, the artificial
cooling of the living room undoubtedly helped turn the typical
American into a year-round TV addict. Without air conditioning,
how many viewers would endure reruns (or even Johnny Carson)
on one of those pestilential summer nights that used to send people
out to collapse on the lawn or to sleep on the roof?

Many of the side effects of air conditioning are far from being   9
fully pinned down. It is a reasonable suspicion, though, that controlled climate, by inducing Congress to stay in Washington longer
than it used to during the swelter season, thus presumably passing
more laws, has contributed to bloated Government. One can only
speculate that the advent of the supercooled bedroom may be
linked to the carnal adventurism associated with the mid-century
sexual revolution. Surely it is a fact—if restaurant complaints
about raised thermostats are to be believed—that air conditioning
induces at least expense-account diners to eat and drink more; if
so, it must be credited with adding to the national fat problem.

Perhaps only a sophist might be tempted to tie the spread of air   10
conditioning to the coincidentally rising divorce rate, but every
attentive realist must have noticed that even a little window unit
can instigate domestic tension and chronic bickering between
couples composed of one who likes it on all the time and another
who does not. In fact, perhaps surprisingly, not everybody likes air
conditioning. The necessarily sealed rooms or buildings make
some feel claustrophobic, cut off from the real world. The rush,
whir and clatter of cooling units annoys others. There are even a
few eccentrics who object to man-made cool simply because they
like hot weather. Still, the overwhelming majority of Americans
have taken to air conditioning like hogs to a wet wallow.

It might be tempting, and even fair, to chastise that vast ma-   11
jority for being spoiled rotten in their cool ascendancy. It would be
more just, however, to observe that their great cooling machine

carries with it a perpetual price tag that is going to provide continued and increasing chastisement during the energy crisis. Ultimately, the air conditioner, and the hermetic buildings it requires, may turn out to be a more pertinent technical symbol of the American personality than the car. While the car has been a fine sign of the American impulse to dart hither and yon about the world, the mechanical cooler more neatly suggests the maturing national compulsion to flee the natural world in favor of a technological cocoon.

Already architectural designers are toiling to find ways out of 12 the technical trap represented by sealed buildings with immovable glass, ways that might let in some of the naturally cool air outside. Some have lately come up with a remarkable discovery: the openable window. Presumably, that represents progress.

QUESTIONS

Understanding

1. Why did air conditioning take hold originally in America, according to Trippett?

2. Trippett says that "two of the effects" of America's addiction to air conditioning are "high cost and easy comfort" (par. 5). How has it also had the effect of transforming "the face of urban America" (par. 6)? What is the result of that transformation?

3. What other effects of universal air conditioning does Trippett identify? Which is he less confident about linking directly with air conditioning, rather than some other cause?

4. Why does Trippett think air conditioning may become a symbol of American character even more apt than the automobile? What does it symbolize about us?

5. Does Trippett seem to think the effects of air conditioning the entire country are largely beneficial or largely detrimental?

Strategies and Structure

1. Does Trippett's essay spend more time analyzing causes or analyzing effects? Explain your answer.

2. In paragraph 6, we are told that air conditioning has made it possible to construct enormous "sealed-in" skyscrapers. This effect, in
turn, says Trippett, has caused urban America to become less liv-
able because less human in scale. Point out several other examples
in his essay of effects that turn into causes.

3. Paragraph 5 here is mainly a TRANSITION paragraph. Which parts
look back to the four opening paragraphs? Which look forward to
the rest? See if you can find other clearly transitional sentences in
Trippett's essay.

4. The opening paragraph of "Cooling Machine" identifies the prime
cause of which the author will subsequently trace the effects: the
wholesale use of air conditioning in America in recent years. However, when Trippett questions "whether air conditioning is the
supreme gift" (par. 1), he sounds more like a writer setting up a
PERSUASIVE ARGUMENT than an essay in CAUSE AND EFFECT. What
is the point of his implied argument?

5. Explain why Trippett's essay is nevertheless one that uses persuasion to support a cause-and-effect analysis (and not the reverse).

6. How might Trippett's analysis of the effects of universal air conditioning serve to support a full-fledged argument that our air
should no longer be "conditioned"?

Words and Figures of Speech

1. What other terms for "effects" does Trippett use in this essay (for
instance, "byproducts" in paragraph 6)?

2. Americans, says Trippett, have taken to air conditioning like "hogs
to a wet wallow" (par. 11). Point out other places in which Trippett uses SLANG or other informal language. Do such words and
phrases belong in an essay on a technical subject such as air conditioning? Why or why not?

3. Does your dictionary list the word *obsoleting* (par. 7)? What part
of speech is *obsolete* usually? Should Trippett have written instead "making obsolete"? Why or why not?

4. In ancient Greece, *Sophists* were philosophers known for their
exceedingly clever (though sometimes hair-splitting) arguments.
How does the word (uncapitalized) apply in this modern context?

Comparing

1. Trippett emphasizes the negative effects of his subject. How does

he compare, in this regard, with Ellen Willis in "Memoirs of a Non-Prom Queen," the next essay in this chapter?

2. Contrast the attitude expressed here toward air conditioning and the architecture it has produced with the attitude of Eugene Raskin toward modern architecture in "Walls and Barriers" (Chapter 6).

3. If Johnson C. Montgomery ("Island of Plenty," Chapter 9) had written an essay on air conditioning and the American way, what differences might you expect between his treatment of the subject and Trippett's?

Discussion and Writing Topics

1. How accurate do you consider the proclamation with which Trippett begins: that air conditioning is America's greatest contribution to civilized living in the twentieth century? What other contenders can you think of?

2. Write an essay in which you analyze the benefits and wholesome effects of air conditioning.

3. Write an essay on the likely effects of some other important technological "advance," such as high-yield fertilizer, containerized freight, wide-body jets, synthetic DNA, or the projected "elevator" that may some day make entry into space easy and inexpensive.

Ellen Willis

Memoirs of
a Non-Prom Queen

*Ellen Willis is a journalist who was born in New York City in 1941
and attended a large "semisuburban" high school in Queens,
before going on to Barnard College and Berkeley. She is a critic of
rock music for The New Yorker and Rolling Stone and the author
of Beginning to See the Light (1981). Willis has also been an
associate or contributing editor of Cheetah magazine, US
magazine, and Ms. and a staff member of Home Front, a center
for antiwar soldiers. "Memoirs of a Non-Prom Queen" is a review
essay insipred by Ralph Keyes's Is There Life after High School?
(1976). It analyzes the lasting psychological effects of Willis's own
less-than-ideal high school years.*

There's a book out called *Is There Life after High School?* 1
It's a fairly silly book, maybe because the subject matter is
the kind that only hurts when you think. Its thesis—that most
people never get over the social triumphs or humiliations of
high school—is not novel. Still, I read it with the respectful
attention a serious hypochondriac accords the lowliest "dear
doctor" column. I don't know about most people, but for me,
forgiving my parents for real and imagined derelictions has
been easy compared to forgiving myself for being a teenage
reject.

Victims of high school trauma—which seems to have af- 2
flicted a disproportionate number of writers, including Ralph
Keyes, the author of this book—tend to embrace the ugly
duckling myth of adolescent social relations: the "innies"

(Keyes's term) are good-looking, athletic mediocrities who will never amount to much, while the "outies" are intelligent, sensitive, creative individuals who will do great things in an effort to make up for their early defeats. Keyes is partial to this myth. He has fun with celebrity anecdotes: Kurt Vonnegut receiving a body-building course as a "gag prize" at a dance; Frank Zappa yelling "fuck you" at a cheerleader; Mike Nichols,[1] as a nightclub comedian, insulting a fan—an erstwhile overbearing classmate turned used-car salesman. In contrast, the ex-prom queens and kings he interviews slink through life, hiding their pasts lest someone call them "dumb jock" or "cheerleader type," perpetually wondering what to do for an encore.

If only it were that simple. There may really be high schools   3 where life approximates an Archie comic, but even in the Fifties, my large (5000 students), semisuburban (Queens, New York), heterogeneous high school was not one of them. The students' social life was fragmented along ethnic and class lines; there was no universally recognized, schoolwide social hierarchy. Being an athlete or a cheerleader or a student officer didn't mean much. Belonging to an illegal sorority or fraternity meant more, at least in some circles, but many socially active students chose not to join. The most popular kids were not necessarily the best looking or the best dressed or the most snobbish or the least studious. In retrospect, it seems to me that they were popular for much more honorable reasons. They were attuned to other people, aware of subtle social nuances. They projected an inviting sexual warmth. Far from being slavish followers of fashion, they were self-confident enough to set fashions. They suggested, initiated, led. Above all—this was their main appeal for me—they knew how to have a good time.

True, it was not particularly sophisticated enjoyment—dancing,   4 pizza eating, hand holding in the lunchroom, the usual. I had friends—precocious intellectuals and bohemians—who were consciously alienated from what they saw as all that teenage crap. Part of me identified with them, yet I badly wanted what they

---

[1] Vonnegut, American novelist, author of *Cat's Cradle* (1963); *God Bless You, Mr. Rosewater* (1964); *Slaughterhouse-Five* (1969); and *Breakfast of Champions* (1973). Zappa was the leader of the rock music group, Mothers of Invention. Nichols is a former night club and television comedian, now a film and stage director.

rejected. Their seriousness engaged my mind, but my romantic and sexual fantasies, and my emotions generally, were obsessively fixed on the parties and dances I wasn't invited to, the boys I never dated. I suppose what says it best is that my "serious" friends hated rock & roll; I loved it.

If I can't rationalize my social ineptitude as intellectual rebel-   5
lion, neither can I blame it on political consciousness. Feminism has inspired a variation of the ugly duckling myth in which high school wallflower becomes feminist heroine, suffering because she has too much integrity to suck up to boys by playing a phony feminine role. There is a tempting grain of truth in this idea. Certainly the self-absorption, anxiety and physical and social awkwardness that made me a difficult teenager were not unrelated to my ambivalent awareness of women's oppression. I couldn't charm boys because I feared and resented them and their power over my life; I couldn't be sexy because I saw sex as a mine field of conflicting, confusing rules that gave them every advantage. I had no sense of what might make me attractive, a lack I'm sure involved unconscious resistance to the game girls were supposed to play (particularly all the rigmarole surrounding clothes, hair and cosmetics); I was a clumsy dancer because I could never follow the boy's lead.

Yet ultimately this rationale misses the point. As I've learned   6
from comparing notes with lots of women, the popular girls were in fact much more in touch with the reality of the female condition than I was. They knew exactly what they had to do for the rewards they wanted, while I did a lot of what feminist organizers call denying the awful truth. I was a bit schizy. Desperate to win the game but unwilling to learn it or even face my feelings about it, I couldn't really play, except in fantasy; paradoxically, I was consumed by it much more thoroughly than the girls who played and played well. Knowing what they wanted and how to get it, they preserved their sense of self, however compromised, while I lost mine. Which is why they were not simply better game players but genuinely more likable than I.

The ugly duckling myth is sentimental. It may soothe the   7
memory of social rejection, but it falsifies the experience, evades its cruelty and uselessness. High school permanently damaged my self-esteem. I learned what it meant to be impotent; what it meant to be invisible. None of this improved my character, spurred my

ambition, or gave me a deeper understanding of life. I know people who were popular in high school who later became serious intellectuals, radicals, artists, even journalists. I regret not being one of those people. To see my failure as morally or politically superior to their success would be to indulge in a version of the Laingian [2] fallacy—that because a destructive society drives people crazy, there is something dishonorable about managing to stay sane.

QUESTIONS

Understanding

1. What was the effect of her high school experience upon the author? In which sentence does she formulate that effect most directly?

2. What specific difficulties during Willis's high school years caused the aftereffects that she describes?

3. Explain the basic idea behind the ugly duckling myth (or the Cinderella story—the two are fundamentally the same). What does the myth have to do with Ralph Keyes's theory (in *Is There Life after High School?*) about the "innies" and the "outies" (par. 2)?

4. Willis agrees that high school can scar its victims for life, but she thinks Keyes's theory about "innies" and "outies" is wrong. Why? What fallacies does she see in Keyes's reasoning?

5. How, according to Willis, has the feminist movement "inspired a variation of the ugly duckling myth" (par. 5)? Who is the swan in this version? How might Willis's essay be interpreted as a more complicated feminist statement?

Strategies and Structure

1. Does Willis devote more attention to causes or to effects in this essay? Assuming that paragraph 1 and 2 constitute her introduction, which specific paragraphs deal with causes? Which deal with effects?

[2] R. D. Laing, the Scottish psychiatrist, argues that personality division is a predictable result of modern life.

2. How efficient do you find the first sentence in paragraph 3 as a TRANSITION sentence? Explain your answer.

3. In paragraph 1 Willis introduces herself as a "serious" hypochondriac, and we smile at the joke. By the end of the essay, how has the non-prom queen's TONE of voice changed?

4. Sentimentality is emotional response out of all proportion to the conditions · that produce it. Willis criticizes the ugly duckling myth for emotional bloat in paragraph 7. Do you think her "memoirs" successfully avoid sentimentality? Why or why not?

5. Why does Willis mention "Archie" comics and the example of her own high school in paragraph 3?

6. In paragraph 3, Willis tells what her high school days look like "in retrospect." What word in the title of her essay alerts us to this backward glance?

Words and Figures of Speech

1. A *rationale* (par. 6) explains the reasons for some course of action. Rationales may turn out to be accurate or inaccurate. *Rationalizations* (par. 5) are always inaccurate. Why? What does the term mean?

2. *Schizy* (par. 6) is short for *schizophrenic*. What psychological condition does the word DENOTE? How does it apply to Willis's state of mind in high school?

3. Willis's vocabulary is sophisticated, even learned; but it includes a smattering of slang and profanity. How might such language be considered appropriate, given the fact that Willis's essay first appeared in *Rolling Stone* magazine?

4. Look up any unfamiliar words in the following list: *thesis* (par. 1), *derelictions* (1), *trauma* (2), *mediocrities* (2), *anecdotes* (2), *erstwhile* (2), *heterogeneous* (3) *hierarchy* (3), *retrospect* (3), *nuances* (3), *slavish* (3), *precocious* (4), *bohemians* (4), *ineptitude* (5), *ambivalent* (5), *impotent* (7).

Comparing

1. Willis says (par. 2) that writers seem especially vulnerable to the traumas of adolescence, and her essay might be seen as a writer's attempt to put a traumatic past into perspective. How does this

therapeutic motive compare with the motive Annie Dillard assigns to the writer in "Transfiguration" (Chapter 7)?

Discussion and Writing Topics

1. Have your high school days left any psychological scars? What traumas caused them?

2. Do you now question any standards or values that you accepted without a second thought in high school? What were they? What caused you to change your mind?

3. Did you know people in high school who were popular for some of the "honorable" reasons Willis mentions in paragraph 3? How did they behave?

4. What is a myth? What kinds of belief do myths reveal within a society or a culture?

Paul Colinvaux

Why Japan
Bombed Pearl Harbor

Professor of zoology at the Ohio State University, Paul Colinvaux
was born in England and served in the Royal Artillery, where he
acquired a knowledge of soldiering that has served him more
recently as a biological historian for whom warfare is ecology.
Besides England and the United States, Colinvaux has lived or
done field work in Germany, Canada, Portugal, Africa, Bermuda,
the Galapagos, and South America. A contributor to Science,
Nature, Ecology, and other journals, he is the author of Why Big
Fierce Animals Are Rare *(1978) and* The Fates of Nations *(1981),*
a Darwinian view of history that links historical change to
variations in national populations and living habits. "Why Japan
Bombed Pearl Harbor" (editor's title), a complete section of this
later book, analyzes the ecological causes leading to an act of
aggression that changed the fate of an ambitious island nation.
The apparently plain style of Colinvaux's essay is eloquent proof
of his contention "that science is so intrinsically interesting that it
only has to be written about beautifully for everybody to
understand all about it."

The Japanese learned of the ways of the European West   1
when their island was feudal, agrarian and crowded. So
crowded were they that, although a country of rural folk and
artisans, Japan actually imported its staple food, rice. Her
feudal masters kept their country and their own power isolated from the expanding West as long as possible, but the
traders came at last. The Americans were first, extracting a
trade treaty with a few thoughtful discharges of their cannon,
and the Europeans were glad enough to follow where the
American cannon went.

It took the Japanese less than ten years to act on the politic ² maxim, "If you can't beat them join them." In a mild revolution the feudal chieftains returned their fiefs; their quaint old retainers, who served as soldiers, were pensioned off, and the people turned their formidable brains to mastering the techniques of Western industry. They also bought or manufactured some cannon as they went along, because they were a trading nation and they had learned from the civilized West that cannon were a very useful aid to trade.

The people learned the new ways in a single generation. Their ³ aspirations bounded high, and so did the country's birth rate. Between the revolution of 1868 and the turn of the century the Japanese bred an extra thirteen million people. They were so crowded to start with that they had to import rice. Now, as an industrial state, they had to import raw materials too. The people felt that they needed to be sure of their supply of resources; they needed to own land with raw materials in it, to control outlets for some of their trade and, perhaps, to have some land where they could deposit surplus people too. They prepared to take what they wanted by force. They studied Western war, made what Western weapons they could, and bought the rest. Britain had the best navy, so the Japanese bought British warships. Germany had Krupp,[1] so they bought German artillery, and so on. Then they beat up some primitive Chinese forces to let them have their way over some minor matters on the mainland, which gave them a chance to try their hands at the new form of soldiering. Practice was necessary because they knew that they must tackle Western power eventually.

What the Japanese wanted first was Korea, a long-coveted piece ⁴ of land which could supply many of their immediate wants. Curious as it may sound, they had to fight Russia for the privilege of conquering Korea, because the Russians felt their vital interest was involved. So they fought the Russians and beat them handsomely in a campaign of 1904, known as the Siege of Port Arthur. They had read the very latest military writers more carefully than had the Russians, and were that much more modern. The Russians let them have Korea. It was a very successful aggression.

[1] Industrial giant known for manufacturing armaments, founded and for 150 years run by the Krupp family.

But, as the population went on growing so did the needs of the   5
people. The Japanese got some more land out of the First World
War when, by a very sensible arrangement for mutual benefit, they
were allied to the British. Their purchase of cannon and warships
was paying off very nicely. No other Asiatic power stood a chance
against Western methods of war, whether these were used by Japanese or by the Europeans who had invented them; and the Japanese had carefully avoided a clash with a major Western power.
Even in their battle with the Russians they had prudently kept
themselves to very limited objectives, avoiding such provocation
that the Russians might think a major war effort was necessary.

But aggressive war was now a Japanese habit, as it is to all   6
nations who pursue it successfully. And the Japanese numbers and
aspirations still continued to grow. Some of the thinking then
common in Japan was written down for us by a young Japanese
naval officer in a book published in 1935 and called *Japan Must
Fight Britain*. The theme is that Japan must expand; therefore,
someone must move over. If not, "Japan must fight Britain," and
if Japan loses that first fight "It is as clear as day that, with her
population and her insufficient resources, it would not be long
before she had to draw her sword and stand up to fight for her
life."

The Japanese were convinced that they must take by force what   7
was needed to give an ever-growing population the standard of life
it thought it deserved. And they did fight. In choosing Britain for
an enemy they were, of course, tackling a weakened power, one
with incompetent generals who had lately preferred horses to tanks
and who had not thought it necessary for Singapore to have guns
on the land side as well as on the sea side. Even so, it was a
dangerous thing to do. But tackling the United States of America
at the same time was so hazardous an undertaking as to be
scarcely believable. The reasons for this desperate venture must
have been very strong indeed.

A wealthy island state, as Japan then was, is predicted by the   8
ecological hypothesis[2] to be extremely prone to start an aggressive
war. The opportunities for a broad niche on the island base must

[2] The theory that changes in human history are caused in part by changes in a
people's numbers and living habits, as with any other animal.

be limited, putting a strong pressure on those desiring wealth to find opportunity elsewhere. Trade must, and always does, become part of the niche-space of the affluent on all islands that achieve moderate wealth. But part of the success in winning niche-space through trade must be spent, through the breeding strategy, in the production of more potential traders. The numbers of the affluent grow, but there is also a worse population consequence as well because imports always include cheap food, which allows the poorer classes to maintain their own, larger breeding effort. The country then becomes dependent on free access to markets to maintain its traditional affluence and must be ready to fight for those markets. A few generations later rising numbers of the wealthier classes find it difficult to provide affluence for their own descendants, which is the essential condition for an aggressive war. Island folk can educate, trade, and breed their way into this condition very easily.

It was clear to the Japanese of 1941 that they had real need of 9 access to other people's land if their new and better way of life was to be maintained. They were quite right. They still need that access forty years later, and are getting it. The large continents of Europe and America are yielding to the Japanese much of their continental living space, welcoming Japanese traders, keeping the sea lanes safe for Japanese commerce with their own navies, accepting Japanese manufactures even at the cost of destroying their own currencies and industries. It is, perhaps, a moot point how long they will feel content to go on doing so. But in 1941 the Japanese were not being so warmly welcomed in the world.

The Japanese had long been fighting to take provinces from 10 China, expanding the continental land they already held in Korea. It was, of course, blatant aggression, sired of ecological necessity and mothered in imitation of the Anglo-Saxon example. Success in this war, long and drawn-out as it came to be, was vital to those who controlled the Japanese government. The people too were deeply conscious of their need, schooled to accept the new Western ways, building a high standard of living by fighting for it. And they were proud.

Then the United States did two things for Japan. They placed an 11 embargo on the sale of the oil needed to sustain Japanese armies, and they put all American warships into one handy disposable package in a harbor in Hawaii. A better combination of stick and carrot to drive the Japanese into war would be hard to imagine. The war chiefs saw their opportunity and struck, and Japan was committed to the forlorn, hopeless adventure. They would take their oil from the British in Burma, by force. They did that. Then they would use valor and skill to make the United States agree to their keeping the loot. But this could not be.

QUESTIONS

Understanding

1. What immediate cause, according to Colinvaux, produced Japan's sudden turn in the 1860s from ancient feudalism to Western ways?
2. One cause of Japan's expansionism early in this century, says Colinvaux, was the unavailability of new land within its own borders. What other causes does he cite?
3. If Colinvaux is right, why are island nations like Japan and England "extremely prone to start an aggressive war" (par. 8)?
4. With any nation, according to Colinvaux, the practice of successful aggression typically has what effect?
5. Of all the causes of aggression that Colinvaux analyzes with the aid of ecological theory, which is "the essential condition" (par. 8) necessary to send an ambitious country to war?
6. In the broadest terms, what other causes of aggression does Colinvaux analyze here by using the example of Japan?
7. In the particular case of Japan's attack on Pearl Harbor, what two immediate causes produced this catastrophic effect?

Strategies and Structure

1. Historians are supposed to be objective toward their subject. Point out additional sentences like the following in which Colinvaux gives the impression of even-handed judgment and sympathy: "It was clear to the Japanese of 1941 that they had real need of access to other people's land. . . . They were quite right" (par. 9).
2. Colinvaux is both a historian and a zoologist. In his essay, how does the scientist accustomed to studying the habits of animals affect the historian who is studying the behavior of a people?

3. The habits of people living in groups are affected by their joint use of tools. Since Colinvaux is studying the Japanese habits of war, he pays special attention to the tools of war. Point out several examples you find especially pertinent.

4. Would you describe the scope of Colinvaux's historical analysis as broad or narrow? Approximately how many years does he cover? For the number of conclusions he draws, does he cite many documentary sources or relatively few, in your opinion?

5. Judging from the number of documentary references in Colinvaux's essay, would you say he is writing primarily for historians, zoologists, or a general audience? Explain your answer.

6. Paragraph 6 cites a book written by a young Japanese naval officer shortly before the bombing of Pearl Harbor. Why do you suppose Colinvaux chose to cite this source rather than other examples of "the thinking then common in Japan" (par. 6), written, say, by army officers or government officials?

7. How effective do you find the reference to rice in paragraph 1? How skillful in general do you find this author at choosing his examples? Explain your answer.

8. America originally opened trade with Japan, writes Colinvaux, by administering some "thoughtful" cannon blasts (par. 1). Try to find other examples of a similar IRONY in this essay. Why might Colinvaux adopt such a TONE when writing for an American readership?

Words and Figures of Speech

1. Both *ecology* and *biology* are words having to do with living things. What are the principal differences in meaning between the two terms?

2. "Agrarianism" (par. 1) refers to a way of making a living. From what? What is *feudalism*? How do these two related words differ in DENOTATION? In CONNOTATION?

3. In the first sentence of paragraph 11, why does Colinvaux use the preposition "for" instead of "to"?

4. What is the difference, exactly, between "politic" (par. 2) and "political"?

5. What are the connotations of the word *bred* in paragraph 3? How can Colinvaux use it here without being insulting?

6. A "maxim" is usually a sober, high-sounding rule for guiding conduct. How would you describe Colinvaux's tone when he says the

Japanese acted on the maxim, "If you can't beat them join them" (par. 2)?

7. Consult your dictionary for any of the following words that are not in your working vocabulary: *artisans* (par. 1), *fiefs* (par. 2), *retainers* (par. 2), *pensioned off* (par. 2), *formidable* (par. 2), *coveted* (par. 3), *provocation* (par. 5), *niche* (par. 8), *moot* (par. 9), *blatant* (par. 10), *embargo* (par. 11).

Comparing

1. How is Colinvaux's analysis of the causes of human aggression confirmed by Loren Eiseley's account of animal behavior in "The Angry Winter" (Chapter 1)?

2. Colinvaux's essay studies a prime example of *offensive* behavior. Desmond Morris's "Barrier Signals" (Chapter 5), on the other hand, looks at *defensive* behavior. What common cause lies behind these contrasting responses of action and reaction as explained in these two essays?

Discussion and Writing Topics

1. Besides changes in breeding and living habits, what other forces do you think can shape and even alter history? (One example might be the emergence of a great leader, such as Abraham Lincoln.)

2. Are you convinced by Colinvaux's analysis of why Japan bombed Pearl Harbor? Why or why not? If not, give your own causal analysis.

3. Who was to blame for Pearl Harbor, according to Colinvaux's account?

4. Is Colinvaux right or wrong to leave out questions of morality when discussing history? Explain your answer.

William Allen
Toward an Understanding of Accidental Knots

William Allen teaches creative writing at the Ohio State University. *He was born in Dallas, Texas, in 1940 and attended the high school he describes in "Haircut"("Paragraphs For Analysis"). A graduate of California State University, Long Beach, he studied creative writing at the University of Iowa (M.F.A., 1970). Editor of the Ohio Journal, he has contributed stories and essays to the New York Times, Saturday Review, Antioch Review, Reader's Digest, and other publications. He is the author of Starkweather (1976), the story of a mass-murderer, and To Tojo from Billy-Bob Jones (1977), a novel. Allen considers himself a regional writer, and he thinks that "every good story should have at least one chicken in it." "Toward an Understanding of Accidental Knots" (from the Atlantic, March 1981) examines the causes and effects of some disturbing kinks in Allen's private world.*

One night a few weeks ago my birdbath caught on fire, and when I ran with what I thought was a neatly coiled hose to put out the blaze, I was yanked up hopelessly short. I looked back and the hose had six knots in it. All those knots appearing just like that seemed impossible, to say nothing of unjust, and it set off something in me that had been brewing for a long time. It made me decide that I was going to unravel forever the mystery surrounding what amounts to half a lifetime of accidental knots.

As a child I thought that any knots in my life must somehow be my fault. Back then I also noticed that knots I wanted tied often wouldn't stay tied—or they turned into knots totally unsuited to my purpose. Later, though I stopped taking the blame for knots, I still hadn't learned how they worked, the way I was sure other people had. Every time I found a knot where I didn't think there should be one, it troubled me. My phone cord has always been in a snarl—I'm used to that—but when it knotted around the stem of my empty wineglass during the night, I needed to know why. Before I died, I wanted to know why the once straight cord to the toaster on my kitchen counter became so knotted that it pulled the appliance up under the cupboard where it was useless, and finally one day caused the toaster to blow up.

I had always assumed a knot required that the end of something   3
be free to go through a loop and then get pulled tight. This assumption was based on the way I had tied knots; but if I was correct, my problem with knots shouldn't exist. If you hold kite string at one end and tie it to a kite at the other, those enormous, hopeless clumps should never develop—especially if the carefully tied knots in the tail are always going to fall loose.

If this seems like a minor issue, let me say that almost everyone   4
I have asked about knots agrees that they are mysterious and need to be better understood. These people also say that my initial conception of a knot ought to be right.

Now, I'm sure that somewhere, in some obscure treatise on   5
some remote library shelf, the answer lies waiting. Sailors and mountain climbers and window washers—or anyone else who depends on the control of knots—certainly must know more than the average person. The cowboys who continually fool with their ropes in movies and rodeos must do so with understanding and purpose. Rope designers and rope makers must know almost everything about knots. But the information has never reached me—and apparently never reached a good many other people as well. What I am about to tell you, then, I have learned on my own.

First, I bought ten feet of common manila rope, tossed it on the   6
middle of the floor, and just watched it for a while. It didn't move, which didn't surprise me, so I left it there overnight.

Next morning I realized that, even though the rope hadn't   7
moved, it looked tangled. I picked up the tangle and, sure enough, it didn't snake out into my ten-foot length of straight manila rope, the way it should have. It came up in a clump. I tried to shake

loose the clump, then pulled on the ends to free it, but this only made it worse. What I had was a tightly tangled mess that required considerable effort to undo.

The rope hadn't been tangled when I bought it, or before I [8] tossed it to the floor, but somehow the *act of tossing* had caused it to converge on itself. It had happened right in front of me, but I hadn't observed it until the next day—which made me aware that, so far, I was bringing an untrained eye to my task.

It became clear that the act of moving the rope in the slightest [9] way tended to cause it to knot. But why? I inspected it more closely. It consisted of three smaller pieces of rope tightly twisted around each other, all with little clinging hemp burrs sticking out of them. Each of the three pieces was made of long, single strands of hemp twisted around each other. When I took it apart, it wanted to kink back up—as if the rope depended on knottiness to exist.

I noticed that if I tossed the rope in the air, freeing it from the [10] force of gravity for a moment, the rope's inherent forces came into play. All the twisting that had gone into the making of the rope had created internal dynamics which made it seek to converge on itself, to continue to twine around itself—most obviously in the form of loops. And a few loops could form a support for yet more rope to gather and wrap around itself. Any collective movement of the rope—any pulling, for instance—made the loops smaller and the tangles tighter. Eventually all this movement was likely to result in a real knot. The bend of a loop, if tight enough, could constitute that free end I originally felt necessary to the creation of a knot.

So now I postulated: *Given the opportunity, a length of some-* [11] *thing with an end or a substitute end will, in general, tangle rather than stay straight.*

But this only formulated the mystery, it didn't solve it. I recently [12] ordered a martini with a twist and noticed that the lemon peel was unusually long, looking like a little yellow snake in my gin. Before the drink was gone, that twist had turned itself into a knot. At this moment, the cord to my desk lamp has a knot in it. (Some people would have plugged it in like that, of course, but I never would.) A couple of years ago I went to great lengths to make sure that the cords running to my new stereo speakers were straight. Now they're snarled and knotted to the point where the little wires inside are broken, causing static when I walk across the living room floor. And then I've got that problem with the vacuum cleaner cord.

When I vacuum the rug, it would be difficult for me consciously 13 to make a knot in the cord, assuming that it was connected to both the wall and the cleaner. I think I would have to pick up my large Eureka upright and put it through an even larger, preformed loop in the cord. But lately I have watched the cord as I vacuum. It goes back and forth, twists this way and that, is constantly being turned—creating tension and a tendency to twine around itself. Then—and this was somehow a surprise to me in its obviousness —I *unplug the cord* in order to move from room to room. For long moments, there is a loose end—sometimes jerked and flying through the air if I'm tired or in a hurry—and with the tension on the cord being what it is, a knot sooner or later will occur.

It all makes sense, more or less. 14

The accidental knotting of my garden hose, however, remains 15 unexplained. I have watched it for some time and can only theorize how a hundred feet of stiff rubber tubing can so easily develop knots. When I discovered those six knots, I thought back and realized that the hose hadn't been moved for over a year, during which time it had, I assumed, been lying in a state of unsnarled rest. The tension from the act of looping those coils the year before, and the tautness resulting from my race to the bird-bath, could certainly explain some snarling, but six knots? The unlikelihood of it has caused me to look in other directions.

I live in the country, and quite a few animals come around that 16 hose at night, drinking from a crock I leave there which is filled by a very slow leak at the point where the hose connects to the faucet. Dogs and cats and raccoons and opossums and who knows what else probably touch the hose from time to time, and just a nudge could activate the tension already in the rubber. Also, the weather could have any variety of effects. High winds and driving rains and accumulations of snow could move the hose from its natural inert state. The change in temperature could cause expansion and contraction—in other words, movement—to occur.

The grass and weeds growing under the hose, the erosion of dirt 17 caused by the leaky faucet, the aging process of the rubber . . . all of these things could combine to make a knot or two while I lie in bed asleep.

But six? It's hard to believe. Possibly other forces, difficult to   [18]
understand but in keeping with the laws of the universe, have
contributed—such as the changing gravitational pull of the moon,
or maybe a preceding configuration of the larger planets. But the
laws themselves are snarled. We are told both that the universe is
expanding and that the natural tendency of all matter is to converge, to pull in upon itself. I have read—and this is disputed—
that our solar system originally formed from condensing hydrogen
plasma which pulled in on itself and hardened into chunks that
became planets and moons that are now locked into orbits about
our sun, which is constantly trying to tug them into its fiery gases.

I've always assumed, as Newton did, that these matters had to   [19]
do with gravity, but cosmologists say they have to do with something called "degree of curvature," and that the quintessence of
curvature—don't ask me how—results in the mysterious black
holes. Some say that the universe is in the shape of a saddle,
except that it has a fourth dimension which perhaps keeps us from
being able to see its tendency toward clumping. Other theorists see
the universe as having the shape of a figure eight—which we all
know is just a yank away from a tangle or a snarl. Whether the
universe is going to tie itself into a knot is still in dispute. The
argument has to do with the need for a free end, which the universe supposedly doesn't have, but I personally think it might have
a tightly bent loop somewhere, which could amount to the same
thing.

Some or perhaps all of the forces in the universe may have   [20]
contributed to the six knots that defeated me the night I ran to put
out the fire in the birdbath. I just don't know. The problem is
baffling. Despite all my research—or perhaps because of it—the
number of knots in that length of rubber hose makes me want to
consider the possibility that they occurred not by accident at all
but by design.

QUESTIONS

Understanding

1. Why does Allen entitle his essay as he does instead of calling it
   simply, "An Understanding of Accidental Knots"?

2. How does Allen define a knot? What does he first think it takes to make one? How does his definition have to be revised?

3. What identifiable physical forces cause the knots (or kinks) in Allen's garden hose? What single physical force is the most essential cause of all accidental knotting, according to Allen's "research"?

4. What attitude does Allen seem to be assuming toward the power of science to supply comprehensible answers to perplexing questions when he writes, "Some say that the universe is in the shape of a saddle, except that it has a fourth dimension which perhaps keeps us from being able to see its tendency toward clumping" (par. 19)?

5. To what final cause of mysterious "accidental" knots is Allen led by his inquiry into its cosmic effects?

Strategies and Structure

1. How does Allen raise the question of responsibility in paragraph 2 for the causes he is inquiring into? How does he return to that issue in paragraph 20?

2. Which phrase in paragraph 14 qualifies Allen's "understanding" of knots? Do you find the short paragraph justified? Why or why not?

3. Why does Allen use italics in paragraph 11?

4. What is the effect of Allen's comparing himself with Newton in paragraph 19?

5. In paragraph 18, where does Allen begin to broaden his research into cosmic reaches? Why is his garden hose example a good link between the domestic world and the greater universe?

6. The inquirer in Allen's essay seems baffled by the conclusions of science but half-convinced by its method of arriving at them. In what ways does his inquiry resemble a scientist's? Where do we see him engaged in mock research using the scientific method?

7. Is Allen speaking entirely tongue-in-cheek here? How do the examples of the flaming bird bath and the exploding toaster help to define his plight?

Words and Figures of Speech

1. In addition to their literal meaning, what METAPHORIC meaning

do knots begin to take on in Allen's essay? What was a Gordian knot in Greek mythology?

2. Allen speaks of his plan to "unravel" (par. 1) a mystery that has been bothering him. Why is this verb especially appropriate to the disquisition that follows?

3. Allen contends that the "internal dynamics" of coiled rope (par. 10) cause it to end up in a "clump" (par. 7). Point out similar instances of scientific language jumbled together with studiedly untechnical language. What is the effect of such a combination?

4. Look up *mystery* in a dictionary of synonyms (available in the reference room of your school library). How is it distinguished from such related words as *enigma, puzzle, conundrum?* Is science more helpful with solving problems or solving mysteries?

5. What is the fundamental difference in meaning between *accident* and *design* (par. 20)?

Comparing

1. In what respects does Allen's inquirer resemble the scientific historian in the preceding essay by Paul Colinvaux? Which has more faith in science?

2. How does the TONE of Allen's essay compare with that of Russell Baker's "A Nice Place to Visit" (Chapter 6)?

Discussion and Writing Topics

1. Do you think Allen is on the right track by the end of his essay? Why or why not?

2. What are the limits of scientific inquiry? What kinds of problems is it *not* likely to explain?

3. Write a mock analysis, using snatches of scientific language, of the causes of some domestic perplexity that has troubled you. Why, for example, do houses make noises at night? What causes keys and wallets to get lost? Why does ketchup explode in the refrigerator or ice cream melt in the freezer?

4. Conduct your own inquiry into the causes of accidental knots.

WRITING TOPICS for Chapter Four
Essays That Analyze Cause and Effect

Write an essay analyzing the probable causes or effects (or both) of one of the following:

1. The energy crisis
2. Pollution
3. Urban blight
4. Drug or alcohol abuse
5. Heart disease, sickle cell anemia, or some other disease
6. Divorce within the first year or two of marriage
7. Loss of religious faith
8. Loss of self-esteem
9. Racial discrimination or ethnic jokes and slurs
10. Success in college
11. Student cheating
12. Sibling rivalry
13. The Civil War or other historical event
14. Invention of the assembly line system
15. Dropping out of high school or college
16. A sudden shift in status: from high school senior to college freshman, for example

5

Essays That Define

To make a basic DEFINITION,[1] put whatever you are defining into a class and then list the characteristics that distinguish it from all other members of that class. The Greek philosopher Plato, for example, defined man by putting him in the class "biped." Then Plato thought of a quality that sets man off from other two-legged creatures. "Man," he said, "is a featherless biped."

When the rival philosopher Diogenes heard this definition, he brought a plucked chicken into the lecture room and observed, "Here is Plato's man." Plato responded by adding that man is a featherless biped "having broad nails." The general principle that Plato was obeying holds for the basic definitions you will write. If at first you choose qualities that do not sufficiently distinguish your subject from others in the same class, refine those attributes until they do.

You can tell when a basic definition is essentially complete by testing whether it is true if reversed. "Man is a biped" proves to be an incomplete definition when we turn it around, for it is not true that "all bipeds are men." Likewise, we know that the final version of Plato's definition is sound because it is truly reversible. All featherless bipeds having broad nails (instead of claws) are indeed humans.

When it can be reversed, a basic definition is complete enough to be accurate; but it still may be scanty or undeveloped. One way of developing a basic definition is by listing qualities or attributes of a thing beyond those needed merely to identify it. Food expert Raymond Sokolov defines

[1] Terms printed in all capitals are defined in the Glossary.

the Florida tomato, for example, as a vegetable that is "mass-produced, artificially ripened, mechanically picked, long-hauled" (all qualities or attributes). "It has no taste and it won't go splat" (more qualities, though negative ones). Sokolov advises that we grow our own tomatoes if we want them to be "antique-style, squishable, blotchy, tart, and sometimes green-dappled."

Another common strategy of basic definition is to define the whole by naming its parts. "Ketchup is long-haul tomatoes combined with sugar, vinegar, salt, onion powder, and 'natural' flavoring." Or you might define a word by tracing its origins: "The English ketchup (or catsup) comes from the Malay word kechap, derived in turn from the Chinese word meaning 'fish brine.'" This word history may seem to take us far from the tomatoes at the base of America's favorite sauce, but it suggests where ketchup originally got its salty taste. Such word histories (or ETYMOLOGIES) can be found in parentheses or brackets before many of the definitions in your dictionary. Woody Allen has fun with etymologies in his essay "Slang Origins," included in this chapter.

Yet another way of developing a basic definition is to give synonyms for the word or concept being defined. A botanist might well tell us that the tomato is a plant used as a vegetable. But if pushed, he would add that the tomato is actually a "berry," or "fleshy fruit," akin to the "hesperidium" and the "pepo." His botanical definition would then proceed to explain what these closely related terms have in common, as well as the shades of difference among them. You can find synonyms for the word you are defining in any good desk dictionary or dictionary of synonyms. (The etymologies usually come at the beginning of a dictionary entry; the "synonymies," or lists of synonyms, at the end.)

The definitions we have discussed so far are short and limited to defining a basic word or phrase. When the strategy of an entire essay is to define something, the author produces what is called an extended definition. Extended definitions seek first and last to explain the nature or meaning of a thing, but they often use many of the other strategies of exposition. An extended definition of the detective story, for example, might divide it into types according to the kind of detective involved: the hard-boiled cop, the bumbling private eye, the clever priest. This would be an example of supporting a definition by CLASSIFICATION.

If we distinguished the detective story from the mystery story

or the thriller, we might go on to define it by COMPARISON AND
CONTRAST with similar forms. If we noted that Edgar Allan Poe
invented the detective story and we gave the history of great detec-
tives from Poe's Dupin to Sherlock Holmes to Columbo, we might
draw upon NARRATIVE. Or if we speculated that the detective story
came into being because Poe wanted to discover a walk of life in
which the scientific mind blended with the poetic mind, we would
be analyzing CAUSE AND EFFECT.

There is no set formula for writing an extended definition, but
here are some questions to keep in mind when working one up:
What is the essential nature or purpose of the thing you are defining? What are its qualities? How does it work? How is it different
from others like it? Why do we need to know about it? In answering these questions, be as specific as you can. Vivid details make
definitions interesting, and interest (after accuracy) is the best test
of a good definition. Plato's definition of man surprises us into
attention by reducing a lofty concept to the homely term "featherless." The poet Emily Dickinson does the same when she defines
Hope as "the thing with feathers." It is the vivid specific detail
that startles us here, as Woody Allen well knows when he reduces
Dickinson's definition to absurdly specific terms: "The thing with
feathers has turned out to be my nephew. I must take him to a
specialist in Zurich."

Desmond Morris

Barrier Signals

Born in Wiltshire, England, in 1928, Desmond Morris is a
zoologist who applies his knowledge of animal behavior to human
beings. Since 1968 he has been a full-time writer, but he maintains an office in the Department of Zoology, Oxford University.
An associate of the Tinbergen research group at Oxford, he is
also an artist, and once organized a gallery sale in London of
abstract paintings by chimpanzees. Morris is best known in this
country as the author of The Naked Ape (1967), a study of the
human animal that was filmed by Universal studios in 1973. His
other books include The Human Zoo (1969); Intimate Behavior
(1971); Manwatching: A Field Guide to Human Behavior (1977);
and the forthcoming Animal Days. "Barrier Signals," a complete
section from Manwatching, is about the gestures we unconsciously
use to say no. It is an extended definition, developed largely by the
use of examples.

People feel safer behind some kind of physical barrier. If a   1
social situation is in any way threatening, then there is an immediate urge to set up such a barricade. For a tiny child faced
with a stranger, the problem is usually solved by hiding behind its mother's body and peeping out at the intruder to see
what he or she will do next. If the mother's body is not
available, then a chair or some other piece of solid furniture
will do. If the stranger insists on coming closer, then the peeping face must be hidden too. If the insensitive intruder continues to approach despite these obvious signals of fear, then
there is nothing for it but to scream or flee.

This pattern is gradually reduced as the child matures. In   2
teenage girls it may still be detected in the giggling cover-up
of the face, with hands or papers, when acutely or jokingly em-

barrassed. But by the time we are adult, the childhood hiding which dwindled to adolescent shyness, is expected to disappear altogether, as we bravely stride out to meet our guests, hosts, companions, relatives, colleagues, customers, clients, or friends. Each social occasion involves us, once again, in encounters similar to the ones which made us hide as scared infants and, as then, each encounter is slightly threatening. In other words, the fears are still there, but their expression is blocked. Our adult roles demand control and suppression of any primitive urge to withdraw and hide ourselves away. The more formal the occasion and the more dominant or unfamiliar our social companions, the more worrying the moment of encounter becomes. Watching people under· these conditions, it is possible to observe the many small ways in which they continue to 'hide behind their mother's skirts'. The actions are still there, but they are transformed into less obvious movements and postures. It is these that are the Barrier Signals of adult life.

The most popular from of Barrier Signal is the Body-cross. In   3
this, the hands or arms are brought into contact with one another in front of the body, forming a temporary 'bar' across the trunk, rather like a bumper or fender on the front of a motor-car. This is not done as a physical act of fending off the other person, as when raising a forearm horizontally across the front of the body to push through a struggling crowd. It is done, usually at quite a distance, as a nervous guest approaches a dominant host. The action is performed unconsciously and, if tackled on the subject immediately afterwards, the guest will not be able to remember having made the gesture. It is always camouflaged in some way, because if it were performed as a primitive fending-off or covering-up action, it would obviously be too transparent. The disguise it wears varies from person to person. Here are some examples:

The special guest on a gala occasion is alighting from his official   4
limousine. Before he can meet and shake hands with the reception committee, he has to walk alone across the open space in front of the main entrance to the building where the function is being held. A large crowd has come to watch his arrival and the press cameras are flashing. Even for the most experienced of celebrities this is a slightly nervous moment, and the mild fear that is felt expresses itself just as he is halfway across the 'greeting-space'. As he walks forward, his right hand reaches across his body and makes

a last-minute adjustment to his left cuff-link. It pauses there momentarily as he takes a few more steps, and then, at last, he is
close enough to reach out his hand for the first of the many hand-
shakes.

On a similar occasion, the special guest is a female. At just the   5
point where her male counterpart would have fiddled with his
cuff, she reaches across her body with her right hand and slightly
shifts the position of her handbag, which is hanging from her left
forearm.

There are other variations on this theme. A male may finger a   6
button or the strap of a wristwatch instead of his cuff. A female
may smooth out an imaginary crease in a sleeve, or re-position a
scarf or coat held over her left arm. But in all cases there is one
essential feature: at the peak moment of nervousness there is a
Body-cross, in which one arm makes contact with the other across
the front of the body, constructing a fleeting barrier between the
guest and the reception committee.

Sometimes the barrier is incomplete. One arm swings across but   7
does not actually make contact with the other. Instead it deals
with some trivial clothing-adjustment task on the opposite side of
the body. With even heavier camouflage, the hand comes up and
across, but goes no further than the far side of the head or face,
with a mild stroking or touching action.

Less disguised forms of the Body-cross are seen with less ex-   8
perienced individuals. The man entering the restaurant, as he
walks across an open space, rubs his hands together, as if washing
them. Or he advances with them clasped firmly in front of him.

Such are the Barrier Signals of the greeting situation, where one   9
person is advancing on another. Interestingly, field observations
reveal that it is most unlikely that both the greeter *and* the greeted
will perform such actions. Regardless of status, it is nearly always
the new arrival who makes the body-cross movement, because it
is he who is invading the home territory of the greeters. They are
on their own ground or, even if they are not, they were there first
and have at least temporary territorial 'rights' over the place. This
gives them an indisputable dominance at the moment of the greeting. Only if they are extremely subordinate to the new arrival, and
perhaps in serious trouble with him, will there be a likelihood of
them taking the 'body-cross role'. And if they do, this will mean
that the new arrival on the scene will omit it as he enters.

These observations tell us something about the secret language 10 of Barrier Signals, and indicate that, although the sending and receiving of the signals are both unconsciously done, the message gets across, none the less. The message says: 'I am nervous but I will not retreat'; and this makes it into an act of subordination which automatically makes the other person feel slightly more dominant and more comfortable.

The situation is different after greetings are over and people are 11 standing about talking to one another. Now, if one man edges too close to another, perhaps to hear better in all the noise of chattering voices, the boxed-in companion may feel the same sort of threatening sensation that the arriving celebrity felt as he walked towards the reception committee. What is needed now, however, is something more long-lasting than a mere cuff-fumble. It is simply not possible to go fiddling with a button for as long as this companion is going to thrust himself forward. So a more composed posture is needed. The favorite Body-cross employed in this situation is the arm-fold, in which the left and right arms intertwine themselves across the front of the chest. This posture, a perfect, frontal Barrier Signal, can be held for a very long time without appearing strange. Unconsciously it transmits a 'come-no-farther' message and is used a great deal at crowded gatherings. It has also been used by poster artists as a deliberate 'They-shall-not-pass!' gesture, and is rather formally employed by bodyguards when standing outside a protected doorway.

The same device of arm-folding can be used in a sitting rela- 12 tionship where the companion is approaching too close, and it can be amplified by a crossing of the legs *away* from the companion. Another variant is to press the tightly clasped hands down on to the crotch and squeeze them there between the legs, as if protecting the genitals. The message of this particular form of barrier is clear enough, even though neither side becomes consciously aware of it. But perhaps the major Barrier Signal for the seated person is that ubiquitous device, the desk. Many a businessman would feel naked without one and hides behind it gratefully every day, wearing it like a vast, wooden chastity-belt. Sitting beyond it he feels fully protected from the visitor exposed on the far side. It is the supreme barrier, both physical and psychological, giving him an immediate and lasting comfort while he remains in its solid embrace.

QUESTIONS

Understanding

1. What is a "barrier signal" as defined by Morris?
2. Why must barrier signals be disguised? What do they mask?
3. Barrier signals as defined by Morris are part of a "secret language" (par. 10) of gestures or signs. How does a sign differ from an action like screaming or running away?
4. In a greeting situation, according to Morris, why is it usually the new arrival who sets up barriers, even when his status is higher than the greeter's?
5. Why are barrier signals of interest to sociologists and anthropologists? What kind of information can they provide?

Strategies and Structure

1. Which sentence in paragraph 2 signals that the author has been constructing a definition?
2. Is the definition in paragraphs 1 and 2 developed primarily by CLASSIFICATION, PROCESS ANALYSIS, CAUSE AND EFFECT analysis, or some combination of these methods? Explain your answer.
3. This essay refers to several different kinds of barrier signals, but it is not really an essay in classification. Why not?
4. The examples in paragraphs 3–8 illustrate "the Body-cross." What else do they also illustrate?
5. In paragraph 12, Morris says that the desk is "the major Barrier Signal for the seated person." Is a desk really a good example of a "signal"? Why or why not?

Words and Figures of Speech

1. Morris is an "ethologist." Look up the definition of this specialty in an unabridged dictionary. How does "Barrier Signals" help to demonstrate what an ethologist does?
2. When he writes such a phrase as "clothing-adjustment task" (par. 7), Morris might be accused of "excess noun-overusage." Point out other examples and suggest less awkward ways for rewriting these phrases-used-as-nouns.

3. How does Morris's METAPHOR of hiding behind mother's skirts (par. 2) apply to barrier signals as he defines them?

4. If you are not sure of any of these words, see how your dictionary defines them: *colleagues* (par. 2), *suppression* (2), *camouflaged* (3), *gala* (4), *status* (9), *subordination* (10), *ubiquitous* (12).

Comparing

1. When you read Barry Lopez's "My Horse" in Chapter 7, look for barrier signals and other symbolic gestures among the Plains Indians that he describes.

2. Compare and contrast Morris's essay with Susan Allen Toth's "Cinematypes" (Chapter 2) as essays about social signals.

Discussion and Writing Topics

1. Elsewhere, Morris defines a "tie" signal as a gesture that indicates a close relationship between two or more people (holding hands, for example). Write an extended definition of "tie signals" in which you cite examples that you have actually observed "in the field."

2. Define *language*. In what sense are most written languages sign languages?

Willard Gaylin

What You See Is the Real You

A native of Cleveland, Ohio, Willard Gaylin, M.D., is professor of clinical psychiatry at Columbia University and president of the Institute of Society, Ethics, and the Life Sciences. Deeply concerned with the ethical issues in biology and medicine, he has taught at colleges and universities throughout the country, including the Columbia School of Law, where he is an adjunct professor. His books include In the Service of Their Country: War Resisters in Prison (1970); Partial Justice: A Study of Bias in Sentencing (1974); and Feelings: Our Vital Signs (1979). What you see in the following essay from the New York Times is a psychiatrist's personal definition of the self, ethics, and the limitations of mental science.

It was, I believe, the distinguished Nebraska financier Father   1
Edward J. Flanagan[1] who professed to having "never met a
bad boy." Having, myself, met a remarkable number of bad
boys, it might seem that either our experiences were drasti-
cally different or we were using the word "bad" differently.
I suspect neither is true, but rather that the Father was ap-
praising the "inner man," while I, in fact, do not acknowledge
the existence of inner people.

Since we psychoanalysts have unwittingly contributed to   2
this confusion, let one, at least, attempt a small rectifying
effort. Psychoanalytic data—which should be viewed as sup-
plementary information—is, unfortunately, often viewed as

1 (1886–1948), founder of Boys' Town orphanage near Omaha, Nebraska.

alternative (and superior) explanation. This has led to the prevalent tendency to think of the "inner" man as the real man and the outer man as an illusion or pretender.

While psychoanalysis supplies us with an incredibly useful tool 3 for explaining the motives and purposes underlying human behavior, most of this has little bearing on the moral nature of that behavior.

Like roentgenology, psychoanalysis is a fascinating, but rela- 4 tively new, means of illuminating the person. But few of us are prepared to substitute an X-ray of Grandfather's head for the portrait that hangs in the parlor. The inside of the man represents another view, not a truer one. A man may not always be what he appears to be, but what he appears to be is always a significant part of what he is. A man is the sum total of *all* his behavior. To probe for unconscious determinants of behavior and then define *him* in their terms exclusively, ignoring his overt behavior altogether, is a greater distortion than ignoring the unconscious completely.

Kurt Vonnegut [2] has said, "You are what you pretend to be," 5 which is simply another way of saying, you are what we (all of us) perceive you to be, not what you think you are.

Consider for a moment the case of the 90-year-old man on his 6 deathbed (surely the Talmud [3] must deal with this?) joyous and relieved over the success of his deception. For 90 years he has shielded his evil nature from public observation. For 90 years he has affected courtesy, kindness, and generosity—suppressing all the malice he knew was within him while he calculatedly and artificially substituted grace and charity. All his life he had been fooling the world into believing he was a good man. This "evil" man will, I predict, be welcomed into the Kingdom of Heaven.

Similarly, I will not be told that the young man who earns his 7 pocket money by mugging old ladies is "really" a good boy. Even my generous and expansive definition of goodness will not accommodate that particular form of self-advancement.

It does not count that beneath the rough exterior he has a 8 heart—or, for that matter, an entire innards—of purest gold,

---

[2] American novelist, author of *Cat's Cradle* (1963); *God Bless You, Mr. Rosewater* (1964); *Slaughterhouse-Five* (1969); and *Breakfast of Champions* (1973).

[3] Book of orthodox Jewish civil and religious law.

locked away from human perception. You are for the most part what you seem to be, not what you would wish to be, nor, indeed, what you believe yourself to be.

Spare me, therefore, your good intentions, your inner sensitivities, your unarticulated and unexpressed love. And spare me also those tedious psychohistories which—by exposing the goodness inside the bad man, and the evil in the good—invariably establish a vulgar and perverse egalitarianism, as if the arrangement of what is outside and what inside makes no moral difference. 9

Saint Francis [4] may, in his unconscious, indeed have been compensating for, and denying, destructive, unconscious Oedipal impulses identical to those which Attila projected and acted on. But the similarity of the unconscious constellations in the two men matters precious little, if it does not distinguish between them. 10

I do not care to learn that Hitler's heart was in the right place. A knowledge of the unconscious life of the man may be an adjunct to understanding his behavior. It is *not* a substitute for his behavior in describing him. 11

The inner man is a fantasy. If it helps you to identify with one, by all means, do so; preserve it, cherish. it, embrace it, but do not present it to others for evaluation or consideration, for excuse or exculpation, or, for that matter, for punishment or disapproval. 12

Like any fantasy, it serves your purposes alone. It has no standing in the real world which we share with each other. Those character traits, those attitudes, that behavior—that strange and alien stuff sticking out all over you—*that's the real you!* 13

QUESTIONS

Understanding

1. How does Gaylin DEFINE the self? How is it different from the self that psychoanalysis usually addresses?

---

[4] Probably St. Francis of Assisi (1182?–1226), Italian monk and founder of the Franciscan Order. The term *Oedipal impulses* refers to a son's sexual attraction to his mother; in Greek mythology, Oedipus, king of Thebes, unwittingly killed his father and married his mother. Attila was the fierce leader of the Huns from 434 to 453; invader of the Roman Empire.

2. What are fantasies, according to Gaylin's definition? What relation do they bear to the outer world?

3. What is the business of psychoanalysis, according to Gaylin? What aspect of human behavior is largely beyond its reach?

4. In paragraphs 1 and 11, what standard does Gaylin assume for judging the morality of human behavior?

Strategies and Structure

1. Like the preceding selection, Gaylin's essay is another instance of definition by example. Which examples do you find most effective? Why?

2. How do the examples of X-ray and portrait (par. 4) contribute to the distinction Gaylin is making between our "selves"?

3. Why do you think Gaylin chose to begin with the example of Father Flanagan? How does this example help to set the TONE of the essay?

4. Gaylin's definition is aided by COMPARISON AND CONTRAST, the EXPOSITORY strategy you will study in Chapter 6. For now, simply point out those examples that establish a contrast.

5. In paragraph 5, Gaylin rephrases Kurt Vonnegut's definition to make it conform with his own definition. Is this a legitimate technique? Why or why not?

Words and Figures of Speech

1. What peculiar meaning does *unconscious* (par. 11) have in the language of psychoanalysis?

2. What modern popular saying does Gaylin's title seem to echo? Why does this slogan, in particular, suit his purpose?

3. Gaylin says that he does "not acknowledge the existence of inner people" (par. 1). How can this HYPERBOLE be reconciled with his statement in paragraph 4 that the "inside view of the man represents another view, not a truer one"?

4. In paragraph 13, Gaylin defines *behavior* as "strange and alien stuff." Point out other passages where he seems to prefer ordinary language to technical language. How does Gaylin's care to avoid psychological jargon help to define his audience?

5. Consult your dictionary if you are not familiar with any of the following words: *financier* (par. 1), *rectify* (2), *roentgenology* (4), *affect* (6), *unarticulated* (9), *vulgar* (9), *perverse* (9), *egalitarianism* (9), *Oedipal* (10), *adjunct* (11).

Comparing

1. How does Gaylin's view of the self compare with the view assumed in Richard Restak's "The Other Difference between Boys and Girls" and Martha Mednick's and Nancy Felipe Russo's "The Sexes Are Not Born with Different Brains" (Chapter 9)?

2. How does the psychology of barrier signals, as explained by Desmond Morris in the preceding essay, *deny* Gaylin's definition of the self?

Discussion and Writing Topics

1. Write a definition of the self as your experience of human nature has led you to perceive it.

2. The main components of the self, according to the psychoanalyst Sigmund Freud, are the *ego*, the *id*, and the *superego*. Define one or more of these concepts.

Ellen Goodman
The Just-Right Wife

A columnist for the Boston Globe, Ellen Goodman (b. 1941)
writes about national but also "private" affairs of home, marriage
and the family, school, and work. Her syndicated column, carried
in over two hundred newspapers throughout the country, was
awarded the 1980 Pulitzer Prize for Commentary. A graduate of
Radcliffe College and a former Nieman Fellow at Harvard,
Goodman is a sometime radio and television commentator and the
author of Turning Points (1979). She lives near Boston with her
daughter. "The Just-Right Wife" is Goodman's definition of
what some marriageable American (and Arab) men are looking for
in a mate. This essay in definition is reprinted from a collection
of her essays on familiar, personal topics, Close to Home (1979).

The upper-middle-class men of Arabia are looking for just   1
the right kind of wife. Arabia's merchant class, reports the
Associated Press, finds the women of Libya too backward, and
the women of Lebanon too forward, and have therefore gone
shopping for brides in Egypt.

Egyptian women are being married off at the rate of thirty   2
a day—an astonishing increase, according to the Egyptian
marriage bureau. It doesn't know whether to be pleased or
alarmed at the popularity of its women. According to one recent Saudi Arabian groom, the Egyptian women are "just
right."

"The Egyptian woman is the happy medium," says Aly   3
Abdul el-Korrary of his bride, Wafaa Ibrahiv (the happy medium herself was not questioned). "She is not too inhibited
as they are in conservative Moslem societies, and not too liberal
like many Lebanese."

Is this beginning to sound familiar? Well, the upper-middle- 4
class, middle-aged, merchant-professional-class man of America
also wants a "happy medium" wife. He is confused. He, too, has a
problem and he would like us to be more understanding.

If it is no longer chic for a sheik to marry a veiled woman, it is 5
somehow no longer "modern" for a successful member of the
liberal establishment to be married to what he used to call a
"housewife" and what he now hears called a "household drudge."

As his father once wanted a wife who had at least started col- 6
lege, now he would like a wife who has a mind, and even a job,
of her own. The younger men in his office these days wear their
wives' occupations on their sleeves. He thinks he, too, would like a
wife—especially for social occasions—whose status would be his
status symbol. A lady lawyer would be nice.

These men, you understand, now say (at least in private to 7
younger working women in their office) that they are bored with
women who "don't do anything." No matter how much some of
them conspired in keeping them at home Back Then, many are
now saying, in the best Moslem style, "I divorce thee." They are
replacing them with more up-to-date models. A Ph.D. candidate
would be nice.

The upper-middle-class, middle-aged man of today wants a wife 8
who won't make him feel guilty. He doesn't want to worry if she's
happy. He doesn't want to hear her complain about her dusty
American history degree. He doesn't want to know if she's crying
at the psychiatrist's office. He most definitely doesn't want to be
blamed. He wants her to fulfill herself already! He doesn't mean
that maliciously.

On the other hand, Lord knows, he doesn't want a wife who is 9
too forward. The Saudi Arabian merchant believes that the Egyptian woman adapts more easily to his moods and needs. The
American merchant also wants a woman who adapts herself to his
moods and needs—his need for an independent woman and a
traditional wife.

He doesn't want to live with a "household drudge," but it would 10
be nice to have an orderly home and well-scrubbed children. Certainly he wouldn't want a wife who got high on folding socks—he
is not a Neanderthal—but it would be nice if she arranged for
these things to get done. Without talking about marriage contracts.

He wants a wife who agreed that "marriage is a matter of give 11 and take, not a business deal and 50–50 chores." It would help if she had just enough conflict herself (for not being her mother) to feel more than half the guilt for a full ashtray.

Of course, he sincerely would like her to be involved in her own [12] work and life. But on the other hand, he doesn't want it to siphon away her energy for him. He needs to be taken care of, nurtured. He would like her to enjoy her job, but be ready to move for his, if necessary (after, of course, a long discussion in which he feels awful about asking and she ends up comforting him and packing).

He wants a wife who is a sexually responsive and satisfied [13] woman, and he would even be pleased if she initiated sex with him. Sometimes. Not too often, however, because then he would get anxious.

He is confused, but he does, in all sincerity (status symbols [14] aside), want a happy marriage to a happy wife. A happy medium. He is not sure exactly what he means, but he, too, would like a wife who is "just right."

The difference is that when the upper-middle-class, middle-aged [15] man of Arabia wants his wife he goes out and buys one. His American "brother" can only offer himself as the prize.

QUESTIONS

Understanding

1. What qualities, as reported by Goodman, make Egyptian women "just-right" in the eyes of today's middle-class Arab men?

2. How have the requirements of American men who go shopping for wives changed since their fathers' day, according to Goodman? By what new standards do they define the just-right wife?

3. What traditional qualities do American men still look for in their wives?

4. Whose needs and opinions are slighted, in Goodman's view, when the ideal American wife gets defined by today's changing standards? What are some of those needs?

5. Goodman treats marriage as a transaction here. Considered as such, what is the main difference she sees between the way Amer-

ican men do business and the practice of their Arab "brothers"? Who offers the better deal for the wife in her view?

Strategies and Structure

1. Who is Goodman addressing primarily when she asks in paragraph 4, "Is this beginning to sound familiar?"

2. In paragraph 3, Goodman writes that "the happy medium herself was not questioned." What pronoun would this construction normally require? Why do you think Goodman used *herself* instead?

3. How do the last sentences in paragraphs 6, 7, and 8 resemble each other in structure? In TONE? Do you find this sort of repetition an effective device? Why or why not?

4. It was Goldilocks who sampled everything in the Three Bears' house until she found the porridge and bed that seemed "just-right" to her taste. What effect does Goodman achieve here by putting Goldilocks's standard of definition in the mouths of men?

5. Goodman's main strategy here is to compare the taste of American men with that of Moslem men, who traditionally prefer wives so subservient that they go about veiled from all other male eyes. Does the comparison work because the parallel is so close and obvious or because it is so unexpected? Explain your answer.

6. Despite the comparison between Moslem men and American men, why is this nevertheless an essay in definition rather than COM-PARISON AND CONTRAST (the strategy defined in Chapter 6)?

Words and Figures of Speech

1. American men, says this essay, want a "medium" wife—not too traditional but not too "forward" either. From the wife's point of view, what is the IRONY in repeatedly calling this kind of standard (and standardizing) "happy"?

2. Do you find "chic for a sheik" (par. 5) just-right or a little too-much?

3. Who was Neanderthal man (par. 10)? What qualities have been (erroneously) associated with him?

4. To what is Goodman comparing women in the METAPHOR "more up-to-date models" (par. 7)? What does the comparison imply about men's treatment of women?

Comparing

1. How might the phrase "happy medium" serve as ammunition for Lindsy Van Gelder's argument against sexist language in "The Great Person-Hole Cover Debate" (Chapter 10)?
2. In what ways does Goodman's point of view resemble that of Susan Allen Toth as she looks at the preferences of men in "Cinematypes" (Chapter 2)?

Discussion and Writing Topics

1. To what extent do you think Goodman is right about what American men want from a wife these days? On what grounds, if any, do you disagree with her definition of the just-right wife?
2. Write your own definition of the perfect spouse.
3. Write a definition of the "just-right" husband that exposes women's selfish demands when looking for a mate.

Woody Allen

Slang Origins

*Allen Stewart Konigsberg (Woody Allen) was born in Brooklyn,
New York, in 1935. Comedian, actor, director, and writer, he
began a busy career while still in high school by making up jokes
for other people; Herb Shriner, Sid Caesar, Art Carney, and Jack
Paar were among his early clients at NBC before Allen himself
went on the stage in 1961. He is probably most famous for his
films, including* Play It Again, Sam *(1972);* Love and Death
(1975); Manhattan *(1979); and* Stardust Memories *(1980). Annie
Hall (1977) won Allen the academy awards for both directing and
screenwriting. Allen's prose writing, which includes* Side Effects
*(1980), has been influenced, he says, by "The Bible, A Boy's Guide
to Forestry, and Advanced Sexual Positions—How to Achieve
Them without Laughing." "Slang Origins," from* Without
Feathers *(1975), shows how to define words by their etymologies
(or linguistic roots). Do not dismiss Allen's ridiculous definitions;
they are funny because they come so close to the standard form.*

How many of you have ever wondered where certain slang   1
expressions come from? Like "She's the cat's pajamas," or to
"take it on the lam." Neither have I. And yet for those who
are interested in this sort of thing I have provided a brief
guide to a few of the more interesting origins.

Unfortunately, time did not permit consulting any of the   2
established works on the subject, and I was forced to either
obtain the information from friends or fill in certain gaps by
using my own common sense.

Take, for instance, the expression "to eat humble pie."   3
During the reign of Louis the Fat, the culinary arts flourished
in France to a degree unequaled anywhere. So obese was the

French monarch that he had to be lowered onto the throne with a winch and packed into the seat itself with a large spatula. A typical dinner (according to DeRochet) consisted of a thin crêpe appetizer, some parsley, an ox, and custard. Food became the court obsession, and no other subject could be discussed under penalty of death. Members of a decadent aristocracy consumed incredible meals and even dressed as foods. DeRochet tells us that M. Monsant showed up at the coronation as a wiener, and Étienne Tisserant received papal dispensation to wed his favorite codfish. Desserts grew more and more elaborate and pies grew larger until the minister of justice suffocated trying to eat a seven-foot "Jumbo Pie." *Jumbo* pie soon became *jumble* pie and "to eat a jumble pie" referred to any kind of humiliating act. When the Spanish seamen heard the word *jumble*, they pronounced it "humble," although many preferred to say nothing and simply grin.

Now, while "humble pie" goes back to the French, "take it on   4
the lam" is English in origin. Years ago, in England, "lamming" was a game played with dice and a large tube of ointment. Each player in turn threw dice and then skipped around the room until he hemorrhaged. If a person threw a seven or under he would say the word "quintz" and proceed to twirl in a frenzy. If he threw over seven, he was forced to give every player a portion of his feathers and was given a good "lamming." Three "lammings" and a player was "kwirled" or declared a moral bankrupt. Gradually any game with feathers was called "lamming" and feathers became "lams." To "take it on the lam" meant to put on feathers and later, to escape, although the transition is unclear.

Incidentally, if two players disagreed on rules, we might say they   5
"got into a beef." This term goes back to the Renaissance when a man would court a woman by stroking the side of her head with a slab of meat. If she pulled away, it meant she was spoken for. If, however, she assisted by clamping the meat to her face and pushing it all over her head, it meant she would marry him. The meat was kept by the bride's parents and worn as a hat on special occasions. If, however, the husband took another lover, the wife could dissolve the marriage by running with the meat to the town square and yelling, "With thine own beef, I do reject thee. Aroo! Aroo!" If a couple "took to the beef" or "had a beef" it meant they were quarreling.

Another marital custom gives us that eloquent and colorful ex-   6 pression of disdain, "to look down one's nose." In Persia it was considered a mark of great beauty for a woman to have a long nose. In fact, the longer the nose, the more desirable the female, up to a certain point. Then it became funny. When a man proposed to a beautiful woman he awaited her decision on bended knee as she "looked down her nose at him." If her nostrils twitched, he was accepted, but if she sharpened her nose with pumice and began pecking him on the neck and shoulders, it meant she loved another.

Now, we all know when someone is very dressed up, we say he   7 looks "spiffy." The term owes its origin to Sir Oswald Spiffy, perhaps the most renowned fop of Victorian England. Heir to treacle millions, Spiffy squandered his money on clothes. It was said that at one time he owned enough handkerchiefs for all the men, women and children in Asia to blow their noses for seven years without stopping. Spiffy's sartorial innovations were legend, and he was the first man ever to wear gloves on his head. Because of extra-sensitive skin, Spiffy's underwear had to be made of the finest Nova Scotia salmon, carefully sliced by one particular tailor. His libertine attitudes involved him in several notorious scandals, and he eventually sued the government over the right to wear earmuffs while fondling a dwarf. In the end Spiffy died a broken man in Chichester, his total wardrobe reduced to kneepads and a sombrero.

Looking "spiffy," then, is quite a compliment, and one who does   8 is liable to be dressed "to beat the band," a turn-of-the-century expression that originated from the custom of attacking with clubs any symphony orchestra whose conductor smiled during Berlioz. "Beating the band" soon became a popular evening out, and people dressed up in their finest clothes, carrying with them sticks and rocks. The practice was finally abandoned, during a performance of the *Symphonie fantastique* [1] in New York when the entire string section suddenly stopped playing and exchanged gunfire with the first ten rows. Police ended the melee but not before a relative of J. P. Morgan's [2] was wounded in the soft palate. After that, for a while at least, nobody dressed "to beat the band."

[1] Symphony composed in 1831 by the Frenchman, Hector Berlioz (1803–1869).

[2] John Pierpont Morgan (1837–1913), American banker and art connoisseur, or his son, J. P. Morgan, Jr. (1867–1943), also an investment banker.

If you think some of the above derivations questionable, you 9
might throw up your hands and say, "Fiddlesticks." This marvelous expression originated in Austria many years ago. Whenever a
man in the banking profession announced his marriage to a circus
pinhead, it was the custom for friends to present him with a
bellows and a three-year supply of wax fruit. Legend has it that
when Leo Rothschild made known his betrothal, a box of cello
bows was delivered to him by mistake. When it was opened and
found not to contain the traditional gift, he exclaimed, "What
are these? Where are my bellows and fruit? Eh? All I rate is fiddlesticks!" The term "fiddlesticks" became a joke overnight in the
taverns amongst the lower classes, who hated Leo Rothschild for
never removing the comb from his hair after combing it. Eventually "fiddlesticks" meant any foolishness.

Well, I hope you've enjoyed some of these slang origins and 10
that they stimulate you to investigate some of your own. And in
case you were wondering about the term used to open this study,
"the cat's pajamas," it goes back to an old burlesque routine of
Chase and Rowe's, the two nutsy German professors. Dressed in
oversized tails, Bill Rowe stole some poor victim's pajamas. Dave
Chase, who got great mileage out of his "hard of hearing" specialty, would ask him:

    CHASE: Ach, Herr Professor. Vot is dot bulge under your pocket? 11
    ROWE: Dot? Dot's de chap's pajamas. 12
    CHASE: The cat's pajamas? Ut mein Gott? 13

Audiences were convulsed by this sort of repartee and only a 14
premature death of the team by strangulation kept them from
stardom.

QUESTIONS

Understanding

1. A parody is a take-off on a literary form. What kind of writing
   is Allen's "study" parodying?

2. Look up *humble pie* in your dictionary. What is the ETYMOLOGY
   of the phrase? Why do you suppose the name of the main ingredient later got confused with the word *humble*?

3. Many words that we use today have their origins in Latin. Check the front or back of your dictionary for a short history of the English language. When and why did Latin most influence English?

Strategies and Structure

1. How soon in paragraph 1 do you know that Allen is "pulling your leg" (to use a phrase that Allen might have "explained" for us)?

2. Describe Allen's TRANSITIONS from word history to word history. How do they contribute to the humor?

3. Allen is not speaking in his own voice here (the voice of Allen Stewart Konigsberg); he is using a persona or stand-in. What is that persona like? How does Allen characterize him? How would you describe the TONE of his voice?

4. Why does Allen end with Rowe and Chase and their strange demise?

5. Allen calls his essay a "guide" (par. 1); it is a form he often uses—"A Brief, Yet Helpful, Guide to Civil Disobedience," for example. Why? What is a "guide" and why might the form appeal to a humorist?

6. Suppose you were explaining what an etymologist is and does. How might you use the etymology of the word itself to help along your DEFINITION?

Words and Figures of Speech

1. Look up several of Woody Allen's words and phrases and "correct" his word histories.

2. Report on the kinds of information to be found in the *Dictionary of American Slang*, edited by Harold Wentworth and Stuart Berg Flexner (available in the reference room of your college or university library.)

3. Look up the word *buxom* in the *Oxford English Dictionary*. (Try the reference room again.) How has the word changed in meaning over the centuries?

Comparing

1. How does Allen's TONE resemble Russell Baker's in "A Nice Place to Visit" (Chapter 6)?

Discussion and Writing Topics

1. Make up your own comic etymologies of the following words and phrases, but adhere as strictly as Allen does to the *form* of definition-by-etymology:

   to fly off the handle
   to go off on a tangent
   squared away
   clean as a whistle
   a horse of another color
   birds of a feather
   a white elephant
   a sacred cow.

WRITING TOPICS for Chapter Five
Essays That Define

Write extended definitions of one or more of the following:

1. Photosynthesis or mitosis
2. Obscenity
3. A liberal education
4. Success
5. A happy marriage
6. A liberated woman
7. A true friend
8. Self-reliance
9. Inertia (physical or spiritual)
10. Non-Euclidian geometry
11. Calculus
12. The big-bang theory of creation
13. Your idea of the ideal society
14. Blues music
15. Tragedy, comedy, romance, novel, satire, or some other literary form

6

Essays That
Compare and Contrast

Before you begin an essay in COMPARISON AND CONTRAST,[1]
it is a good idea to make a list of the qualities of the two
objects or ideas to be compared. Suppose, for example, that
our "objects" were all-time basketball greats Wilt ("The
Stilt") Chamberlain and Bill Russell. Our lists might look
like this:

Chamberlain	Russell
7-feet-3-inches tall	6-feet-9-inches tall
good team	better team
fast	faster
style	discipline
loser (almost)	winner (almost)
Goliath	David

Each of these lists is an abbreviated DESCRIPTION of the
player whose attributes it compiles. At this early stage, our
comparison and contrast essay seems indistinguishable from
descriptive writing. As soon as we bring our two lists
together, however, the descriptive impulse yields to the
impulse to explain. Consider the following excerpt from
an actual comparison of Chamberlain with Russell by sportswriter Jeremy Larner:

Wilt's defenders could claim with justice that Russell played
with a better team, but it was all too apparent that Boston was
better partly because Russell played better with them. Russell
has been above all a team player—a man of discipline, self-

[1] Terms printed in all capitals are defined in the Glossary.

denial and killer instinct; in short, a *winner*, in the best American
Calvinist tradition. Whereas Russell has been able somehow to
squeeze out his last ounce of ability, Chamberlain's performances
have been marked by a seeming nonchalance—as if, recognizing his
Giantistic fate, he were more concerned with personal style than
with winning. "I never want to set records. The only thing I
strive for is perfection" Chamberlain has said. When Wilt goes
into his routine, his body proclaims from tip to toe, it's not my
fault, folks, honestly—and though I've got to lose, if you look close,
you'll see I'm beautiful through and through!

Even though it describes the two men in some detail, this passage
is EXPOSITION rather than description. Like most comparative writing, its comparisons are cast as statements or propositions: Russell
is more efficient than Chamberlain; Chamberlain is concerned
with style, while Russell plays to win. The controlling proposition
of Larner's entire essay is that Chamberlain was a Goliath "type-
cast" by fans to lose to Russell the giant-killer; but Chamberlain
broke the stereotype to become the greatest basketball player ever.

We can take a number of hints from Jeremy Larner about
writing comparison and contrast essays. First, stick to two and only
two subjects at a time. Second, choose subjects that invite comparison because they belong to the same general class: two athletes,
two religions, two sororities, two mammals. (In "The Black and
White Truth about Basketball," reprinted in this chapter, another
sports enthusiast, Jeff Greenfield, compares two styles of playing
the same game.) You might point out many differences between a
mattress and a steamboat, but no one is likely to be impressed by
this exercise in the obvious. The third lesson is that you do not
have to give equal weight to similarities and differences. Larner
assumes the similarities between Chamberlain and Russell (both
are towering champions), but he works carefully through the
differences. An essay that compares a turtle to a tank, on the other
hand, might concentrate upon the similarities of the two if it proposes that both belong to the class of moving things with armor.

Our example suggests, finally, that comparison and contrast
essays proceed by alternation. From paragraph to paragraph, Larner
dispenses his subject in "slices." His assertion that Russell is a
team player is followed immediately by the counterassertion that
Chamberlain plays to a private standard. Chamberlain's free throws

are always uncertain; Russell's are accurate in the clutch. And so on, point by point. Another way of comparing and contrasting is in "chunks." Larner might have said all he had to say about Russell in several paragraphs and then followed up with all of his remarks on Chamberlain. Either method (or a combination of the two) is correct if it works. The aim is to set forth clear alternatives.

Bruce Catton

Grant and Lee: A Study in Contrasts

A native of Michigan who attended Oberlin College, Bruce Catton was a former newspaper reporter, a one-time editor of American Heritage, and a noted historian of the Civil War. A Stillness at Appomattox (1953) won both the Pulitzer Prize and the National Book Award for history in 1954. It was not, said Catton, "the strategy or political meanings" that fascinated him but the "almost incomprehensible emotional experience which this war brought to our country." Among Catton's many other books are This Hallowed Ground (1956); The Coming Fury (1961); The Army of the Potomac (1962); Terrible Swift Sword (1963); Never Call Retreat (1965); Grant Takes Command (1969); and Michigan: A Bicentennial History (1976). "Grant and Lee: A Study in Contrasts" is reprinted from a collection of essays by distinguished historians.

When Ulysses S. Grant and Robert E. Lee met in the parlor of a modest house at Appomattox Court House, Virginia, on April 9, 1865, to work out the terms for the surrender of Lee's Army of Northern Virginia, a great chapter in American life came to a close, and a great new chapter began. 1

These men were bringing the Civil War to its virtual finish. To be sure, other armies had yet to surrender, and for a few days the fugitive Confederate government would struggle desperately and vainly, trying to find some way to go on living now that its chief support was gone. But in effect it was all 2 over when Grant and Lee signed the papers. And the little room where they wrote out the terms was the scene of one of the poignant, dramatic contrasts in American history.

They were two strong men, these oddly different generals, and they represented the strengths of two conflicting currents that, through them, had come into final collision.   3

Back of Robert E. Lee was the notion that the old aristocratic concept might somehow survive and be dominant in American life.   4

Lee was tidewater Virginia, and in his background were family, culture, and tradition . . . the age of chivalry transplanted to a New World which was making its own legends and its own myths. He embodied a way of life that had come down through the age of knighthood and the English country squire. America was a land that was beginning all over again, dedicated to nothing much more complicated than the rather hazy belief that all men had equal rights and should have an equal chance in the world. In such a land Lee stood for the feeling that it was somehow of advantage to human society to have a pronounced inequality in the social structure. There should be a leisure class, backed by ownership of land; in turn, society itself should be keyed to the land as the chief source of wealth and influence. It would bring forth (according to this ideal) a class of men with a strong sense of obligation to the community; men who lived not to gain advantage for themselves, but to meet the solemn obligations which had been laid on them by the very fact that they were privileged. From them the country would get its leadership; to them it could look for the higher values—of thought, of conduct, of personal deportment—to give it strength and virtue.   5

Lee embodied the noblest elements of this aristocratic ideal. Through him, the landed nobility justified itself. For four years, the Southern states had fought a desperate war to uphold the ideals for which Lee stood. In the end, it almost seemed as if the Confederacy fought for Lee; as if he himself was the Confederacy . . . the best thing that the way of life for which the Confederacy stood could ever have to offer. He had passed into legend before Appomattox. Thousands of tired, underfed, poorly clothed Confederate soldiers, long since past the simple enthusiasm of the early days of the struggle, somehow considered Lee the symbol of everything for which they had been willing to die. But   6 they could not quite put this feeling into words. If the Lost Cause, sanctified by so much heroism and so many deaths, had a living justification, its justification was General Lee.

Grant, the son of a tanner on the Western frontier, was every- 7 thing Lee was not. He had come up the hard way and embodied nothing in particular except the eternal toughness and sinewy fiber of the men who grew up beyond the mountains. He was one of a body of men who owed reverence and obeisance to no one, who were self-reliant to a fault, who cared hardly anything for the past but who had a sharp eye for the future.

These frontier men were the precise opposites of the tidewater 8 aristocrats. Back of them, in the great surge that had taken people over the Alleghenies and into the opening Western country, there was a deep, implicit dissatisfaction with a past that had settled into grooves. They stood for democracy, not from any reasoned conclusion about the proper ordering of human society, but simply because they had grown up in the middle of democracy and knew how it worked. Their society might have privileges, but they would be privileges each man had won for himself. Forms and patterns meant nothing. No man was born to anything, except perhaps to a chance to show how far he could rise. Life was competition.

Yet along with this feeling had come a deep sense of belonging 9 to a national community. The Westerner who developed a farm, opened a shop, or set up in business as a trader, could hope to prosper only as his own community prospered—and his community ran from the Atlantic to the Pacific and from Canada down to Mexico. If the land was settled, with towns and highways and accessible markets, he could better himself. He saw his fate in terms of the nation's own destiny. As its horizons expanded, so did his. He had, in other words, an acute dollars-and-cents stake in the continued growth and development of his country.

And that, perhaps, is where the contrast between Grant and Lee 10 becomes most striking. The Virginia aristocrat, inevitably, saw himself in relation to his own region. He lived in a static society which could endure almost anything except change. Instinctively, his first loyalty would go to the locality in which that society existed. He would fight to the limit of endurance to defend it, because in defending it he was defending everything that gave his own life its deepest meaning.

The Westerner, on the other hand, would fight with an equal 11 tenacity for the broader concept of society. He fought so because everything he lived by was tied to growth, expansion, and a constantly widening horizon. What he lived by would survive or fall with the nation itself. He could not possibly stand by unmoved in the face of an attempt to destroy the Union. He would combat it with everything he had, because he could only see it as an effort to cut the ground out from under his feet.

So Grant and Lee were in complete contrast, representing two [12] diametrically opposed elements in American life. Grant was the modern man emerging; beyond him, ready to come on the stage, was the great age of steel and machinery, of crowded cities and a restless burgeoning vitality. Lee might have ridden down from the old age of chivalry, lance in hand, silken banner fluttering over his head. Each man was the perfect champion of his cause, drawing both his strengths and his weaknesses from the people he led.

Yet it was not all contrast, after all. Different as they were—in [13] background, in personality, in underlying aspiration—these two great soldiers had much in common. Under everything else, they were marvelous fighters. Furthermore, their fighting qualities were really very much alike.

Each man had, to begin with, the great virtue of utter tenacity [14] and fidelity. Grant fought his way down the Mississippi Valley in spite of acute personal discouragement and profound military handicaps. Lee hung on in the trenches at Petersburg after hope itself had died. In each man there was an indomitable quality . . . the born fighter's refusal to give up as long as he can still remain on his feet and lift his two fists.

Daring and resourcefulness they had, too; the ability to think [15] faster and move faster than the enemy. These were the qualities which gave Lee the dazzling campaigns of Second Manassas and Chancellorsville and won Vicksburg for Grant.

Lastly, and perhaps greatest of all, there was the ability, at the [16] end, to turn quickly from war to peace once the fighting was over. Out of the way these two men behaved at Appomattox came the possibility of a peace of reconciliation. It was a possibility not wholly realized, in the years to come, but which did, in the end, help the two sections to become one nation again . . . after a war whose bitterness might have seemed to make such a reunion wholly impossible. No part of either man's life became him more than the part he played in this brief meeting in the McLean house

at Appomattox. Their behavior there put all succeeding generations of Americans in their debt. Two great Americans, Grant and
Lee—very different, yet under everything very much alike. Their
encounter at Appomattox was one of the great moments of
American history.

QUESTIONS

Understanding

1. Catton writes that generals Lee and Grant represented two opposing currents (par. 3) of American culture. What were they?
   Describe the contrasting qualities and ideals that Catton associates
   with each man.

2. What qualities, according to Catton, did Grant and Lee have in
   common?

3. With Lee's surrender, says Catton, "a great new chapter" (par.
   1) of American history began. He is referring, presumably, to the
   period of expansion between the Civil War and World War I,
   when industrialization really took hold in America. What characteristics of the new era does his description of Grant anticipate?

4. Catton does not describe, in any detail, how Grant and Lee behaved as they worked out the terms of peace at Appomattox; but
   what does he *imply* about the conduct of the two generals? Why
   was their conduct important to "all succeeding generations" (par.
   16) of Americans?

5. Catton gives no specific reasons for the Confederacy's defeat. He
   says nothing, for example, about the Union's greater numbers or
   its superior communications system. What general explanation
   does he imply, however, when he associates Lee with a "static"
   society (par. 10) and Grant with a society of "restless burgeoning
   vitality" (par. 12)?

Strategies and Structure

1. Beginning with paragraph 3, Catton gets down to the particulars
   of his contrast between the two generals. Where does the contrast end? In which paragraph does he begin to list similarities
   between the two men?

2. Except for mentioning their strength, Catton says little about the unique physical appearance of either Grant or Lee. Is this a weakness in his essay or is there some justification for avoiding such details? Explain your answer.

3. Which sentence in paragraph 16 brings together the contrasts and the similarities of the preceding paragraphs? How does this final paragraph recall the opening paragraphs of the essay? Why might Catton end with an echo of his beginning?

4. Would you say that the historian's voice in this essay is primarily DESCRIPTIVE, NARRATIVE, or EXPOSITORY? Explain your answer.

Words and Figures of Speech

1. Catton describes the parlor where Grant and Lee met as the *scene* of a *dramatic* contrast (par. 2), and he says in paragraph 12 that the post–Civil War era was "ready to come on stage." Where do such METAPHORS come from, and what view of history do they suggest?

2. What is the Lost Cause of paragraph 6, and what does the phrase (in capital letters) CONNOTE?

3. Catton does not use the phrase *noblesse oblige*, but it could be applied to General Lee's beliefs as Catton defines them. What does the phrase mean?

4. What is the precise meaning of *obeisance* (par. 7), and why might Catton have chosen it instead of the more common *obedience* when describing General Grant?

5. Look up any of these words with which you are not on easy terms: *fugitive* (par. 2), *poignant* (2), *chivalry* (5), *sinewy* (7), *implicit* (8), *tenacity* (11), *diametrically* (12), *acute* (14), *profound* (14), and *indomitable* (14).

Comparing

1. Both Catton and Alex Haley in "My Furthest-Back Person—'The African'" (Chapter 1) are writing about the past from vantage points in the present. How do they differ in their approaches to history and to the historian's role?

2. Catton speaks often of the "conduct" and "deportment" of Grant and Lee. How does his idea of human behavior compare with

that of sociologist Desmond Morris in "Barrier Signals" (Chapter 5)?

Discussion and Writing Topics

1. Write an essay contrasting Thomas Jefferson and Alexander Hamilton (or John F. Kennedy and Richard Nixon) as men who represented the conflicting forces of their time.

2. "America," Catton writes, "was a land that was beginning all over again . . ." (par. 5). Discuss this idea as one way of formulating the "American dream."

3. Grant, we are told, saw the nation's "destiny" (par. 9) as coinciding with his own. What was the notion of "Manifest Destiny," and how did it help to shape American history?

4. Do you agree with Catton's assessment of General Lee as a man of the past and, therefore, a fitting emblem of the South? Why or why not?

5. Is history the story of forces acting through great personalities (as Catton assumes) or of great personalities who control forces? Or neither? Explain your answer.

Russell Baker
A Nice Place to Visit

For many years now, Russell Baker has lived and worked in New
York City. To an insider's familiarity with the manners and folk-
ways of that city, however, he brings the perspective of a relative
late-comer who was born in Virginia in 1925 and lived first in
Baltimore and then Washington, D.C., before coming to the Big
Apple. Since 1962, Baker has contributed to the New York Times
his nationally syndicated "Observer" column, known both for its
keen eye upon American politics and its attentive ear to the
English language. A contributor to such other periodicals as the
Saturday Evening Post, Sports Illustrated, and Ladies' Home
Journal, Baker is also the author of numerous books and collections
of essays, including Baker's Dozen (1964), Our Next President
(1968), Poor Russell's Almanac (1972), The Upside-down Man
(1977), and So This Is Depravity (1980), from which "A Nice
Place to Visit" is taken in its entirety. A life-long observer of cities,
Baker here contrasts his mannerly Canadian neighbor, Toronto,
with the adoptive American metropolis he loves to hate.

Having heard that Toronto was becoming one of the con-   1
tinent's noblest cities, we flew from New York to investigate.
New Yorkers jealous of their city's reputation and concerned
about challenges to its stature have little to worry about.

After three days in residence, our delegation noted an ab-   2
sence of hysteria that was almost intolerable and took to con-
suming large portions of black coffee to maintain our normal
state of irritability. The local people to whom we complained
in hopes of provoking comfortably nasty confrontations declined to become bellicose. They would like to enjoy a gratify-
ing big-city hysteria, they said, but believed it would seem
ill-mannered in front of strangers.

Extensive field studies—our stay lasted four weeks—persuaded ³
us that this failure reflects the survival in Toronto of an ancient
pattern of social conduct called "courtesy."

"Courtesy" manifests itself in many quaint forms appalling to ⁴
the New Yorker. Thus, for example, Yankee fans may be aston-
ished to learn that at the Toronto baseball park it is considered
bad form to heave rolls of toilet paper and beer cans at players on
the field.

Official literature inside Toronto taxicabs includes a notification ⁵
of the proper address to which riders may mail the authorities not
only complaints but also compliments about the cabbie's behavior.

For a city that aspires to urban greatness, Toronto's entire taxi ⁶
system has far to go. At present, it seems hopelessly bogged down
in civilization. One day a member of our delegation listening to a
radio conversation between a short-tempered cabbie and the dispatcher distinctly heard the dispatcher say, "As Shakespeare said,
if music be the food of love, play on, give me excess of it."

This delegate became so unnerved by hearing Shakespeare ⁷
quoted by a cab dispatcher that he fled immediately back to New
York to have his nerves abraded and his spine rearranged in a real
big-city taxi.

What was particularly distressing as the stay continued was the ⁸
absence of shrieking police and fire sirens at 3 A.M.—or any other
hour, for that matter. We spoke to the city authorities about this.
What kind of city was it, we asked, that expected its citizens to
sleep all night and rise refreshed in the morning? Where was the
incentive to awaken gummy-eyed and exhausted, ready to scream
at the first person one saw in the morning? How could Toronto
possibly hope to maintain a robust urban divorce rate?

Our criticism went unheeded, such is the torpor with which ⁹
Toronto pursues true urbanity. The fact appears to be that
Toronto has very little grasp of what is required of a great city.

Consider the garbage picture. It seems never to have occurred to ¹⁰
anybody in Toronto that garbage exists to be heaved into the
streets. One can drive for miles without seeing so much as a ba-
nana peel in the gutter or a discarded newspaper whirling in the
wind.

Nor has Toronto learned about dogs. A check with the authori- ¹¹
ties confirmed that, yes, there are indeed dogs resident in Toronto,

but one would never realize it by walking the sidewalks. Our delegation was shocked by the presumption of a town's calling itself a city, much less a great city, when it obviously knows nothing of either garbage or dogs.

The subway, on which Toronto prides itself, was a laughable   12
imitation of the real thing. The subway cars were not only spotlessly clean, but also fully illuminated. So were the stations. To New Yorkers, it was embarrassing, and we hadn't the heart to tell the subway authorities that they were light-years away from greatness.

We did, however, tell them about spray paints and how effec-   13
tively a few hundred children equipped with spray-paint cans could at least give their subway the big-city look.

It seems doubtful they are ready to take such hints. There is a   14
disturbing distaste for vandalism in Toronto which will make it hard for the city to enter wholeheartedly into the vigor of the late twentieth century.

A board fence surrounding a huge excavation for a new high-   15
rise building in the downtown district offers depressing evidence of Toronto's lack of big-city impulse. Embedded in the fence at intervals of about fifty feet are loudspeakers that play recorded music for passing pedestrians.

Not a single one of these loudspeakers has been mutilated.   16
What's worse, not a single one has been stolen.

It was good to get back to the Big Apple. My coat pocket was   17
bulging with candy wrappers from Toronto and—such is the lingering power of Toronto—it took me two or three hours back in New York before it seemed natural again to toss them into the street.

QUESTIONS

Understanding

1. When Toronto authorities pay no attention to Baker's advice about the need for sirens at 3:00 A.M., he remarks how slowly the city "pursues true urbanity" (par. 9). What definition of "urbanity" is Baker humorously assuming here and throughout his comparison of New York and Toronto?

2. What are some of the main conditions in Toronto that seem particularly backward to a New Yorker? How might New Yorkers define the idea of "civilization" in which the Canadian city is "hopelessly bogged down" (par. 6).

3. What specific living conditions does Baker attribute to New York by contrast with the appallingly genteel ways of life in Toronto?

4. When Baker returns home from Canada, it takes "two or three hours" (par. 17) before he can start throwing litter in the streets again. How "lingering," actually, is the influence of the Canadian city upon the true New Yorker?

Strategies and Structure

1. In comparing the two cities, Baker does not so much tell us what New York is like as what Toronto is *not* like. How, then, does he nevertheless get across a clear picture of life in the American city?

2. Baker's IRONY is especially thick in sentences such as this, "What kind of a city was it, we asked, that expected its citizens to sleep all night and rise refreshed in the morning" (par. 8)? Point out other examples in which his mock exasperation is particularly transparent. Do you find such irony an effective device? Why or why not?

3. Why does the author of this essay adopt the plural pronoun "we" instead of saying "I"? Is his reason solely that he went to Canada with several other people?

4. Why does Baker refer to his ramblings in Toronto as "extensive field studies" (par. 3)? What is the difference between an expedition and a trip, or visit?

5. Baker uses a number of highly formal constructions: "our delegation noted an absence" (par. 2), "local people . . . declined to become bellicose" (par. 2), " 'courtesy' manifests itself in many quaint forms" (par. 4). Why might Baker adopt such ponderous SYNTAX, given the role he assumes in this essay.

6. Point out grammatical constructions that show Baker knows how to write in a plainer style.

7. What is a parody? What sort of language and general point of view is Baker having fun with here?

Words and Figures of Speech

1. Baker's title is the first half of an observation that returning travel-

ers often make about strange, impressive places. What is the other half? How does it apply to the case of a dyed-in-the-wool New Yorker?

2. Why does Baker put the word *courtesy* (pars. 5 and 6) in quotation marks?

3. How would you describe Baker's vocabulary most of the time in this essay? Which is more typical of his diction throughout: words like *gummy-eyed* (par. 8) or like *bellicose* (par. 2)? Why the preponderance of such words?

4. What are the CONNOTATIONS of *robust* (par. 8)? Has Baker failed to consider the implications of the word? What reason might he have for choosing it in the context of divorce rates?

5. "What's worse" (par. 16) is a good example of verbal irony, that is, words that say one thing and mean another. In Baker's opening paragraph, what phrase is to be taken equally ironically? What is Baker really saying in both cases?

Comparing

1. Baker's assumed attitude toward the subject of his field studies closely resembles that of Horace Miner in "Body Ritual among the Nacirema" (Chapter 8). What do the assumed roles of both writers have in common? What similar effects do they achieve by adopting them?

Discussion and Writing Topics

1. What is your opinion of the true American urbanite's understanding of urbanity, as reported by Baker? Is Baker being fair to New York and New Yorkers?

2. Confirmed urban dwellers, especially those born and bred in New York City have been called the country's greatest provincials. Do you agree? Why or why not?

3. Compare and contrast two cities or towns of your acquaintance by assuming the prejudices of one and revealing the "faults" of the other in the glaring light of those prejudices.

Jeff Greenfield

The Black and White Truth about Basketball

*Jeff Greenfield is a political analyst and sportswriter. He was born
in New York in 1943, the son of a lawyer; he attended the University of Wisconsin and Yale (LL.B., 1967). Once a speechwriter
and legislative aide to Robert F. Kennedy and former Mayor
Lindsay of New York, he is the co-author of* The Advance Man
(1971) and A Populist Manifesto *(1972). In 1973, pursuing other
interests, Greenfield published* Where Have You Gone, Joe
Dimaggio? *Among his other works are* The World's Greatest Team:
A Portrait of the Boston Celtics *(1976) and* Playing to Win: An
Insider's Guide to Politics *(1980). "The Black and White Truth
about Basketball," from* Esquire *magazine, contrasts two styles of
play; it carries the subtitle, "A Skin-Deep Theory of Style." This is
primarily an essay in comparison and contrast, but it also analyzes*
CAUSE AND EFFECT.

The dominance of black athletes over professional basketball   1
is beyond dispute. Two thirds of the players are black, and the
number would be greater were it not for the continuing practice of picking white bench warmers for the sake of balance.
The Most Valuable Player award of the National Basketball
Association has gone to blacks for sixteen of the last twenty
years, and in the newer American Basketball Association,
blacks have won it all but once in the league's eight years. In
the 1974–75 season, four of the top five All-Stars and seven of
the top ten were black. The N.B.A. was the first pro sports
league of any stature to hire a black coach (Bill Russell of the
Celtics) and the first black general manager (Wayne Embry
of the Bucks). What discrimination remains—lack of opportunity for lucrative benefits such as speaking engagements and
product endorsements—has more to do with society than with
basketball.

This dominance reflects a natural inheritance; basketball is a   2
pastime of the urban poor. The current generation of black athletes are heirs to a tradition half a century old: in a neighborhood
without the money for bats, gloves, hockey sticks, tennis rackets,
or shoulder pads, basketball is accessible. "Once it was the game
of the Irish and Italian Catholics in Rockaway and the Jews on
Fordham Road in the Bronx," writes David Wolf in his brilliant
book, *Foul!* "It was recreation, status, and a way out." But now
the ethnic names are changed; instead of Red Holzmans, Red
Auerbachs, and McGuire brothers, there are Earl Monroes and
Connie Hawkins and Nate Archibalds. And professional basketball is a sport with a national television contract and million-
dollar salaries.

But the mark on basketball of today's players can be measured   3
by more than money or visibility. It is a question of style. For
there is a clear difference between "black" and "white" styles of
play that is as clear as the difference between 155th Street at
Eighth Avenue and Crystal City, Missouri. Most simply (remembering we are talking about culture, not chromosomes), "black"
basketball is the use of superb athletic skill to adapt to the limits
of space imposed by the game. "White" ball is the pulverization
of that space by sheer intensity.

It takes a conscious effort to realize how constricted the space   4
is on a basketball court. Place a regulation court (ninety-four by
fifty feet) on a football field, and it will reach from the back of
the end zone to the twenty-one-yard line; its width will cover less
than a third of the field. On a baseball diamond, a basketball
court will reach from home plate to just beyond first base. Compared to its principal indoor rival, ice hockey, basketball covers
about one fourth the playing area. And during the normal flow of
the game, most of the action takes place on about the third of the
court nearest the basket. It is in this dollhouse space that ten
men, each of them half a foot taller than the average man, come
together to battle each other.

There is, thus, no room; basketball is a struggle for the edge: the   5
half step with which to cut around the defender for a lay-up, the
half second of freedom with which to release a jump shot, the in-
stant a head turns allowing a pass to a teammate breaking for
the basket. It is an arena for the subtlest of skills: the head fake,
the shoulder fake, the shift of body weight to the right and the

sudden cut to the left. Deception is crucial to success; and to young men who have learned early and painfully that life is a battle for survival, basketball is one of the few games in which the weapon of deception is a legitimate rule and not the source of trouble.

If there is, then, the need to compete in a crowd, to battle for the edge, then the surest strategy is to develop the *unexpected*; to develop a shot that is simply and fundamentally different from the usual methods of putting the ball in the basket. Drive to the hoop, but go under it and come up the other side; hold the ball at waist level and shoot from there instead of bringing the ball up to eye level; leap into the air and fall away from the basket instead of toward it. All these tactics take maximum advantage of the crowding on a court; they also stamp uniqueness on young men who may feel it nowhere else.

"For many young men in the slums," David Wolf writes, "the school yard is the only place they can feel true pride in what they do, where they can move free of inhibitions and where they can, by being spectacular, rise for the moment against the drabness and anonymity of their lives. Thus, when a player develops extraordinary 'school yard' moves and shots . . . [they] become his measure as a man."

So the moves that begin as tactics for scoring soon become calling cards. You don't just lay the ball in for an uncontested basket; you take the ball in both hands, leap as high as you can, and slam the ball through the hoop. When you jump in the air, fake a shot, bring the ball back to your body, and throw up a shot, all without coming back down, you have proven your worth in uncontestable fashion.

This liquid grace is an integral part of "black" ball, almost exclusively the province of the playground player. Some white stars like Richie Guerin, Bob Cousy, and Billy Cunningham have it: the body control, the moves to the basket, the free-ranging mobility. They also have the surface ease that is integral to the "black" style; an incorporation of the ethic of mean streets—to "make it" is not just to have wealth, but to have it without strain. Whatever the muscles and organs are doing, the face of the "black" star almost never shows it. Bob McAdoo of the Buffalo Braves can drive to the basket with two men on him, pull up, turn around, and hit a basket without the least flicker of emotion. The

Knicks' Walt Frazier, flamboyant in dress, cars, and companions, displays nothing but a quickly raised fist after scoring a particularly important basket. (Interestingly, the black coaches in the N.B.A. exhibit far less emotion on the bench than their white counterparts; Washington's K. C. Jones and Seattle's Bill Russell are statuelike compared with Tommy Heinsohn, Jack Ramsey, or Dick Motta.)

If there is a single trait that characterizes "black" ball it is leaping agility. Bob Cousy, ex-Celtic great and former pro coach, says that "when coaches get together, one is sure to say, 'I've got the one black kid in the country who can't jump.' When coaches see a white boy who can jump or who moves with extraordinary quickness, they say, 'He should have been born black, he's that good.'" [10]

Don Nelson of the Celtics recalls that in 1970, Dave Cowens, then a relatively unknown Florida State graduate, prepared for his rookie season by playing in the Rucker League, an outdoor Harlem competition that pits pros against playground stars and college kids. So ferocious was Cowens' leaping power, Nelson says, that "when the summer was over, everyone wanted to know who the white son of a bitch was who could jump so high." That's another way to overcome a crowd around the basket—just go over it. [11]

Speed, mobility, quickness, acceleration, "the moves"—all of these are catch-phrases that surround the "black" playground style of play. So does the most racially tinged of attributes, "rhythm." Yet rhythm is what the black stars themselves talk about; feeling the flow of the game, finding the tempo of the dribble, the step, the shot. It is an instinctive quality, one that has led to difficulty between systematic coaches and free-form players. "Cats from the street have their own rhythm when they play," said college dropout Bill Spivey, onetime New York high-school star. "It's not a matter of somebody setting you up and you shooting. You *feel* the shot. When a coach holds you back, you lose the feel and it isn't fun anymore." [12]

Connie Hawkins, the legendary Brooklyn playground star, said of Laker coach Bill Sharman's methodical style of teaching, "He's systematic to the point where it begins to be a little too much. It's such an action-reaction type of game that when you have to do everything the same way, I think you lose something." [13]

There is another kind of basketball that has grown up in America. It is not played on asphalt playgrounds with a crowd of [14] kids competing for the court; it is played on macadam driveways by one boy with a ball and a backboard nailed over the garage; it is played in Midwestern gyms and on Southern dirt courts. It is a mechanical, precise development of skills (when Don Nelson was an Iowa farm boy his incentive to make his shots was that an errant rebound would land in the middle of chicken droppings), without frills, without flow, but with effectiveness. It is "white" basketball: jagged, sweaty, stumbling, intense. A "black" player overcomes an obstacle with finesse and body control; a "white" player reacts by outrunning or outpowering the obstacle.

By this definition, the Boston Celtics and the Chicago Bulls are 15
classically "white" teams. The Celtics almost never use a player with dazzling moves; that would probably make Red Auerbach swallow his cigar. Instead, the Celtics wear you down with execution, with constant running, with the same play run again and again. The rebound triggers the fast break, with everyone racing downcourt; the ball goes to John Havlicek, who pulls up and takes the jump shot, or who fakes the shot and passes off to the man following, the "trailer," who has the momentum to go inside for a relatively easy shot.

The Bulls wear you down with punishing intensity, hustling, 16
and defensive tactics which are either aggressive or illegal, depending on what side you're on. The Bulls—particularly Jerry Sloan and Norm Van Lier (one white, one black for the quota-minded)— seem to reject the concept of an out-of-bounds line. They are as likely to be found under the press table or wrapped around the ushers as on the court.

Perhaps the most classically "white" position is that of the quick 17
forward, one without great moves to the basket, without highly developed shots, without the height and mobility for rebounding effectiveness. What does he do? He runs. He runs from the opening jump to the last horn. He runs up and down the court, from base line to base line, back and forth under the basket, looking for the opening, for the pass, for the chance to take a quick step and the high-percentage shot. To watch Boston's Don Nelson, a player without speed or moves, is to wonder what this thirty-five-year-old is doing in the N.B.A.—until you see him swing free and throw up a shot that, without demanding any apparent skill, somehow goes in the basket more frequently than the shots of any of his teammates. And to watch his teammate John Havlicek, also thirty-five, is to see "white" ball at its best.

Havlicek stands in dramatic contrast to Julius Erving of the New [18] York Nets. Erving has the capacity to make legends come true; leaping from the foul line and slam-dunking the ball on his way down; going up for a lay-up, pulling the ball to his body and throwing under and up the other side of the rim, defying gravity and probability with moves and jumps. Havlicek looks like the living embodiment of his small-town Ohio background. He brings the ball downcourt, weaving left, then right, looking for the path. He swings the ball to a teammate, cuts behind a pick, takes the pass and releases the shot in a flicker of time. It looks plain, unvarnished. But there are not half a dozen players in the league who can see such possibilities for a free shot, then get that shot off as quickly and efficiently as Havlicek.

To Jim McMillian of Buffalo, a black with "white" attributes, [19] himself a quick forward, "it's a matter of environment. Julius Erving grew up in a different environment from Havlicek—John came from a very small town in Ohio. There everything was done the easy way, the shortest distance between two points. It's nothing fancy, very few times will he go one-on-one; he hits the lay-up, hits the jump shot, makes the free throw, and after the game you look up and you say, 'How did he hurt us that much?' "

"White" ball, then, is the basketball of patience and method. [20] "Black" ball is the basketball of electric self-expression. One player has all the time in the world to perfect his skills, the other a need to prove himself. These are slippery categories, because a poor boy who is black can play "white" and a white boy of middle-class parents can play "black." K. C. Jones and Pete Maravich are athletes who seem to defy these categories. And what makes basketball the most intriguing of sports is how these styles do not necessarily clash; how the punishing intensity of "white" players and the dazzling moves of the "blacks" can fit together, a fusion of cultures that seems more and more difficult in the world beyond the out-of-bounds line.

QUESTIONS

Understanding

1. What are the most important aspects of "black" basketball as Greenfield defines it? Of "white" basketball?

2. Why is basketball basically a city game, according to this essay? In particular, what has space in the city to do with the "black" player's approach to space on the court?

3. Why are "black" players and coaches more poker-faced than their "white" counterparts? What strategy and what ethic contribute to this seeming unconcern?

4. What does Greenfield mean when he reminds us that "we are talking about culture, not chromosomes" (par. 3)? How does this statement fit in with the subtitle of his essay "A Skin-Deep Theory of Style"?

Strategies and Structure

1. Greenfield starts to compare the two styles of play in paragraph 3; which sentence signals this intention?

2. Greenfield's method of development is to concentrate on one style before going on to the other. Where does his explanation of the "black" style end? Where does his explanation of the "white" style begin? Which paragraph brings the two together in summation?

3. Paragraph 2 in this essay serves to explain the origin of basketball in general before the author goes on to define two different types. What is the purpose of paragraph 1, in which basketball is considered not so much a game as a social phenomenon?

4. Paragraph 4 (about the size of a basketball court in comparison to the playing areas of other sports) looks at first like a digression from the matter of style, introduced in paragraph 3. Is Greenfield really off the track here? Why or why not?

5. How effective do you find the example of Jim McMillian in paragraph 19? Why? Of Don Nelson in paragraph 14? Why?

6. Why do you think Greenfield ends his essay by referring to "the world beyond the out-of-bounds line" (par. 20)? What is he implying about the common ground of both "white" and "black" basketball?

Words and Figures of Speech

1. What is the pun in Greenfield's title? How effective is it? Why does Greenfield put "black" and "white" in quotation marks throughout his essay?

2. Why is Greenfield nervous about using the word *rhythm* in paragraph 12? How does he legitimize his use of the term?

3. What attribute is "only skin-deep" according to the proverb? In what sense does Greenfield reverse the meaning of the proverb when adapting it to a discussion of style?

4. What does Greenfield's use of the phrase, "for the quota-minded" (par. 16), imply about his own feelings about quotas?

5. If you are not sure of any of the following words, look them up in your dictionary: *lucrative* (par. 1), *inhibitions* (7), *anonymity* (7), *province* (9), *ethic* (9), *flamboyant* (9), *catch-phrases* (12), *finesse* (14). Why do you think a sports article might have relatively few unfamiliar words?

Comparing

1. Would you describe David Dubber's athletic style in "Crossing the Bar on a Fiberglas Pole" (Chapter 1) as essentially "black" or "white"? Why?

2. Greenfield points out that basketball (the city game) occupies much less space than does baseball (the country game). How is *time* treated in basketball in contrast to baseball's time, described by Roger Angell in "Time Out" ("Paragraphs for Analysis")?

3. In "Haircut" ("Paragraphs for Analysis"), William Allen defines style as form or arrangement (to be distinguished from content or substance). Apply Allen's definition to "black" style as defined by Greenfield? How well does it fit "white" style?

Discussion and Writing Topics

1. Compare and contrast the traditional role of a basketball forward with that of a guard or center.

2. What does it mean to be "cool"? What conditions encourage coolness, and what sports express that virtue?

3. What are the purposes of boundary lines in sports? Why might an athlete, a musician, or an artist welcome limits and boundaries in his or her field of endeavor?

4. Contrast the style of a typical professional tennis player, boxer, or golfer with the style of a typical amateur.

Eugene Raskin
Walls and Barriers

*Eugene Raskin is an architect, playwright, and composer. Born
in New York in 1909, he was educated at Columbia University
and the University of Paris. He joined the Columbia faculty as a
professor of architecture in 1942, became a Langley fellow of the
American Institute of Architects in 1952, and in 1963 won first
prize at the American Film Festival for the documentary, How to
Look at a City. Author of* Architecturally Speaking *(1954) and*
The Post-Urban Society *(1969), Raskin has also written a number
of plays, including* One's a Crowd *(1951);* Amata *(1952);* Last
Island *(1954); and* Stranger in My Arms *(1971). Among his
published songs was the international hit, "Those Were the
Days." "Walls and Barriers" contrasts the modern notion of
wall-as-window with the ancient conception of wall-as-barrier.*

My father's reaction to the bank building at 43rd Street   1
and Fifth Avenue in New York City was immediate and definite: "You won't catch me putting my money in *there!*" he
declared. "Not in that glass box!"

Of course, my father is a gentleman of the old school, a   2
member of the generation to whom a good deal of modern
architecture is unnerving; but I suspect—I more than suspect,
I am convinced—that his negative response was not so much
to the architecture as to a violation of his concept of the
nature of money.

In his generation money was thought of as a tangible com-   3
modity—bullion, bank notes, coins—that could be hefted,
carried, or stolen. Consequently, to attract the custom of a
sensible man, a bank had to have heavy walls, barred windows, and bronze doors, to affirm the fact, however untrue,

that money would be safe inside. If a building's design made it appear impregnable, the institution was necessarily sound, and the meaning of the heavy wall as an architectural symbol dwelt in the prevailing attitude toward money, rather than in any aesthetic theory.

But that attitude toward money has of course changed. Excepting pocket money, cash of any kind is now rarely used; money as a tangible commodity has largely been replaced by credit; a bookkeeping-banking matter. A deficit economy, accompanied by huge expansion, has led us to think of money as a product of the creative imagination. The banker no longer offers us a *safe*, he offers us a *service*—a service in which the most valuable elements are dash and a creative flair for the invention of large numbers. It is in no way surprising, in view of this change in attitude, that we are witnessing the disappearance of the heavy-walled bank. The Manufacturers Trust, which my father distrusted so heartily, is a great cubical cage of glass whose brilliantly lighted interior challenges even the brightness of a sunny day, while the door to the vault, far from being secluded and guarded, is set out as a window display. 4

Just as the older bank asserted its invulnerability, this bank *by its architecture* boasts of its imaginative powers. From this point of view it is hard to say where architecture ends and human assertion begins. In fact, there is no such division; the two are one and the same. 5

It is in the understanding of architecture as a medium for the expression of human attitudes, prejudices, taboos, and ideals that the new architectural criticism departs from classical aesthetics. The latter relied upon pure proportion, composition, etc., as bases for artistic judgment. In the age of sociology and psychology, walls are not simply walls but physical symbols of the barriers in men's minds. 6

In a primitive society, for example, men pictured the world as large, fearsome, hostile, and beyond human control. Therefore they built heavy walls of huge boulders, behind which they could feel themselves to be in a delimited space that was controllable and safe; these heavy walls expressed man's fear of the outer world and his need to find protection, however illusory. It might be argued that the undeveloped technology of the period precluded the construction of more delicate walls. This is of course true. 7

Still, it was not technology, but a fearful attitude toward the world, which made people want to build walls in the first place. The greater the fear, the heavier the wall, until in the tombs of ancient kings we find structures that are practically all wall, the fear of dissolution being the ultimate fear.

And then there is the question of privacy—for it *has* become   8 questionable. In some Mediterranean cultures it was not so much the world of nature that was feared, but the world of men. Men were dirty, prying, vile, and dangerous. One went about, if one could afford it, in guarded litters; women went about heavily veiled, if they went about at all. One's house was surrounded by a wall, and the rooms faced not out, but in, toward a patio, express- ing the prevalent conviction that the beauties and values of life were to be found by looking inward, and by engaging in the inti- mate activities of a personal as against a public life. The rich intricacies of the decorative arts of the period, as well as its con- templative philosophies, are as illustrative of this attitude as the walls themselves.

We feel different today. For one thing, we place greater reliance   9 upon the control of human hostility, not so much by physical barriers, as by the conventions of law and social practice—as well as the availability of motorized police. We do not cherish privacy as much as did our ancestors. We are proud to have our women seen and admired, and the same goes for our homes. We do not seek solitude; in fact, if we find ourselves alone for once, we flick a switch and invite the whole world in through the television screen. Small wonder, then, that the heavy surrounding wall is obsolete, and we build, instead, membranes of thin sheet metal or glass.

The principal function of today's wall is to separate possibly   10 undesirable outside air from the controlled conditions of tempera- ture and humidity which we have created inside. Glass may accom- plish this function, though there are apparently a good many people who still have qualms about eating, sleeping, and dressing under conditions of high visibility; they demand walls that will at least give them a sense of adequate screening. But these shy ones are a vanishing breed. The Philip Johnson [1] house in Connecticut,

---

[1] American architect, born 1906; in 1949 he designed and constructed the Glass House for his residence in New Canaan, Connecticut.

which is much admired and widely imitated, has glass walls all
the way around, and the only real privacy is to be found in the
bathroom, the toilette taboo being still unbroken, at least in
Connecticut.

To repeat, it is not our advanced technology, but our changing   11
conceptions of ourselves in relation to the world that determine
how we shall build our walls. The glass wall expresses man's conviction that he can and does master nature and society. The "open
plan" and the unobstructed view are consistent with his faith in
the eventual solution of all problems through the expanding efforts
of science. This is perhaps why it is the most "advanced" and
"forward-looking" among us who live and work in glass houses.
Even the fear of the cast stone has been analyzed out of us.

QUESTIONS

Understanding

1. Raskin is contrasting ancient walls and modern walls. According
   to him, what was the function of walls in primitive society? What
   attitude toward nature is expressed by the glass walls of modern
   society?
2. Why has the function of walls changed, according to Raskin?
3. Raskin is also contrasting "classical" and "new" (par. 6) theories
   of architecture. Which stresses form? Which stresses function?
4. How, according to Raskin, has our culture's view of money
   changed since his father's day?

Strategies and Structure

1. Why do you think Raskin begins by quoting his father? Do you
   think this is an effective opening? Why or why not?
2. Is Raskin's father in any way a confusing example? He has an
   old-fashioned view of money; what is his view of architecture?
3. The "cast stone" (par. 11) of Raskin's last sentence echoes the
   proverb, "People who live in glass houses should not throw
   stones." How does this reference to traditional wisdom at the
   end resemble Raskin's reference to his father at the beginning?

4. Which phrase in his last paragraph (par. 11) signals that the author is summing up what he has to say?

5. Does the paragraph on Mediterranean houses (par. 8) continue or diverge from the preceding paragraph (par. 7) on walls in primitive culture?

Words and Figures of Speech

1. What is the meaning of the proverb about glass houses? Under what conditions might it be applied?

2. Which of the two key words in the title applies to primitive walls as Raskin describes them?

3. Paragraph 6 mentions "architectural criticism." What does *criticism* mean here and in phrases like "art criticism" or "literary criticism"?

4. In paragraph 4, Raskin says that the bright interior of the new bank "challenges" the daylight. How does that word apply to modern man's attitude toward nature as Raskin defines it?

5. Look up any of the following words that you do not already know: *tangible* (par. 3), *impregnable* (3), *aesthetic* (3), *deficit* (4), *taboos* (6), *composition* (6), *illusory* (7), *dissolution* (7), and *membrane* (9).

Comparing

1. How does Desmond Morris's explanation of the origin of barrier signals in Chapter 5 confirm what Raskin says about the original purpose of walls?

2. William Allen's "Haircut" (in "Paragraphs for Analysis") deals with a structure and the aesthetic theory that produced it. Is Allen's theory "classic" or modern by Raskin's standards? Explain your answer.

Discussion and Writing Topics

1. Raskin says we do not cherish privacy as much as our fathers did. Agree or disagree with this view by comparing and contrasting life in an old-fashioned single-family dwelling with life in a high-rise apartment or condominium.

2. What is the "international style" in modern architecture? Contrast it with what Raskin calls the "classical" style.

3. American architect Louis Sullivan (1856–1924) said that "form follows function" in architecture. By "follows" he meant "depends upon." Is his theory modern or classical by Raskin's standards?

4. Recall an old building in your hometown (a high school, library, or courthouse, for example) that has been replaced by a new building. Compare and contrast the two.

5. What is a proverb? How does it differ from a parable?

WRITING TOPICS for Chapter Six
Essays That Compare and Contrast

Write a comparison and contrast essay on one of the following topics:

1. Two different cities (for example, New York and Washington, D.C.)

2. The same city at different times of day or in different seasons

3. Two World War II generals (for example, Patton and Eisenhower)

4. Two teachers you have admired

5. Two neighborhoods you have lived in

6. The haves and the have-nots in your hometown

7. Two of your classmates from different geographical regions

8. Two roommates you have had

9. A job versus a profession

10. Modern versus old-fashioned families (or marriages)

11. Two churches or synagogues in your hometown

12. Life in a democracy versus life under some other form of government

13. Two styles of playing football, baseball, tennis, or golf

14. The styles of two political (or social) leaders on your campus

15. The styles of two national politicians

16. The work of two painters, singers, musicians, or writers

17. Two newspaper columns or magazines that you read

18. Two comic strips

7
Essays That Use
Metaphor and Analogy

METAPHORS [1] and ANALOGIES are FIGURES OF SPEECH or
"turns" of language that use words symbolically rather than
literally. The poet Carl Sandburg created a metaphor when
he wrote, "The woman named Tomorrow/sits with a hair-
pin in her teeth/and takes her time. . . ." His friend and
fellow poet, Robert Frost, was developing an analogy when
he told Sandburg that writing poetry without regular meter
and rhyme is like playing tennis with the net down. Metaphors and analogies (or "extended metaphors"), then, are
comparisons that reveal an object, event, or quality by identifying it with another object, event, or quality (usually one
more familiar than the first, as tennis is more familiar to
most of us than the rules of poetry).

The kinds of comparisons that metaphors and analogies
make, however, should not be confused with those discussed
in the last chapter ("Essays That Compare and Contrast").
When Bruce Catton compared Grant and Lee, he was as
much interested in one general as the other. COMPARISON
AND CONTRAST essays may not attend equally to the similarities and differences between their subjects, but they usually
give equal weight to the subjects themselves. Essays that use
metaphor and analogy, on the other hand, have a primary
subject, which the object of comparison is introduced to
explain. When Ernest Hemingway declared, for example,
that a fine English sentence has the clean grace of a mata-
dor's sweeping cape, he was talking about writing, not
bullfighting.

[1] Terms printed in all capitals are defined in the Glossary.

One common use of such comparisons is to advance an ARGU-
MENT. If you were trying to convince a friend that the government
should spend more money on the space program, you might argue
that Americans have a pioneering spirit and that outer space is like
the western frontier of a century ago; to advance across this new
frontier is simply to fulfill our national destiny. Such a line of
reasoning is an "argument by analogy." It assumes that, because
two entities or ideas are alike in some ways, they are alike in other
significant ways. An argument by analogy is the most vulnerable
form of argument; it is only as strong as the analogy is close and
complete. Your argument would collapse if your friend observed
that spaceships are much more expensive than covered wagons and
that the original frontier was conquered by exploiting the first
Americans.

Another common function of analogies is to explain; the EXPOSI-
TORY essays in the following pages are used for this purpose. "On
Societies as Organisms" by Lewis Thomas, for example, teaches us
something about humans in groups by comparing their social
activity to the bustle of an insect colony. In finished essays, such
analogies are primarily organizing devices; but when you are pre-
paring an essay, they may actually aid you in finding something
to say.

Suppose you were getting ready to write an essay on the expansion of the universe, and you were puzzled by the problem of
locating the center of expansion. From our galaxy, all the other
galaxies seem to be rushing out and away; yet astrophysicists tell
us that we would experience the same sense of being left behind
if we visited any other galaxy in the universe. To write your essay,
you must resolve this apparent contradiction.

Now, suppose you hit upon the analogy of the balloon. (Your
subject is the universe, remember, not balloons; an analogy illumi-
nates a primary subject, it does not replace it with another.) You
might begin to think of the many galaxies of our expanding universe as spots of dark paint dotting the surface of the inflating
balloon. As the rubber surface expands, every dot draws apart from
every other dot. Whichever dot you single out will appear to be
the "center" of a surface that has no fixed middle point. Having
used this analogy to grasp your subject, you may then turn around
and use it to explain your complicated ideas to the reader.

Keep the following pointers in mind when developing an essay by analogy. Although an analogy will not "hold" if it compares objects that are too disparate, avoid obvious, trivial, or tired comparisons: life to a brief parade, a face without a smile to a day without sunshine. Analogies often liken the unfamiliar and the complicated to the common and the simple, but an analogy may also compare its primary subject with something exotic in order to discover the unexpected in the familiar. (This is Barry Lopez's strategy in "My Horse," an essay that is really about his Dodge van.) And, finally, try to compare your primary subject with something that is interesting and original in its own right. You are not likely to impress your reader if you explain the idea of blind choice by analogy with a stab in the dark or a number drawn from a hat.

Lewis Thomas

On Societies as Organisms

Lewis Thomas, M.D., a neurologist by training, is president and
chief executive officer of the Memorial Sloan-Kettering Cancer
Center in New York City. He was born in Flushing, New York,
and attended Princeton University and Harvard Medical School
(M.D., 1937). A member of the council of the Institute of Medicine, he has contributed many articles to scientific journals. In
1971, Thomas began writing "Notes of a Biology Watcher" for
less specialized readers in the New England Journal of Medicine.
His Lives of a Cell (1974), from which the following essay is
taken, won the National Book Award for arts and letters in 1975.
Another collection of Thomas's essays, The Medusa and the Snail,
was published in 1979. "On Societies as Organisms" begins by
comparing ants to humans—not the other way around—and goes
on to draw an extended analogy between all social groups and the
activity of living beings.

Viewed from a suitable height, the aggregating clusters of [1]
medical scientists in the bright sunlight of the boardwalk at
Atlantic City, swarmed there from everywhere for the annual
meetings, have the look of assemblages of social insects. There
is the same vibrating, ionic movement, interrupted by the
darting back and forth of jerky individuals to touch antennae
and exchange small bits of information; periodically, the mass
casts out, like a trout-line, a long single file unerringly toward
Childs's.[1] If the boards were not fastened down, it would not
be a surprise to see them put together a nest of sorts.

It is permissible to say this sort of thing about humans. [2]
They do resemble, in their most compulsively social behavior,

---

[1] A local restaurant.

ants at a distance. It is, however, quite bad form in biological circles to put it the other way round, to imply that the operation of insect societies has any relation at all to human affairs. The writers of books on insect behavior generally take pains, in their prefaces, to caution that insects are like creatures from another planet, that their behavior is absolutely foreign, totally unhuman, unearthly, almost unbiological. They are more like perfectly tooled but crazy little machines, and we violate science when we try to read human meanings in their arrangements.

It is hard for a bystander not to do so. Ants are so much like human beings as to be an embarrassment. They farm fungi, raise aphids as livestock, launch armies into wars, use chemical sprays to alarm and confuse enemies, capture slaves. The families of weaver ants engage in child labor, holding their larvae like shuttles to spin out the thread that sews the leaves together for their fungus gardens. They exchange information ceaselessly. They do everything but watch television. 3

What makes us most uncomfortable is that they, and the bees and termites and social wasps, seem to live two kinds of lives: they are individuals, going about the day's business without much evidence of thought for tomorrow, and they are at the same time component parts, cellular elements, in the huge, writhing, ruminating organism of the Hill, the nest, the hive. It is because of this aspect, I think, that we most wish for them to be something foreign. We do not like the notion that there can be collective societies with the capacity to behave like organisms. If such things exist, they can have nothing to do with us. 4

Still, there it is. A solitary ant, afield, cannot be considered to have much of anything on his mind; indeed, with only a few neurons strung together by fibers, he can't be imagined to have a mind at all, much less a thought. He is more like a ganglion on legs. Four ants together, or ten, encircling a dead moth on a path, begin to look more like an idea. They fumble and shove, gradually moving the food toward the Hill, but as though by blind chance. It is only when you watch the dense mass of thousands of ants, crowded together around the Hill, blackening the ground, that you begin to see the whole beast, and now you observe it thinking, planning, calculating. It is an intelligence, a kind of live computer, with crawling bits for its wits. 5

At a stage in the construction, twigs of a certain size are needed, 6 and all the members forage obsessively for twigs of just this size. Later, when outer walls are to be finished, thatched, the size must change, and as though given new orders by telephone, all the workers shift the search to the new twigs. If you disturb the arrangement of a part of the Hill, hundreds of ants will set it vibrating, shifting, until it is put right again. Distant sources of food are somehow sensed, and long lines, like tentacles, reach out over the ground, up over walls, behind boulders, to fetch it in.

Termites are even more extraordinary in the way they seem to 7 accumulate intelligence as they gather together. Two or three termites in a chamber will begin to pick up pellets and move them from place to place, but nothing comes of it; nothing is built. As more join in, they seem to reach a critical mass, a quorum, and the thinking begins. They place pellets atop pellets, then throw up columns and beautiful, curving, symmetrical arches, and the crystalline architecture of vaulted chambers is created. It is not known how they communicate with each other, how the chains of termites building one column know when to turn toward the crew on the adjacent column, or how, when the time comes, they manage the flawless joining of the arches. The stimuli that set them off at the outset, building collectively instead of shifting things about, may be pheromones [2] released when they reach committee size. They react as if alarmed. They become agitated, excited, and then they begin working, like artists.

Bees live lives of organisms, tissues, cells, organelles, all at the 8 same time. The single bee, out of the hive retrieving sugar (instructed by the dancer: "south-southeast for seven hundred meters, clover—mind you make corrections for the sundrift") is still as much a part of the hive as if attached by a filament. Building the hive, the workers have the look of embryonic cells organizing a developing tissue; from a distance they are like the viruses inside a cell, running off row after row of symmetrical polygons as though laying down crystals. When the time for swarming comes, and the old queen prepares to leave with her part of the population, it is as though the hive were involved in mitosis. There is an agitated moving of bees back and forth, like granules in cell sap. They distribute themselves in almost precisely equal parts, half to the departing queen, half to the new one. Thus, like an egg, the great,

[2] Hormones secreted by insects when communicating with other insects.

hairy, black and golden creature splits in two, each with an equal share of the family genome.

The phenomenon of separate animals joining up to form an [9] organism is not unique in insects. Slime-mold cells do it all the time, of course, in each life cycle. At first they are single amebocytes swimming around, eating bacteria, aloof from each other, untouching, voting straight Republican. Then, a bell sounds, and acrasin [3] is released by special cells toward which the others converge in stellate ranks, touch, fuse together, and construct the slug, solid as a trout. A splendid stalk is raised, with a fruiting body on top, and out of this comes the next generation of amebocytes, ready to swim across the same moist ground, solitary and ambitious.

Herring and other fish in schools are at times so closely inte- [10] grated, their actions so coordinated, that they seem to be functionally a great multi-fish organism. Flocking birds, especially the seabirds nesting on the slopes of offshore islands in Newfoundland, are similarly attached, connected, synchronized.

Although we are by all odds the most social of all social animals [11] —more interdependent, more attached to each other, more inseparable in our behavior than bees—we do not often feel our conjoined intelligence. Perhaps, however, we are linked in circuits for the storage, processing, and retrieval of information, since this appears to be the most basic and universal of all human enterprises. It may be our biological function to build a certain kind of Hill. We have access to all the information of the biosphere, arriving as elementary units in the stream of solar photons. When we have learned how these are rearranged against randomness, to make, say, springtails, quantum mechanics, and the late quartets, we may have a clearer notion how to proceed. The circuitry seems to be there, even if the current is not always on.

The system of communications used in science should provide [12] a neat, workable model for studying mechanisms of information-building in human society. Ziman, in a recent *Nature* essay, points out, "the invention of a mechanism for the systematic publication of *fragments* of scientific work may well have been the key event in the history of modern science." He continues:

---

[3] Chemical attractant named after the class (Acrasiae) to which these special slime molds belong.

A regular journal carries from one research worker to another the various . . . observations which are of common interest. . . . A typical scientific paper has never pretended to be more than another little piece in a larger jigsaw—not significant in itself but as an element in a grander scheme. *This technique, of soliciting many modest contributions to the store of human knowledge, has been the secret of Western science since the seventeenth century, for it achieves a corporate, collective power that is far greater than any one individual can exert* [italics mine].

With some alternation of terms, some toning down, the passage could describe the building of a termite nest.   13

It is fascinating that the word "explore" does not apply to the searching aspect of the activity, but has its origins in the sounds we make while engaged in it. We like to think of exploring in science as a lonely, meditative business, and so it is in the first stages, but always, sooner or later, before the enterprise reaches completion, as we explore, we call to each other, communicate, publish, send letters to the editor, present papers, cry out on finding.   14

QUESTIONS

Understanding

1. In paragraph 1, what is Thomas comparing to what? In paragraph 3? Which of the two paragraphs formulates the ANALOGY that Thomas will develop throughout his essay?

2. The title of Thomas's essay expresses his main analogy in its most general terms. Which term applies to individual human beings? Which applies to *groups* of insects, fish, birds, or humans?

3. What is an organism? How does it differ from a mechanism, one of the "crazy little machines" that Thomas refers to in paragraph 2?

4. Why, according to Thomas, are we reluctant to attribute human characteristics to insect colonies? How might people in Russia or Communist China be expected to react to such comparisons?

5. Thomas says that, like the ant's, mankind's biological function is "to build a certain kind of Hill" (par. 11). What, specifically, is

the basic enterprise of human society in Thomas's view? What kind of hill is the human community erecting?

Strategies and Structure

1. In the opening paragraph, Thomas looks down upon his fellow medical scientists from a "suitable height." Why do you suppose he establishes this perspective? Why does Thomas call himself a "bystander" in paragraph 3?

2. How might paragraph 5 be interpreted as a mini-version of Thomas's entire essay?

3. Thomas develops a single elaborate analogy by building upon a number of smaller analogies. To what specialized human beings does he compare the builder termites in paragraph 7? Why does an egg provide a fitting analogy for describing the swarming bee colony in paragraph 8? What analogy is suggested by "voting straight Republican" in paragraph 9?

4. Throughout most of this essay, the author is applying what he knows about human society to learn more about insect behavior. When does he begin to reverse this procedure? In what sense is Thomas's essay not about insects at all?

5. Thomas is writing here for a more general audience than a convention of medical specialists at Atlantic City, but he nevertheless speaks with the authority of a trained scientist. How is that authority conveyed to us?

6. Explain the analogy in paragraphs 12, 13, and 14. Does it make for a satisfying ending to Thomas's essay? Why or why not?

Words and Figures of Speech

1. Look up the root meaning of *explore* (par. 14). Applied to scientific investigation, how does the word in its original meaning support Thomas's analogy in paragraphs 12–14?

2. Look up *biology* in your dictionary. In which sense is Thomas using the word when he refers to insects as "unbiological" (par. 2) and to the "biological function" of humanity (par. 11)?

3. Why do you think Thomas applies such terms as *quorum* and *committee* (par. 7) to groups of insects that begin to act intelligently?

4. In paragraph 11, when Thomas says that "the current is not always on," to what circuit is he referring? Why is the METAPHOR amusing?

5. Consult your dictionary for definitions of the following words: *ionic* (par. 1), *ruminating* (1), *ganglion* (5), *critical mass* (7), *organelles* (8), *embryonic* (8), *mitosis* (8), *genome* (8), *amebocytes* (9), *stellate* (9), *biosphere* (11), *photons* (11), *springtails* (11), and *quantum mechanics* (11).

Comparing

1. If you compare Thomas's essay with Alexander Petrunkevitch's "The Spider and the Wasp" (Chapter 3), which reads more like a technical scientific report? Explain your answer.

2. In its use of analogy does Thomas's essay more closely resemble Petrunkevitch's or Virginia Woolf's "The Death of the Moth" (Chapter 8)? Explain your answer.

Discussion and Writing Topics

1. Describe some human social enterprise—a party, field trip, class session, convention, or bargain sale—by analogy with a collective gathering of insects.

2. Thomas suggests that human beings work collectively to gather information. Speculate on other motives for human social activity —companionship, for example.

3. If societies are organisms with a group mind or will, what becomes of the individual's responsibility for his or her behavior when he or she acts as part of a group? Is a lynch mob, say, an amoral thing like a cold virus?

Barry Lopez

My Horse

The son of a publisher, Barry Lopez is a full-time writer and free-lance photographer. He was born in Port Chester, New York, but now lives with his wife in Finn Rock, Oregon. He was educated at Notre Dame and the University of Oregon. A contributor to Harper's, the North American Review, and Audubon, among other magazines, he is the author of a collection of American Indian trickster tales, a book on wolves (illustrated with his own photographs) called Of Wolves and Men (1979), Desert Notes: Reflections in the Eye of a Raven (1976), and River Notes: The Dance of the Herons (1979). Lopez is now at work on "Animal Notes." "My Horse," which originally appeared in the North American Review, draws an analogy between the author's Dodge Sportsman 300 van and Coke High, a quarter horse that Lopez rode as a wrangler in Wyoming.

It is curious that Indian warriors on the northern plains in   1
the nineteenth century, who were almost entirely dependent on the horse for mobility and status, never gave their horses names. If you borrowed a man's horse and went off raiding for other horses, however, or if you lost your mount in battle and then jumped on mine and counted coup [1] on an enemy— well, those horses would have to be shared with the man whose horse you borrowed, and that coup would be mine, not yours. Because even if I gave him no name, he was my horse.

If you were a Crow warrior and I a young Teton Sioux out   2
after a warrior's identity and we came over a small hill some-

---

[1] The custom among the Plains Indians of striking or touching an enemy as a sign of courage.

where in the Montana prairie and surprised each other, I could tell a lot about you by looking at your horse.

Your horse might have feathers tied in his mane, or in his tail, or a medicine bag tied around his neck. If I knew enough about the Crow, and had looked at you closely, I might make some sense of the decoration, even guess who you were if you were well-known. If you had painted your horse I could tell even more, because we both decorated our horses with signs that meant the same things. Your white handprints high on his flanks would tell me you had killed an enemy in a hand-to-hand fight. Small horizontal lines stacked on your horse's foreleg, or across his nose, would tell me how many times you had counted coup. Horse hoof marks on your horse's rump, or three-sided boxes, would tell me how many times you had stolen horses. If there was a bright red square on your horse's neck I would know you were leading a war party and that there were probably others out there in the coulees behind you.   3

You might be painted all over as blue as the sky and covered with white dots, with your horse painted the same way. Maybe hailstorms were your power—or if I chased you a hailstorm might come down and hide you. There might be lightning bolts on the horse's legs and flanks, and I would wonder if you had lightning power, or a slow horse. There might be white circles around your horse's eyes to help him see better.   4

Or you might be like Crazy Horse,[2] with no decoration, no marks on your horse to tell me anything, only a small lightning bolt on your cheek, a piece of turquoise tied behind your ear.   5

You might have scalps dangling from your rein.   6

I could tell something about you by your horse. All this would come to me in a few seconds. I might decide this was my moment and shout my war cry—*Hoka hey!* Or I might decide you were like the grizzly bear: I would raise my weapon to you in salute and go my way, to see you again when I was older.   7

I do not own a horse. I am attached to a truck, however, and I have come to think of it in a similar way. It has no name; it never occurred to me to give it a name. It has little decoration; neither   8

---

[2] (1849?–1877), a Sioux chief, born in Nebraska; he fought General Custer at the Little Big Horn.

of us is partial to decoration. I have a piece of turquoise in the truck because I had heard once that some of the southwestern tribes tied a small piece of turquoise in a horse's hock to keep him from stumbling. I like the idea. I also hang sage in the truck when I go on a long trip. But inside, the truck doesn't look much different from others that look just like it on the outside. I like it that way. Because I like my privacy.

For two years in Wyoming I worked on a ranch wrangling   9
horses. The horse I rode when I had to have a good horse was a quarter horse and his name was Coke High. This name came with him. At first I thought he'd been named for the soft drink. I'd known stranger names given to horses by whites. Years later I wondered if some deviant Wyoming cowboy wise to cocaine had not named him. Now I think he was probably named after a rancher, an historical figure of the region. I never asked the people who owned him for fear of spoiling the spirit of my inquiry.

We were running over a hundred horses on this ranch. They all   10
had names. After a few weeks I knew all the horses and the names too. You had to. No one knew how to talk about the animals or put them in order or tell the wranglers what to do unless they were using the names—Princess, Big Red, Shoshone, Clay.

My truck is named Dodge. The name came with it. I don't   11
know if it was named after the town or the verb or the man who invented it. I like it for a name. Perfectly anonymous, like Rex for a dog, or Old Paint. You can't tell anything with a name like that.

The truck is a van. I call it a truck because it's not a car and   12
because "van" is a suburban sort of consumer word, like "oxford loafer," and I don't like the sound of it. On the outside it looks like any other Dodge Sportsman 300. It's a dirty tan color. There are a few body dents, but it's never been in a wreck. I tore the antenna off against a tree on a pinched mountain road. A boy in Midland, Texas, rocked one of my rear view mirrors off. A logging truck in Oregon squeeze-fired a piece of debris off the road and shattered my windshield. The oil pan and gas tank are pug-faced from high-centering on bad roads. (I remember a horse I rode for a while named Targhee whose hocks were scarred from tangles in barbed wire when he was a colt and who spooked a lot in high grass, but these were not like "dents." They were more like bad tires.)

I like to travel. I go mostly in the winter and mostly on two-   13
lane roads. I've driven the truck from Key West to Vancouver,
British Columbia, and from Yuma to Long Island over the past
four years. I used to ride Coke High only about five miles every
morning when we were rounding up horses. Hard miles of twisting
and turning. About six hundred miles a year. Then I'd turn him
out and ride another horse for the rest of the day. That's what was
nice about having a remuda.[3] You could do all you had to do and
not take it all out on your best horse. Three car family.

My truck came with a lot of seats in it and I've never really   14
known what to do with them. Sometimes I put the seats in and go
somewhere with a lot of people, but most of the time I leave them
out. I like riding around with that empty cavern of space behind
my head. I know it's something with a history to it, that there's
truth in it, because I always rode a horse the same way—with
empty saddle bags. In case I found something. The possibility
of finding something is half the reason for being on the road.

The value of anything comes to me in its use. If I am not using   15
something it is of no value to me and I give it away. I wasn't
always that way. I used to keep everything I owned—just in case.
I feel good about the truck because it gets used. A lot. To haul
hay and firewood and lumber and rocks and garbage and animals.
Other people have used it to haul furniture and freezers and dirt
and recycled newspapers. And to move from one house to another.
When I lend it for things like that I don't look to get anything
back but some gas (if we're going to be friends). But if you go way
out in the country to a dump and pick up the things you can still
find out there (once a load of cedar shingles we sold for $175 to
an architect) I expect you to leave some of those things around
my place when you come back—if I need them.

When I think back, maybe the nicest thing I ever put in that   16
truck was timber wolves. It was a long night's drive from Oregon
up into British Columbia. We were all very quiet about it; it was
like moving clouds across the desert.

Sometimes something won't fit in the truck and I think about   17

---

[3] In the Southwest, a herd of horses from which ranch hands choose their
mounts.

improving it—building a different door system, for example. I am forever going to add better gauges on the dash and a pair of driving lamps and a sunroof, but I never get around to doing any of it. I remember I wanted to improve Coke High once too, especially the way he bolted like a greyhound through patches of cottonwood on a river flat. But all I could do with him was to try to rein him out of it. Or hug his back.

Sometimes, road-stoned in a blur of country like southwestern [18] Wyoming or North Dakota, I talk to the truck. It's like wandering on the high plains under a summer sun, on plains where, George Catlin [4] wrote, you were "out of sight of land." I say what I am thinking out loud, or point at things along the road. It's a crazy, sun-stroked sort of activity, a sure sign it's time to pull over, to go for a walk, to make a fire and have some tea, to lie in the shade of the truck.

I've always wanted to pat the truck. It's basic to the relation- [19] ship. But it never works.

I remember when I was on the ranch, just at sunrise, after I'd [20] saddled Coke High, I'd be huddled down in my jacket smoking a cigarette and looking down into the valley, along the river where the other horses had spent the night. I'd turn to Coke and run my hand down his neck and slap-pat him on the shoulder to say I was coming up. It made a bond, an agreement we started the day with.

I've thought about that a lot with the truck, because we've gone [21] out together at sunrise on so many mornings. I've even fumbled around trying to do it. But metal won't give.

The truck's personality is mostly an expression of two ideas: [22] "with-you" and "alone." When Coke High was "with-you" he and I were the same animal. We could have cut a rooster out of a flock of chickens, we were so in tune. It's the same with the truck: rolling through Kentucky on a hilly two-lane road, three in the morning under a full moon and no traffic. Picture it. You roll like water.

There are other times when you are with each other but there's [23] no connection at all. Coke got that way when he was bored and we'd fight each other about which way to go around a tree. When

---

[4] (1796–1872), American artist and writer who lived among the Indians.

the truck gets like that—"alone"—it's because it feels its Detroit fat-ass design dragging at its heart and making a fool out of it.

I can think back over more than a hundred nights I've slept in   24
the truck, sat in it with a lamp burning, bundled up in a parka, reading a book. It was always comfortable. A good place to wait out a storm. Like sleeping inside a buffalo.

The truck will go past 100,000 miles soon. I'll rebuild the engine   25
and put a different transmission in it. I can tell from magazine advertisements that I'll never get another one like it. Because every year they take more of the heart out of them. One thing that makes a farmer or a rancher go sour is a truck that isn't worth a shit. The reason you see so many old pickups in ranch country is because these are the only ones with any heart. You can count on them. The weekend rancher runs around in a new pickup with too much engine and not enough transmission and with the wrong sort of tires because he can afford anything, even the worst. A lot of them have names for their pickups too.

My truck has broken down, in out of the way places at the worst   26
of times. I've walked away and screamed the foulness out of my system and gotten the tools out. I had to fix a water pump in a blizzard in the Panamint Mountains in California once. It took all day with the Coleman stove burning under the engine block to keep my hands from freezing. We drifted into Beatty, Nevada, that night with it jury-rigged together with—I swear—baling wire, and we were melting snow as we went and pouring it in to compensate for the leaks.

There is a dent next to the door on the driver's side I put there   27
one sweltering night in Miami. I had gone to the airport to meet my wife, whom I hadn't seen in a month. My hands were so swollen with poison ivy blisters I had to drive with my wrists. I had shut the door and was locking it when the window fell off its runners and slid down inside the door. I couldn't leave the truck unlocked because I had too much inside I didn't want to lose. So I just kicked the truck a blow in the side and went to work on the window. I hate to admit kicking the truck. It's like kicking a dog, which I've never done.

Coke High and I had an accident once. We hit a badger hole   28
at a full gallop. I landed on my back and blacked out. When I

came to, Coke High was about a hundred yards away. He stayed a hundred yards away for six miles, all the way back to the ranch.

I want to tell you about carrying those wolves, because it was a 29 fine thing. There were ten of them. We had four in the truck with us in crates and six in a trailer. It was a five hundred mile trip. We went at night for the cool air and because there wouldn't be as much traffic. I could feel from the way the truck rolled along that its heart was in the trip. It liked the wolves inside it, the sweet odor that came from the crates. I could feel that same tireless wolf-lope developing in its wheels; it was like you might never have to stop for gas, ever again.

The truck gets very self-focused when it works like this; its 30 heart is strong and it's good to be around it. It's good to be *with* it. You get the same feeling when you pull someone out of a ditch. Coke High and I pulled a Volkswagen out of the mud once, but Coke didn't like doing it very much. Speed, not strength, was his center. When the guy who owned the car thanked us and tried to pat Coke, the horse snorted and swung away, trying to preserve his distance, which is something a horse spends a lot of time on.

So does the truck. 31

Being distant lets the truck get its heart up. The truck has been 32 cold and alone in Montana at 38 below zero. It's climbed horrible, eroded roads in Idaho. It's been burdened beyond overloading, and made it anyway. I've asked it to do these things because they build heart, and without heart all you have is a machine. You have nothing. I don't think people in Detroit know anything at all about heart. That's why everything they build dies so young.

One time in Arizona the truck and I came through one of the 33 worst storms I've ever been in, an outrageous, angry blizzard. But we went down the road, right through it. You couldn't explain our getting through by the sort of tires I had on the truck, or the fact that I had chains on, or was a good driver, or had a lot of weight over my drive wheels or a good engine, because it was more than this. It was a contest between the truck and the blizzard— and the truck wouldn't quit. I could have gone to sleep and the truck would have just torn a road down Interstate 40 on its own. It scared the hell out of me; but it gave me heart, too.

We came off the Mogollon Rim that night and out of the storm 34 and headed south for Phoenix. I pulled off the road to sleep for a few hours, but before I did I got out of the truck. It was raining. Warm rain. I tied a short piece of red avalanche cord into the grill. I left it there for a long time, like an eagle feather on a horse's tail. It flapped and spun in the wind. I could hear it ticking against the grill when I drove.

When I have to leave that truck I will just raise up my left   35
arm—*Hoka hey!*—and walk away.

QUESTIONS

Understanding

1. Which is the *primary* subject of Lopez's ANALOGY, his truck or his horse? Explain your answer.
2. What does Lopez mean by "heart" (par. 32)? How does his account of the drive through the blizzard (par. 33) help to define this virtue?
3. Why does Lopez admire Crazy Horse (par. 5)? How is his truck like Crazy Horse's mount?
4. How does Lopez resemble the young Teton Sioux at the beginning of his essay? How has he changed (almost) by the end? What accounts for the change?
5. Lopez says of riding in his empty truck that "it's something with a history to it, that there's truth in it" (par. 14). What does he mean by this statement? How has it been anticipated earlier?
6. What does Detroit come to signify in this essay?
7. When friends borrow Lopez's truck, they are expected to share what they find with it, even though he otherwise shuns possessions. Why? What tradition does this custom recall?

Strategies and Structure

1. Lopez's analogy between truck and horse is largely unstated; he does not often refer explicitly to the fact of resemblance. Instead, he proceeds by alternating between his two subjects until they blend and merge. Cite several examples of this technique.
2. Sometimes Lopez's analogy shifts unexpectedly from one subject

back to the other. Which examples do you find particularly surprising? How does Lopez use this technique to end his essay?

3. In what sense does the last line of paragraph 13 reverse Lopez's
basic analogy? Where else in his essay does this sort of reversal
occur?

4. Lopez's basic analogy is between his truck and a horse, but this
is not the only analogy in his essay. To what else, particularly
animals, does he compare his truck?

5. Lopez admits that his basic analogy breaks down in one respect.
How is his truck *not* like a horse? How does he turn this exception to advantage?

6. Lopez is drawing analogies here, but his essay also uses many of
the techniques of NARRATION. What are some of these techniques?
Point to specific examples.

Words and Figures of Speech

1. Names usually signify identity, but Lopez is glad that his truck
is named "Dodge" because it is thus *anonymous* (par. 11), like an
Indian pony. Look up the root meaning of this word. Why is it
appropriate here?

2. In a way, this is an essay about sign language. To whose language
does the word *van* (par. 12) belong, according to Lopez? What
does it signify or "sign"?

3. Some cultures assume that "signs" and the ideas they represent
are separate and distinct. Other cultures blur this distinction and
tend to *identify* a sign with what it refers to. Which is the case
with Lopez and his Indians? Explain your answer.

4. Is Coke High a METAPHOR for Lopez's truck or a SIMILE? Explain
your opinion.

5. If Lopez's horse stands for his truck, what does his truck stand
for?

Comparing

1. Describe how Barry Lopez's use of language resembles that of
Chief Seattle in his "Reply to the U.S. Government" (Chapter
10).

2. How does the sign language of Lopez's Indians resemble the

"secret language" that Desmond Morris defines in "Barrier Signals" (Chapter 5)?

3. Compare Lopez's attitude toward new-fangled gadgets and soft living with that of Frank Trippett in "The Great American Cooling Machine" (Chapter 4).

Discussion and Writing Topics

1. If you know someone who identifies with his or her car, motorcycle, or bike, develop an analogy between them.

2. Develop an analogy between someone you know and his or her pet.

3. Some tasks and responsibilities (raising a colt, harvesting a crop, maintaining a boat) have been considered as aids to growing up. Describe some such task as a metaphor for coming-of-age.

Annie Dillard

Transfiguration

Annie Dillard was born in Pittsburgh in 1945, attended Hollins College, and lived in Virginia's Roanoke Valley from 1965 to 1975, when she moved to an island in Puget Sound for a period of meditation. She has written a book of poems, Tickets for a Prayer Wheel (1974); her Pilgrim at Tinker Creek (1974), an account of mystical contact with the natural world, won the Pulitzer Prize. (One critic called that book a "psalm of terror and celebration.") "Transfiguration" (editor's title) is from Part One of her latest book, Holy the Firm (1977). The students mentioned in it studied with Dillard at Western Washington State College in Bellingham.

I live on northern Puget Sound, in Washington State, alone. 1
I have a gold cat, who sleeps on my legs, named Small. In the morning I joke to her blank face, Do you remember last night? Do you remember? I throw her out before breakfast, so I can eat.

There is a spider, too, in the bathroom, with whom I keep 2
a sort of company. Her little outfit always reminds me of a certain moth I helped to kill. The spider herself is of uncertain lineage, bulbous at the abdomen and drab. Her six-inch mess of a web works, works somehow, works miraculously, to keep her alive and me amazed. The web itself is in a corner behind the toilet, connecting tile wall to tile wall and floor, in a place where there is, I would have thought, scant traffic. Yet under the web are sixteen or so corpses she has tossed to the floor.

The corpses appear to be mostly sow bugs, those little 3

armadillo creatures who live to travel flat out in houses, and die round. There is also a new shred of earwig, three old spider skins crinkled and clenched, and two moth bodies, wingless and huge and empty, moth bodies I drop to my knees to see.

Today the earwig shines darkly and gleams, what there is of   4
him: a dorsal curve of thorax and abdomen, and a smooth pair of cerci [1] by which I knew his name. Next week, if the other bodies are any indication, he will be shrunken and gray, webbed to the floor with dust. The sow bugs beside him are hollow and empty of color, fragile, a breath away from brittle fluff. The spider skins lie on their sides, translucent and ragged, their legs drying in knots. And the moths, the empty moths, stagger against each other, headless, in a confusion of arching strips of chitin like peeling varnish, like a jumble of buttresses for cathedral domes, like nothing resembling moths, so that I should hesitate to call them moths, except that I have had some experience with the figure Moth reduced to a nub.

Two summers ago I was camping alone in the Blue Ridge   5
Mountains in Virginia. I had hauled myself and gear up there to read, among other things, James Ramsey Ullman's *The Day on Fire*, a novel about Rimbaud that had made me want to be a writer when I was sixteen; [2] I was hoping it would do it again. So I read, lost, every day sitting under a tree by my tent, while warblers swung in the leaves overhead and bristle worms trailed their inches over the twiggy dirt at my feet; and I read every night by candlelight, while barred owls called in the forest and pale moths massed round my head in the clearing, where my light made a ring.

Moths kept flying into the candle. They would hiss and recoil,   6
lost upside down in the shadows among my cooking pans. Or they would singe their wings and fall, and their hot wings, as if melted, would stick to the first thing they touched—a pan, a lid, a spoon— so that the snagged moths could flutter only in tiny arcs, unable to struggle free. These I could release by a quick flip with a stick; in the morning I would find my cooking stuff gilded with torn flecks

[1] Plural of *cercus*, posterior "feeler" of an insect.
[2] French poet Arthur Rimbaud (1854–1891) himself began writing at age sixteen and produced his major work before he was twenty. Ullman's novel was published in 1958.

of moth wings, triangles of shiny dust here and there on the aluminum. So I read, and boiled water, and replenished candles, and read on.

One night a moth flew into the candle, was caught, burnt dry, and held. I must have been staring at the candle, or maybe I looked up when a shadow crossed my page; at any rate, I saw it all. A golden female moth, a biggish one with a two-inch wingspan, flapped into the fire, dropped her abdomen into the wet wax, stuck, flamed, frazzled and fried in a second. Her moving wings ignited like tissue paper, enlarging the circle of light in the clearing and creating out of the darkness the sudden blue sleeves of my sweater, the green leaves of jewelweed by my side, the ragged red trunk of a pine. At once the light contracted again and the moth's wings vanished in a fine, foul smoke. At the same time her six legs clawed, curled, blackened, and ceased, disappearing utterly. And her head jerked in spasms, making a spattering noise; her antennae crisped and burned away and her heaving mouth parts crackled like pistol fire. When it was all over, her head was, so far as I could determine, gone, gone the long way of her wings and legs. Had she been new, or old? Had she mated and laid her eggs, had she done her work? All that was left was the glowing horn shell of her abdomen and thorax—a fraying, partially collapsed gold tube jammed upright in the candle's round pool.

And then this moth-essence, this spectacular skeleton, began to act as a wick. She kept burning. The wax rose in the moth's body from her soaking abdomen to her thorax to the jagged hole where her head should be, and widened into flame, a saffron-yellow flame that robed her to the ground like any immolating monk. That candle had two wicks, two flames of identical height, side by side. The moth's head was fire. She burned for two hours, until I blew her out.

She burned for two hours without changing, without bending or leaning—only glowing within, like a building fire glimpsed through silhouetted walls, like a hollow saint, like a flame-faced virgin gone to God, while I read by her light, kindled, while Rimbaud in Paris burnt out his brains in a thousand poems, while night pooled wetly at my feet.

And that is why I believe those hollow crisps on the bathroom floor are moths. I think I know moths, and fragments of moths, and chips and tatters of utterly empty moths, in any state. How many of you, I asked the people in my class, which of you want to give your lives and be writers? I was trembling from coffee, or cigarettes, or the closeness of faces all around me. (Is this what we live for? I thought; is this the only final beauty: the color of any skin in any light, and living, human eyes?) All hands rose to the question. (You, Nick? Will you? Margaret? Randy? Why do I want them to mean it?) And then I tried to tell them what the choice must mean: you can't be anything else. You must go at your life with a broadax. . . . They had no idea what I was saying. (I have two hands, don't I? And all this energy, for as long as I can remember. I'll do it in the evenings, after skiing, or on the way home from the bank, or after the children are asleep. . . .) They thought I was raving again. It's just as well.

I have three candles here on the table which I disentangle from   11
the plants and light when visitors come. Small usually avoids them, although once she came too close and her tail caught fire; I rubbed it out before she noticed. The flames move light over everyone's skin, draw light to the surface of the faces of my friends. When the people leave I never blow the candles out, and after I'm asleep they flame and burn.

QUESTIONS

Understanding

1. What is the most important ANALOGY in Dillard's essay? What is she comparing to what?

2. What is Dillard referring to in paragraph 10 when she says, "I'll do it in the evening, after skiing, or on the way home from the bank . . ."?

3. At what cost does Dillard seem to think the writer does her (or his) work?

4. When Dillard draws an analogy between the moth and an "immolating monk" (par. 8) or a "flame-faced virgin" (par. 9), she gets beyond the realm of merely natural phenomena. Into what?

5. What is "miraculous" about the spider's web in paragraph 2? Of

all nature as Dillard sees it? What miracle does she celebrate throughout the essay?

6. Why does Dillard refer to the corpses of the moths beneath the spider web in her bathroom?

7. What kind of beauty does Dillard have in mind when she refers to "the color of any skin in any light, and living, human eyes" (par. 10)?

8. What is the significance of the book Dillard is reading when the moth burns?

Strategies and Structure

1. When did you first realize that Dillard's essay draws an extended analogy between the writer and the moth? How does she introduce the comparison without saying flatly, "The writer is like . . ."?

2. How does Dillard's main analogy help to explain the kind of beauty the writer seeks? Her (or his) dedication to her art?

3. How does Dillard's main analogy convey her own sense of awe and wonder at the sacredness of the writer's calling?

4. What analogy is Dillard drawing in the line, "You must go at your life with a broadax . . ." (par. 10)?

5. What is the effect of Dillard's calling the moth "she" instead of "it"? Of Dillard's wondering whether the moth has finished her earthly work (par. 7)?

6. How effective do you find the specific details of the DESCRIPTION in paragraph 3? Explain your answer.

7. How does Dillard give the impression of seeing her world intently, as if through a magnifying glass?

8. In paragraph 9, moth and candle seem almost to be holding the night at bay. How does Dillard create this impression? How does she get across to us the sudden flare of the moth as it first hits the flame?

9. Dillard's analogies are developed through a personal NARRATIVE of the sort exemplified in Chapter 1. Which parts of her narrative are set in the present (the time at which she writes)? Where is she located physically in the present time?

10. In what *two* places is the past action of Dillard's narrative located? When does she return to the present?

11. How does Dillard achieve a welcome comic relief in paragraph 11?

Words and Figures of Speech

1. What is the effect of Dillard's including "like a jumble of but-tresses for cathedral domes" in the list of SIMILES at the end of paragraph 4?
2. Look up *transfiguration* in your dictionary. What does it mean in religious terms? How does it apply to Dillard's essay?
3. Why do you think Dillard uses such technical terms as *thorax, cerci,* and *chitin* (par. 4)?
4. How effective do you find the phrase "scant traffic" in paragraph 2? What is the effect of the word *raving* in paragraph 10?
5. Why does Dillard capitalize *Moth* in paragraph 4?
6. Consult your dictionary as necessary for the following words: *lineage* (par. 2), *bulbous* (2), *dorsal* (4), *thorax* (4), *translucent* (4), *chitin* (4), *buttresses* (4), *gilded* (6), *replenished* (6), *essence* (8), *immolating* (8).

Comparing

1. Which of the insects described in Lewis Thomas's "On Societies as Organisms" (Chapter 7) most closely resembles Dillard's burning moth?
2. In a sense, Dillard's account of the death of a moth and Virginia Woolf's account of the same phenomenon (in the next chapter) come to opposite conclusions. What are those conclusions? Explain the contrast.

Discussion and Writing Topics

1. Draw an analogy between human life and a bird flying through a house.
2. Compare the artist's or the musician's task to that of a champion athlete.
3. Draw an analogy between a nun, priest, rabbi, or other religious figure and a bridge; between a church or synagogue and a ship or city.

WRITING TOPICS for Chapter Seven
Essays That Use Metaphor and Analogy

1. Explain your inner self by analogy with a car, truck, motorcycle, boat, or other vehicle that you consider to be a means of self-expression.

2. Write an essay using the shrinking size of American automobiles as indexes to the country's economic condition.

3. Describe a house you have seen as an emblem of the people that you know or imagine to inhabit it.

4. Define several different kinds of human intelligence by associating each type with a game that exemplifies it.

5. Explain how to develop self-confidence by comparing the process of acquiring it to weaving a design, cultivating a garden, or building a fire.

6. Explain the kind of education your college or university offers by comparing it to a meal in a restaurant or cafeteria.

7. Describe a typical day in your life as if you were threading your way through a maze.

8. Compare the maneuvers and challenges of the dating game to the activities of a disco lounge or other night spot.

9. Recall formative events of your past life by associating them with objects in an attic or pictures in a photo album.

10. Explain the typical life cycle of a human being by likening it to that of an insect or animal.

)

|

Description

8

Essays That Appeal to the Senses

DESCRIPTION [1] is the MODE of writing that appeals most directly to the senses either by telling us the qualities of a person, place, or thing or by showing them. For example, here are two descriptions of cemeteries. The first, from Natural History magazine, is written in the language of detached observation:

An old and popular New England tradition for resident and visitor alike, is a relaxing walk through one of our historical cemeteries. . . .

Haphazard rows of slate tablets give way in time to simple marble tablets bearing urn and willow motifs. The latter in turn lose popularity to marble gravestones of a variety of sizes and shapes and often arranged in groups or family plots. The heyday of ornate marble memorials lasted into the 1920s, when measured rows of uniformly sized granite blocks replaced them.

Compare this passage with novelist John Updike's far-from-detached description of the cemetery in the town where he lives:

The stones are marble, modernly glossy and simple, though I suppose that time will eventually reveal them as another fashion, dated and quaint. Now, the sod is still raw, the sutures of turf are unhealed, the earth still humped, the wreaths scarcely withered. . . . I remember my grandfather's funeral, the hurried cross of sand the minister drew on the coffin lid, the whine of the lowering straps, the lengthening, cleanly cut sides of clay, the thought of air, the lack of air forever in the close dark space lined with pink satin. . . .

[1] Terms printed in all capitals are defined in the Glossary.

Our first example relies heavily upon adjectives: "historical," "haphazard," "simple," "ornate," "measured," "uniformly sized." Except when they identify minerals—slate tablets, marble memorials—these adjectives tend to be ABSTRACT. Indeed, the movement of the entire passage is away from the particular. No single grave is described in detail. Even the "urn and willow motifs" adorn a number of tombs. The authors seem interested in the whole sweep of the cemetery from the haphazard rows of the oldest section to the ordered ranks of modern headstones in the newest. It is the arrangement, or shift in arrangement, that most concerns them.

Arrangement is an abstract concept, and we should remember that description is not limited to people or things that can be perceived directly by the physical senses. Description may also convey ideas: the proportions of a building, the style of a baseball player, the infinitude of space. Our first description of cemeteries, in fact, moves from the concrete to the abstract because it was written to support ideas. It is part of a sociological study of cemeteries as they reveal changing American attitudes toward death, family, and society. The authors take their "relaxing walk" not because they want to examine individual tombstones but because they want to generalize from a multitude of physical evidence. As reporters, they stand between us and the actual objects they tell about.

By contrast, the movement of the Updike passage is from the general to the particular. Starting where the other leaves off—with a field of glossy modern slabs—it focuses quickly upon the new-dug graves and then narrows even more sharply to a single grave kept fresh in the author's memory. This time the adjectives are CONCRETE: "raw," "unhealed," "humped," "withered," "hurried," "close," "dark." The nouns are concrete too: "sod" and "earth" give way to the "space" lined with satin. Death is no abstraction for Updike; it is the suffocating loss of personal life. Updike makes us experience the finality of death by recreating his own sensations of claustrophobia at his grandfather's funeral.

Different as they are, these two passages illustrate a single peculiarity of description as a mode: it seldom stands alone. As in our first example, "scientific" description shades easily into exposition. As in our second, "evocative" description shades just as easily into narration. The authors of example number one describe the changes in a cemetery in order to explain (EXPOSITION) what those changes mean for American culture. After evoking his feelings about a past event, the author of example number two goes on in later lines to show what happened (NARRATION) when his reverie was interrupted by his son, who was learning to ride a bicycle in the peaceful cemetery. Which kind of description is better—telling or showing, scientific or evocative? Neither is inherently better or worse than the other. The kind of description that a writer chooses depends upon what he wants to do with it.

Updike's reference to the "sutures" of "unhealed" turf suggests how easily description also falls into METAPHOR, SIMILE, and ANALOGY. This is hardly surprising, for we often describe a thing in everyday speech by telling what it is like. A thump in your closet at night sounds like an owl hitting a haystack. A crowd stirs like a jellyfish. The seams of turf on new graves are like the stitches binding a human wound.

The ease with which description shifts into other MODES does not mean that a good description has no unity or order of its own, however. When writing description, keep in mind that every detail should contribute to a dominant impression, mood, or purpose. The dominant impression he wanted to convey when describing his grandfather's funeral, says Updike, was "the foreverness, the towering foreverness." Updike creates this impression by moving from the outside to the inside of the grave. Depending upon the object or place you are describing, you may want to move from the inside out, from left to right, top to bottom, or front to back. Whatever arrangement you choose, present the details of your description systematically; but do not call so much attention to your system of organization that it dominates the thing you are describing.

What impression, mood, or purpose is your description intended to serve? What specific objects can contribute to it? What do they look, feel, smell, taste, or sound like? Does your object or place suggest any natural order of presentation? These are the questions to ask when you begin a descriptive essay.

Francis X. Clines
Eggbag

Francis X. Clines is a reporter on the national staff of the New
York Times. Reared in Brooklyn, he now lives outside Washington,
D.C., with his wife and four children. For three years, Clines had
the enviable assignment of roaming New York City for his newspaper and filing reports three times weekly on whatever aspect of
city life he chose. His editors at the Times put no restrictions on
him, besides deadlines, "because they wanted the story of the
quality of the city that defies the usual categories of journalism."
The result was Clines's first book, About New York (1980), a
volume subtitled "Sketches of the City." "Eggbag" is one of those
sketches. With a reporter's eye and story teller's voice, it describes
the scene and perpetrators, human as well as feline, of a little magic
on Eighth Avenue, a place where enchantment is usually hard to
come by.

Eggbag the cat is asleep in the back of the magic shop, and   1
Eighth Avenue looks almost greasy with the afternoon rain.
There isn't much magic on the avenue and the hookers stand
out under their golf umbrellas.

In the magic store where Eggbag the cat sleeps, with a   2
pawnshop on one side and a naked-lady emporium on the
other, a few locals wait for the cat to wake up and do his
card trick. They kill time talking of human magicians.

"Have you seen the new guy, Presto?" Johnny Burns asks,   3
leaning on the counter that has all the magic magazines and
the false fruit and fish to squeeze into tiny balls for hiding.
"Presto is great. A black guy, fantastic magician, can blind
you up close or way back."

Two officers from the beat come in to buy some magic   4
stuff, and the owner of the store, Russ Delmar, an old vaude-

villian, goes into some lovely sleight-of-hand with them, doing the shifting silver dollars, the moving pen and an eight-card cover ending with all the cards the same.

The shorter officer of the two loves it when Russ makes him blow   5
extra hard for the abracadabra moment. Russ has strong, clean hands, and the tricks go perfectly and he kids his audience. "You're not too smart—How'd you ever get to be a cop?"

"Nice, Russ," the officer says, still watching his hands. The   6
police enjoy themselves. It's better than standing outside with the hookers and golf umbrellas.

They buy a dirty illusion to put on the lieutenant's chair back   7
in the precinct, an old New York favorite—imitation dog-dropping. It's not first-line magic, but Russ sells some of the usual novelties, too, along with professional grade tricks and illusions. His biggest illusion now is the shoot-the-woman, which goes for $150. (You want to know what it is, buy it. Or, as Russ says: "How do I do it? I do it very well.")

Russ's store, the Magic Center, has been scaled down in its   8
thirty years on the west side of Eighth Avenue north of 46th Street. Once he had ten salesmen demonstrating tricks costing up to $600. He still has good stuff, says his friend, Ken Martin, a local actor, magician and Chinese food chef. But Russ has scaled down, mainly enjoying showing magic to the kids who come by and taking care of Eggbag the cat, who was named after the trick in which an egg is palmed out of a felt purse. Russ is near seventy years old, but he looks fifteen younger from all the adagio dancing and unicycle juggling he did fifty years ago in vaudeville.

Where is Eggbag the cat? We want to see him do his card trick.   9
"Eggbag will be along," Russ says. Well either that or we'll go for this guy Presto. "Presto is like wine," Johnny Burns says. "He is good."

Strange-looking people come in out of the rain, a few looking   10
desperate, and stunned, as if they had come from an accident. But it is only the neighborhood they're coming from. Russ is friendly to all and does sleight-of-hand, even when he gives a quarter to a panhandler, and the panhandler appreciates the magic.

"Wait till you see the cat," Ken Martin says. "I saw that trick   11
first time, I almost fell on the floor."

Russ goes back where Eggbag the cat sleeps. Once three hook-   12

ers came in and offered to rent the backroom for $100 a day if
Russ would put a cot in. He said no for morality reasons as well as
the fact that Eggbag slept there.

After a while, Eggbag the cat comes out. He is an even gray-   13
white color, like a shirt that's been washed without bleach. He
ignores everyone and yawns elaborately, stretching his front paws
out and curving his back up the sudden way humans pop their
knuckles.

What Eggbag really wants is to steal one of the magicians'   14
dummy mice from the glass showcase, as he does every day, and
knock it around the floor for his daily macho hunter fix. (He has
never gone back out on Eighth Avenue since he sneaked into the
store two years ago.) But Russ keeps hauling the cat to the
counter. It's show time.

"Pick a card," Russ says to a visitor, holding a deck out. (It is   15
the three of hearts, but don't tell the cat.)

Russ puts the card back in the pack, has the visitor straighten   16
the deck. Russ fans the cards in front to Eggbag the cat. "C'mon,
Eggbag."

Eggbag the cat sprawls on the counter as if he is trying out for a   17
Mae West movie. Even his whiskers are blasé.

"C'mon, Eggbag," Russ says, kind of pushing the fan of cards   18
toward the cat, and the cat suddenly bites one, as if it were the
hand of human kindness, and he pulls it out in his teeth and lets it
flutter down. It is the same three of hearts.

He does it two more times. Not bad for a cat. One of the visitors   19
confides that it clearly was a trick.

Granted. But what can you expect on a rainy day on Eighth   20
Avenue in a place called the Magic Center—divinity?

QUESTIONS

Understanding

1. Clines describes an Eighth Avenue neighborhood in New York
   City. What sort of neighborhood is it? How are the people affected by this street environment?

2. What "miracle" has Clines come to the magic shop especially to witness?

3. Inside the magic shop, how does Russ Delmar, the magician, pass the time as everyone waits?

4. How has the shop changed over the years? How has its proprietor changed? In what fundamental ways have he and the shop remained untouched by time?

5. What does Eggbag look like physically? Would he win any prizes at a cat show? How about his mood and manner?

6. What is the mood of the people inside the shop? Of those "strange-looking people" who wander in from the outside?

7. Eggbag does the great trick, but who is the master illusionist in the shop? What power transforms his audience, no matter where they come from?

Strategies and Structure

1. Clines's essay is divided into three parts: the third describes Eggbag and his trick; the second describes the proprietor and the inside of the shop. The first part describes the inside, too—but by contrast with what?

2. How does Clines separate the two locales of his essay? Which is represented by the policemen? How do they behave while inside the shop? What do they take away with them?

3. Why do you suppose Clines never describes the back room where Eggbag sleeps? What is the effect of his telling us that the magician once declined to rent that space to prostitutes?

4. Clines delays any complete physical description of the magacian until paragraph 8. What part of him does the writer describe earlier? Why this part and no more?

5. Why is Johnny Burns mentioned twice in Clines's description? What do he and Ken Martin (also mentioned more than once) have in common? How much of their speech (and which parts) does Clines quote?

6. How does the rain contribute to the atmosphere of Clines's description? To what part of the scene is the rain confined?

7. Why might Clines stress the very ordinariness of the magic cat: "like a shirt that's been washed without bleach" (par. 13)?

8. What is the TONE of the final line about "divinity" on Eighth Avenue? of the writer's parenthetical comments in paragraphs 7 and 15?

Words and Figures of Speech

1. "Eggbag" is named after a serviceable but not very flashy trick that is an old stand-by with magicians. Why is it a good name for a cat, especially this cat?

2. By the time Clines repeats the name of the magic shop in the last paragraph, it has taken on the function of more than a label. What has "The Magic Center" come to signify?

3. What is "sleight-of-hand" exactly? How is it different from other kinds of magic, for example grand stage illusions that can be witnessed by a huge audience? Why is sleight-of-hand the appropriate kind of magic for *this* magician in *this* place?

4. Clines says the walk-in strangers look "as if they had come from an accident" (par. 10). Why is this SIMILE appropriate, given where they actually have come from?

5. What alternative implications do the following words take on in the context Clines gives them: "better than standing outside" (par. 6) and "he still has good stuff" (par. 8)?

6. Look up *abracadabra* in the Oxford English Dictionary (OED) in the reference room of your school library. How old a word is it? Where does it probably come from?

Comparing

1. What does the interior of Russ Delmar's magic shop have in common with the floor of Annie Dillard's bathroom in "Transfiguration" (Chapter 7)?

2. How does Clines's description of Eight Avenue square with Russell Baker's general description of New York City in "A Nice Place to Visit" (Chapter 6)?

Discussion and Writing Topics

1. Describe a shop or business you know about—a tattoo parlor, a tiny restaurant, a museum—that seems like a retreat from its depressing surroundings.

2. Describe a supposedly hallowed place that struck you as inescapably profane, for example: a funeral parlor, a cemetery, a shop devoted to religious supplies, a church that looks like a factory.

3. As a good reporter, should Clines have told us how Eggbag did his trick? Why or why not?

Horace Miner

Body Ritual
among the Nacirema

Horace Miner is professor of social anthropology at the University
of Michigan; he is an authority on African cultures. A native of
St. Paul, Minnesota, he studied at the University of Kentucky and
the University of Chicago (Ph.D., 1937). He joined the faculty
at Michigan in 1946 after teaching at Wayne State University
and serving in the wartime army. Miner is the author of The
Primitive City of Timbuctoo (1953); Oasis and Casbah (1960);
and The City in Modern Africa (1967). "Body Ritual among the
Nacirema" first appeared in The American Anthropologist; it
uses the methods and language of social anthropology to describe
a curious North American tribe.

The anthropologist has become so familiar with the diversity [1]
of ways in which different peoples behave in similar situations
that he is not apt to be surprised by even the most exotic customs. In fact, if all of the logically possible combinations of
behavior have not been found somewhere in the world, he is
apt to suspect that they must be present in some yet unde-
scribed tribe. This point has, in fact, been expressed with
respect to clan organization by Murdock.[1] In this light, the
magical beliefs and practices of the Nacirema present such
unusual aspects that it seems desirable to describe them as an
example of the extremes to which human behavior can go.

Professor Linton first brought the ritual of the Nacirema [2]
to the attention of anthropologists twenty years ago, but the

[1] American anthropologist George Peter Murdock (b. 1897), authority
on primitive cultures.

245

culture of this people is still very poorly understood. They are a North American group living in the territory between the Canadian Cree, the Yaqui and Tarahumare of Mexico, and the Carib and Arawak of the Antilles.[2] Little is known of their origin, although tradition states that they came from the east. . . .

Nacirema culture is characterized by a highly developed market 3
economy which has evolved in a rich natural habitat. While much of the people's time is devoted to economic pursuits, a large part of the fruits of these labors and a considerable portion of the day are spent in ritual activity. The focus of this activity is the human body, the appearance and health of which loom as a dominant concern in the ethos of the people. While such a concern is certainly not unusual, its ceremonial aspects and associated philosophy are unique.

The fundamental belief underlying the whole system appears to 4
be that the human body is ugly and that its natural tendency is to debility and disease. Incarcerated in such a body, man's only hope is to avert these characteristics through the use of the powerful influences of ritual and ceremony. Every household has one or more shrines devoted to this purpose. The more powerful individuals in the society have several shrines in their houses and, in fact, the opulence of a house is often referred to in terms of the number of such ritual centers it possesses. Most houses are of wattle and daub construction, but the shrine rooms of the more wealthy are walled with stone. Poorer families imitate the rich by applying pottery plaques to their shrine walls.

While each family has at least one such shrine, the rituals as- 5
sociated with it are not family ceremonies but are private and secret. The rites are normally only discussed with children, and then only during the period when they are being initiated into these mysteries. I was able, however, to establish sufficient rapport with the natives to examine these shrines and to have the rituals described to me.

The focal point of the shrine is a box or chest which is built 6
into the wall. In this chest are kept the many charms and magical potions without which no native believes he could live. These preparations are secured from a variety of specialized practitioners.

___

[2] Native American tribes formerly inhabiting the Saskatchewan region of Canada, the Sonora region of Mexico, and the West Indies.

The most powerful of these are the medicine men, whose assistance must be rewarded with substantial gifts. However, the medicine men do not provide the curative potions for their clients, but decide what the ingredients should be and then write them down in an ancient and secret language. This writing is understood only by the medicine men and by the herbalists who, for another gift, provide the required charm.

The charm is not disposed of after it has served its purpose, but   7 is placed in the charm-box of the household shrine. As these magical materials are specific for certain ills, and the real or imagined maladies of the people are many, the charm-box is usually full to overflowing. The magical packets are so numerous that people forget what their purposes were and fear to use them again. While the natives are very vague on this point, we can only assume that the idea in retaining all the old magical materials is that their presence in the charm-box, before which the body rituals are conducted, will in some way protect the worshipper.

Beneath the charm-box is a small font. Each day every member   8 of the family, in succession, enters the shrine room, bows his head before the charm-box, mingles different sorts of holy water in the font, and proceeds with a brief rite of ablution. The holy waters are secured from the Water Temple of the community, where the priests conduct elaborate ceremonies to make the liquid ritually pure.

In the hierarchy of magical practitioners, and below the medi-   9 cine men in prestige, are specialists whose designation is best translated "holy-mouth-men." The Nacirema have an almost pathological horror of and fascination with the mouth, the condition of which is believed to have a supernatural influence on all social relationships. Were it not for the rituals of the mouth, they believe that their teeth would fall out, their gums bleed, their jaws shrink, their friends desert them, and their lovers reject them. They also believe that a strong relationship exists between oral and moral characteristics. For example, there is a ritual ablution of the mouth for children which is supposed to improve their moral fiber.

The daily body ritual performed by everyone includes a mouth-   10 rite. Despite the fact that these people are so punctilious about care of the mouth, this rite involves a practice which strikes the uninitiated stranger as revolting. It was reported to me that the ritual consists of inserting a small bundle of hog hairs into the mouth, along with certain magical powders, and then moving the bundle in a highly formalized series of gestures.

In addition to the private mouth-rite, the people seek out a 11 holy-mouth-man once or twice a year. These practitioners have an impressive set of paraphernalia, consisting of a variety of augers, awls, probes, and prods. The use of these objects in the exorcism of the evils of the mouth involves almost unbelievable ritual torture of the client. The holy-mouth-man opens the client's mouth and, using the above mentioned tools, enlarges any holes which decay may have created in the teeth. Magical materials are put into these holes. If there are not naturally occurring holes in the teeth, large sections of one or more teeth are gouged out so that the supernatural substance can be applied. In the client's view, the purpose of these ministrations is to arrest decay and to draw friends. The extremely sacred and traditional character of the rite is evident in the fact that the natives return to the holy-mouth-men year after year, despite the fact that their teeth continue to decay.

It is to be hoped that, when a thorough study of the Nacirema 12 is made, there will be careful inquiry into the personality structure of these people. One has but to watch the gleam in the eye of a holy-mouth-man, as he jabs an awl into an exposed nerve, to suspect that a certain amount of sadism is involved. If this can be established, a very interesting pattern emerges, for most of the population shows definite masochistic tendencies. It was to these that Professor Linton referred in discussing a distinctive part of the daily body ritual which is performed only by men. This part of the rite involves scraping and lacerating the surface of the face with a sharp instrument. Special women's rites are performed only four times during each lunar month, but what they lack in frequency is made up in barbarity. As part of this ceremony, women bake their heads in small ovens for about an hour. The theoretically interesting point is that what seems to be a preponderantly masochistic people have developed sadistic specialists.

The medicine men have an imposing temple, or *latipso*, in 13 every community of any size. The more elaborate ceremonies required to treat very sick patients can only be performed at this temple. These ceremonies involve not only the thaumaturge but a

permanent group of vestal maidens who move sedately about the
temple chambers in distinctive costume and headdress.

The *latipso* ceremonies are so harsh that it is phenomenal that   14
a fair proportion of the really sick natives who enter the temple
ever recover. Small children whose indoctrination is still incomplete have been known to resist attempts to take them to the
temple because "that is where you go to die." Despite this fact,
sick adults are not only willing but eager to undergo the pro-
tracted ritual purification, if they can afford to do so. No matter
how ill the supplicant or how grave the emergency, the guardians
of many temples will not admit a client if he cannot give a rich
gift to the custodian. Even after one has gained admission and
survived the ceremonies, the guardians will not permit the neophyte to leave until he makes still another gift.

The supplicant entering the temple is first stripped of all his or   15
her clothes. In everyday life the Nacirema avoids exposure of his
body and its natural functions. Bathing and excretory acts are
performed only in the secrecy of the household shrine, where they
are ritualized as part of the body-rites. Psychological shock results
from the fact that body secrecy is suddenly lost upon entry into
the *latipso*. A man, whose own wife has never seen him in an
excretory act, suddenly finds himself naked and assisted by a vestal
maiden while he performs his natural functions into a sacred ves-
sel. This sort of ceremonial treatment is necessitated by the fact
that the excreta are used by a diviner to ascertain the course and
nature of the client's sickness. Female clients, on the other hand,
find their naked bodies are subjected to the scrutiny, manipulation
and prodding of the medicine men.

Few supplicants in the temple are well enough to do anything   16
but lie on their hard beds. The daily ceremonies, like the rites of
the holy-mouth-men, involve discomfort and torture. With ritual
precision, the vestals awaken their miserable charges each dawn
and roll them about on their beds of pain while performing ablu-
tions, in the formal movements of which the maidens are highly
trained. At other times they insert magic wands in the supplicant's
mouth or force him to eat substances which are supposed to be
healing. From time to time the medicine men come to their
clients and jab magically treated needles into their flesh. The fact
that these temple ceremonies may not cure, and may even kill the

neophyte, in no way decreases the people's faith in the medicine men.

There remains one other kind of practitioner, known as a [17] "listener." This witchdoctor has the power to exorcise the devils that lodge in the heads of people who have been bewitched. The Nacirema believe that parents bewitch their own children. Mothers are particularly suspected of putting a curse on children while teaching them the secret body rituals. The counter-magic of the witchdoctor is unusual in its lack of ritual. The patient simply tells the "listener" all his troubles and fears, beginning with the earliest difficulties he can remember. The memory displayed by the Nacirema in these exorcism sessions is truly remarkable. It is not uncommon for the patient to bemoan the rejection he felt upon being weaned as a babe, and a few individuals even see their troubles going back to the traumatic effects of their own birth.

In conclusion, mention must be made of certain practices which [18] have their base in native esthetics but which depend upon the pervasive aversion to the natural body and its functions. There are ritual fasts to make fat people thin and ceremonial feasts to make thin people fat. Still other rites are used to make women's breasts larger if they are small, and smaller if they are large. General dissatisfaction with breast shape is symbolized in the fact that the ideal form is virtually outside the range of human variation. A few women afflicted with almost inhuman hyper-mammary development are so idolized that they make a handsome living by simply going from village to village and permitting the natives to stare at them for a fee.

Reference has already been made to the fact that excretory [19] functions are ritualized, routinized, and relegated to secrecy. Natural reproductive functions are similarly distorted. Intercourse is taboo as a topic and scheduled as an act. Efforts are made to avoid pregnancy by the use of magical materials or by limiting intercourse to certain phases of the moon. Conception is actually very infrequent. When pregnant, women dress so as to hide their condition. Parturition takes place in secret, without friends or relatives to assist, and the majority of women do not nurse their infants.

Our review of the ritual life of the Nacirema has certainly [20] shown them to be a magic-ridden people. It is hard to understand how they have managed to exist so long under the burdens which they have imposed upon themselves. But even such exotic customs as these take on real meaning when they are viewed with the insight provided by Malinowski[3] when he wrote:

"Looking from far and above, from our high places of safety in   21
the developed civilization, it is easy to see all the crudity and irrelevance of magic. But without its power and guidance early man could not have mastered his practical difficulties as he has done, nor could man have advanced to the higher stages of civilization."

QUESTIONS

Understanding

1. Who are these strange people, the Nacirema? How did they get their name?
2. What are "shrine rooms" (par. 4) and "charm-boxes"(par. 7) used in the morning rituals of the Nacirema?
3. Why do the Nacirema put "hog hairs" (par. 10) in their mouths? What is the "ritual ablution of the mouth" (par. 9) believed to improve the moral fiber of children?
4. Who is the "listener" (par. 17), and why do the Nacirema think that "parents bewitch their own children" (par. 17)?
5. Having closely observed their private behavior, Miner concludes that the Nacirema base their body rituals on the belief that "the human body is ugly" (par. 4) in its natural state. Do you agree? Why or why not?
6. What is the "real meaning" (par. 20) of the Nacirema's exotic customs when viewed in the light of Malinowski's statement in paragraph 21?

Strategies and Structure

1. When did you first suspect that Miner is writing tongue-in-cheek? What specific details in his DESCRIPTION tipped you off?
2. From what perspective is Miner describing the Nacirema? How

---

[3] Bronislaw Kasper Malinowski (1884–1942), Polish-born anthropologist, who came to America in 1938.

do paragraphs 1, 3, and 21 help to establish his "cultural" and professional vantage point?

3. Descriptions often strive to make the strange seem familiar, but Miner's makes the familiar seem strange. Give several examples, and analyze how they reverse the usual procedure.

4. What is the serious purpose behind Miner's "joke"? Do you think a mock-scientific paper is an effective means of accomplishing that purpose? Why or why not?

5. A social anthropologist, Miner originally wrote his "study" for *The American Anthropologist*, a journal whose audience expected writing in their field to follow conventional forms. How does Miner give his essay the flavor of a scientific (as opposed to a "literary") article or report? Pay special attention to paragraphs 1–3 and 18–21.

6. How can Miner's essay be seen in any way to SATIRIZE the methods and language of social anthropology?

Words and Figures of Speech

1. Where did the Nacirema get the word *latipso* (par. 13) for their temples of the sick?

2. Miner's last paragraph could be considered a non-sequitur, or conclusion that does not logically follow from the evidence it is built upon. What is wrong, logically, with the quoted statement? Why might Miner choose to end his essay with this device?

3. What is a *thaumaturge* (par. 13)? Given his true subject, what is the effect of Miner's using that term and such related terms as *herbalist* (par. 6), *medicine men* (par. 6), *holy-mouth-men* (par. 9), and *diviner* (par. 15)?

4. For which one of these practitioners does Miner have to invent a name? What does the lack of a standard term for it in the language of anthropology suggest about this role in modern society?

5. Why do you think Miner uses such clinical terms as *excreta* (par. 15), *hyper-mammary* (par. 18), and *parturition* (par. 19)?

6. Consult your dictionary for any of the following words you do not already know: *ethos* (par. 3), *incarcerated* (4), *opulence* (4), *ablution* (8), *pathological* (9), *punctilious* (10), *paraphernalia* (11), *sadism* (12), *masochistic* (12), *supplicant* (14), *neophyte* (14), *scrutiny* (15), *aversion* (18), *taboo* (19), *parturition* (19).

Comparing

1. Both Miner and Russell Baker ("A Nice Place to Visit," Chapter 6) describe "alien" cultures. What does the language of both "interpreters" have in common?

2. How does Miner's perspective here resemble William Allen's in "Toward an Understanding of Accidental Knots" in Chapter 4?

3. Miner's irony is similar to Jonathan Swift's in "A Modest Proposal" ("Essays For Further Reading"); when you read Swift, ask yourself how the speakers in the two essays resemble each other.

Discussion and Writing Topics

1. Describe other rituals of the Nacirema—for example, those associated with wearing clothes and with transportation—that bear out Miner's findings about the tribe's distaste for the human body.

2. Although Miner says that the Nacirema have a "highly developed market economy" (par. 3), he says little about it. Describe their "economic pursuits" (par. 3) in such a way as to "prove" that these people who find the body ugly nevertheless find treasure beautiful.

3. Describe a barber or beauty shop or an exercise salon as if you were seeing one for the first time and so did not know the names or purposes of anything. Make up descriptive names for people and objects and assign causes according to the surface appearance of events.

Richard Selzer

The Discus Thrower

Richard Selzer is a surgeon. From his native Troy, New York, he attended Union College and Albany Medical College (M.D., 1953). After postdoctoral study at Yale, he entered private practice in 1960. A fellow of Ezra Stiles College of Yale University, he also teaches surgery at Yale Medical School. Selzer has contributed stories and essays to Harper's, Esquire, Redbook, Mademoiselle, and other popular magazines. His Rituals of Surgery, a collection of short stories, appeared in 1974. Selzer is best known for his essays of the doctor's life, some of which are collected in Mortal Lessons (1977) and Confessions of a Knife (1979). He is now at work on more essays and stories and on a mythological treatment of the Civil War. "The Discus Thrower" was published in Harper's with the subtitle "Do Not Go Gentle"; it describes a terminally ill patient in a bare hospital room.

I spy on my patients. Ought not a doctor to observe his ¹ patients by any means and from any stance, that he might the more fully assemble evidence? So I stand in the doorways of hospital rooms and gaze. Oh, it is not all that furtive an act. Those in bed need only look up to discover me. But they never do.

From the doorway of Room 542 the man in the bed seems ² deeply tanned. Blue eyes and close-cropped white hair give him the appearance of vigor and good health. But I know that his skin is not brown from the sun. It is rusted, rather, in the last stage of containing the vile repose within. And the blue eyes are frosted, looking inward like the windows of a snowbound cottage. This man is blind. This man is also legless—the right leg missing from midthigh down, the left from just below the knee. It gives him the look of a bonsai, roots and branches pruned into the dwarfed facsimile of a great tree.

Propped on pillows, he cups his right thigh in both hands. Now   3
and then he shakes his head as though acknowledging the intensity of his suffering. In all of this he makes no sound. Is he mute as well as blind?·

The room in which he dwells is empty of all possessions—no   4
get-well cards, small, private caches of food, day-old flowers, slippers, all the usual kickshaws of the sickroom. There is only the bed, a chair, a nightstand, and a tray on wheels that can be swung across his lap for meals.

"What time is it?" he asks.   5
"Three o'clock."   6
"Morning or afternoon?"   7
"Afternoon."   8
He is silent. There is nothing else he wants to know.   9
"How are you?" I say.   10
"Who is it?" he asks.   11
"It's the doctor. How do you feel?"   12
He does not answer right away.   13
"Feel?" he says.   14
"I hope you feel better," I say.   15
I press the button at the side of the bed.   16
"Down you go," I say.   17
"Yes, down," he says.   18
He falls back upon the bed awkwardly. His stumps, unweighted   19
by legs and feet, rise in the air, presenting themselves. I unwrap the bandages from the stumps, and begin to cut away the black scabs and the dead, glazed fat with scissors and forceps. A shard of white bone comes loose. I pick it away. I wash the wounds with disinfectant and redress the stumps. All this while, he does not speak. What is he thinking behind those lids that do not blink? Is he remembering a time when he was whole? Does he dream of feet? Of when his body was not a rotting log?

He lies solid and inert. In spite of everything, he remains im-   20
pressive, as though he were a sailor standing athwart a slanting deck.

"Anything more I can do for you?" I ask.   21

For a long moment he is silent. 22

"Yes," he says at last and without the least irony. "You can 23
bring me a pair of shoes."

In the corridor, the head nurse is waiting for me. 24

"We have to do something about him," she says. "Every morn- 25
ing he orders scrambled eggs for breakfast, and, instead of eating
them, he picks up the plate and throws it against the wall."

"Throws his plate?" 26

"Nasty. That's what he is. No wonder his family doesn't come 27
to visit. They probably can't stand him any more than we can."

She is waiting for me to do something. 28

"Well?" 29

"We'll see," I say. 30

The next morning I am waiting in the corridor when the 31
kitchen delivers his breakfast. I watch the aide place the tray on
the stand and swing it across his lap. She presses the button to
raise the head of the bed. Then she leaves.

In time the man reaches to find the rim of the tray, then on to 32
find the dome of the covered dish. He lifts off the cover and places
it on the stand. He fingers across the plate until he probes the
eggs. He lifts the plate in both hands, sets it on the palm of his
right hand, centers it, balances it. He hefts it up and down
slightly, getting the feel of it. Abruptly, he draws back his right
arm as far as he can.

There is the crack of the plate breaking against the wall at the 33
foot of his bed and the small wet sound of the scrambled eggs
dropping to the floor.

And then he laughs. It is a sound you have never heard. It is 34
something new under the sun. It could cure cancer.

Out in the corridor, the eyes of the head nurse narrow. 35

"Laughed, did he?" 36

She writes something down on her clipboard. 37

A second aide arrives, brings a second breakfast tray, puts it on 38
the nightstand, out of his reach. She looks over at me shaking her
head and making her mouth go. I see that we are to be accomplices.

"I've got to feed you," she says to the man. 39

"Oh, no you don't," the man says. 40

"Oh, yes I do," the aide says, "after the way you just did. Nurse 41
says so."

"Get me my shoes," the man says.   42

"Here's oatmeal," the aide says. "Open." And she touches the   43
spoon to his lower lip.

"I ordered scrambled eggs," says the man.   44

"That's right," the aide says.   45

I step forward.   46

"Is there anything I can do?" I say.   47

"Who are you?" the man asks.   48

In the evening I go once more to that ward to make my rounds.   49
The head nurse reports to me that Room 542 is deceased. She
has discovered this quite by accident, she says. No, there had been
no sound. Nothing. It's a blessing, she says.

I go into his room, a spy looking for secrets. He is still there in   50
his bed. His face is relaxed, grave, dignified. After a while, I turn
to leave. My gaze sweeps the wall at the foot of the bed, and I see
the place where it has been repeatedly washed, where the wall
looks very clean and very white.

QUESTIONS

Understanding

1. Why does Selzer's dying patient throw his breakfast against the
   wall?

2. What is the significance of the patient's repeatedly calling for
   shoes? Of his reminding the aide in paragraph 44 that he had
   ordered scrambled eggs?

3. Selzer says that the discus thrower is "impressive" (par. 19) despite his mutilation. Why is he impressive to the doctor?

4. What is the significance of the patient's question about time in
   paragraph 7?

5. What attitude is revealed by the doctor's questions to his patient?
   What is revealed by the dying patient's responses, "Who is it?"
   (par. 11) and "Who are you?" (par. 48)?

6. How might the doctor's response to the nurse (par. 30) be interpreted to carry the "mortal lesson" of Selzer's entire essay?

Strategies and Structure

1. The doctor's role throughout this essay is to DESCRIBE without interpreting. How is this role anticipated in paragraph 1? Why do you think Selzer adopts it?
2. How does the doctor's physical stance during much of the essay contribute to the POINT OF VIEW from which it is told?
3. Selzer's essay alternates between dialogue and description, with little commentary on the meaning of what he describes. Point out the few passages of actual commentary or interpretation. Would Selzer's essay have been more or less successful with more such commentary? Explain your answer.
4. Analyze the TONE of Selzer's description of dressing his patient's stumps in paragraph 19. How well does the tone comport with the doctor's role throughout the essay?
5. How does Selzer avoid sentimentality in his description of the dying man?
6. Describe the function of the head nurse in this essay.
7. What is the effect of Selzer's using the second PERSON "you" in paragraph 34?
8. Why does Selzer end his essay with a reference to the wall?

Words and Figures of Speech

1. An *epithet* is a descriptive title or name for a person, such as "giant-killer" for Jack in the fairy tale. What are the implications of Selzer's main epithet for this patient?
2. Why is the "rotting log" METAPHOR appropriate (par. 19)?
3. The second nurse's aide and the doctor are said to be "accomplices" (par. 38). What does this term CONNOTE? Why does Selzer use it? What similar term does he use in paragraph 1?
4. A *kickshaw* (par. 4) is a trinket or other little gift, often of food. What does Selzer's reference to kickshaws show about his patient? About the doctor?
5. HYPERBOLE is exaggeration. How effective is Selzer's use of this figure of speech in paragraph 34? Explain your answer.
6. Selzer's alternate title, or subtitle, for "The Discus Thrower" is "Do Not Go Gentle," an ALLUSION to the Dylan Thomas poem,

"Do Not Go Gentle into That Good Night." Find a copy of the poem in your school library and explain why Selzer refers to it.

Comparing

1. Both Selzer's essay and the next one (by Virginia Woolf), deal with death; but Woolf's essay, you will find, includes much more commentary on what it describes. What accounts for this difference, and how does it influence our response in each case?
2. What attitudes (both physical and intellectual) does the speaker in Selzer's essay share with the speaker in Lewis Thomas's "On Societies as Organisms" (Chapter 7)?

Discussion and Writing Topics

1. Write a description of a person in a place or situation that is characteristic of him or her. Use dialogue to support your description.
2. Describe the "kickshaws" of any sickroom or rooms with which you have been acquainted. Try to suggest the emotions that those objects represent or fail to represent.
3. Define and describe the role of the physician, as you see it, after his or her patient is beyond the help of medicine.

Virginia Woolf

The Death of the Moth

Virginia Woolf (1882–1941), the distinguished novelist, was the
daughter of Leslie Stephen, a Victorian literary critic. She became the center of the "Bloomsbury Group" of writers and artists
that flourished in London from about 1907 to 1930. Terrified by
the return of her recurring mental depression, she drowned herself
in the river Ouse near her home at Rodmell, England. The
Voyage Out (1915), Mrs. Dalloway (1925), To the Lighthouse
(1927), Orlando (1928), and The Waves (1931) are among the
works with which she helped to alter the course of the English
novel. Today she is recognized as a psychological novelist especially gifted at exploring the minds of her female characters.
"The Death of the Moth" is the title essay of a collection published soon after her suicide; it describes "a tiny bead of pure
life."

Moths that fly by day are not properly to be called moths; 1
they do not excite that pleasant sense of dark autumn nights
and ivy-blossom which the commonest yellow underwing
asleep in the shadow of the curtain never fails to rouse in us.
They are hybrid creatures, neither gay like butterflies nor
sombre like their own species. Nevertheless the present specimen, with his narrow hay-coloured wings, fringed with a tassel
of the same colour, seemed to be content with life. It was a
pleasant morning, mid-September, mild, benignant, yet with
a keener breath than that of the summer months. The plough
was already scoring the field opposite the window, and where
the share had been, the earth was pressed flat and gleamed
with moisture. Such vigour came rolling in from the fields

and the down beyond that it was difficult to keep the eyes strictly
turned upon the book. The rooks too were keeping one of their
annual festivities; soaring round the tree-tops until it looked as if
a vast net with thousands of black knots in it has been cast up into
the air; which, after a few moments sank slowly down upon the
trees until every twig seemed to have a knot at the end of it. Then,
suddenly, the net would be thrown into the air again in a wider
circle this time, with the utmost clamour and vociferation, as
though to be thrown into the air and settle slowly down upon the
tree-tops were a tremendously exciting experience.

The same energy which inspired the rooks, the ploughmen, the   2
horses, and even, it seemed, the lean bare-backed downs, sent the
moth fluttering from side to side of his square of the window-pane.
One could not help watching him. One was, indeed, conscious of
a queer feeling of pity for him. The possibilities of pleasure seemed
that morning so enormous and so various that to have only a
moth's part in life, and a day moth's at that, appeared a hard fate,
and his zest in enjoying his meagre opportunities to the full,
pathetic. He flew vigorously to one corner of his compartment,
and, after waiting there a second, flew across to the other. What
remained for him but to fly to a third corner and then to a fourth?
That was all he could do, in spite of the size of the downs, the
width of the sky, the far-off smoke of houses, and the romantic
voice, now and then, of a steamer out at sea. What he could do he
did. Watching him, it seemed as if a fiber, very thin but pure, of
the enormous energy of the world had been thrust into his frail
and diminutive body. As often as he crossed the pane, I could
fancy that a thread of vital light became visible. He was little or
nothing but life.

Yet, because he was so small, and so simple a form of the energy   3
that was rolling in at the open window and driving its way through
so many narrow and intricate corridors in my own brain and in
those of other human beings, there was something marvelous as
well as pathetic about him. It was as if someone had taken a tiny
bead of pure life and decking it as lightly as possible with down
and feathers, had set it dancing and zigzagging to show us the true
nature of life. Thus displayed one could not get over the strangeness of it. One is apt to forget all about life, seeing it humped
and bossed and garnished and cumbered so that it has to move
with the greatest circumspection and dignity. Again, the thought

of all that life might have been had he been born in any other shape caused one to view his simple activities with a kind of pity.

After a time, tired by his dancing apparently, he settled on the window ledge in the sun, and the queer spectacle being at an end, I forgot about him. Then, looking up, my eye was caught by him. He was trying to resume his dancing, but seemed either so stiff or so awkward that he could only flutter to the bottom of the window-pane; and when he tried to fly across it he failed. Being intent on other matters I watched these futile attempts for a time without thinking, unconsciously waiting for him to resume his flight, as one waits for a machine, that has stopped momentarily, to start again without considering the reason for its failure. After perhaps a seventh attempt he slipped from the wooden ledge and fell, fluttering his wings, on to his back on the window-sill. The helplessness of his attitude roused me. It flashed upon me that he was in difficulties; he could no longer raise himself; his legs struggled vainly. But, as I stretched out a pencil, meaning to help him to right himself, it came over me that the failure and awkwardness were the approach of death. I laid the pencil down again.

The legs agitated themselves once more. I looked as if for the enemy against which he struggled. I looked out of doors. What had happened there? Presumably it was midday, and work in the fields had stopped. Stillness and quiet had replaced the previous animation. The birds had taken themselves off to feed in the brooks. The horses stood still. Yet the power was there all the same, massed outside indifferent, impersonal, not attending to anything in particular. Somehow it was opposed to the little hay-coloured moth. It was useless to try to do anything. One could only watch the extraordinary efforts made by those tiny legs against an oncoming doom which could, had it chosen, have submerged an entire city, not merely a city, but masses of human beings; nothing, I knew, had any chance against death. Nevertheless after a pause of exhaustion the legs fluttered again. It was superb this last protest, and so frantic that he succeeded at last in righting himself. One's sympathies, of course, were all on the side of life. Also, when there was nobody to care or to know, this gigantic effort on the part of an insignificant little moth, against a power of such magnitude, to retain what no one else valued or desired to keep, moved one strangely. Again, somehow, one saw life, a pure bead. I lifted the pencil again, useless though I knew it to be. But even as I did so, the unmistakable tokens of death showed themselves. The body relaxed, and instantly grew stiff. The struggle was over. The insignificant little creature now knew death. As I looked at the dead moth, this minute wayside triumph of so great a force over so mean an antagonist filled me with wonder. Just as life had been strange a few minutes before, so death was now as strange. The moth having righted himself now lay most decently and uncomplainingly composed. O yes, he seemed to say, death is stronger than I am.

QUESTIONS

Understanding

1. The author of this essay is describing much more than just an insect. What is the true object of her studied observation? What name does she give it in paragraph 3?
2. What does Woolf's tiny moth have in common with the rooks, ploughmen, horses, and fields? Why does the moth's dance seem "strange" (par. 3) to Woolf?
3. If "the true nature of life" (par. 3) is animation, or mere movement, what is the essence of death as Woolf describes it?
4. What role is the speaker in Woolf's essay vainly assuming when she starts to interpose a pencil between the moth and death? Why does she tell us so little about who or what set the moth dancing in the first place?

Strategies and Structure

1. Woolf's essay opens with a DESCRIPTION of moths in general. In which sentence does she begin to describe a particular moth? Through what specific details?
2. How does Woolf use the window to help organize her description?
3. Paragraphs 1 and 3 picture the same scene outside Woolf's window. How has the picture altered in the second version? How does she convey the change?

4. What is the observer in this essay doing when she is not watching the moth or looking out the window?

5. Approximately how much time elapses during the course of this essay? How does Woolf indicate the passage of time?

6. What time of year is Woolf describing here? How does she give us a sense of the season?

7. At first, the speaker in this essay feels pity for the limitations of the moth's life. When the moth struggles against death at the end, how has her attitude changed?

8. Woolf does not use the first PERSON until she says (almost half-way through her essay), "I could fancy that a thread of vital light became visible" (par. 2). What effect does she achieve with such phrases as "in us," "the eyes," "one was," and "one could" (pars. 1 and 2)?

Words and Figures of Speech

1. Paragraph 3 describes the moth's "down and feathers." Why does Woolf choose to "deck" her specimen in the lightest of garments? What property or quality is expressed by "humped," "bossed," "garnished," and "cumbered" (also in par. 3)?

2. Which of the following possible definitions of *vigor* (par. 1) best fits the content of Woolf's essay: 1) physical or mental strength; 2) healthy growth; 3) intensity or force; 4) validity? Explain your choice.

3. Why does Woolf use the METAPHOR of the dance to describe the moth's frantic movements? How does the moth's dance resemble the flight of the rooks?

Comparing

1. Which essay—Woolf's or Annie Dillard's in the preceding chapter—do you find more effective as a description of a physical phenomenon? Explain your preference.

2. Woolf equates the moth's life with movement; to what does Dillard compare the "moth-essence" in "Transfiguration"? Which of the two essays seems more "religious"? Why?

Discussion and Writing Topics

1. Describe a pond, a dance, a journey, or a mountain as an emblem of life or one of life's phases.
2. Have you ever been tempted to interfere with a natural process or to save some animal from a natural enemy? Describe what you did and how you felt.

Describe one of the following:

1. The oldest person you know

2. Your dream house

3. The place you associate most closely with family vacations

4. A ghost town or dying neighborhood you have visited

5. A shipyard, dock, or harbor you have seen

6. The worst storm you can remember and its aftermath

7. A room in a hospital or rest home

8. An old-fashioned general store, hardware store, or drugstore

9. A carnival or fair

10. A building, street, or town that has given you a glimpse of foreign culture

11. A statue that seems out of place to you

12. A tropical garden

13. The waiting room of a bus or train station

14. The main reading room of a public library

15. An expensive sporting goods store

16. A factory or plant you have worked in or visited

17. A well-run farm

18. A junkyard

Persuasion and
Argumentation

9

Essays That Appeal to Reason

PERSUASION [1] is the strategic use of language to move an audience to action or belief. In persuasive writing, readers can be moved in three ways: (1) by appealing to their reason; (2) by appealing to their emotions; and (3) by appealing to their sense of ethics (their standards of what constitutes proper behavior). The first of these, often called ARGUMENTATION, is discussed in this chapter; the other two will be taken up in Chapter 10.

Argumentation, as the term is used here, refers both to logical thinking and to the expression of that thought in such a way as to convince others to accept it. Argumentation, in other words, analyzes a subject or problem in order to induce belief. It may or may not go on to urge a course of action. In "Capital Punishment," for example, you will find William F. Buckley, Jr., laying out the case for the death penalty "without wholeheartedly endorsing it." Buckley wants to convince us that there are valid reasons for the death penalty, but he is also aware of good arguments on the other side. So he analyzes the issues; he takes a position; but he does not tell us to get out and write our congressman. Like most persuasive arguments, however, Buckley's at least implies a course of action.

Whether they induce action or belief or both, persuasive arguments appeal through logic to our capacity to reason. There are two basic kinds of logical reasoning: INDUCTION and DEDUCTION. When we deduce something, we reason from general premises to particular conclusions. When we

[1] Terms printed in all capitals are defined in the Glossary.

reason by induction, we proceed the other way—from particulars to generalities.

In Edgar Allan Poe's "The Murders in the Rue Morgue," master detective Auguste Dupin is investigating two brutal killings. One victim has been jammed up a chimney further than the strength of a normal man could have shoved her; the other lies in the courtyard below. Dupin notices a lightning-rod extending from the courtyard past the victims' window, but it is too far for an escaping man to negotiate. Putting these and other particulars together, Dupin reasons inductively that the murderer is not a man but a giant ape. Yet how did the animal escape?—the two windows of the apartment are nailed shut and the doors are locked from the inside. Reasoning deductively now, Dupin begins with the premise that a "material" killer—not the supernatural agent the authorities half-suspect—must have "escaped materially." Thus the closed windows must have the power of closing themselves: Dupin examines one window and finds a hidden spring; but the nail fastening the window is still intact. Therefore, Dupin reasons, the ape "must have escaped through the other window" and "there must be found a difference between the nails." Dupin examines the nail in the second window and, sure enough, it is broken; outside, moveover, hangs a shutter on which the animal could have swung to the lightning-rod. Dupin advertises for the owner of a missing orangutang, and that very night, a sailor appears at his door.

Inductive reasoning, then, depends upon examples—like the minute clues that lead Poe's Dupin to suspect an orangutang—and in many cases the validity of an inductive argument increases as the sheer number of examples increases. We are more likely to believe that UFOs exist if they have been sighted by ten thousand witnesses than by one thousand. In a short essay we seldom have room for more than a few examples, however. (You will be surprised how often they are reduced to the "magic" number three.) So we must select the most telling and representative ones.

Deductive reasoning depends upon the "syllogism." Here is Aristotle's famous example of this basic pattern of logical thinking:

Major premise: All men are mortal.
Minor premise: Socrates is a man.
Conclusion: Therefore, Socrates is mortal.

If we grant Aristotle's major assumption that all men must die and his minor (or narrower) assumption that Socrates is a man, the conclusion follows inevitably that Socrates must die. (Since Socrates had died about fifteen years before Aristotle was born, Aristotle was reasonably confident that his example would not be seriously challenged.)

When a conclusion follows from the premises or (in inductive reasoning) from the examples, we say that the argument is "valid." An invalid argument is one that jumps to conclusions: the conclusion does not follow logically from the premises or examples. Inductive arguments (from particulars to generalizations) are often invalid because they use too few examples, because the examples are not representative, or because the examples depend upon faulty authorities or faulty comparisons of the sort the Duchess makes in Lewis Carroll's Alice in Wonderland. In your own reasoning, strive to think like Alice:

> "Very true," said the Duchess: "flamingoes and mustard both bite. And the moral of that is—'Birds of a feather flock together.'"
>
> "Only mustard isn't a bird," Alice remarked.
>
> "Right, as usual," said the Duchess: "what a clear way you have of putting things!"

A deductive argument may be valid without being true, of course. Consider this valid argument by satirist Ambrose Bierce:

> Major Premise: Sixty men can do a piece of work sixty times as quickly as one man.
> Minor Premise: One man can dig a posthole in sixty seconds; therefore—
> Conclusion: Sixty men can dig a posthole in one second.

As Bierce was aware, this argument is valid but untrue. It would get too crowded around that posthole for efficiency. The trouble here, and with all deductive arguments that are valid but untrue, is a faulty premise. Sixty men cannot do work sixty times as fast as one if they have no place to stand. We can see why Bierce's Devil's Dictionary defines the syllogism as a "logical formula consisting of a major and a minor assumption and an inconsequent." The syllogism provides a manner for thinking logically; but as Bierce's irony would warn us, it does not provide the matter of logical thought. We have to supply that ourselves.

In real-life persuasive arguments, we seldom use the formal syllogism. We are much more likely to assert, "If one man can dig a posthole in sixty seconds, sixty men can do it in one." Or: "You know he is an atheist because he doesn't go to church." We can meet such faulty arguments more effectively if we realize that they are abbreviated syllogisms with one premise left unsaid. Stated as a formal syllogism, our second example would look like this:

> *Major premise:* All people who do not go to church are atheists.
> *Minor premise:* He does not go to church.
> *Conclusion:* Therefore, he is an atheist.

The implied premise here is the major premise: "All people who do not go to church are atheists." Usually the implied premise is the weak spot in your opponent's argument. If you can challenge it, your own position has won an excellent foothold.

Most extended debates in real life arise because the parties disagree over the truth or untruth of one or more primary assumptions. "The U.S. should stay out of South American affairs." "Inflation will drop sharply next year." "All women should work." Propositions like these cannot be assumed; they must be debated. But in your own persuasive writing, be sure of your logic first. If it can be shown that your conclusions do not follow from your premises, the debate will be over before the crucial issue of truth can be raised.

In a short essay, you should not depend rigidly upon logical forms, and you cannot hope to prove anything worth proving to an absolute certainty. But an argumentative essay does not have to prove, remember. It has only to convince. Be as convincing as you reasonably can by appealing to your audience's reason.

Thomas Jefferson

The Declaration of Independence

The third American president, Thomas Jefferson (1743–1826) was born in Virginia, attended William and Mary College, and practiced law for several years. He entered local politics in 1769, was elected to the Continental Congress, and drafted the Declaration of Independence in 1776. After serving as Virginia's governor during the revolution, he became American minister to France and later Washington's secretary of state. His conflict with Alexander Hamilton contributed to the formation of separate political parties in America. Jefferson became vice-president of the United States in 1796 and president in 1801. During the first (and more successful) of his two terms, he engineered the Louisiana Purchase. Retiring to his estate, Monticello, in 1809, he died there on the fifteenth anniversary of American independence, July 4, 1826. Jefferson preferred the role of the philosopher to that of the politician, and the Declaration of Independence, which announced the thirteen colonies' break with England, was as much an essay on human rights as a political document. It is based upon the natural-rights theory of government, derived from eighteenth-century rationalism. The Declaration, written by Jefferson, was revised by Benjamin Franklin, John Adams, and the Continental Congress at large. The fifty-six colonial representatives signed it on August 2, 1776.

When in the course of human events, it becomes necessary ¹ for one people to dissolve the political bands which have connected them with another, and to assume among the Powers of the earth, the separate and equal station to which the Laws of Nature and of Nature's God entitle them, a decent respect to the opinions of mankind requires that they should declare the causes which impel them to the separation.

We hold these truths to be self-evident, that all men are created 2 equal, that they are endowed by their Creator with certain unalienable Rights, that among these are Life, Liberty and the pursuit of Happiness. That to secure these rights, Governments are instituted among Men, deriving their just powers from the consent of the governed. That whenever any Form of Government becomes destructive of these ends, it is the Right of the People to alter or to abolish it, and to institute new Government, laying its foundation on such principles and organizing its powers in such form, as to them shall seem most likely to effect their Safety and Happiness. Prudence, indeed, will dictate that Governments long established should not be changed for light and transient causes; and accordingly all experience hath shown, that mankind are more disposed to suffer, while evils are sufferable, than to right themselves by abolishing the forms to which they are accustomed. But when a long train of abuses and usurpations pursuing invariably the same Object evinces a design to reduce them under absolute Despotism, it is their right, it is their duty, to throw off such government, and to provide new Guards for their future security. Such has been the patient sufferance of these Colonies; and such is now the necessity which constrains them to alter their former Systems of Government. The history of the present King of Great Britain [1] is a history of repeated injuries and usurpations, all having in direct object the establishment of absolute Tyranny over these States. To prove this, let Facts be submitted to a candid world.

He has refused his Assent to Laws, the most wholesome and 3 necessary for the public good.

He has forbidden his Governors to pass Laws of immediate and 4 pressing importance, unless suspended in their operation till his Assent should be obtained; and when so suspended, he has utterly neglected to attend to them.

He has refused to pass other Laws for the accommodation of 5 large districts of people, unless those people would relinquish the right of Representation in the Legislature, a right inestimable to them and formidable to tyrants only.

---

[1] George III (ruled 1761–1820).

He has called together legislative bodies at places unusual, uncomfortable, and distant from the depository of their Public Records, for the sole purpose of fatiguing them into compliance with his measures. [6]

He has dissolved Representative Houses repeatedly, for opposing with manly firmness his invasions on the rights of the people. [7]

He has refused for a long time, after such dissolutions, to cause others to be elected; whereby the Legislative Powers, incapable of Annihilation, have returned to the People at large for their exercise; the State remaining in the mean time exposed to all the dangers of invasion from without, and convulsions within. [8]

He has endeavoured to prevent the population of these States; for that purpose obstructing the Laws of Naturalization of Foreigners; refusing to pass others to encourage their migration hither, and raising the conditions of new Appropriations of Lands. [9]

He has obstructed the Administration of Justice, by refusing his Assent to Laws for establishing Judiciary Powers. [10]

He has made Judges dependent on his Will alone, for the tenure of their offices, and the amount and payment of their salaries. [11]

He has erected a multitude of New Offices, and sent hither swarms of Officers to harass our People, and eat out their substance. [12]

He has kept among us, in time of peace, Standing Armies without the Consent of our Legislature. [13]

He has affected to render the Military independent of and superior to the Civil Power. [14]

He has combined with others to subject us to jurisdictions foreign to our constitution, and unacknowledged by our laws; giving us Assent to their acts of pretended Legislation: [15]

For quartering large bodies of armed troops among us: [16]

For protecting them, by a mock Trial, from Punishment for any Murders which they should commit on the Inhabitants of these States: [17]

For cutting off our Trade with all parts of the world: [18]

For imposing Taxes on us without our Consent: [19]

For depriving us in many cases, of the benefits of Trial by Jury: [20]

For transporting us beyond Seas to be tried for pretended offenses: [21]

For abolishing the free System of English Laws in a Neighbouring Province, establishing therein an Arbitrary government, and enlarging its boundaries so as to render it at once an example and [22] fit instrument for introducing the same absolute rule into these Colonies:

For taking away our Charters, abolishing our most valuable Laws, and altering fundamentally the Forms of our Governments: [23]

For suspending our own Legislatures, and declaring themselves invested with Power to legislate for us in all cases whatsoever. [24]

He has abdicated Government here, by declaring us out of his Protection and waging War against us. [25]

He has plundered our seas, ravaged our Coasts, burnt our towns and destroyed the Lives of our people. [26]

He is at this time transporting large Armies of foreign Mercenaries to complete the works of death, desolation and tyranny, already begun with circumstances of Cruelty & perfidy scarcely paralleled in the most barbarous ages, and totally unworthy the Head of a civilized nation. [27]

He has constrained our fellow Citizens taken Captive on the high Seas to bear Arms against their Colony, to become the executioners of their friends and Brethren, or to fall themselves by their Hands. [28]

He has excited domestic insurrections amongst us, and has endeavoured to bring on the inhabitants of our frontiers, the merciless Indian Savages, whose known rule of warfare, is an undistinguished destruction of all ages, sexes and conditions. [29]

In every stage of these Oppressions We have Petitioned for Redress in the most humble terms: Our repeated petitions have been answered only by repeated injury. A Prince, whose character is thus marked by every act which may define a Tyrant, is unfit to be the ruler of a free People. [30]

Nor have We been wanting in attention to our British brethren. We have warned them from time to time of attempts by their legislature to extend an unwarrantable jurisdiction over us. We have reminded them of the circumstances of our emigration and settlement here. We have appealed to their native justice and magnanimity and we have conjured them by the ties of our common kindred to disavow these usurpations, which would inevitably interrupt our connections and correspondence. They too have been deaf to the voice of justice and of consanguinity. We must, therefore acquiesce in the necessity, which denounces our Separation, and hold them, as we hold the rest of mankind, Enemies in War, in Peace Friends. [31]

We, therefore, the Representatives of the United States of 32
America, in General Congress, Assembled, appealing to the Supreme Judge of the world for the rectitude of our intentions, do,
in the Name, and by Authority of the good People of these Colonies, solemnly publish and declare, That these United Colonies
are, and of Right ought to be Free and Independent States; that
they are Absolved from all Allegiance to the British Crown, and
that all political connection between them and the State of Great
Britain, is and ought to be totally dissolved; and that as Free and
Independent States, they have full power to levy War, conclude
Peace, contract Alliances, establish Commerce, and to do all other
Acts and Things which Independent States may of right do. And
for the support of this Declaration, with a firm reliance on the
protection of Divine Providence, we mutually pledge to each other
our lives, our Fortunes and our sacred Honor.

QUESTIONS

Understanding

1. What is the purpose of government, according to Thomas
   Jefferson?
2. Where, in Jefferson's view, does a ruler get his authority?
3. "We hold these truths to be self-evident . . ." (par. 2). Another
   name for a self-evident "truth" granted at the beginning of an
   ARGUMENT is a *premise*. Briefly summarize the initial premises on
   which Jefferson's entire argument is built.
4. Which of Jefferson's premises is most crucial to his logic?
5. What is the ultimate conclusion of Jefferson's argument? Where
   is it stated?
6. Which of the many "injuries and usurpations" (par. 2) attributed
   by Jefferson to the British king seem most intolerable to you?
   Why?

Strategies and Structure

1. Jefferson gives the impression that the colonies are breaking away
   with extreme reluctance and only because of forces beyond any

colonist's personal power to overlook them. How does he create this impression?

2. What is the function of paragraph 31, which seems to be a digression from Jefferson's main line of argument?

3. A *hypothesis* is a theory or supposition to be tested by further proof. What is the hypothesis, introduced in paragraph 2, that Jefferson's long list of "Facts" is adduced to test?

4. Where is Jefferson's hypothesis restated (indirectly) as an established conclusion? Is the process of arriving at this conclusion basically INDUCTION (from examples to generalizations) or DEDUCTION (from premises to particular conclusions)?

5. Jefferson's conclusion to this line of argument might be restated simply as, "King George is a tyrant." We can take this conclusion as the *minor premise* of the underlying argument of the entire Declaration. If the *major premise* is "Tyrannical governments may be abolished by the People," what is the *conclusion* of that underlying argument?

6. Which sentence in paragraph 2 states Jefferson's major premise in so many words?

7. Is this underlying argument of the Declaration basically inductive or deductive? Explain your answer.

8. The signers of the Declaration of Independence wanted to appear as men of right reason, and they approved the logical form that Jefferson gave that document. Many of the specific issues their reason addressed, however, were highly emotional. What traces of strong feelings can you detect in Jefferson's wording of individual charges against the king?

9. The eighteenth-century is said to have admired and imitated "classical" balance and symmetry (as in the facade of Jefferson's Monticello). Does the form of the Declaration confirm or deny this observation? Explain your answer.

Words and Figures of Speech

1. Look up *unalienable* (or *inalienable*) in your dictionary. Considering that the Declaration was addressed, in part, to a "foreign" tyrant, why might Jefferson have chosen this adjective (par. 2) instead of, say, *natural, God-given,* or *fundamental*?

2. A *proposition* is a premise that is waiting to be approved. What single word signals us each time that Jefferson introduces a new proposition in his argument?

3. What is *consanguinity* (par. 31)? How may it be said to have a "voice"?

4. Look up *metonymy* under FIGURES OF SPEECH in the Glossary. What example of this figure can you find in paragraph 32?

5. For any of the following words you are not quite sure of, consult your dictionary: *transient* (par. 2), *usurpations* (2), *evinces* (2), *despotism* (2), *constrains* (2), *candid* (2), *abdicated* (25), *perfidy* (27), *redress* (30), *magnanimity* (31), *conjured* (31), *acquiesce* (31), *rectitude* (32).

Comparing

1. Like the Declaration of Independence, Chief Seattle's "Reply" (Chapter 10) is addressed to a "superior" head of state. Unlike Jefferson's, however, Chief Seattle's nation was toppling instead of rising. How does this difference in circumstances change the way the two speakers address their adversaries?

Discussion and Writing Topics

1. Compose a reply to Jefferson's charges by King George in defense of his actions and policies toward the colonies.

2. Jefferson lists "the pursuit of Happiness" (par. 2) as one of our basic rights. Construct an argument urging that this promise was unwise, that happiness cannot be guaranteed, and, therefore, that Americans have been set up for inevitable disappointment by the founding fathers. Your argument will have to anticipate the objection that the Declaration protects the *pursuit* of happiness, not happiness itself.

3. Some "loyalists" remained true to England at the time of the American Revolution. How might they have justified their "patriotism"?

William F. Buckley, Jr.
Capital Punishment

William F. Buckley, Jr., is a columnist, debater, conservative
politician, novelist, and sailor. One of ten children of a father
with oil interests in seven countries, he was born in New York
City in 1925 and lived in England and France for a time. He
studied at the University of Mexico and Yale (B.A., 1950). The
founder of the National Review in 1955, Buckley ran as Conservative party candidate for mayor of New York City in 1965, and
began the weekly television show, Firing Line, in 1966. He writes
three syndicated newspaper columns a week and contributes to,
among others, Esquire, Saturday Review, Harper's, Motor Boat-
ing, and Atlantic. His books include God and Man at Yale
(1951); Up from Liberalism (1959); The Unmaking of a Mayor
(1966); The United Nations Journal (1975); Saving the Queen
(1976); Stained Glass (1978); and Who's on First (1980). "Capital
Punishment" is one essay in the collection Execution Eve, and
Other Contemporary Ballads (1975).

There is national suspense over whether capital punishment   1
is about to be abolished, and the assumption is that when it
comes it will come from the Supreme Court. Meanwhile, (a)
the prestigious State Supreme Court of California has interrupted executions, giving constitutional reasons for doing so;
(b) the death wings are overflowing with convicted prisoners;
(c) executions are a remote memory; and—for the first time
in years—(d) the opinion polls show that there is sentiment
for what amounts to the restoration of capital punishment.

The case for abolition is popularly known. The other case   2
less so, and (without wholeheartedly endorsing it) I give it as

it was given recently to the Committee of the Judiciary of the House of Representatives by Professor Ernest van den Haag, under whose thinking cap groweth no moss. Mr. van den Haag, a professor of social philosophy at New York University, ambushed the most popular arguments of the abolitionists, taking no prisoners.

(1) The business about the poor and the black suffering excessively from capital punishment is no argument against capital punishment. It is an argument against the *administration* of justice, not against the penalty. Any punishment can be unfairly or unjustly applied. Go ahead and reform the processes by which capital punishment is inflicted, if you wish; but don't confuse maladministration with the merits of capital punishment.   3

(2) The argument that the death penalty is "unusual" is circular.[1] Capital punishment continues on the books of a majority of states, the people continue to sanction the concept of capital punishment, and indeed capital sentences are routinely handed down. What has made capital punishment "unusual" is that the courts and, primarily, governors have intervened in the process so as to collaborate in the frustration of the execution of the law. To argue that capital punishment is unusual, when in fact it has been made unusual by extra-legislative authority, is an argument to expedite, not eliminate, executions.   4

(3) Capital punishment is cruel. That is a historical judgment. But the Constitution suggests that what must be proscribed as cruel is (a) a particularly painful way of inflicting death, or (b) a particularly undeserved death; and the death penalty, as such, offends neither of these criteria and cannot therefore be regarded as objectively "cruel."   5

Viewed the other way, the question is whether capital punishment can be regarded as useful, and the question of deterrence arises.   6

(4) Those who believe that the death penalty does not intensify the disinclination to commit certain crimes need to wrestle with statistics that, in fact, it can't be proved that *any* punishment does that to any particular crime. One would rationally suppose that two years in jail would cut the commission of a crime if not exactly by 100 percent more than a penalty of one year in jail, at least that   7

---

[1] The Eighth Amendment to the U.S. Constitution (part of the Bill of Rights) forbids "cruel and unusual" punishment.

it would further discourage crime to a certain extent. The proof is unavailing. On the other hand, the statistics, although ambiguous, do not show either (a) that capital punishment net discourages; or (b) that capital punishment fails net to discourage. "The absence of proof for the additional deterrent effect of the death penalty must not be confused with the presence of proof for the absence of this effect."

The argument that most capital crimes are crimes of passion   8
committed by irrational persons is no argument against the death penalty, because it does not reveal how many crimes might, but for the death penalty, have been committed by rational persons who are now deterred.

And the clincher. (5) Since we do not know for certain whether   9
or not the death penalty adds deterrence, we have in effect the choice of two risks.

Risk One: If we execute convicted murderers without thereby   10
deterring prospective murderers beyond the deterrence that could have been achieved by life imprisonment, we may have vainly sacrificed the life of the convicted murderer.

Risk Two: If we fail to execute a convicted murderer whose   11
execution might have deterred an indefinite number of prospective murderers, our failure sacrifices an indefinite number of victims of future murderers.

"If we had certainty, we would not have risks. We do not have   12
certainty. If we have risks—and we do—better to risk the life of the convicted man than risk the life of an indefinite number of innocent victims who might survive if he were executed."

QUESTIONS

Understanding

1. If you have trouble keeping Buckley's ARGUMENT straight, make a list that states each proposition as briefly and simply as possible. How many items will be on your list?

2. What is the conclusion that Buckley's (and van den Haag's) entire argument is intended to prove?

author of the essay. Why might Buckley want to end with another writer's words (and conclusion)?

8. Buckley's argument is really a counterargument that proceeds by addressing propositions already raised by others. Is this a legitimate tactic of debate? Explain your answer.

9. The great eighteenth-century man of reason, Samuel Johnson, once observed: "It is always easy to be on the negative. If a man were now to deny that there is salt upon the table you could not reduce him to an absurdity." How might Dr. Johnson's observation about negative reasoning be applied to Buckley's argument concerning deterrence?

10. How might Buckley turn Dr. Johnson's observation back on those who argue that the statistics do not prove the deterrent value of capital punishment?

11. In that part of paragraph 7 where he deals with statistics, is Buckley's method of reasoning basically INDUCTIVE (from particulars to generalizations) or DEDUCTIVE (from premises to conclusions)? In paragraphs 9–12?

Words and Figures of Speech

1. Professor van den Haag, Buckley tells us, "ambushed the most popular arguments of the abolitionists, taking no prisoners." How does this METAPHOR, particularly the word *ambushed*, reflect Buckley's mixed feelings toward what he is reporting?

2. When he says that no moss "groweth" under van den Haag's thinking cap, Buckley is purposely concocting an absurdity. Why might he want to do so, especially this early in his essay?

3. The phrase "does not intensify the disinclination" seems wordy and stilted. How might it be justified in its touchy context, nevertheless?

4. Describe the effect of Buckley's use of the word *indefinite* when he explains "Risk Two" (par. 11). How *low* might the number conceivably be?

Comparing

1. The bulk of Jefferson's reasoning in the Declaration of Independence is inductive; what about Buckley's? Does he reason most of the time by induction or deduction? Explain your answer.

3. What is the gist of Buckley's complicated reasoning in paragraph 7?

4. Paragraph 5 says it is a historical judgment to say that capital punishment is cruel. What does Buckley mean by a "historical" judgment? What alternate standard does he put forth?

5. Paragraph 5 of this essay can be restated as a syllogism with the following minor premise: "The death penalty is neither painful nor undeserved." What would be the conclusion of this syllogism? What would be the major premise?

6. When Buckley argues (par. 5) that only a "particularly undeserved death" is cruel, he assumes that some deaths are "deserved." What do you think of this unstated assumption?

7. Granted that Buckley's argument is *logical*, how might your reaction to his assumption about "deserved" deaths influence whether or not you grant the *truth* of Buckley's entire argument?

Strategies and Structure

1. What do Buckley's numbers in parentheses refer to? Do you find them an effective organizing device? Why or why not? How have we been prepared for them by paragraph 1?

2. Why do you think Buckley mentions public opinion polls in the first paragraph even though he does not refer to them again in the essay?

3. Buckley gives the case against abolishing the death penalty "without wholeheartedly endorsing it" (par. 2). Is this a legitimate strategy? Why or why not?

4. Buckley is making the case against abolition; where does he first address the case *for* it? What do you make of the *length* of his treatment?

5. In paragraph 4 Buckley writes that the argument condemning the death penalty as unusual is "circular." What is a circular argument? What is logically wrong with one?

6. Where does Buckley begin the part of his argument dealing with deterrence? How does his fifth proposition (in pars. 9–12) bear upon this argument?

7. This essay ends abruptly—with a quotation from Professor van den Haag's testimony instead of a summarizing statement by the

2. Buckley is often called a "conservative," and the term could be applied with equal justice to Johnson C. Montgomery's position in the next essay, "The Island of Plenty." Judging from these two essays, how would you define a "conservative"?

3. Buckley's primary weapon is logic. What does Jonathan Swift say about the limits of this method of thinking in "A Modest Proposal" ("Essays For Further Reading")?

Discussion and Writing Topics

1. From Buckley's counterarguments, reconstruct the positive case for, and argue in favor of, abolishing capital punishment.

2. Make up your own positive argument *against* abolishing the death penalty.

3. Should the U.S. Constitution and other laws ultimately determine what is a "deserved" death and a "cruel" punishment, or are such questions beyond the scope of the law? Give your opinion in the form of a coherent logical argument.

4. What is the difference between a social philosopher and a sociologist?

5. The field of the social philosopher (as of all philosophers) is one of the "humanities." Do you find it at all strange that a philosopher should argue in favor of capital punishment? How could van den Haag's argument be interpreted, in the long run, as a "humanistic" argument?

Johnson C. Montgomery
The Island of Plenty

Johnson C. Montgomery was a California attorney and an early member of the Zero Population Growth organization. Born in 1934, Montgomery attended Harvard University and the Stanford University Law School; he was admitted to the California bar in 1960. "The Island of Plenty," in his own words, is an "elitist" argument in favor of American social isolationism. Until we have enough food to feed ourselves, he says, we owe it to future generations not to share our material resources with other countries of the world.

The United States should remain an island of plenty in a sea   1
of hunger. The future of mankind is at stake. We are not responsible for the rest of humanity. We should not accept responsibility for all humanity. We owe more to the hundreds of billions of *Homo futurans* than we do to the hungry millions—soon to be billions—of our own generation.

Ample food and resources exist to nourish man and all   2
other creatures indefinitely into the future. This planet is indeed an Eden—to date our only Eden. Admittedly our Eden is plagued by pollution. Some of us have polluted the planet by reproducing too many of us. Too many people have made excessive demands on the long-range carrying capacity of our garden; and during the last 200 years there has been dramatic, ever-increasing destruction of the web of life on earth. If we try to save the starving millions today, we will simply destroy what's left of Eden.

The problem is not that there is too little food. The problem is there are too many people—many too many. It is not that the children should never have been born. It is simply that we have mindlessly tried to cram too many of us into too short a time span. Four billion humans are fine—but they should have been spread over several hundred years.

But the billions are already here. What should we do about them? Should we send food, knowing that each child saved in Southeast Asia, India or Africa will probably live to reproduce and thereby bring more people into the world to live even more miserably? Should we eat the last tuna fish, the last ear of corn and utterly destroy the garden? That is what we have been doing for a long time and all the misguided efforts have merely increased the number who go to bed hungry each night. There have never been more miserable, deprived people in the world than there are right now.

It was obvious even in the late 1950s that the famine the world now faces was coming unless people immediately began exercising responsibility for reducing population levels. It was also obvious that too many people contributed to the risk of nuclear war, global pestilence, illiteracy and even to many problems that are usually classified as purely economic. For example, unemployment is having too many people for the available jobs. Inflation is in part the result of too much demand from too many people. But in the 1950s, population control was taboo and those who warned of impending disasters received a cool reception.

By the time Zero Population Growth, Inc., was formed, those of us who wanted to do something useful decided to concentrate our initial efforts on our own families and friends and then on the white American middle and upper classes. Our belief was that by setting an example, we could later insist that others pay attention to our proposals.

I think I was the first in the original ZPG group to have had a vasectomy. Nancy and I had two children—each doing superbly well and each getting all the advantages of the best nutrition, education, attention, love and other resources available. I think Paul Ehrlich [1] (one child) was the next. Now don't ask me to

---

[1] Biology professor at Stanford, founder and past-president of Zero Population Growth.

cut my children back to the same number of calories that children from large families eat. In fact, don't ask me to cut my children back on anything. I won't do it without a fight; and in today's world, power is in knowledge, not numbers. Nancy and I made a conscious decision to limit the number of our children so each child could have a larger share of whatever we could make available. We intend to keep the best for them.

The future of mankind is indeed with the children. But it is   8 with the nourished, educated and loved children. It is not with the starving, uneducated and ignored. This is of course a highly elitist point of view. But that doesn't make the view incorrect. As a matter of fact, the lowest reproductive rate in the nation is that of one of the most elite groups in the world—black, female Ph.D.'s. They had to be smart and effective to make it. Having made it, they are smart enough not to wreck it with too many kids.

We in the United States have made great progress in lowering   9 our birth rates. But now, because we have been responsible, it seems to some that we have a great surplus. There is, indeed, waste that should be eliminated, but there is not as much fat in our system as most people think. Yet we are being asked to share our resources with the hungry peoples of the world. But why should we share? The nations having the greatest needs are those that have been the least responsible in cutting down on births. Famine is one of nature's ways of telling profligate peoples that they have been irresponsible in their breeding habits.

Naturally, we would like to help; and if we could, perhaps we   10 should. But we can't be of any use in the long run—particularly if we weaken ourselves.

Until we have at least a couple of years' supply of food and   11 other resources on hand to take care of our own people and until those asking for handouts are doing at least as well as we are at reducing existing excessive population-growth rates, we should not give away our resources—not so much as one bushel of wheat. Certainly we should not participate in any programs that will increase the burden that mankind is already placing on the earth. We should not deplete our own soils to save those who will only die equally miserably a decade or so down the line—and in many cases only after reproducing more children who are inevitably doomed to live and die in misery.

We know the world is finite. There is only so much pie. We 12
may be able to expand the pie, but at any point in time, the pie
is finite. How big a piece each person gets depends in part on how
many people there are. At least for the foreseeable future, the
fewer of us there are, the more there will be for each. That is
true on a family, community, state, national and global basis.

At the moment, the future of mankind seems to depend on our 13
maintaining the island of plenty in a sea of deprivation. If everyone shared equally, we would all be suffering from protein-defi-
ciency brain damage—and that would probably be true even if we
ate every last animal on earth.

As compassionate human beings, we grieve for the condition of 14
mankind. But our grief must not interfere with our perception of
reality and our planning for a better future for those who will
come after us. Someone must protect the material and intellectual
seed grain for the future. It seems to me that that someone is the
U.S. We owe it to our children—and to their children's children's
children's children.

These conclusions will be attacked, as they have been within 15
Zero Population Growth, as simplistic and inhumane. But truth
is often very simple and reality often inhumane.

QUESTIONS

Understanding

1. What is Montgomery's main proposition in this essay? In which
   two paragraphs is it stated most directly?

2. What other general propositions does he put forth in support of
   his main proposition?

3. In paragraph 4, what is the last sentence (about the number of
   miserable people in the world) intended to prove?

4. Montgomery warns us not to "ask me to cut my children back on
   anything" (par. 7). How is this position consistent with what he
   says about the planet's not having enough to go around?

Strategies and Structure

1. The logic of Montgomery's basic ARGUMENT can be represented by a syllogism. *Major premise:* To provide undamaged human stock for the future, some people must remain healthy. *Minor premise:* All will suffer if all share equally in the world's limited bounty. *Conclusion:* Some must not share what they have. How sound is this logic? Will you grant Montgomery's premises? Why or why not?

2. Montgomery's hard-headed realism would show us the "truth" (par. 15) of the human condition; but it would also move us to action. What would Montgomery have us do?

3. Logic is only part of Montgomery's persuasive arsenal. Which paragraphs in his essay appeal more to emotion and ethics than to logic?

4. Montgomery seems to be speaking from authority. Where does he get his authority, and how much weight should it carry?

5. Montgomery admits that his position is "elitist" (par. 8). How does he head off the charge that it is racist?

6. Is Montgomery's last paragraph necessary? Why or why not?

7. Are you persuaded by Montgomery's essay? Why or why not?

Words and Figures of Speech

1. How does the METAPHOR of the island contribute to Montgomery's argument? Is there any IRONY in his title?

2. For the sake of the future, says Montgomery, we must save some "material and intellectual seed grain" (par. 14). Explain this metaphor: What is being compared to what? Why is the metaphor appropriate?

3. How is Montgomery altering the traditional definition of Eden? Is he rejecting the traditional idea altogether? Explain your answer.

4. *Homo futurans* (par. 1), meaning "man of the future," is modeled after such scientific terms as *Homo erectus* ("upright man") and *Homo sapiens* ("thinking man"). Why might Montgomery choose to use the language of science at the beginning of his argument?

5. How does Montgomery's use of the word *mindlessly* (par. 3) fit in with his entire argument?

6. What is the meaning of *profligate* (par. 9)?

Comparing

1. By comparison with William F. Buckley's "Capital Punishment," does "The Island of Plenty" seem more concerned with analyzing a condition or with persuading the reader to act? Explain.

2. Opponents of Montgomery's argument might charge that he has written "a modest proposal." What would they mean by this? Would they be justified? (See Jonathan Swift's "A Modest Proposal" in "Essays For Further Reading.")

Discussion and Writing Topics

1. Attack Montgomery's position on the grounds that he is confusing compassion with weakness.

2. Defend Montgomery's assertion that "there is not as much fat in our system as most people think" (par. 9).

3. Write your own "modest proposal" (for feeding the world, curing inflation, regulating human breeding habits, or some other "simple" task).

Richard M. Restak
The Other Difference between Boys and Girls

Born in Wilmington, Delaware, in 1942 and trained at hospitals
in New York City and Washington, D.C., Dr. Richard Restak is a
Washington neurologist. He is the author of Premeditated Man:
The Bioethics and Control of Future Human Life (1975) and The
Brain: The Last Frontier (1979). The most controversial of
Restak's conclusions from his studies in neurology is that the brains
of men and women function differently—the "other difference"
between the sexes proclaimed in the following essay from the
Washington Post. Restak argues for social and educational changes
based upon an open recognition that men and women do not think
alike. For a rebuttal attacking his argument on logical grounds, see
the next essay in this chapter, "The Sexes Are Not Born with
Different Brains," by Martha Mednick and Nancy Felipe Russo.
Giving his own brain a change of pace, Restak is presently at work
on a series of profiles of contemporary scientists. He also hopes
someday to write a biography of British novelist Somerset Maugham.

Boys think differently from girls. Recent research on brain   1
behavior makes that conclusion inescapable, and it is unrealistic to keep denying it.

I know how offensive that will sound to feminists and others   2
committed to overcoming sexual stereotypes. As the father of
three daughters, I am well aware of the discrimination girls
suffer. But social equality for men and women really depends
on recognizing these differences in brain behavior.

At present, schooling and testing discriminate against both   3
boys and girls in different ways, ignoring differences that have
been observed by parents and educators for years. Boys suffer
in elementary school classrooms, which are ideally suited to

the way girls think. Girls suffer later on, in crucial ways, taking scholarship tests that are geared for male performance.

Anyone who has spent time with children in a playground or school setting is aware of differences in the way boys and girls respond to similar situations. Think of the last time you supervised a birthday party attended by five-year-olds. It's not usually the girls who pull hair, throw punches or smear each other with food.

Usually such differences are explained on a cultural basis. Boys are expected to be more aggressive and play rough games, while girls are presumably encouraged to be gentle, nonassertive and passive. After several years of exposure to such expectations, the theory goes, men and women wind up with widely varying behavioral and intellectual repertoires. As a corollary to this, many people believe that if child-rearing practices could be equalized and sexual stereotypes eliminated, most of these differences would eventually disappear. As often happens, however, the true state of affairs is not that simple.

Undoubtedly, many of the differences traditionally believed to exist between the sexes are based on stereotypes. But despite this, evidence from recent brain research indicates that many behavioral differences between men and women are based on differences in brain functioning that are biologically inherent and unlikely to be modified by cultural factors alone.

The first clue to brain differences between the sexes came from observations of male and female infants. From birth, female infants are more sensitive to sounds, particularly to their mother's voice. In a laboratory, if the sound of the mother's voice is displaced to another part of the room, female babies will react while male babies usually seem oblivious to the displacement. Female babies are also more easily startled by loud noises. In fact, their enhanced hearing performance persists throughout life, with females experiencing a fall-off in hearing much later than males.

Tests involving girls old enough to cooperate show increased skin sensitivity, particularly in the fingertips, which have a lower threshold for touch identification. Females are also more proficient at fine motor performance. Rapid tapping movements are carried out quickly and more efficiently by girls than by boys.

In addition, there are differences in what attracts a girl's attention. Generally, females are more attentive to social contexts—

faces, speech patterns and subtle vocal cues. By four months of age, a female infant is socially aware enough to distinguish photographs of familiar people, a task rarely performed well by boys of that age. Also at four months, girls will babble to a mother's face, seemingly recognizing her as a person, while boys fail to distinguish between a face and a dangling toy, babbling equally to both.

Female infants also speak sooner, have larger vocabularies and   10
rarely demonstrate speech defects. Stuttering, for instance, occurs almost exclusively among boys.

Girls can also sing in tune at an earlier age. In fact, if we think   11
of the muscles of the throat as muscles of fine control—those in which girls excel—then it should come as no surprise that girls exceed boys in language abilities. This early linguistic bias often prevails throughout life. Girls read sooner, learn foreign languages more easily and, as a result, are more likely to enter occupations involving language mastery.

Boys, in contrast, show an early visual superiority. They are   12
also clumsier, performing poorly at something like arranging a row of beads, but excel at other activities calling on total body coordination. Their attentional mechanisms are also different. A boy will react to an inanimate object as quickly as he will to a person. A male baby will often ignore the mother and babble to a blinking light, fixate on a geometric figure and, at a later point, manipulate it and attempt to take it apart.

A study of nursery preschool children carried out by psycholo-   13
gist Diane McGuinness of Stanford University found boys more curious, especially in regard to exploring their environment. McGuinness' studies also confirmed that males are better at manipulating three-dimensional space. When boys and girls are asked to mentally rotate or fold an object, boys overwhelmingly outperform girls. "I folded it in my mind" is a typical male response. Girls, when explaining how they perform the same task, are likely to produce elaborate verbal descriptions which, because they are less appropriate to the task, result in frequent errors.

In an attempt to understand the sex differences in spatial ability,   14
electroencephalogram (EEG) measurements have recently been made of the accompanying electrical events going on within the brain.

Ordinarily, the two brain hemispheres produce a similar electri-   15 cal background that can be measured by an EEG. When a person is involved in a mental task—say, subtracting 73 from 102—the hemisphere that is activated will demonstrate a change in its electrical background. When boys are involved in tasks employing spatial concepts, such as figuring out mentally which of three folded shapes can be made from a flat, irregular piece of paper, the right hemisphere is activated consistently. Girls, in contrast, are more likely to activate both hemispheres, indicating that spatial ability is more widely dispersed in the female brain.

When it comes to psychological measurements of brain functioning between the sexes, unmistakable differences emerge. In 11 subtests of the most widely used test of general intelligence, only two subtests reveal similar mean scores for males and females. These sex differences have been substantiated across cultures and are so consistent that the standard battery of this intelligence test now contains a masculinity-femininity index. [16]

Further support for sex differences in brain functioning comes from experience with subtests that eventually had to be omitted from the original test battery. A cube-analysis test, for example, was excluded because, after testing thousands of subjects, a large sex bias appeared to favor males. In all, over 30 tests eventually had to be eliminated because they discriminated in favor of one or the other sex. One test, involving mentally working oneself through a maze, favored boys so overwhelmingly that, for a while, some psychologists speculated that girls were totally lacking in a "spatial factor." [17]

Most thought-provoking of all is a series of findings by Eleanor Maccoby and Carol Nagly Jacklin of Stanford on personality traits and intellectual achievement. They found that girls whose intellectual achievement is greatest tend to be unusually active, independent, competitive and free of fear or anxiety, while intellectually outstanding boys are often timid, anxious, not overtly aggressive and less active. [18]

In essence, Maccoby and Jacklin's findings suggest that intellectual performance is incompatible with our stereotype of femininity in girls or masculinity in boys. [19]

Research evidence within the last six months indicates that many of these brain sex differences persist over a person's lifetime. In a study at the University Hospital in Ontario that compared [20] verbal and spatial abilities of men and women after a stroke, the women did better than men in key categories tested. After the stroke, women tended to be less disabled and recovered more quickly.

Research at the National Institute of Mental Health is even un- [21] covering biochemical differences in the brains of men and women. Women's brains, it seems, are more sensitive to experimentally administered lights and sounds. The investigator in charge of this research, Dr. Monte Buchsbaum, speculates that the enhanced response of the female brain depends on the effect of sex hormones on the formation of a key brain chemical. This increased sensibility to stimuli by the female brain may explain why women more often than men respond to loss and stress by developing depression.

It's important to remember that we're not talking about one sex [22] being generally superior or inferior to another. Rather, psychobiological research is turning up important functional differences between male and female brains. The discoveries might possibly contribute to further resentments and divisions in our society. But must they? Why are sex differences in brain functioning disturbing to so many people? And why do women react so vehemently to findings that, if anything, indicate enhanced capabilities in the female brain?

It seems to me that we can make two responses to these findings [23] on brain-sex differences. First, we can use them to help bring about true social equity. One way of doing this might be to change such practices as nationwide competitive examinations. If boys, for instance, truly do excel in right-hemisphere tasks, then tests such as the National Merit Scholarship Examination should be radically redesigned to assure that both sexes have an equal chance. As things now stand, the tests are heavily weighted with items that virtually guarantee superior male performance.

Attitude changes are also needed in our approach to "hyperac [24] tive" or "learning disabled" children. The evidence for sex differences here is staggering: More than 95 percent of hyperactives are males. And why should this be surprising in light of the sex differences in brain function that we've just discussed?

The male brain learns by manipulating its environment, yet the [25] typical student is forced to sit still for long hours in the classroom. The male brain is primarily visual, while classroom instruction demands attentive listening. Boys are clumsy in fine hand coordination, yet are forced at an early age to express themselves in writing. Finally, there is little opportunity in most schools, other than during recess, for gross motor movements or rapid muscular responses. In essence, the classrooms in most of our nation's primary grades are geared to skills that come naturally to girls but develop very slowly in boys. The results shouldn't be surprising: a "learning disabled" child who is also frequently "hyperactive."

"He can't sit still, can't write legibly, is always trying to take [26] things apart, won't follow instructions, is loud, and, oh yes, terribly clumsy," is a typical teacher description of male hyperactivity. We now have the opportunity, based on emerging evidence of sex differences in brain functioning, to restructure elementary grades so that boys find their initial educational contacts less stressful.

At more advanced levels of instruction, efforts must be made to [27] develop teaching methods that incorporate verbal and linguistic approaches to physics, engineering and architecture (to mention only three fields where women are conspicuously underrepresented and, on competitive aptitude tests, score well below males).

The second alternative is, of course, to do nothing about brain [28] differences and perhaps even deny them altogether. Certainly there is something to be said for this approach too. In the recent past, enhanced social benefit has usually resulted from stressing the similarities between people rather than their differences. We ignore brain-sex differences, however, at the risk of confusing biology with sociology, and wishful thinking with scientific facts.

The question is not, "Are there brain-sex differences?" but [29] rather, "What is going to be our response to these differences?" Psychobiological research is slowly but surely inching toward scientific proof of a premise first articulated by the psychologist David Wechsler more than 20 years ago:

"The findings suggest that women seemingly call upon different [30] resources or different degrees of like abilities in exercising whatever it is we call intelligence. For the moment, one need not be concerned as to which approach is better or 'superior.' But our findings do confirm what poets and novelists have often asserted, and the average layman long believed, namely, that men not only behave, but 'think' differently from women."

QUESTIONS

Understanding

1. The major premise of Restak's essay is that "Boys think differently from girls" (par. 1). What does he mean when he says, "Usually such differences are explained on a cultural basis" (par. 5)?

2. How would Restak, as a neurologist, explain the "difference in brain functioning" (par. 6) between boys and girls?

3. Why might some women be disturbed by Restak's explanation for intellectual differences between males and females? (He says he makes no judgments about "inferior" and "superior" brains and that his findings might even be interpreted to favor women.)

4. What answer does Restak give in advance to "feminists" and others who may be expected to take exception to his views?

5. Neurologists believe that the right hemisphere of the brain dominates our handling of visual and spatial data and that the left hemisphere has more to do with language acquisition and use. By comparison with girls, do boys tend to be more "right-brained" or "left-brained," according to Restak's analysis of the research? How about girls? Which are they?

6. Restak has examined research dealing with both physiological and psychological data. Which kind is provided by electroencephalograms (pars. 14 and 15)? By intelligence tests and subtests (pars. 16 and 17)? By recent research with lights and sounds at the National Institute of Mental Health (par. 21)?

7. According to Restak, what were the conclusions of the thought-provoking Maccoby-Jacklin experiments at Stanford (par. 18)? How does Restak himself interpret their findings? What conclusion does he draw from their conclusion?

8. One public response to the new understanding of brain differences, says Restak, is to do nothing or "perhaps even deny them altogether" (par. 28). What advantage might conceivably be gained from this negative response? Why is doing nothing, however, the wrong way to react in Restak's opinion?

9. What does Restak consider the proper, positive reaction to the new findings? How, specifically, would he change traditional teaching and testing methods in the schools?

Strategies and Structure

1. A good strategy in logical argument is always to anticipate objections that might be raised against your reasoning. Restak begins

almost immediately to defend his position against "feminists and others committed to overcoming sexual stereotypes" (par. 2). What concession does he make to the opposition? Where does he take up the line of defense again toward the end of his essay? Is he still making concessions, or is he arguing more aggressively? Explain your answer.

2. Why does Restak mention that he is the father of three daughters (par. 2)?

3. Restak's essay combines INDUCTIVE reasoning (from particular observations to general principles) with DEDUCTIVE reasoning (from general principles to conclusions). If the "inescapable" conclusion of his inductive argument is that "boys think differently from girls" (anticipated in par. 1), which paragraph begins to recite the specific bits of evidence upon which this conclusion rests?

4. Where does Restak end the survey of the evidence (and thus the deductive part of his argument)?

5. The conclusion of Restak's inductive argument—that the sexes have different brains—becomes the major premise of a deductive argument in the last third of his essay. If the implied minor premise is that differences among the sexes are socially undesirable, what is the conclusion of Restak's deductive argument? Where is it stated?

6. When Restak launches into his inductive argument in paragraph 7, he suspends the deductive part for some time. We know to expect it eventually, however, because of clear signals in the opening six paragraphs. Where exactly does Restak anticipate his deductive argument in favor of reform in educating and testing the sexes?

7. There is a considerable difference between arguing that males and females develop different brains and arguing that they are *born* with those differences. In which early paragraph does Restak switch ground toward the second, more radical view?

8. Restak notes that boys activate the right hemisphere of the brain when working with shapes, while girls activate both hemispheres. From such data he concludes (par. 15) that "spatial ability is more widely dispersed" in girls (and therefore, presumably, more watered down). Is this a logical conclusion? Why or why not? What different conclusion is possible from these same data?

9. Should Restak have cited more or less research to buttress his findings, or has he selected about the right amount? What do you think and why?

Words and Figures of Speech

1. Which single word in paragraph 1 anticipates Restak's later con-

tention that people who ignore brain differences between the sexes confuse "biology with sociology, and wishful thinking with scientific facts" (par. 28)?

2. What are the implications of the phrase "biologically inherent" (par. 6)? Why is it a crucial part of Restak's argument? Does he call attention to the importance of this phrase or leave it to be discovered by the reader? Why?

3. Do you find Restak's title effective and accurate? Why or why not?

4. The word *stereotypes* (pars. 2, 5, 6, 19) comes from printing; it refers to metal plates of type, or other design, cast from a mold. What does the word mean when applied to people? Why is it appropriate here for describing behavior that is imposed rather than inherited?

5. Sociologists and psychologists speak not only of "behavior" but also of "behaviors" (plural). The way male babies respond to lights is one behavior; to sounds, another. What is meant by the technical use of this term?

6. Look up in a good desk dictionary any of these words that you do not recognize immediately: *cultural* (par. 5), *repertoires* (par. 5), *corollary* (par. 5), *modified* (par. 6), *oblivious* (par. 7), *enhanced* (pars. 7, 21, 22), *threshold* (par. 8), *inanimate* (par. 12), *fixate* (par. 12), *stimuli* (par. 21), *depression* (par. 21), *equity* (par. 23), *hyperactivity* (par. 26), *linguistic* (par. 27).

7. Judging from this list, how would you characterize Dr. Restak's vocabulary?

Comparing

1. How does Restak's premise that intelligence is inherent rather than learned compare with Ellen Willis's explanation of how personalities are formed in "Memoirs of a Non-Prom Queen" (Chapter 4)?

2. Examine the following counter argument ("The Sexes Are Not Born with Different Brains") in which Martha Mednick and Nancy Felipe Russo directly respond to Dr. Restak's argument. On what grounds do they disagree? Where do they concur, if at all?

3. Like Thomas Jefferson in the "Declaration of Independence" (earlier in this chapter), Restak combines inductive and deductive reasoning. How close is the parallel as far as logic is concerned?

Discussion and Writing Topics

1. From Restak's argument, are you convinced that the sexes have different brains? That they are *born* with them? That the differences should be acknowledged and taken into account? Explain your answer to each of these separate questions.

2. Are most scientific arguments based on the evidence of research more like to be inductive or deductive? Why?

3. Using Restak's own report of the research, attack or defend his conclusions.

Martha Mednick
and Nancy Felipe Russo

The Sexes Are Not Born with Different Brains

Born in New York City, Martha Mednick (Ph.D., Northwestern) is professor of psychology at Howard University and co-author of Women and Achievement (1975). A native Californian, her collaborator, Nancy Felipe Russo (Ph.D., Cornell), has administered the women's programs of the American Psychological Association since 1977. She is the author of The Motherhood Mandate (1979). As research psychologists, teachers, and writers, Mednick and Russo share a common interest in the psychology of women and in social influences upon women's careers and sex-roles. "The Sexes Are Not Born with Different Brains" first appeared in the Washington Post as a direct response to neurologist Richard Restak's "The Other Difference between Boys and Girls." (Published earlier in the "Outlook" section of the Post, Restak's article is reprinted here as the preceding essay in persuasion.) The titles of the two essays neatly demarcate the grounds on which their authors disagree about the psychology of sex. The subtitle of the essay by Mednick and Russo is "How Misleading Thinking Can Lead to Illogical Results."

For many years some people have been searching for differ- [1]
ences in the brains of men and women in an attempt to explain
differences in behavior between the sexes.

For a while in the 19th century it was the smaller absolute [2]
brain size of females that was said to account for a supposed
lesser ability among women. In the mid-1800s some researchers
concentrated on the fact that men have more developed frontal lobes than women. Then attention switched to the parietal
lobes, which were regarded as the seat of the intellect at that
time.

Now we have neurologist Richard Restak reviewing a large   3
number of research findings and researching the "inescapable"
conclusion that in many respects boys and girls think differently.
As there are male and female reproductive systems, Restak tells us
in the June 24 "Outlook," so there are in effect male and female
brains.

Restak contends that "many behavioral differences between   4
men and women are based on differences in brain functioning that
are biologically inherent and unlikely to be modified by cultural
factors alone." "We ignore brain-sex differences," he says, "at
the risk of confusing biology with sociology, and wishful thinking
with scientific fact."

But if ever there was an example of wishful thinking disguised   5
as scientific objectivity, it is in the distorted evidence and shaky
logic exhibited by Restak.

Granted, Restak asserts that "we're not talking about one sex   6
being superior or inferior to the other," and he says that his proposal to restructure the educational, social and work worlds of
men and women is intended to help every person fully realize his
or her own potential. But he is naïve if he believes that his work
will not be used by some to help justify the low numbers of women
in many professions, and his proposal could not conceivably ac-
complish what he says he intends.

Let us begin, then, with his misleading review of the research.   7
If we look at children just after birth, before the sexes have been
extensively exposed to differential treatment, we do not find the
sex differences in sensation, perception and motor behavior that
Restak suggests are inherent.

Yvonne Brackbill, a noted authority on infant development, re-   8
cently completed a major review of all recent research published in
the United States and England dealing with the behavior of babies
from 1 to 30 days of age. She could find no sex difference in *any* of
these important aspects of behavior. Even sleep patterns, indi-
cators of brain activity, were not found to differ for the sexes.

Similarly, Restak's assertion that females are more sensitive to   9
sound while males show an "early visual superiority" is based on
an incomplete evaluation of the literature. In a comprehensive
review of research in these areas, for one example, Eleanor
Maccoby and Carol Nagly Jacklin of Stanford University con-

cluded that "it has not been demonstrated that either sex is more 'visual' or more 'auditory' than the other."

It would be surprising, of course, if different treatment of boys [10] and girls did not in time have some effect. As Restak notes, in American society girls on the average eventually achieve verbal superiority over boys, while boys eventually excel on the average in spatial ability. But he is sorely mistaken in suggesting that these differences are universal or immodifiable.

The female verbal superiority in this country which Restak at- [11] tributes to "the female brain" is not found in Germany, as Michele Wittig and Anne Petersen report in their recent book, "Sex-Related Cognitive Differences." Amiah Lieblich of Hebrew University similarly has found that boys in Israel perform equal to or better than girls at all ages on measures of verbal ability.

Nor is male superiority in spatial ability found in all cultures. [12] J. W. Berry and R. McArthur, for example, conducted separate and independent studies among Canadian Eskimos and found no sex differences in measures of spatial ability. Moreover, there is no doubt that where lower female performance in spatial ability is found among adolescents, in this country or elsewhere, it can be changed by training.

A more serious error by Restak, though, is the way he leaps to [13] cause-and-effect conclusions in linking behavior differences between the sexes to "biologically inherent" differences in brain functioning. It is believed, for example, that the left hemisphere of the brain plays a dominant role in language functions and that the right hemisphere is dominant for processing spatial information. Restak reports that on tests of spatial ability, boys used the right sides of their brains while girls were more likely to activate both sides. Fine.

But then he jumps to the unfounded conclusion that this differ- [14] ence is caused by something inherent about male and female brains, and that it is related to a detriment in performance for females. He does not even consider the fact that after boys are "trained" for years in our society to emphasize tasks involving spatial abilities, it would be surprising if their brains did not react differently to spatial tasks. Which is really the cause and which the effect?

Any weight watcher or body builder will tell you that one's [15] biological status at any moment is a complex expression of the effect of both one's heredity and one's environment. The brain is not exempt from this principle. It is exceedingly difficult to sort out the contributions of genetics, biology and environment to the development of sex differences in hemispheric activity.

In the same way, it cannot automatically be *assumed* that a sex [16] difference in one area such as the brain's hemispheric activity is linked to another area such as spatial tasks. For example, a study that recently appeared in *Science,* the journal of the American Association for the Advancement of Science, raises questions about the behavioral effects of sex differences in hemispheric activity that Restak cites so definitively.

In that study, psychologists Joseph Cioffi and Gilray Kandel of [17] the Rensselaer Polytechnic Institute found that in contrast to earlier work, both boys and girls identify shapes better by touch with their left hand than with their right. Both sexes also identified words better by touch with their right hand than with their left. Girls performed no differently on these tasks than boys.

The researchers did find a difference in the hand best used to [18] identify bigrams (two letters that do not form a word, such as XH), but both sexes nonetheless were equally accurate in identifying the bigrams. Further, some girls did better with their left hand, and some boys did better with their right. The authors concluded that any assertions about the differential organization of the brains of boys and girls must be carefully qualified.

Perhaps the most profound and consequential mistake Restak [19] makes, however, is in his confusion between groups and individuals, particularly as it affects his prescriptions for general changes in education and elsewhere.

When group differences are found, it is always an average com- [20] paring large numbers of people. While a small average difference can be significant to a statistician, it tells very little about individuals. As Leona E. Tyler, past president of the American Psychological Association and a noted authority on individual differences, has observed, average differences in tests "are trifling as compared with the individual differences in each sex."

Any approach that ignores individual variation is naive and [21] harmful. It also leads to tortured semantics. In dealing with hemispheric activities, for example, Restak says that girls, on the average, are more *likely* to demonstrate such differences, yet he talks about "biologically inherent" characteristics of male and female brains. Does he mean to imply that the many girls within the average who perform the tasks "the way the boys do it" (on the average) have inherited "male brains"? Do the many boys who do better than many other girls on verbal measures have "female brains"?

When society bases educational, occupational and social poli-   22
cies on studies of group differences, there obviously are devastating consequences for individuals.

Whether one is talking about brain size in the 19th century or   23
hemispheric activity in the 20th, then, there is no body of scientific fact proving that sex differences in behavior are caused by inherent differences in brain characteristics. The failure of science to establish this link is not surprising, given the powerful forces that have been demonstrated to shape boys and girls into fulfilling the expectations of our sex-role stereotypes.

That is not to say that both genetic and biological considera-   24
tions for individuals are not important. But the strength of the contribution of genetic factors depends directly on how differently people are treated on the basis of their sex. If society treated the sexes in a totally equivalent fashion, differences between male and females would reflect inherent characteristics. We do not live in such a society.

What it comes down to is that some boys think differently from   25
some girls. They also think differently from each other. The same holds for girls. We are beginning to understand the many factors that create this rich diversity. There is a new sophistication in much of the research that focuses on the interaction of genetic, biological and environmental factors, and the results of this work may, indeed, eventually lead to the full realization of the potential within each person.

QUESTIONS

Understanding

1. Mednick and Russo agree with neurologist Richard M. Restak ("The Other Difference between Boys and Girls," preceding essay) that the brains of males and females may respond differently to the

same task (for example, learning a language or solving problems in spatial relations). They vehemently disagree, however, with Restak's "unfounded conclusion" (par. 14) about the cause of such differences. To what ultimate cause does Restak attribute brain differences between the sexes? To what do Mednick and Russo attribute them?

2. Mednick and Russo are reluctant even to grant Restak's basic premise, that "boys think differently from girls." How would they qualify this assertion about *uniform* brain differences between the sexes?

3. Mednick and Russo accuse Restak of misevaluating research on sensation and perception among infants. What conclusions do they reach from their own evaluation of the research in paragraphs 7–12? What conclusions do they attribute to Dr. Restak?

4. What social effects do Mednick and Russo fear from the "biologically inherent" theory of intellectual differences between males and females?

5. Restak argues that those who reject the notion of male and female brains are "unrealistic." What quality of mind do Mednick and Russo, in turn, charge against Restak for believing that his interpretation of the evidence will not be misused?

6. What is Restak's most serious error as Mednick and Russo see it? How does this "mistake" (par. 19), in their view, nullify Restak's argument that all girls need to be educated differently from all boys?

Strategies and Structure

1. Why do you think Mednick and Russo begin with a historical perspective?

2. Which part of Restak's thesis do they contest more vigorously—the proposition that the sexes have different brains or that they are born with those differences? Where is the issue first raised in their rebuttal?

3. Mednick and Russo accuse Restak of distorting evidence (par. 5). The first evidence they themselves cite is the research compiled by Yvonne Brackbill (par. 8). What makes this study especially helpful to their case against Dr. Restak?

4. What is the evidence cited in paragraphs 11 and 12 intended to prove? Where else in the essay do Mednick and Russo address the issue of brain modification?

5. Mednick and Russo also chide Restak for "shaky logic" (par. 5). The logical blunder they cite is that of "leaping" to a false conclusion about causation (par. 13), a fallacy that usually occurs with INDUCTIVE rather than DEDUCTIVE arguments. The portion of Restak's argument that Mednick and Russo seem to have in mind is that set forth in paragraphs 13–17 of the preceding essay. Look closely at those paragraphs. Is the charge of shaky logic justified? Why or why not?

6. In paragraph 4, Mednick and Russo quote from Dr. Restak's argument and then (par. 5) turn his words back on him. How effective do you consider this as a technique of rebuttal?

7. In paragraph 23, Mednick and Russo argue a negative: "there is no body of scientific fact proving that sex differences in behavior are caused by inherent differences in brain characteristics." What would be the positive version of this proposition? Would their argument have been stronger if they had cast it this way? Why didn't they?

8. What counter arguments, if any, might be raised against the argument set forth here by Mednick and Russo?

Words and Figures of Speech

1. When applied to language, "semantics" refers to the study of the *meanings* of words. Mednick and Russo say that ignoring brain differences among individuals of the same sex leads to "tortured semantics" (par. 21). What new, clumsy meanings of *male* and *female* do they make fun of?

2. How effective do you find the ANALOGY between brain performance and body building or weight watching (par. 15)?

3. In logic, what is a *non sequitur*? (Your dictionary will tell you.) What *non sequitur*, in particular, do Mednick and Russo attribute to Dr. Restak's argument?

4. Which single word in paragraph 6 lets you know that the authors are agreeing with their opponent only to disagree with him soon after?

5. A single word, *fine*, does duty for a whole sentence at the end of paragraph 13 of this essay. Why are the authors so terse? Is the device "correct" or "incorrect"? Why?

6. Consult your dictionary for the following words if you do not know them already: *parietal* (par. 2), *spatial* (par. 12), *detriment* (par. 14), *genetics* (par. 15), *consequential* (par. 19), *prescriptions*

(par. 19), *statistician* (par. 20), *verbal* (par. 21), *sophistication* (par. 25).

7. What is the difference between *verbal* (par. 21) and *oral*?

Comparing

1. "The Sexes Are Not Born with Different Brains" is a direct rebuttal to the preceding essay by Richard Restak, "The Other Difference between Boys and Girls." Which do you find more convincing as a logical argument (even if you do not agree with the truth of the conclusions or premises). Why?

2. Both Restak (pars. 18 and 19 of the preceding essay) and the co-authors of this essay cite the work of Maccoby and Jacklin at Stanford University. How do their interpretations of this research compare? Who is right? Is there enough evidence to tell?

Discussion and Writing Topics

1. How would you go about resolving differences in the interpretation of the same evidence, reported in brief, by different experts? Is it possible for well-informed, well-intentioned people to interpret the same body of evidence diversely? Explain your opinion?

2. What advantages might an unanswered rebuttal (like Mednick's and Russo's) have in debate over the original argument it attacks? Can you think of any disadvantages or limitations imposed upon the author of a rebuttal?

3. Take a side in this debate about inherent differences in male and female brains and argue your case using different evidence or the same evidence interpreted differently.

4. Inductive arguments can lead to faulty generalizations when they are based on insufficient evidence, bad authorities, or good authorities quoted inaccurately or out of context. Do any of these fallacies apply to the logic of this essay or the preceding one by Richard Restak? If so, how might they be corrected?

Essays That Appeal to Reason

Write a logical argument defending one of the following propositions:

1. Buying a house, condominium, or trailer makes (does not make) better sense in the long run than renting one

2. Grading standards are (are not) slipping in American colleges and universities

3. College students are (are not) as bright now as they used to be

4. College graduates get (do not get) better jobs than those who do not go to college

5. Graduate or professional school is (is not) worth the expense these days

6. Smoking is (is not) hazardous to your health

7. America has (has not) developed into a "welfare state"

8. Farm-life is (is not) a dying institution in America

9. Cities are (are not) dying in America

10. Women's liberation has (has not) produced desirable results

11. The "revolution" in sexual morality is (is not) a myth

12. Religion is (is not) reviving in America

13. Pollution is (is not) avoidable

14. Our society has (has not) curtailed racism

10

Essays That Appeal to Emotion and Ethics

PERSUASION,[1] we have said, is the strategic use of language to move an audience to action or belief. It works by appealing to our reason through logical ARGUMENT (the MODE OF PERSUASION discussed in Chapter 9). It also works by appealing to our emotions and to our sense of ethics.

The APPEAL TO EMOTION is nicely exemplified in "Being Prepared in Suburbia," the first essay in this chapter. Writing about gun-control legislation, Roger Verhulst deliberately sets aside reason and logic. He could produce statistics to show how many deaths will soon be caused by privately owned firearms, says Verhulst; but he finds "no point in citing those statistics again; they may prove something, but they're not likely to prompt any concrete action. There is nothing moving about statistics."

Here is the essence of the emotional appeal. It assumes, in Verhulst's words, that "what is needed to produce results is passion"; it aims at "the gut." Even if his own passion has cooled in the process of writing it down—and what passion can flare through several rewritings?—the author of an emotional appeal must kindle his original feelings in the reader. He cannot do this, however, simply by being emotional.

It is a fallacy to think that you can appeal to an emotion in your reader by imitating it: hysteria by being hysterical, anger by raging. Often the best measure is to appear calm, detached, thoroughly in control of your feelings—now. However intensely felt, your testimony must be orderly, or at least coherent. You may want to recreate the circumstances or perception that first excited in you the emotions that you

---

[1] Terms printed in all capitals are defined in the Glossary.

want to excite in your readers (as Fred Reed does so viscerally in "A Veteran Writes"); but here again your narrative must be controlled and directed toward its desired effect. Even your choice of individual words cannot be haphazard; you must pay close attention to their CONNOTATIONS. If you are addressing a labor union, for example, it will make a great difference whether you refer to the members as drones, workers, comrades, or just people.

The APPEAL TO ETHICS is an appeal to the reader's sense of how people ought to behave. This mode of persuasion convinces the reader that it is written by a person of good character whose judgment should be heeded. We are moved by the force of the speaker's personality.

Because the author's personality is so important in an appeal to ethics, great care must be taken to measure his or her tone of voice. TONE is an author's revealed attitude toward the material; it conveys his or her temper. A writer can be a decent human being and may have the reader's best interests at heart; but the reader may not trust the writer if the tone clashes with the message. Sincerity is the soul of the ethical appeal, and a writer must take pains to appear trustworthy as well as to be so.

To appear trustworthy, the writer must seem to be not only a person of good character and even temper but also a person who is well-informed. When noted attorney F. Lee Bailey tells us to "watch out for trial lawyers" because too many are competent only in the research library, we tend to believe him. Bailey's own expertise in the courtroom makes him an expert witness. The appeal of the expert witness, in fact, is one of the most common modern forms of the appeal to ethics. We are won over not by the moral uprightness of the expert but by his or her knowledge and intellectual integrity.

For study purposes, the appeals to emotion and to ethics have been separated here from the appeal to reason and from each other. (The first two essays in this chapter appeal to emotions; the last three appeal to ethics.) In practice you may want to combine all three modes of persuasion in the same essay (as Lindsy Van Gelder does in "The Great Person-Hole Cover Debate"). The goal of persuasive writing is to bring others around to your way of thinking in a good cause. Any honest means to this end is sound RHETORIC.

Roger Verhulst

Being Prepared in Suburbia

*Roger Verhulst lives with his wife and two sons in Grand Rapids,
Michigan, where he writes about books and games. A former sup-
porter of gun-control legislation, he recently became the co-leader
of a Cub Scout den and acquired his first gun, a Crossman 760,
because the scouts wanted target practice. "Being Prepared in
Suburbia" testifies to a conversion, of sorts, that followed. Verhulst
found, he says, that the owners of guns have an irrational attach-
ment to their weapons that is stronger than the rational arguments against owning deadly firearms. In an essay analyzing the
emotion it arouses, Verhulst would persuade us that gun control
is as dead as the victims of uncontrolled guns.*

Gun legislation is dead for another year. As a result, if sta-   1
tistics are any guide, there's every likelihood that a lot of people now living will also be dead before the year is over.

There's no point in citing those statistics again; they may   2
prove something, but they're not likely to prompt any concrete action. There is nothing very moving about statistics.

What is needed to produce results is passion—and that's   3
where the antigun-control lobby has it all over the rest of
us. Those who favor stronger gun legislation—a solid majority
of Americans—can't hold a candle to the lovers of guns when
it comes to zeal.

I had a taste of that passion recently, and I begin to under-   4
stand something of what it is that fosters in gun libbers such
dedicated resolve. Thanks to a bunch of Cub Scouts and an
absurd little creature that went bump in the night, I've begun
to realize why cold, unemotional tabulations of gun deaths will

never lead to effective gun control. It's because of what can happen to people—even sane, rational, firearm-hating people like me—when they get their hands on a genuine, authentic, real-life gun.

Until last fall, I had never owned any weapon more lethal than 5
a water pistol. I opposed guns as esthetically repugnant, noisy, essentially churlish devices whose only practical purpose was to blast holes of various sizes in entities that would thereby be rendered less functional than they would otherwise have been. I didn't object merely to guns that killed people; I also objected to guns that killed animals, or shattered windows, or plinked away at discarded beer bottles. Whenever a gun was put to effective use, I insisted, something broke; and it seemed absurd to go through life breaking things.

With arguments such as these, bolstered by assorted threats, I 6
tried to instill holey terror also in my sons. Initially, I imposed an absolute ban on even toy guns. When that didn't work—their determination to possess such toys exceeding by scores of decibels my determination to ban them—I tried substituting lectures on the merits of nonviolence and universal love. Nice try.

Then, last fall, I became co-leader of a Cub Scout den here in 7
Grand Rapids, Mich., consisting of half a dozen 9-, 10- and 11-year-old boys. Sharing the leadership responsibilities with me was a kind and gentle man named Mickey Shea, who happens to be extremely fond of outdoor activities—including, of course, hunting.

It was in Mickey's basement, in full view of an imposing gun 8
rack, that I yielded to the pressure of pleading Cubbers and agreed to add target shooting to our scheduled activities. (Though I should make it clear that it wasn't Mickey who forced, or even strongly urged, that agreement; it was rather a wish to be accepted by the boys—to be regarded as appropriately adult and masculine—that prompted my decision. I've no one to blame but myself.)

So, for the sake of my kids and under the auspices of the Boy 9
Scouts of America, I bought a gun—a Crossman Power Master 760 BB Repeater pump gun, with bolt action, adjustable sight and a satisfying heft. It was capable of putting holes in all sorts of things.

A few nights later we got the Cubs together and spent an hour 10
or two aiming and firing at targets taped to paper-filled cardboard cartons. After which I unloaded the gun and locked it in my study, intending to leave it there until future target shoots came along

to justify bringing it out again. But a roving opossum that took up residence in our garage for a few cold nights in January undermined my good intentions.

We were entertained, at first. We called the kids down to see [11] our visitor perched on the edge of the trash barrel; we recorded the event on film. We regarded the presence of authentic wild animals in our corner of suburbia as delightfully diverting.

Almost at once, however, the rat-faced prowler began to make [12] himself obnoxious. There was the midnight clatter of falling objects, and the morning-after disarray of strewn garbage. The possum, we decided, would have to go.

But he proved to be not only an unwelcome but also a recal- [13] citrant guest. It was cold outside, and rather than waddling willingly back through the open garage door he took refuge behind a pile of scrap lumber; my vigorous thrusts with a broomstick were parried by obstinacy, and an occasional grunt.

I was cold, too, by now; and tired; and becoming frustrated. [14] Drastic action was indicated; I poured a handful of BB's into the Crossman 760, pumped it up, pointed the barrel blindly into the woodpile and pulled the trigger.

Nothing happened. The opossum did not move. Shivering, I [15] went back inside the house, still holding my weapon. I sat down with a drink and a cigarette to warm up.

With little else to do, I put the gun to my shoulder and aimed [16] it idly at the clock above the fireplace; I aimed it at a light fixture across the room, pressing gently against the trigger; I aimed it at a row of glasses behind the bar, imagining the snap and shatter of breaking glass; I aimed it at my own reflection in the TV set, thinking how absurdly easy it would be to eliminate television from my life.

The more imaginary targets I selected, the stronger became the [17] urge to shoot—something, anything. The gun extended my potential range of influence to everyone within sight; I could alter the world around me without even moving from the couch, simply by pulling the trigger. Gun in hand, I was bravely prepared to defend myself against any intruder, man or beast. I felt omnipotent as Zeus,[1] with lightning bolts at my fingertips.

No wonder, I thought, that people become hooked on guns. [18]

---

[1] Ruler of the Greek gods; lightning was his special weapon.

This is the feeling that explains their passion, their religious fervor, their refusal to yield. It's rooted in the gut, not in the head. And in the recurrent struggle over gun legislation it is no wonder that their stamina exceeds mine.

I can understand that passion because I've felt it in my own   19
gut. I've felt the gun in my hand punch psychic holes in my intellectual convictions. And having felt all that, I do not have much hope that private ownership of deadly weapons will be at all regulated or controlled in the foreseeable future.

QUESTIONS

Understanding

1. According to Verhulst, what is the appeal of guns to those who own them? In which paragraph does he explain that appeal most explicitly?

2. Verhulst thinks that gun-control legislation is doomed. Why? What is his main reason?

3. Verhulst says that he yielded to the scouts' demand for target practice because he wished "to be accepted by the boys—to be regarded as appropriately adult and masculine" (par. 8). How far does this motive go toward explaining why some men like guns? How "sane" is it?

4. Why do you think Verhulst takes pains to point out that he came into contact with guns through the Cub Scouts?

5. In paragraph 19, Verhulst says that his gun opened "psychic holes" in his resolve. Which earlier paragraphs of his essay does this statement hark back to? How? With what unexpected twist has Verhulst's original theory about guns been confirmed?

6. Why is Verhulst's subject especially suited to an appeal to emotion?

Strategies and Structure

1. Verhulst writes as a "convert," an opponent of free guns who has come reluctantly to understand the appeal of firearms. Would his prediction about the failure of gun control be more or less con-

vincing if he were speaking as a long-time gun enthusiast? Explain your answer.

2. By telling the story of the author's conversion, this essay uses NARRATION to help achieve its persuasive purpose. Where does the narration begin? Where does it end? How compelling do you find Verhulst's narrative? Why?

3. As a general rule, do you think narration is more likely to be found in an APPEAL TO REASON or an APPEAL TO EMOTION? Why?

4. What is the strategy of Verhulst's first and second paragraphs? How successful is it?

5. Verhulst says that his sons' demand for toy guns exceeded "by scores of decibels" (par. 6) his resistance. What is the TONE of this remark? Of "Nice try" in the same paragraph? Describe Verhulst's TONE throughout the essay.

6. Why does Verhulst make himself look foolish, even mean, in the encounter with the "possum"?

7. How do the length and rhythm of the single sentence in paragraph 16 capture the author's state of mind at that point in his essay?

8. Far from assuming that a writer stirs emotion simply by being emotional, Verhulst comes across as remarkably cool-headed. How does he create this impression?

9. Whom do you take to be Verhulst's audience? In which paragraph does he, in effect, define it? Why is his cool-headed approach a good one for this audience?

10. When do you think a writer is better advised to be emotional (not just to describe emotions and appeal to them in the reader) — when he is addressing an audience that essentially agrees with him or one that disagrees? Why?

Words and Figures of Speech

1. Why does Verhulst use the word *hooked* in paragraph 18? What are the CONNOTATIONS of the term?

2. "Holey terror" (par. 6) and "delightfully diverting" (par. 11) represent two different LEVELS OF DICTION. Define the two levels and point out other examples of each. Why do you think Verhulst mixes the two?

3. *Psychic* (par. 19) has two basic meanings. What are they? Which one is intended here?

4. Look up the following words in your dictionary: *churlish* (par. 5), *decibels* (6), *auspices* (9), *obnoxious* (12), *recalcitrant* (13), *obstinacy* (13), *frustrated* (14), *omnipotent* (17), *fervor* (18).

Comparing

1. Compare and contrast "Being Prepared in Suburbia" with William F. Buckley's "Capital Punishment" (Chapter 9) as representative examples of two different MODES OF PERSUASION: the appeal to reason and the appeal to emotion, respectively.
2. Consider both Verhulst's essay and Deairich Hunter's "Ducks vs. Hard Rocks" (Chapter 2) as commentaries on why people resort to violence. Do they square with each other?

Discussion and Writing Topics

1. Write a persuasive essay in favor of gun-control legislation that appeals to emotion and that argues that guns are "esthetically repugnant, noisy, essentially churlish devices" (par. 5).
2. Construct a persuasive rational argument *against* gun-control legislation, the sort of argument, though on the opposite side, that Verhulst declines to make at the start of his essay.
3. If Verhulst's experience is at all typical, under what circumstances do our irrational impulses come forth? Are they any less real for being irrational? Why or why not?

Fred Reed

A Veteran Writes

*Fred Reed is a former U. S. Marine, a veteran of the Vietnam
War. As a stringer for the Army Times he witnessed the fall of
Saigon and Phnom Penh. Reed lingered in Southeast Asia because,
like many veterans, he liked it there. When he came home, he felt
bored and angry that veterans were not really welcome to those
who knew nothing of war at first-hand; he drifted for a while until
he learned "that aberrant behavior, when written about, is literature." His memories of Vietnam are as lush, vivid, and frightening
as a napalm flash. "A Veteran Writes," from Harper's, might have
been placed in the "Description" section of this book—its pictures
are so powerful—but even more powerful is the message of silence
it carries for non-veterans who criticize G.I.'s for not adjusting
gracefully to "real" life back home.*

I begin to weary of the stories about veterans that are now   1
in vogue with the newspapers, the stories that dissect the
veteran's psyche as if prying apart a laboratory frog—patronizing stories written by style-section reporters who know all
there is to know about chocolate mousse, ladies' fashions, and
the wonderful desserts that can be made with simple jello. I
weary of seeing veterans analyzed and diagnosed and explained
by people who share nothing with veterans, by people who,
one feels intuitively, would regard it as a harrowing experience
to be alone in a backyard.

Week after week the mousse authorities tell us what is   2
wrong with the veteran. The veteran is badly in need of adjustment, they say—lacks balance, needs fine tuning to whatever
it is in society that one should be attuned to. What we have
here, all agree, with omniscience and veiled condescension, is

a victim: The press loves a victim. The veteran has bad dreams, say the jello writers, is alienated, may be hostile, doesn't socialize well—isn't, to be frank, quite right in the head.

But perhaps it is the veteran's head to be right or wrong in, and   3
maybe it makes a difference what memories are in the head. For the jello writers the war was a moral fable on Channel Four, a struggle hinging on Nixon and Joan Baez and the inequities of this or that. I can't be sure. The veterans seem to have missed the war by having been away in Vietnam at the time and do not understand the combat as it raged in the internecine cocktail parties of Georgetown.[1]

Still, to me Vietnam was not what it was to the jello writers, not   4
a ventilation of pious simplisms, not the latest literary interpretation of the domino theory. It left me memories the fashion writers can't imagine. It was the slums of Truong Minh Ky, where dogs' heads floated in pools of green water and three-inch roaches droned in sweltering back-alley rooms and I was happy. Washington knows nothing of hot, whorerich, beery Truong Minh Ky. I remember riding the bomb boats up the Mekong to Phnom Penh, with the devilish brown river closing in like a vise and rockets shrieking from the dim jungle to burst against the sandbagged wheelhouse, and crouching below the waterline between the diesel tanks. The mousse authorities do not remember this. I remember the villa on Monivong in Phnom Penh, with Sedlacek, the balding Australian hippie, and Naoki, the crazy freelance combat photographer, and Zoco, the Frenchman, when the night jumped and flickered with the boom of artillery and we listened to Mancini on shortwave and watched Nara dance. Washington's elite did not know Nara. They know much of politicians and of furniture.

If I try to explain what Vietnam meant to me—I haven't for   5
years, and never will again—they grow uneasy at my intensity. *My God,* their eyes say, *he sounds as though he liked it over there. Something in the experience clearly snapped an anchoring ligament in his mind and left him with odd cravings, a perverse view of life—nothing dangerous, of course, but. . . . The war did that to them,* they say. *War is hell.*

Well, yes, they may have something there. When you have seen   6

[1] A well-to-do section of Washington, D.C., where many high government officials reside.

a peasant mother screaming over three pounds of bright red mush that, thanks to God and a Chicom 107, is no longer precisely her child, you see that Sherman may have been on to something.[2] When you have eaten fish with Khmer troops in charred Cambodian battlefields, where the heat beats down like a soft rubber truncheon and a wretched stink comes from shallow graves, no particular leap of imagination is necessary to notice that war is no paradise. I cannot say that the jello writers are wrong in their understanding of war. But somehow I don't like hearing pieties about the war from these sleek, wise people who never saw it. It offends propriety.

There were, of course, veterans and veterans. Some hated the war, some didn't. Some went around the bend down in IV Corps, where leeches dropped softly down collars like green sausages and death erupted unexpected from the ungodly foliage. To the men in the elite groups—the Seals, Special Forces, Recondos, and Lurps who spent years in the Khmer bush, low to the ground where the ants bit hard—the war was a game with stakes high enough to engage their attention. They liked to play.   7

To many of us there, the war was the best time of our lives, almost the only time. We loved it because in those days we were alive, life was intense, the pungent hours passed fast over the central event of the age and the howling jets appeased the terrible boredom of existence. Psychologists, high priests of the mean, say that boredom is a symptom of maladjustment; maybe, but boredom has been around longer than psychologists have.   8

The jello writers would say we are mad to remember fondly anything about Nixon's war that Kennedy started. They do not remember the shuddering flight of a helicopter high over glowing green jungle that spread beneath us like a frozen sea. They never made the low runs a foot above treetops along paths that led like rivers through branches that clawed at the skids, never peered down into murky clearings and bubbling swamps of sucking snake-ridden muck. They do not remember monsoon mornings in the   9

---

[2] General William Tecumseh Sherman (1820–1891): "I am tired and sick of war. Its glory is all moonshine. It is only those who have neither fired a shot nor heard the shrieks and groans of the wounded who cry aloud for blood, more vengeance, more desolation. War is hell." Chicom 107: Chinese communist rocket.

highlands where dragons of mist twisted in the valleys, coiling lazily on themselves, puffing up and swallowing whole villages in their dank breath. The mousse men do not remember driving before dawn to Red Beach, when the headlights in the blackness caught ghostly shapes, maybe VC,[3] thin yellow men mushroom-headed in the night, bicycling along the alien roads. As nearly as I can tell, jello writers do not remember anything.

Then it was over. The veterans came home. Suddenly the world   10
seemed to stop dead in the water. Suddenly the slant-eyed hookers were gone, as were the gunships and the wild drunken nights in places that the jello writers can't picture. Suddenly the veterans were among soft, proper people who knew nothing of what they had done and what they had seen, and who, truth to be told, didn't much like them.

Nor did some of us much like the people at home—though it   11
was not at first a conscious distaste. Men came home with wounds and terrible memories and dead friends to be greeted by that squalling she-ass of Tom Hayden's,[4] to find a country that viewed them as criminals. Slowly, to more men than will admit to it, the thought came: *These are the people I fought for?* And so we lost a country.

We looked around us with new eyes and saw that, in a sense the   12
mousse people could never understand, we had lost even our dignity. I remember a marine corporal at Bethesda Naval Hospital who, while his wounds healed, had to run errands for the nurses, last year's co-eds. "A hell of a bust," he said with the military's sardonic economy of language. "Machine gunner to messenger boy."

It wasn't exactly that we didn't fit. Rather, we saw what there   13
was to fit with—and recoiled. We sought jobs, but found offices where countless bureaucrats shuffled papers at long rows of desks, like battery hens awaiting the laying urge, their bellies billowing over their belts. Some of us joined them but some, in different ways, fled. A gunship pilot of my acquaintance took to the law, and to drink, and spent five years discovering that he really wanted to be in Rhodesia. Others went back into the death-in-the-bushes outfits, where the hard old rules still held. I drifted across Asia,

---

[3] Viet Cong, communist guerillas.
[4] Hayden is married to actress and antiwar activist Jane Fonda.

Mexico, Wyoming, hitchhiking and sleeping in ditches a lot until I learned that aberrant behavior, when written about, is literature.

The jello writers were quickly upon us. We were morose, they said, sullen. We acted strangely at parties, sat silently in corners and watched with noncommittal stares. Mentally, said the fashion experts, we hadn't made the trip home. ⁱ⁴

It didn't occur to them that we just had nothing to say about jello. Desserts mean little to men who have lain in dark rifle pits over Happy Valley in rainy season, watching mortar flares tremble in low-lying clouds that flickered like the face of God, while in the nervous evening safeties clicked off along the wire and amtracs rumbled into alert idles, coughing and waiting. ⁱ⁵

Once, after the GIs had left Saigon, I came out of a bar on Cach Mang and saw a veteran with a sign on his jacket: VIET NAM: IF YOU HAVEN'T BEEN THERE, SHUT THE FUCK UP. Maybe, just maybe, he had something. ⁱ⁶

QUESTIONS

Understanding

1. Why, according to Reed, did he (and some other veterans) love a war that he recognized as hellish?

2. If this essay is right, why have Reed and many other veterans had trouble getting over their experiences in Vietnam? What do they carry home with them?

3. What aspect of "normal" life back home did Reed himself find hardest to adjust to?

4. What are some examples of the kind of behavior, according to Reed, that non-veterans consider disturbing and anti-social?

5. The newspaper commentators are right, Reed agrees, when they say that war is hell. Why, then, does he get angry with them for mouthing "pieties" (par. 6) anyway? What disqualifies them from commenting, even accurately, on the war in Reed's opinion?

6. How does Reed's opinion of psychologists resemble his opinion of the commentators?

7. Reed's essay is a vivid piece of descriptive writing, but it is also an essay in persuasion. What is Reed trying to persuade readers unacquainted directly with Vietnam to do or accept?

8. Does Reed claim that all veterans reacted as he did to the business of returning to civilian life? How did some others react?

9. How much faith does Reed appear to place in the importance of political forces and policies upon the war in Vietnam?

Strategies and Structure

1. The thrust of Reed's appeal to emotion is that those who have not fought in Vietnam should not presume to explain the experience to those who have. On what authority does he base this appeal? Is he convincing? Why or why not?

2. Why does Reed end his essay by referring to the veteran with the sign on his jacket? Is the profanity justified or not? Why or why not?

3. Reed does not organize his essay according to the steps of a logical proof—logicality is one of the attitudes Reed is attacking here—but as a series of memories. What emotions do these memories appeal to? Which passages do you find most effective, given the author's purpose.

4. In what sense is Reed's persuasive appeal also a definition? What is he defining and for whom?

5. Where do you see traces of a chronological ordering in Reed's essay?

6. Reed's essay at times resembles a harangue, a form of speech in which the speaker faces his audience and repeatedly confronts them with his complaint. Point out other repetitive elements like the following that give Reed's essay the feeling of being spoken, almost chanted: "They do not remember the shuddering flight . . ."; "They do not remember monsoon mornings . . ."; "The mousse men do not remember driving before dawn . . ." (par. 9).

7. What do the italicized portions signify in Reed's essay? What is his TONE in them?

8. "It offends propriety," says Reed (par. 7) of non-veterans who pronounce truisms about war. Why do you suppose Reed chooses this particular defense? How might he respond to the charge that his essay offends propriety with its undisguised anger and unwholesome images?

9. What indications of emotional sensitivity do you discern in this veteran's tough stand against uncomprehending non-veterans?

10. What reason for being sore does Reed suggest when he says of

veterans like himself that some non-veteran critics of the war
"viewed them as criminals" (par. 11)?

Words and Figures of Speech

1. What is the effect of Reed's repetition of epithets such as "mousse
   men" and "jello writers" (par. 9)?
2. Why might epithets (name-calling) fit neatly into a harangue?
3. What is the effect of Reed's choosing the word *precisely* in paragraph 6? Of his choice of *ventilation* in paragraph 4?
4. "And so we lost a country" (par. 11) is a good example of UNDER-
   STATEMENT. Point out other examples of Reed's use of this device.
5. "They know much of politicians and of furniture," says Reed of
   non-veterans he meets or overhears at cocktail parties. What is the
   effect of juxtaposing the last two nouns in this biting sentence?
6. Which sense of *mean* is Reed using in paragraph 8?
7. Explain the METAPHOR, "the world seemed to stop dead in the
   water" (par. 10). To what is Reed comparing the world? Also explain his "fine tuning" metaphor in paragraph 2.
8. Look up any of the following words that you may have paused
   over: *psyche* (par. 1), *patronizing* (par. 1), *omniscience* (par. 2),
   condescension (par. 2), *alienated* (par. 2), *internecine* (par. 3),
   perverse (par. 5), *pieties* (par. 6), *appeased* (par. 8), *sardonic* (par.
   12), *aberrant* (par. 13), *morose* (par. 14).

Comparing

1. Contrast Reed's presence and voice in this essay with those of
   another veteran soldier delivering a haranque, Chief Seattle in his
   "Reply to the U. S. Government" at the end of this chapter.
2. How does "A Veteran Writes" confirm George Orwell's charge in
   "Politics and the English Language" ("Essays for Further Reading") that political lies erode the power of language to aid clear
   thinking?

Discussion and Writing Topics

1. Do you find Reed's descriptions of his experience in Vietnam to
   be beautiful or appalling or both? Explain your reaction?

2. Do you agree with Reed's assumption that one must be an eye-witness of events in order to understand them? Why or why not?

3. If you are a veteran, use your experience to refute or support the position of non-veterans who say that those who fought in Vietnam or elsewhere are criminals.

4. If you are not a veteran, try to get a friend or relative who is to confide his or her experiences to you. Then take a position on this same issue using what you have learned about how one veteran feels.

Lindsy Van Gelder

The Great Person-Hole Cover Debate

Lindsy Van Gelder is a frequent contributor to Ms. magazine and a reporter on feminist topics, in this case, the English language. She was born in Plainfield, New Jersey, in 1944 and attended Sarah Lawrence College and Northwestern. Van Gelder now lives in New York City, where she has worked for the World-Telegram and Sun, United Press International, and station WNEW-TV; she has also taught journalism at New York University graduate school. Her articles and essays can be found in Redbook, Esquire, Rolling Stone, and New York magazine. "The Great Person-Hole Cover Debate" (reprinted from Ms.) is a witty proposal for abolishing (or inverting) sexism in our language. On a subject that has too often inspired humorless diatribe as well as tortured syntax, Van Gelder appeals to opponents as a person who should be heard because of her good humor and good will. (That an idea is good because it comes from a just or knowledgeable person is the heart of the appeal to ethics.)

I wasn't looking for trouble. What I was looking for, actually, was a little tourist information to help me plan a camping trip to New England.

But there it was, on the first page of the 1979 edition of the State of Vermont *Digest of Fish and Game Laws and Regulations*: a special message of welcome from one Edward F. Kehoe, commissioner of the Vermont Fish and Game Department, to the reader and would-be camper, *i.e.*, me.

This person (*i.e.*, me) is called "the sportsman."

"We have no 'sportswomen, sportspersons, sportsboys, or sportsgirls,'" Commissioner Kehoe hastened to explain, obviously anticipating that some of us sportsfeminists might feel a bit overlooked. "But," he added, "we are pleased to report that we do have many great sportsmen who are women, as well as young people of both sexes."

It's just that the Fish and Game Department is trying to keep 5 things "simple and forthright" and to respect "long-standing tradition." And anyway, we really ought to be flattered, "sportsman" being "a meaningful title being earned by a special kind of dedicated man, woman, or young person, as opposed to just any hunter, fisherman, or trapper."

I have heard this particular line of reasoning before. In fact, I've 6 heard it so often that I've come to think of it as The Great Person-Hole Cover Debate, since gender-neutral manholes are invariably brought into the argument as evidence of the lengths to which humorless, Newspeak-spouting feminists will go to destroy their mother tongue.

Consternation about woman-handling the language comes from 7 all sides. Sexual conservatives who see the feminist movement as a unisex plot and who long for the good olde days of *vive la différence,* when men were men and women were women, nonetheless do not rally behind the notion that the term "mankind" excludes women.

But most of the people who choke on expressions like "spokes- 8 person" aren't right-wing misogynists, and this is what troubles me. Like the undoubtedly well-meaning folks at the Vermont Fish and Game Department, they tend to reassure you right up front that they're only trying to keep things "simple" and to follow "tradition," and that some of their best men are women, anyway.

Usually they wind up warning you, with great sincerity, that 9 you're jeopardizing the worthy cause of women's rights by focusing on "trivial" side issues. I would like to know how anything that gets people so defensive and resistant can possibly be called "trivial," whatever else it might be.

The English language is alive and constantly changing. Progress 10 —both scientific and social—is reflected in our language, or should be.

Not too long ago, there was a product called "flesh-colored" 11 Band-Aids. The flesh in question was colored Caucasian. Once the civil rights movement pointed out the racism inherent in the name, it was dropped. I cannot imagine reading a thoughtful, well-intentioned company policy statement explaining that while the Band-Aids would continue to be called "flesh-colored" for old time's sake, black and brown people would now be considered honorary whites and were perfectly welcome to use them.

Most sensitive people manage to describe our national religious traditions as "Judeo-Christian," even though it takes a few seconds longer to say than "Christian." So why is it such a hardship to say "he or she" instead of "he"? [12]

I have a modest proposal for anyone who maintains that "he" is just plain easier: since "he" has been the style for several centuries now—and since it really includes everybody anyway, right?—it seems only fair to give "she" a turn. Instead of having to ponder over the intricacies of, say, "Congressman" versus "Congressperson" versus "representative," we can simplify things by calling them all "Congresswoman." [13]

Other clarifications will follow: "a woman's home is her castle . . ." "a giant step for all womankind" . . . "all women are created equal" . . . "Fisherwoman's Wharf." . . . [14]

And don't be upset by the business letter that begins "Dear Madam," fellas. It means you, too. [15]

QUESTIONS

Understanding

1. What is the "great person-hole cover debate," as Van Gelder has come to call it? Where did the debate get its name?

2. Van Gelder finds Commissioner Kehoe's "particular line of reasoning" (par. 6) typical of the arguments on one side of the debate. This side, according to Van Gelder, objects on four main grounds to making the English language more sensitive to gender. The fourth is that such fuss trivializes the just cause of women's rights. What are the other three grounds?

3. What "modest" solution to the debate does Van Gelder propose?

4. Why should the "sexual conservatives" of paragraph 7 be upset, in Van Gelder's view, that words like *mankind* exclude women?

5. Does Van Gelder think that most of the people, like Commissioner Kehoe, who resist change in the gender conventions of English grammar are militant anti-feminists? How does she feel about the majority?

6. Why does Van Gelder think debates about "person-hole" covers and "congresspersons" are *not* trivial?

Strategies and Structure

1. Why do you think Van Gelder singled out the Vermont fish and game regulations to typify the kind of argument she is contesting? Was this a good choice of a prime example? Why or why not?

2. Where and how does Van Gelder counter the argument that essays like hers address a "trivial" issue?

3. How well does Van Gelder's proposed "solution" fit the first three basic criteria that the opposition typically advances in support of its own position. Which of the three arguments is her conclusion (par. 15) intended to counter? How effective, logically, do you find this kind of turning the tables?

4. In paragraph 11, Van Gelder is arguing by analogy. To what is she comparing sexist language? Do you find this standard strategy of logical argument more or less convincing here? (Arguments by analogy are usually as strong as the analogy is close.) Explain your answer.

5. Where else does Van Gelder argue by analogy in her essay?

6. Besides logic, Van Gelder's counter argument makes an ethical appeal. The opposition attributes her kind of argument to "humorless" (par. 6) militants who bloat their native language with jargon. How does Van Gelder create the opposite impression here, so that she becomes someone the opposition must listen to if they are not to abandon their own ethical standards?

7. How does Van Gelder give the impression of tolerance as well as good humor?

8. Linguists tell us that a living language changes whether we want it to or not. How and where does Van Gelder turn this linguistic fact of life to the advantage of her argument?

9. Paragraph 8 makes it clear that Van Gelder is not merely addressing "right-wing misogynists" who, in her view, resist all changes in sexual conventions. For whom is she writing then? How are her manner and TONE tailored for an audience that is not absolutely hostile but not necessarily on her side either?

Words and Figures of Speech

1. What is a *misogynist* (par. 8)?

2. According to your dictionary, what are the full form and meaning of the Latin abbreviation, *i.e.* (pars. 2 and 3)? How does it differ in meaning and application from *e.g.*?

3. Why do you think Van Gelder chose the word "overlooked" in paragraph 4 instead of "slighted," "mistreated," or "abused"? How effective do you find her choice of words here? In paragraph 14, when she refers to "clarifications"?

4. Van Gelder renovates a number of CLICHÉS in paragraph 14. We normally think of clichés as weary words to be avoided; should she have selected less familiar phrases here? Why or why not?

5. Why does Van Gelder spell *olde* with an "e" in paragraph 7?

6. *Vive la différence* in the same paragraph means simply, "Long live the difference." What difference exactly? Why does Van Gelder put a French phrase, especially this phrase, into the mouths of the "conservatives"?

7. To what word in paragraph 3 is *Madame* (par. 15) the feminist equivalent?

Comparing

1. How does George Orwell define "Newspeak" (par. 6) in "Politics and the English Language," reprinted in "Essays for Further Reading" at the end of this book?

2. Orwell connects the breakdown of language with political collapse and corruption. How might Orwell's analysis of the politics of language be applied in the great person-hole cover debate? What political views do some radical feminists ascribe to those who resist changes in the gender conventions of the English language?

3. Van Gelder's "modest proposal" in paragraph 13 alludes to the essay of that title by Jonathan Swift (also reprinted in "Essays for Further Reading"). How does the modesty of Van Gelder's proposal compare with that of Swift's outrageous "projector"? How likely to be adopted does Van Gelder consider her proposal when she draws the comparison with Swift?

4. Compare and contrast Van Gelder's counter argument with that of Martha Mednick and Nancy Felipe Russo in the preceding chapter. In what sense is the essay by Mednick and Russo an appeal to ethics like Van Gelder's?

Discussion and Writing Topics

1. Are you convinced by Van Gelder's argument? Why or why not?

2. Is the controversy over gender in English composition trivial in your opinion? Why or why not?

3. Write an essay attacking such locutions as "his/her," "mail-person," "person-hole cover," and "man- and woman-kind" on the grounds that they make for clumsy writing. Try to think of serious alternatives that will be both gramatically smooth and non-sexist.

4. Write your own modest proposal for (or against) making English a more feminine mother tongue.

Chief Seattle

Reply to the U.S. Government

Chief Seattle (c. 1786–1866) was the leader of the Dwamish, Suquamish, and allied Native American tribes living in the region of the city that now bears his name. He welcomed white settlers from the time of their first arrival and loyally resisted uprisings against them. He later converted to Roman Catholicism and began holding morning and evening services among the tribe. He was not pleased when the village of Seattle, Washington, took his name because he believed that his spirit would be disturbed in the afterlife each time his name was spoken by mortals. Toward the end of his life, Seattle exacted compensation for his broken sleep by seeking gifts among citizens of the region. The "Reply" printed here was Chief Seattle's response to the U.S. government's offer to buy two million acres of Indian land. The offer was made in 1854 through Governor Isaac Stevens of the Washington Territory. For his formal answer, spoken in the Dwamish language, Seattle gathered the tribe around him and placed his hand on Governor Stevens's head. He stood a foot taller than the governor, and his voice could be heard for half a mile. Henry A. Smith translated the speech. Seattle considered the government's proposal (as he promises to do here), decided to accept it, and signed the treaty of Point Elliott on January 22, 1855.

Yonder sky that has wept tears of compassion upon my people for centuries untold, and which to us appears changeless and eternal, may change. Today is fair. Tomorrow may be overcast with clouds. My words are like the stars that never change. Whatever Seattle says the great chief at Washington can rely upon with as much certainty as he can upon the return of the sun or the seasons. The White Chief says that Big Chief at Washington sends us greetings of friendship and goodwill. That is kind of him for we know he has little need of our friendship in return. His people are many. They are like the grass that covers vast prairies. My people are few. They resemble the scattering trees of a storm-swept plain. The great, and—I presume—good, White Chief sends us word that he wishes to buy our lands but is willing to allow us enough to live comfortably. This indeed appears just, even generous, for the Red Man no longer has rights that he need respect, and the offer may be wise also, as we are no longer in need of an extensive country. . . . I will not dwell on, nor mourn over, our untimely decay, nor reproach our paleface brothers with hastening it, as we too may have been somewhat to blame.

Youth is impulsive. When our young men grow angry at some   2
real or imaginary wrong, and disfigure their faces with black paint, it denotes that their hearts are black, and then they are often cruel and relentless, and our old men and old women are unable to restrain them. Thus it has ever been. Thus it was when the white men first began to push our forefathers further westward. But let us hope that the hostilities between us may never return. We would have everything to lose and nothing to gain. Revenge by young men is considered gain, even at the cost of their own lives, but old men who stay at home in times of war, and mothers who have sons to lose, know better.

Our good father at Washington—for I presume he is now our   3
father as well as yours, since King George [1] has moved his boundaries further north—our great good father, I say, sends us word that if we do as he desires he will protect us. His brave warriors will be to us a bristling wall of strength, and his wonderful ships of war will fill our harbors so that our ancient enemies far to the northward—the Hydas and Tsimpsians—will cease to frighten our women, children, and old men. Then in reality will he be our father and we his children. But can that ever be? Your God is not our God! Your God loves your people and hates mine. He folds his strong and protecting arms lovingly about the paleface and leads him by the hand as a father leads his infant son—but He

[1] George IV, king of England from 1820 to 1830.

has forsaken His red children—if they really are his. Our God, the Great Spirit, seems also to have forsaken us. Your God makes your people wax strong every day. Soon they will fill the land. Our people are ebbing away like a rapidly receding tide that will never return. The white man's God cannot love our people or He would protect them. They seem to be orphans who can look nowhere for help. How then can we be brothers? How can your God become our God and renew our prosperity and awaken in us dreams of returning greatness? If we have a common heavenly father He must be partial—for He came to his paleface children. We never saw Him. He gave you laws but He had no word for His red children whose teeming multitudes once filled this vast continent as stars fill the firmament. No; we are two distinct races with separate origins and separate destinies. There is little in common between us.

To us the ashes of our ancestors are sacred and their resting   4
place is hallowed ground. You wander far from the graves of your ancestors and seemingly without regret. Your religion was written upon tables of stone by the iron finger of your God so that you could not forget. The Red Man could never comprehend nor remember it. Our religion is the traditions of our ancestors—the dreams of our old men, given them in solemn hours of night by the Great Spirit; and the visions of our sachems; and it is written in the hearts of our people.

Your dead cease to love you and the land of their nativity as   5
soon as they pass the portals of the tomb and wander way beyond the stars. They are soon forgotten and never return. Our dead never forget the beautiful world that gave them being.

Day and night cannot dwell together. The Red man has ever   6
fled the approach of the White Man, as the morning mist flees before the morning sun. However, your proposition seems fair and I think that my people will accept it and will retire to the reservation you offer them. Then we will dwell apart in peace, for the words of the Great White Chief seem to be the words of nature speaking to my people out of dense darkness.

It matters little where we pass the remnant of our days. They   7
will not be many. A few more moons; a few more winters—and not one of the descendants of the mighty hosts that once moved over this broad land or lived in happy homes, protected by the Great Spirit, will remain to mourn over the graves of a people

once more powerful and hopeful than yours. But why should I mourn at the untimely fate of my people? Tribe follows tribe, and nation follows nation, like the waves of the sea. It is the order of nature, and regret is useless. Your time of decay may be distant, but it will surely come, for even the White Man whose God walked and talked with him as friend with friend, cannot be exempt from the common destiny. We may be brothers after all. We will see.

We will ponder your proposition, and when we decide we will   8
let you know. But should we accept it, I here and now make this condition that we will not be denied the privilege without molestation of visiting at any time the tombs of our ancestors, friends and children. Every part of this soil is sacred in the estimation of my people. Every hillside, every valley, every plain and grove, has been hallowed by some sad or happy event in days long vanished. . . . The very dust upon which you now stand responds more lovingly to their footsteps than to yours, because it is rich with the blood of our ancestors and our bare feet are conscious of the sympathetic touch. . . . Even the little children who lived here and rejoiced here for a brief season will love these somber solitudes and at eventide they greet shadowy returning spirits. And when the last Red Man shall have perished, and the memory of my tribe shall have become a myth among the White Men, these shores will swarm with the invisible dead of my tribe, and when your children's children think themselves alone in the field, the store, the shop, upon the highway, or in the silence of the pathless woods, they will not be alone. . . . At night when the streets of your cities and villages are silent and you think them deserted, they will throng with the returning hosts that once filled and still love this beautiful land. The White Man will never be alone.

Let him be just and deal kindly with my people, for the dead   9
are not powerless. Dead, did I say? There is no death, only a change of worlds.

QUESTIONS

Understanding

1. For what is Chief Seattle appealing to the White Man? What slightly veiled threat does he make in the last two paragraphs of his speech?

2. Describe the single condition that Chief Seattle puts upon his probable acceptance of the government's offer to buy the tribe's land. Why does he make this condition? What does it show about the basis of his religion?

3. How does this belief help to explain why many Native Americans moved onto the reservation only with the greatest reluctance?

4. The last paragraph of Chief Seattle's speech sounds at first like a Christian denial of death and affirmation of heavenly life, but what does he mean by "a change of worlds" (par. 9)? What other differences does Chief Seattle mention between his religion and Christianity?

5. Why does the Dwamish chief doubt that the White Man and the Red Man will ever be brothers? In what grim sense may they prove "brothers after all" (par. 7)?

6. Why, according to Chief Seattle, did the young men of his tribe paint their faces and go to war? What was their motive, and what was the meaning of their war-paint?

7. Chief Seattle refuses to mourn the "untimely fate" (par. 7) of his people or to grant the eternal supremacy of his conquerors. Why? Explain the pervasive theme of his speech.

Strategies and Structure

1. Does Chief Seattle appear trustworthy to you? Why or why not?

2. How does he attempt to establish his authority and trustworthiness in paragraph 1? What equivalent devices might you find in a modern speech?

3. What personal qualities do you attribute to Chief Seattle after reading his entire speech? Point out specific statements and phrases that help to characterize him.

4. How does paragraph 2 show Chief Seattle's wisdom?

5. What distinction is Chief Seattle making when he refers to the "great, and—I presume—good, White Chief" (par. 1)? How does his being anxious to draw this distinction help to qualify the chief as a person worthy to make an APPEAL TO ETHICS?

6. The Dwamish chief shows his respect for the Big Chief at Washington by thanking him for "his greetings of friendship and goodwill" (par. 1) and by addressing him as "our good father" (par. 3). How does he also show that he is not afraid of the Big Chief?

7. Seattle's voice is said to have rumbled like the iron engine of a train when he delivered his speech. How is this rumbling quality conveyed in the sentence patterns of paragraphs 1 and 7? Why is an "iron" pace appropriate to Seattle's message?

8. Seattle begins his appeal by acknowledging the justice (even the generosity) and the power of the government; but he declines to make up his mind at once, and ends by asserting that the Red Man retains a degree of power. Is the order significant here? How would Seattle's speech have been changed if the order had been reversed?

9. When arguing at a disadvantage (against a popular opinion, for example), should you admit that disadvantage early on, mention it in closing, or not acknowledge it at all? Explain your answer.

10. Chief Seattle's ethical appeal also makes use of the APPEAL TO EMOTION. Discuss where and how the two work together. What emotion or emotions does his oration speak to?

Words and Figures of Speech

1. The White Man, we are told, is like "the grass that covers vast prairies" (par. 1) and the Indian is like "scattering trees" (par. 1) or the "receding tide" (par. 3), though once he was like the "stars" (par. 3). How do these natural METAPHORS fit in with Chief Seattle's general references to decay and to the cycle of the seasons?

2. What are the implications of the metaphor, "Day and night cannot dwell together" (par. 6)?

3. In what sense is the translator using the word *sympathetic* when he reports Seattle as saying that "our bare feet are conscious of the sympathetic touch" (par. 8)?

4. What analogy does Chief Seattle draw when he describes the role of the ideal leader or chief in paragraph 3?

Comparing

1. A representative of the old, dying order, Seattle resembles General Lee as Bruce Catton portrays him in "Grant and Lee: A Study in Contrasts" (Chapter 6). Pursue the parallel between the two men and the cultures they represent.
2. Analyze and explain what Barry Lopez in "My Horse" (Chapter 7) has "learned" from Chief Seattle's braves.
3. Compare and contrast Seattle's view of nature with Annie Dillard's in "Transfiguration" (Chapter 7).
4. Apply Horace Miner's explanation of how superstition and magic work in a primitive society ("Body Ritual Among the Nacirema," Chapter 8) to the society of the Dwamish tribe as revealed by Chief Seattle.

Discussion and Writing Topics

1. Speaking on behalf of the government, compose an appropriate reply to Chief Seattle's speech.
2. Write a persuasive ethical appeal in which you contend that it is not possible to restore all their lands to the Native Americans but that some reparation for past injustices is due them.
3. Judging from Chief Seattle's speech, why do you think Indian literature is full of natural metaphors?

Steven Brill

When Lawyers Help Villains

Steven Brill is a contributing editor of Esquire Fortnightly, *for which he writes a regular column entitled, "The Law." He is a graduate of Yale and the Yale Law School and was once an assistant to former New York mayor John V. Lindsay. He has written articles on law, firearms, and presidential politics for* Harper's, New York, *and other magazines. He is also the author of* Firearm Abuse: A Research and Policy Report *(1977) and* The Teamsters *(1978). Editor Clay Felker of* New York *magazine has called Brill "a fantastic reporter, a trained lawyer who is not afraid to look at a document for the facts." Brill's critics charge that his objectivity is sometimes overwhelmed by his liberal's zeal. "When Lawyers Help Villains" is one of his* Esquire *essays; it gives an expert witness's testimony about the moral tightrope that lawyers must walk in order to maintain our present judicial system.*

Leroy "Nicky" Barnes is one-hundred-percent villain. Recently he was convicted in federal court in New York of masterminding one of the city's largest heroin-dealer networks. A millionaire who spent lavishly on cars, homes and furs with the profits he made from delivering heroin to the veins of the men, women and children of Harlem, Barnes had been called Mr. Untouchable because his lawyers had in the past gotten him off when he faced charges of murder, gun possession, heroin dealing and bribery.

Barnes's lawyer is a young former assistant district attorney named David Breitbart. He has handled Barnes's court fights since 1973. Sources close to this most recent case claim that Barnes gave Breitbart a million dollars in cash to split between himself and lawyers working for Barnes's codefendants.

Armed with that tip and curious to meet the man who'd argued with a straight face that his client was an innocent man framed by the government, I went to see Breitbart soon after the trial.

Breitbart's office is in a run-down building at Broadway and 3 Canal Street. There Breitbart adamantly denied the story of the million-dollar fee, saying only that "Barnes paid me well."

"*If* you believed Barnes really was a top heroin dealer," I asked, 4 "and he was supplying, even helping to hook, children on the stuff, would you have any qualms about working for him?" "Not at all," Breitbart shot back. "I don't care what he's done. . . . A criminal lawyer is an advocate. . . . If a man's got the price, I'll try his case and do everything I can to get him off. And I do a great job of it. . . ." Would there ever be a case he wouldn't take? "Well, I suppose if they found a Nazi who'd killed millions of Jews and put him on trial here, I'd have problems taking his case. But, you know, most of us are whores, and I guess if they offered me enough money for it I'd take it. . . ."

What's great about Nicky Barnes and David Breitbart is that 5 they sharpen an issue about lawyers and lawyering that otherwise tends to be much fuzzier. For several days after the interview with Breitbart, I talked about it with several lawyer friends who work at prestigious New York firms. All seemed to have the same reaction—that Breitbart is a detestable type, hardly a credit to the bar.

But Breitbart isn't really much different from other lawyers. 6 Give him some nicely tailored wools to replace his double knits, a hundred-lawyer office in a classy skyscraper, an Ivy League diploma and some skill at editing what he says to reporters, and he could be any of my lawyer friends who snickered at him, or, for that matter, any of the nation's respected attorneys who, for the right price, will take on clients engaged in all kinds of antisocial activities.

For example, there's Thomas Sullivan, a longtime criminal law- 7 yer and a partner in the Chicago firm of Jenner & Block. In early 1975, Sullivan was the lead lawyer defending several organized-crime figures charged with defrauding the Teamsters' $1.6 billion Central States Pension Fund. His clients were accused of using a Teamster pension-fund loan to take over a small manufacturer, then siphoning off the loaned money from the company until it went bankrupt.

The jury found them not guilty. One reason was that one of   8
two star witnesses was shotgunned to death several weeks before
the trial. (The F.B.I. later found that the title to a getaway car
used by the murderers was under a phony name but had been
notarized by a secretary who worked for Sullivan's client.) Another
reason for the verdict was Tom Sullivan. He was brilliant. Trial
rules didn't allow the prosecution to mention the past organized-
crime activities of any of the defendants, and Sullivan got the jury
to accept the proposition that these were innocent entrepreneurs
whose dream of manufacturing plastic pails had failed.

Today, Sullivan is the United States attorney for the Northern   9
District of Illinois, which includes Chicago. President Carter appointed him last year. No reservations were expressed by the Sen-
ate committee that voted on his nomination or by the press about
his role in the Teamster-Mafia case or in cases where he had
defended other alleged pension-fund embezzlers and corrupt government officials.

That's the way it should be. Sullivan has an unblemished repu-   10
tation as an honest lawyer and a decent guy who has been involved
in a number of bar-related civic activities. Carter's decision to
replace Sullivan's Republican-appointed predecessor, like his more
recent dismissal of the U.S. attorney in Philadelphia, was not
based on merit. But the choice of Sullivan as a replacement was.
He was a good lawyer willing to cut his income to about a fourth
of what it had been in order to enter public service.

Sullivan has resolved conflict-of-interest problems by removing   11
himself from involvement in any case concerning former clients of
his, or his old law firm. With this restriction invoked, his side
switching—common among prosecutors and defense lawyers—becomes a plus. Who's better qualified to win cases for the government than a man who has beaten it so many times in the past?

On the other hand, isn't there something we should dislike   12
about men like Thomas Sullivan or David Breitbart, whose ethical
compasses, or lack thereof, allow them to make lots of money defending mobsters or heroin dealers?

Few lawyers see it that way. In broad terms, the lawyers' Code   13
of Professional Responsibility entitles the impeccably evil Nicky
Barnes to the best lawyer he can buy. It allows—in fact, encourages—lawyers to be vigorous advocates of their clients' cases re-

gardless of what they personally believe about their clients' guilt or goodness (as long as they don't knowingly present perjured evidence).

There's good logic in these standards. If lawyers refused to rep- 14 resent clients because they felt they were guilty, many defendants wouldn't be able to find good lawyers and we'd have replaced a jury-trial system that puts the burden of proof on the government with one in which an accused person's fate is decided by the first-impression judgments of lawyers. Also, if lawyers were scared away from defending unpopular clients or people involved in unpopular issues, unpopular *innocent* people (the targets of a Joe McCarthy-type witch-hunt,[1] for instance) would suffer.

Most lawyers aren't as free of qualms as Breitbart in taking 15 clients. Sullivan, for example, says he'd never defend a heroin dealer.

Still, these personal hesitations rarely interfere with the general 16 willingness of lawyers to take any clients with cases falling within the bounds of their practices. The reason Breitbart sharpens this issue so nicely is not just that he apparently has none of these hang-ups but also that his practice is in a particularly unseemly field. He forces us to consider the most troubling consequence of the principle that lawyers shouldn't allow distaste for a client or an issue to dissuade them from taking a case and that lawyers who do take such cases should not be identified negatively with their clients for doing so—namely, that this often allows people like Barnes to go free. But there just isn't a better way to preserve a rule of law that resolves most civil disputes peaceably and does much to make sure that the government can't cut corners to put one of us in jail.

But look where that leaves lawyers. It makes them amoral auto- 17 matons. At a time when so many other pillars of our social and economic establishment, spurred by the Watergate and the corporate-bribery disclosures, are reassessing the ethical consequences of their conduct, lawyers have immunity from the new morality. They're in the unique, if not enviable, position of holding them-

[1] Persecution based on rumor: In the early 1950s, with little evidence, Joseph Raymond McCarthy, U.S. senator from Wisconsin (1946–1957), led an investigation of "un-American" activities in the army that extended to private citizens.

selves out as hired guns, allowed by their own code to be above the moral implications of their work because, as Breitbart puts it, "it's our tough advocacy that keeps the system honest."

Faced with the Breitbart lawyer-amorality question, one Wall   18 Street lawyer suggested that if we give lawyers a free pass on worrying about the moral consequences of what they do for a particular client, then maybe we should try to take something in return by asking them to do a set amount of noncompensated work for charitable or public-interest groups. Requiring such *pro bono* [2] work, or even defining what qualifies as such, has obvious practical pitfalls. Even so, many lawyers already do some charitable work. But if lawyers are going to lessen the growing public distrust and resentment of their profession, it would seem that they'd want to do something in a concrete, organized way to show that they're more than the "whores" Breitbart thinks they are.

QUESTIONS

Understanding

1. Brill says that heroin dealer "Nicky" Barnes and his attorney, David Breitbart, nicely "sharpen an issue about lawyers and lawyering" (par. 5). What is the issue and what makes their case such a clear-cut example?

2. How, according to Breitbart, do lawyers usually answer the charge that they should not defend men they know to be guilty?

3. Brill himself obviously has mixed feelings about this issue. Describe those mixed feelings and explain where he comes out— with or against the lawyers?

4. What additional issue does Brill introduce in paragraphs 17 and 18?

5. What are "conflict-of-interest problems" (par. 11)? Under what circumstances do they arise in business and politics?

6. To what extent do you agree with Brill's assertion that Breitbart "isn't really much different from other lawyers" (par. 6)? How important are the differences he mentions?

[2] *Pro bono publico*, "for the public good."

Strategies and Structure

1. Brill's essay is an APPEAL TO ETHICS in two senses: (1) it appeals to the ethical standards of its audience; (2) it is an appeal made by an ethical person. How does Brill create the impression that he has a highly developed sense of ethics?

2. In general, how are these two aspects of the appeal to ethics related? Why might an essay that adopts one of these strategies also be expected to adopt the other?

3. The first twelve paragraphs of Brill's essay contribute to an INDUCTIVE argument that ends, after a break, in paragraph 16. What is the conclusion of this argument? In which lines is it stated?

4. The word *logic* in paragraph 14 should alert us to look for a DEDUCTIVE argument. Analyze the reasoning in this paragraph.

5. Brill's inductive and deductive arguments come together in paragraph 16. Which sentence in that paragraph states the conclusion of his *deductive* line of reasoning?

6. How many examples does Brill use for the *inductive* part of his argument? How (and in which paragraph) does he justify so few? Is this a legitimate tactic in persuasive writing?

7. Explain why paragraphs 17 and 18 carry Brill's essay beyond logical argumentation and into the realm of ethical appeal. To whom are these final paragraphs directed? What do they urge that audience to do?

8. How effective do you find Brill's use of several different MODES OF PERSUASION in the same essay? Is this sort of combining a good idea as a general strategy of persuasive writing? Explain your answer.

Words and Figures of Speech

1. Brill says that the legal system puts lawyers in the position of being *automatons* (par. 17). What is an automaton and what qualities does the METAPHOR ascribe to lawyers?

2. *Villain* is a term often used in the theater and in sentimental literature. Why does Brill use it here?

3. Why do you think Brill uses the informal *fuzzier* in paragraph 5?

4. How effective do you find the "hired guns" ANALOGY in paragraph 17? Is it fair to lawyers?

5. In the last sentence, Brill turns attorney Breitbart's analogy against him and against the legal profession. How effective is this tactic? Why does attorney Breitbart draw the analogy in the first place?

Comparing

1. In "What You See Is the Real You" (Chapter 5), Willard Gaylin argues that morality is gauged by behavior. How well does this principle hold up in Brill's examination of legal ethics? Explain your answer.
2. Can Brill's charge that attorneys are "amoral automatons" (par. 17) be applied with any justice to attorney Johnson C. Montgomery's position in "Island of Plenty" (Chapter 9)? Why or why not?

Discussion and Writing Topics

1. Brill asserts that "side switching" (par. 11) is a "plus" when the lawyer moves from the side of the criminals to the side of the government. What about the morality of switching the other way, a common enough occurrence? Construct a persuasive argument in which you attack the ethics of this practice.
2. Defend the proposition that even "a Nazi who'd killed millions of Jews" (par. 4) is entitled to his day in court.
3. It was "trial rules" (par. 8), according to Brill, that kept out of court the information that attorney Sullivan's clients had ties with organized crime. How serious a stumbling block to justice do you consider rules of evidence, plea bargaining, and other "technical" aspects of our legal system? Write an appeal to ethics on this issue.
4. How important is the right to a speedy trial? Advance your opinion in a persuasive essay.

WRITING TOPICS for Chapter Ten
Essays That Appeal to Emotion and Ethics

Write an emotional or ethical appeal on one of the following subjects:

1. Marriage is (is not) a wretched institution

2. Doctors are (are not) technicians rather than healers

3. Lawyers are (are not) a dishonest breed

4. College athletics should (should not) be abolished

5. ROTC should (should not) be abolished on college campuses

6. Universities should (should not) allow radicals to speak in their facilities

7. Teachers should (should not) pass judgment on their students' work

8. Public schools are (are not) more responsive to the whole person than are private schools

9. Most college requirements are (are not) worthwhile

10. Seeking psychiatric help is (is not) a sign of weakness

11. The drug laws should (should not) be tightened up

12. Exercise: Analyze the appeal of several newspaper or magazine advertisements: For what audience are they intended? How do they attract that audience? What unstated assumptions do they make?

Essays for
Further Reading

Jonathan Swift
A Modest Proposal

The great satirist, Jonathan Swift (1667–1745), was born in Dub-
lin, Ireland, and educated at Trinity College, Dublin, where he
was censured for breaking the rules of discipline and graduated
only by "special grace." He was ordained an Anglican clergyman
in 1694 and became Dean of St. Patrick's, Dublin in 1713. His
satires in prose and verse addressed three main issues: political
relations between England and Ireland; Irish social questions; and
matters of church doctrine. He is most famous for The Battle of
the Books (1704); A Tale of a Tub (1704); and Gulliver's Travels
(1726). His best-known essay was published in 1729 under the full
title, "A Modest Proposal for Preventing the Children of Poor
People from Being a Burden to Their Parents or the Country."
Assuming a mask, or persona, Swift poured into the essay his con-
tempt for human materialism and for logic without compassion.

It is a melancholy object to those who walk through this great ¹
town ¹ or travel in the country, when they see the streets, the
roads, and cabin doors, crowded with beggars of the female sex,
followed by three, four, or six children, all in rags and impor-
tuning every passenger for an alms. These mothers, instead of
being able to work for their honest livelihood, are forced to
employ all their time in strolling to beg sustenance for their
helpless infants, who, as they grow up, either turn thieves for
want of work, or leave their dear native country to fight for
the Pretender in Spain, or sell themselves to the Barbadoes.²

¹ Dublin, capital city of Ireland.
² The pretender to the throne of England was James Stuart (1688–1766),
son of the deposed James II. Barbados is an island in the West Indies.

I think it is agreed by all parties that this prodigious number of ² children in the arms, or on the backs, or at the heels of their mothers, and frequently of their fathers, is in the present deplorable state of the kingdom a very great additional grievance; and therefore whoever could find out a fair, cheap, and easy method of making these children sound, useful members of the commonwealth would deserve so well of the public as to have his statue set up for a preserver of the nation.

But my intention is very far from being confined to provide only ³ for the children of professed beggars; it is of a much greater extent, and shall take in the whole number of infants at a certain age who are born of parents in effect as little able to support them as those who demand our charity in the streets.

As to my own part, having turned my thoughts for many years ⁴ upon this important subject, and maturely weighed the several schemes of other projectors,³ I have always found them grossly mistaken in their computation. It is true, a child just dropped from its dam may be supported by her milk for a solar year, with little other nourishment; at most not above the value of two shillings,⁴ which the mother may certainly get, or the value in scraps, by her lawful occupation of begging; and it is exactly at one year old that I propose to provide for them in such a manner as instead of being a charge upon their parents or the parish, or wanting food and raiment for the rest of their lives, they shall on the contrary contribute to the feeding, and partly to the clothing, of many thousands.

There is likewise another great advantage in my scheme, that it ⁵ will prevent those voluntary abortions, and that horrid practice of women murdering their bastard children, alas, too frequent among us, sacrificing the poor innocent babes, I doubt, more to avoid the expense than the shame, which would move tears and pity in the most savage and inhuman breast.

The number of souls in this kingdom being usually reckoned ⁶ one million and a half, of these I calculate there may be about two hundred thousand couple whose wives are breeders; from which number I subtract thirty thousand couples who are able to

---

³ Men whose heads were full of foolish schemes or projects.
⁴ The British pound sterling was made up of twenty shillings; five shillings made a crown.

maintain their own children, although I apprehend there cannot be so many under the present distress of the kingdom; but this being granted, there will remain an hundred and seventy thousand breeders. I again subtract fifty thousand for those women who miscarry, or whose children die by accident or disease within the year. There only remain an hundred and twenty thousand children of poor parents annually born. The question therefore is, how this number shall be reared and provided for, which, as I have already said, under the present situation of affairs, is utterly impossible by all the methods hitherto proposed. For we can neither employ them in handicraft or agriculture; we neither build houses (I mean in the country) nor cultivate land. They can very seldom pick up a livelihood by stealing till they arrive at six years old, except where they are of towardly parts;[5] although I confess they learn the rudiments much earlier, during which time they can however be looked upon only as probationers, as I have been informed by a principal gentleman in the county of Cavan, who protested to me that he never knew above one or two instances under the age of six, even in a part of the kingdom so renowned for the quickest proficiency in that art.

I am assured by our merchants that a boy or a girl before twelve   7
years old is no salable commodity; and even when they come to this age they will not yield above three pounds, or three pounds and half a crown at most on the Exchange; which cannot turn to account either to the parents or the kingdom, the charge of nutriment and rags having been at least four times that value.

I shall now therefore humbly propose my own thoughts, which   8
I hope will not be liable to the least objection.

I have been assured by a very knowing American of my ac-   9
quaintance in London, that a young healthy child well nursed is at a year old a most delicious, nourishing, and wholesome food, whether stewed, roasted, baked, or boiled; and I make no doubt that it will equally serve in a fricassee or a ragout.

I do therefore humbly offer it to public consideration that of   10
the hundred and twenty thousand children, already computed, twenty thousand may be reserved for breed, whereof only one fourth part to be males, which is more than we allow to sheep, black cattle, or swine; and my reason is that these children are

[5] Having natural ability.

seldom the fruits of marriage, a circumstance not much regarded by our savages, therefore one male will be sufficient to serve four females. That the remaining hundred thousand may at a year old be offered in sale to the persons of quality and fortune through the kingdom, always advising the mother to let them suck plentifully in the last month, so as to render them plump and fat for a good table. A child will make two dishes at an entertainment for friends; and when the family dines alone, the fore or hind quarter will make a reasonable dish, and seasoned with a little pepper or salt will be very good boiled on the fourth day, especially in winter.

I have reckoned upon a medium that a child just born will 11 weigh twelve pounds, and in a solar year if tolerably nursed increaseth to twenty-eight pounds.

I grant this food will be somewhat dear, and therefore very 12 proper for landlords, who, as they have already devoured most of the parents, seem to have the best title to the children.

Infant's flesh will be in season throughout the year, but more 13 plentiful in March, and a little before and after. For we are told by a grave author, an eminent French physician,[6] that fish being a prolific diet, there are more children born in Roman Catholic countries about nine months after Lent than at any other season; therefore, reckoning a year after Lent, the markets will be more glutted than usual, because the number of popish infants is at least three to one in this kingdom; and therefore it will have one other collateral advantage, by lessening the number of Papists among us.

I have already computed the charge of nursing a beggar's child 14 (in which list I reckon all cottagers, laborers, and four fifths of the farmers) to be about two shillings per annum, rags included; and I believe no gentleman would repine to give ten shillings for the carcass of a good fat child, which, as I have said, will make four dishes of excellent nutritive meat, when he hath only some particular friend or his own family to dine with him. Thus the squire will learn to be a good landlord, and grow popular among the tenants; the mother will have eight shillings net profit, and be fit for work till she produces another child.

Those who are more thrifty (as I must confess the times re- 15

---

[6] François Rabelais (1494?–1553), French satirist.

quire) may flay the carcass; the skin of which artificially [7] dressed
will make admirable gloves for ladies, and summer boots for fine
gentlemen.

As to our city of Dublin, shambles [8] may be appointed for this   16
purpose in the most convenient parts of it, and butchers we may
be assured will not be wanting; although I rather recommend buying the children alive, and dressing them hot from the knife as we
do roasting pigs.

A very worthy person, a true lover of his country, and whose   17
virtues I highly esteem, was lately pleased in discoursing on this
matter to offer a refinement upon my scheme. He said that many
gentlemen of this kingdom, having of late destroyed their deer, he
conceived that the want of venison might be well supplied by the
bodies of young lads and maidens, not exceeding fourteen years of
age nor under twelve, so great a number of both sexes in every
country being now ready to starve for want of work and service;
and these to be disposed of by their parents, if alive, or otherwise
by their nearest relations. But with due deference to so excellent
a friend and so deserving a patriot, I cannot be altogether in his
sentiments; for as to the males, my American acquaintance assured
me from frequent experience that their flesh was generally tough
and lean, like that of our schoolboys, by continual exercise, and
their taste disagreeable; and to fatten them would not answer the
charge. Then as to the females, it would, I think with humble sub-
mission, be a loss to the public, because they soon would become
breeders themselves: and besides, it is not improbable that some
scrupulous people might be apt to censure such a practice (although indeed very unjustly) as a little bordering upon cruelty;
which, I confess, hath always been with me the strongest objection
against any project, how well soever intended.

But in order to justify my friend, he confessed that this ex-   18
pedient was put into his head by the famous Psalmanazar,[9] a
native of the island Formosa, who came from thence to London
above twenty years ago, and in conversation told my friend that in
his country when any young person happened to be put to death,
the executioner sold the carcass to persons of quality as a prime

---

[7] Skillfully, artfully.
[8] Slaughterhouses.
[9] George Psalmanazar (1679?–1763), a Frenchman, fooled English society for
several years by masquerading as a pagan Formosan.

dainty; and that in his time the body of a plump girl of fifteen, who was crucified for an attempt to poison the emperor, was sold to his Imperial Majesty's prime minister of state, and other great mandarins of the court, in joints from the gibbet, at four hundred crowns. Neither indeed can I deny that if the same use were made of several plump young girls in this town, who without one single groat to their fortunes cannot stir abroad without a chair, and appear at the playhouse and assemblies in foreign fineries which they never will pay for, the kingdom would not be the worse.

Some persons of a desponding spirit are in great concern about   19
that vast number of poor people who are aged, diseased, or maimed, and I have been desired to employ my thoughts what course may be taken to ease the nation of so grievous an encumbrance. But I am not in the least pain upon that matter, because it is very well known that they are every day dying and rotting by cold and famine, and filth and vermin, as fast as can be reasonably expected. And as to the younger laborers, they are now in almost as hopeful a condition. They cannot get work, and consequently pine away for want of nourishment to a degree that if at any time they are accidentally hired to common labor, they have not strength to perform it; and thus the country and themselves are happily delivered from the evils to come.

I have too long digressed, and therefore shall return to my sub-   20
ject. I think the advantages by the proposal which I have made are obvious and many, as well as of the highest importance.

For first, as I have already observed, it would greatly lessen the   21
number of Papists, with whom we are yearly overrun, being the principal breeders of the nation as well as our most dangerous enemies; and who stay at home on purpose to deliver the kingdom to the Pretender, hoping to take their advantage by the absence of so many good Protestants, who have chosen rather to leave their country than stay at home and pay tithes against their conscience to an Episcopal curate.[1]

Secondly, the poorer tenants will have something valuable of   22
their own, which by law may be made liable to distress, and help

---

[1] Swift blamed much of Ireland's poverty upon large landowners who avoided church tithes by living (and spending their money) abroad.

to pay their landlord's rent, their corn and cattle being already seized and money a thing unknown.

Thirdly, whereas the maintenance of an hundred thousand chil- 23 dren, from two years old and upward, cannot be computed at less than ten shillings a piece per annum, the nation's stock will be thereby increased fifty thousand pounds per annum, besides the profit of a new dish introduced to the tables of all gentlemen of fortune in the kingdom who have any refinement in taste. And the money will circulate among ourselves, the goods being entirely of our own growth and manufacture.

Fourthly, the constant breeders, besides the gain of eight shil- 24 lings sterling per annum by the sale of their children, will be rid of the charge of maintaining them after the first year.

Fifthly, this food would likewise bring great custom to taverns, 25 where the vintners will certainly be so prudent as to procure the best receipts for dressing it to perfection, and consequently have their houses frequented by all the fine gentlemen, who justly value themselves upon their knowledge in good eating; and a skillful cook, who understands how to oblige his guests, will contrive to make it as expensive as they please.

Sixthly, this would be a great inducement to marriage, which all 26 wise nations have either encouraged by rewards or enforced by laws and penalties. It would increase the care and tenderness of mothers toward their children, when they were sure of a settlement for life to the poor babes, provided in some sort by the public, to their annual profit instead of expense. We should see an honest emulation among the married women, which of them could bring the fattest child to the market. Men would become as fond of their wifes during the time of their pregnancy as they are now of their mares in foal, their cows in calf, or sows when they are ready to farrow; nor offer to beat or kick them (as is too frequent a prac- tice) for fear of a miscarriage.

Many other advantages might be enumerated. For instance, the 27 addition of some thousand carcasses in our exportation of barreled beef, the propagation of swine's flesh, and improvement in the art of making good bacon, so much wanted among us by the great destruction of pigs, too frequent at our tables, which are no way comparable in taste or magnificence to a well-grown, fat, yearling child, which roasted whole will make a considerable figure at a lord mayor's feast or any other public entertainment. But this and many others I omit, being studious of brevity.

Supposing that one thousand families in this city would be constant customers for infants' flesh, besides others who might have it at merry meetings, particularly weddings and christenings, I compute that Dublin would take off annually about twenty thousand carcasses, and the rest of the kingdom (where probably they will be sold somewhat cheaper) the remaining eighty thousand.   28

I can think of no one objection that will possibly be raised against this proposal, unless it should be urged that the number of people will be thereby much lessened in the kingdom. This I freely own, and it was indeed one principal design in offering it to the world. I desire the reader will observe, that I calculate my remedy for this one individual kingdom of Ireland and for no other that ever was, is, or I think ever can be upon earth. Therefore let no man talk to me of other expedients [2]: of taxing our absentees at five shillings a pound: of using neither clothes nor household furniture except what is of our own growth and manufacture: of utterly rejecting the materials and instruments that promote foreign luxury: of curing the expensiveness of pride, vanity, idleness, and gaming in our women: of introducing a vein of parsimony, prudence, and temperance: of learning to love our country, in the want of which we differ even from Laplanders and the inhabitants of Topinamboo [3]: of quitting our animosities and factions, nor acting any longer like the Jews, who were murdering one another at the very moment their city [4] was taken: of being a little cautious not to sell our country and conscience for nothing: of teaching landlords to have at least one degree of mercy toward their tenants: lastly, of putting a spirit of honesty, industry, and skill into our shopkeepers; who, if a resolution could now be taken to buy only our native goods, would immediately unite to cheat and exact upon us in the price, the measure, and the goodness, nor could ever yet be brought to make one fair proposal of just dealing, though often and earnestly invited to it.   29

Therefore I repeat, let no man talk to me of these and the like   30

[2] The following are all measures that Swift himself proposed in various pamphlets.
[3] In Brazil.
[4] Jerusalem, sacked by the Romans in A.D. 70.

expedients, till he hath at least some glimpse of hope that there will ever be some hearty and sincere attempt to put them in practice.

But as to myself, having been wearied out for many years with offering vain, idle, visionary thoughts, and at length utterly despairing of success, I fortunately fell upon this proposal, which, as it is wholly new, so it hath something solid and real, of no expense and little trouble, full in our own power, and whereby we can incur no danger in disobliging England. For this kind of commodity will not bear exportation, the flesh being of too tender a consistence to admit a long continuance in salt, although perhaps I could name a country [5] which would be glad to eat up our whole nation without it.

After all, I am not so violently bent upon my own opinion as to reject any offer proposed by wise men, which shall be found equally innocent, cheap, easy, and effectual. But before something of that kind shall be advanced in contradiction to my scheme, and offering a better, I desire the author or authors will be pleased maturely to consider two points. First, as things now stand, how they will be able to find food and raiment for an hundred thousand useless mouths and backs. And secondly, there being a round million of creatures in human figure throughout this kingdom, whose sole subsistence put into a common stock would leave them in debt two millions of pounds sterling, adding those who are beggars by profession to the bulk of farmers, cottagers, and laborers, with their wives and children who are beggars in effect; I desire those politicians who dislike my overture, and may perhaps be so bold to attempt an answer, that they will first ask the parents of these mortals whether they would not at this day think it a great happiness to have been sold for food at a year old in the manner I prescribe, and thereby have avoided such a perpetual scene of misfortunes as they have since gone through by the oppression of landlords, the impossibility of paying rent without money or trade, the want of common sustenance, with neither house nor clothes to cover them from the inclemencies of the weather, and the most inevitable prospect of entailing the like or greater miseries upon their breed forever.

[5] England.

I profess, in the sincerity of my heart, that I have not the least 33 personal interest in endeavoring to promote this necessary work, having no other motive than the public good of my country, by advancing our trade, providing for infants, relieving the poor, and giving some pleasure to the rich. I have no children by which I can propose to get a single penny; the youngest being nine years old, and my wife past childbearing.

James Thurber

University Days

James Thurber (1894–1961) was one of America's leading humor-
ists, essayists, and cartoonists. He grew up in Columbus, Ohio,
and attended the Ohio State University. In 1925 he joined the
Staff of The New Yorker, where E. B. White (see the next essay)
helped him to perfect his prose style. Aware that the humorist's
imagination is "set in motion by the damp hand of melancholy,"
Thurber once defined humor as "a kind of emotional chaos told
about calmly and quietly in retrospect." Among Thurber's books
of stories, essays, and the drawings that Dorothy Parker called
"unbaked cookies" are: Is Sex Necessary? (1929 with E. B.
White); The Owl in the Attic (1931); The Middle-Aged Man on
the Flying Trapeze (1935); Let Your Mind Alone! (1937); My
World—and Welcome to It (1942); The Thurber Carnival
(1945); Alarms and Diversions (1957); The Years with Ross
(1959); Lanterns and Lances (1961) and Credos and Curios
(1962). "University Days" appears in one of Thurber's most successful books, My Life and Hard Times (1933).

I passed all the other courses that I took at my University,   1
but I could never pass botany. This was because all botany
students had to spend several hours a week in a laboratory
looking through a microscope at plant cells, and I could never
see through a microscope. I never once saw a cell through a
microscope. This used to enrage my instructor. He would
wander around the laboratory pleased with the progress all
the students were making in drawing the involved and, so I
am told, interesting structure of flower cells, until he came to
me. I would just be standing there. "I can't see anything," I

would say. He would begin patiently enough, explaining how anybody can see through a microscope, but he would always end up in a fury; claiming that I could *too* see through a microscope but just pretended that I couldn't. "It takes away from the beauty of flowers anyway," I used to tell him. "We are not concerned with beauty in this course," he would say. "We are concerned solely with what I may call the *mechanics* of flars." "Well," I'd say. "I can't see anything." "Try it just once again," he'd say, and I would put my eye to the microscope and see nothing at all, except now and again a nebulous milky substance—a phenomenon of maladjustment. You were supposed to see a vivid, restless clockwork of sharply defined plant cells. "I see what looks like a lot of milk," I would tell him. This, he claimed, was the result of my not having adjused the microscope properly, so he would readjust it for me, or rather, for himself. And I would look again and see milk.

I finally took a deferred pass, as they called it, and waited a   2
year and tried again. (You had to pass one of the biological sciences or you couldn't graduate.) The professor had come back from vacation brown as a berry, bright-eyed, and eager to explain cell-structure again to his classes. "Well," he said to me, cheerily, when we met in the first laboratory hour of the semester, "we're going to see cells this time, aren't we?" "Yes, sir," I said. Students to the right of me and left of me and in front of me were seeing cells; what's more, they were quietly drawing pictures of them in their notebooks. Of course, I didn't see anything.

"We'll try it," the professor said to me, grimly, "with every   3
adjustment of the microscope known to man. As God is my witness, I'll arrange this glass so that you see cells through it or I'll give up teaching. In twenty-two years of botony, I—" He cut off abruptly for he was beginning to quiver all over, like Lionel Barrymore,[1] and he genuinely wished to hold onto his temper; his scenes with me had taken a great deal out of him.

So we tried it with every adjustment of the microscope known   4
to man. With only one of them did I see anything but blackness or the familiar lacteal opacity, and that time I saw, to my pleasure and amazement, a variegated constellation of flecks, specks, and dots. These I hastily drew. The instructor, noting my activity,

[1] (1878–1954), American actor.

came from an adjoining desk, a smile on his lips and his eyebrows high in hope. He looked at my cell drawing. "What's that?" he demanded, with a hint of squeal in his voice. "That's what I saw," I said. "You didn't, you didn't, you *didn*'t!" he screamed, losing control of his temper instantly, and he bent over and squinted into the microscope. His head snapped up. "That's your eye!" he shouted. "You've fixed the lens so that it reflects! You've drawn your eye!"

Another course that I didn't like, but somehow managed to   5 pass, was economics. I went to that class straight from the botany class, which didn't help me any in understanding either subject. I used to get them mixed up. But not as mixed up as another student in my economics class who came there direct from a physics laboratory. He was a tackle on the football team, named Bolenciecwcz. At that time Ohio State University had one of the best football teams in the country, and Bolenciecwcz was one of its outstanding stars. In order to be eligible to play it was necessary for him to keep up in his studies, a very difficult matter, for while he was not dumber than an ox he was not any smarter. Most of his professors were lenient and helped him along. None gave him more hints, in answering questions, or asked him simpler ones than the economics professor, a thin, timid man named Bassum. One day when we were on the subject of transportation and distribution, it came Bolenciecwcz's turn to answer a question. "Name one means of transportation," the professor said to him. No light came into the big tackle's eyes. "Just any means of transportation," said the professor. Bolenciecwcz sat staring at him. "That is," pursued the professor, "any medium, agency, or method of going from one place to another." Bolenciecwcz had the look of a man who is being led into a trap. "You may choose among steam, horse-drawn, or electrically propelled vehicles," said the instructor. "I might suggest the one which we commonly take in making long journeys across land." There was a profound silence in which everybody stirred uneasily, including Bolenciecwcz and Mr. Bassum. Mr. Bassum abruptly broke this silence in an amazing manner. "Choo-choo-choo," he said, in a low voice, and turned instantly scarlet. He glanced appealingly around the room. All of us, of course, shared Mr. Bassum's desire that Bolenciecwcz should stay abreast of the class in economics, for the Illinois game, one of the hardest and most important of the season, was only a week off. "Toot, toot, too-tooooooot!" some student with a deep voice moaned, and we all looked encouragingly at Bolenciecwcz. Somebody else gave a fine imitation of a locomotive letting off steam. Mr. Bassum himself rounded off the little show. "Ding, dong, ding, dong," he said, hopefully. Bolenciecwcz was staring at the floor now, trying to think, his great brow furrowed, his huge hands rubbing together, his face red.

"How did you come to college this year, Mr. Bolenciecwcz?" 6
asked the professor. "*Chuf*fa chuffa, *chuf*fa chuffa."

"M'father sent me," said the football player.   7

"What on?" asked Bassum.   8

"I git an 'lowance," said the tackle, in a low, husky voice,   9
obviously embarrassed.

"No, no," said Bassum. "Name a means of transportation.   10
What did you *ride* here on?"

"Train," said Bolenciecwcz.   11

"Quite right," said the professor. "Now, Mr. Nugent, will you   12
tell us—"

If I went through anguish in botany and economics—for dif-   13
ferent reasons—gymnasium work was even worse. I don't even like to think about it. They wouldn't let you play games or join in the exercises with your glasses on and I couldn't see with mine off. I bumped into professors, horizontal bars, agricultural students, and swinging iron rings. Not being able to see, I could take it but I couldn't dish it out. Also, in order to pass gymnasium (and you had to pass it to graduate) you had to learn to swim if you didn't know how. I didn't like the swimming pool, I didn't like swimming, and I didn't like the swimming instructor, and after all these years I still don't. I never swam but I passed my gym work anyway, by having another student give my gymnasium number (978) and swim across the pool in my place. He was a quiet, amiable blonde youth, number 473, and he would have seen through a microscope for me if we could have got away with it, but we couldn't get away with it. Another thing I didn't like about gymnasium work was that they made you strip the day you registered. It is impossible for me to be happy when I am stripped and being asked a lot of questions. Still, I did better than a lanky agricultural student who was cross-examined just before I was. They asked

each student what college he was in—that is, whether Arts, Engineering, Commerce, or Agriculture. "What college are you in?" the instructor snapped at the youth in front of me. "Ohio State University," he said promptly.

It wasn't that agricultural student but it was another a whole lot like him who decided to take up journalism, possibly on the ground that when farming went to hell he could fall back on newspaper work. He didn't realize, of course, that that would be very much like falling back full-length on a kit of carpenter's tools. Haskins didn't seem cut out for journalism, being too embarassed to talk to anybody and unable to use a typewriter, but the editor of the college paper assigned him to the cow barns, the sheep house, the horse pavilion, and the animal husbandry department generally. This was a genuinely big "beat," for it took up five times as much ground and got ten times as great a legislative appropriation as the College of Liberal Arts. The agricultural student knew animals, but nevertheless his stories were dull and colorlessly written. He took all afternoon on each one of them, on account of having to hunt for each letter on the typewriter. Once in a while he had to ask somebody to help him hunt. "C" and "L," in particular, were hard letters for him to find. His editor finally got pretty much annoyed at the farmer-journalist because his pieces were so uninteresting. "See here, Haskins," he snapped at him one day, "why is it we never have anything hot from you on the horse pavilion? Here we have two hundred head of horses on this campus—more than any other university in the Western Conference except Purdue—and yet you never get any real low down on them. Now shoot over to the horse barns and dig up something lively." Haskins shambled out and came back in about an hour; he said he had something. "Well, start it off snappily," said the editor. "Something people will read." Haskins set to work and in a couple of hours brought a sheet of typewritten paper to the desk; it was a two-hundred word story about some disease that had broken out among the horses. Its opening sentence was simple but arresting. It read: "Who has noticed the sores on the tops of the horses in the animal husbandry building?"

Ohio State was a land grant university and therefore two years of military drill was compulsory. We drilled with old Springfield rifles and studied the tactics of the Civil War even though the

14

15

World War was going on at the time.[2] At 11 o'clock each morning thousands of freshmen and sophomores used to deploy over the campus, moodily creeping up on the old chemistry building. It was good training for the kind of warfare that was waged at Shiloh but it had no connection with what was going on in Europe. Some people used to think there was German money behind it, but they didn't dare say so or they would have been thrown in jail as German spies. It was a period of muddy thought and marked, I believe, the decline of higher education in the Middle West.

As a soldier I was never any good at all. Most of the cadets were [16] glumly indifferent soldiers, but I was no good at all. Once General Littlefield, who was commandant of the cadet corps, popped up in front of me during regimental drill and snapped, "You are the main trouble with this university!" I think he meant that my type was the main trouble with the university but he may have meant me individually. I was mediocre at drill, certainly—that is, until my senior year. By that time I had drilled longer than anybody else in the Western Conference, having failed at military at the end of each preceding year so that I had to do it all over again. I was the only senior still in uniform. The uniform which, when new, had made me look like an interurban railway conductor, now that it had become faded and too tight made me look like Bert Williams in his bellboy act. This had a definitely bad effect on my morale. Even so, I had become by sheer practice little short of wonderful at squad manoeuvres.

One day General Littlefield picked our company out of the [17] whole regiment and tried to get it mixed up by putting it through one movement after another as fast as we could execute them: squads right, squads left, squads on right into line, squads right about, squads left front into line etc. In about three minutes one hundred and nine men were marching in one direction and I was marching away from them at an angle of forty degrees, all alone. "Company, halt!" shouted General Littlefield, "That man is the only man who has it right!" I was made a corporal for my achievement.

---

[2] The World War I armistice was signed November 11, 1918, two days before Thurber landed in Paris as a code clerk for the state department.

The next day General Littlefield summoned me to his office. [18] He was swatting flies when I went in. I was silent and he was silent too, for a long time. I don't think he remembered me or why he had sent for me, but he didn't want to admit it. He swatted some more flies, keeping his eyes on them narrowly before he let go with the swatter. "Button up your coat!" he snapped. Looking back on it now I can see that he meant me although he was looking at a fly, but I just stood there. Another fly came to rest on a paper in front of the general and began rubbing its hind legs together. The general lifted the swatter cautiously. I moved restlessly and the fly flew away. "You startled him!" barked General Littlefield, looking at me severely. I said I was sorry. "That won't help the situation!" snapped the General, with cold military logic. I didn't see what I could do except offer to chase some more flies toward his desk, but I didn't say anything. He stared out the window at the faraway figures of co-eds crossing the campus toward the library. Finally, he told me I could go. So I went. He either didn't know which cadet I was or else he forgot what he wanted to see me about. It may have been that he wished to apologize for having called me the main trouble with the university; or maybe he had decided to compliment me on my brilliant drilling of the day before and then at the last minute decided not to. I don't know. I don't think about it much any more.

E. B. White

Once More to the Lake

Elwyn Brooks White, the dean of American essayists, a story-teller and a poet, was born in Mount Vernon, New York, in 1899. After studying at Cornell University, he joined the staff of The New Yorker in 1926. A gifted reporter of urban life, White was to find the city too "seductive," and he gradually spent more and more time on his farm in Maine, where he moved more or less permanently in 1957. Widely praised for his prose style, White wrote a regular column, "One Man's Meat" for Harper's and many editorials for The New Yorker. He has published nineteen books, including Charlotte's Web (1952, for children); The Second Tree from the Corner (1954); The Elements of Style (1959, an enlargement of William Strunk's handbook for writers); The Points of My Compass (1962); and The Letters of E. B. White (1976). "Once More to the Lake," a narrative about the generations, is reprinted from Essays of E. B. White (1977); written in August 1941, it originally appeared in Harper's and later in One Man's Meat (1942).

One summer, along about 1904, my father rented a camp on a lake in Maine and took us all there for the month of August. We all got ringworm from some kittens and had to rub Pond's Extract on our arms and legs night and morning, and my father rolled over in a canoe with all his clothes on; but outside of that the vacation was a success and from then on none of us ever thought there was any place in the world like that lake in Maine. We returned summer after summer— always on August 1 for one month. I have since become a salt-water man, but sometimes in summer there are days when the restlessness of the tides and the fearful cold of the sea water and the incessant wind that blows across the afternoon and into the evening make me wish for the placidity of a lake in the woods. A few weeks ago this feeling got so strong I bought myself a couple of bass hooks and a spinner and returned to the lake where we used to go, for a week's fishing and to revisit old haunts.

I took along my son, who had never had any fresh water up his   2
nose and who had seen lily pads only from train windows. On the journey over to the lake I began to wonder what it would be like. I wondered how the time would have marred this unique, this holy spot—the coves and streams, the hills that the sun set behind, the camps and the paths behind the camps. I was sure that the tarred road would have found it out, and I wondered in what other ways it would be desolated. It is strange how much you can re-member about places like that once you allow your mind to return into the grooves that lead back. You remember one thing, and that suddenly reminds you of another thing. I guess I remembered clearest of all the early mornings, when the lake was cool and motionless, remembered how the bedroom smelled of the lumber it was made of and of the wet woods whose scent entered through the screen. The partitions in the camp were thin and did not extend clear to the top of the rooms, and as I was always the first up I would dress softly so as not to wake the others, and sneak out into the sweet outdoors and start out in the canoe, keeping close along the shore in the long shadows of the pines. I remem-bered being very careful never to rub my paddle against the gun-wale for fear of disturbing the stillness of the cathedral.

The lake had never been what you would call a wild lake. There   3
were cottages sprinkled around the shores, and it was in farming country although the shores of the lake were quite heavily wooded. Some of the cottages were owned by nearby farmers, and you would live at the shore and eat your meals at the farmhouse. That's what our family did. But although it wasn't wild, it was a fairly large and undisturbed lake and there were places in it that, to a child at least, seemed infinitely remote and primeval.

I was right about the tar: it led to within half a mile of the   4
shore. But when I got back there, with my boy, and we settled into a camp near a farmhouse and into the kind of summertime I had known, I could tell that it was going to be pretty much the same as it had been before—I knew it, lying in bed the first morn-

ing, smelling the bedroom and hearing the boy sneak quietly out and go off along the shore in a boat. I began to sustain the illusion that he was I, and therefore, by simple transposition, that I was my father. This sensation persisted, kept cropping up all the time we were there. It was not an entirely new feeling, but in this setting, it grew much stronger. I seemed to be living a dual existence. I would be in the middle of some simple act, I would be picking up a bait box or laying down a table fork, or I would be saying something, and suddenly it would be not I but my father who was saying the words or making the gesture. It gave me a creepy sensation.

We went fishing the first morning. I felt the same damp moss   5 covering the worms in the bait can, and saw the dragonfly alight on the tip of my rod as it hovered a few inches from the surface of the water. It was the arrival of this fly that convinced me beyond any doubt that everything was as it always had been, that the years were a mirage and that there had been no years. The small waves were the same, chucking the rowboat under the chin as we fished at anchor, and the boat was the same boat, the same color green and the ribs broken in the same places, and under the floorboards the same fresh-water leavings and débris—the dead helgramite, the wisps of moss, the rusty discarded fishhook, the dried blood from yesterday's catch. We stared silently at the tips of our rods, at the dragonflies that came and went. I lowered the tip of mine into the water, tentatively, pensively dislodging the fly, which darted two feet away, poised, darted two feet back, and came to rest again a little farther up the rod. There had been no years between the ducking of this dragonfly and the other one— the one that was part of memory. I looked at the boy, who was silently watching his fly, and it was my hands that held his rod, my eyes watching. I felt dizzy and didn't know which rod I was at the end of.

We caught two bass, hauling them in briskly as though they   6 were mackerel, pulling them over the side of the boat in a businesslike manner without any landing net, and stunning them with a blow on the back of the head. When we got back for a swim before lunch, the lake was exactly where we had left it, the same number of inches from the dock, and there was only the merest suggestion of a breeze. This seemed an utterly enchanted sea, this lake you could leave to its own devices for a few hours and come back to, and find that it had not stirred, this constant and trust-worthy body of water. In the shallows, the dark, water-soaked sticks and twigs, smooth and old, were undulating in clusters on the bottom against the clean ribbed sand, and the track of the mussel was plain. A school of minnows swam by, each minnow with its small individual shadow, doubling the attendance, so clear and sharp in the sunlight. Some of the other campers were in swimming, along the shore, one of them with a cake of soap, and the water felt thin and clear and unsubstantial. Over the years there had been this person with the cake of soap, this cultist, and here he was. There had been no years.

Up to the farmhouse to dinner through the teeming, dusty field, 7 the road under our sneakers was only a two-track road. The middle track was missing, the one with the marks of the hooves and the splotches of dried, flaky manure. There had always been three tracks to choose from in choosing which track to walk in; now the choice was narrowed down to two. For a moment I missed ter-ribly the middle alternative. But the way led past the tennis court, and something about the way it lay there in the sun reassured me; the tape had loosened along the backline, the alleys were green with plantains and other weeds, and the net (installed in June and removed in September) sagged in the dry noon, and the whole place steamed with midday heat and hunger and emptiness. There was a choice of pie for dessert, and one was blueberry and one was apple, and the waitresses were the same country girls, there having been no passage of time, only the illusion of it as in a dropped cur-tain—the waitresses were still fifteen; their hair had been washed, that was the only difference—they had been to the movies and seen the pretty girls with the clean hair.

Summertime, oh, summertime, pattern of life indelible, the 8 fade-proof lake, the woods unshatterable, the pasture with the sweetfern and the juniper forever and ever, summer without end; this was the background, and the life along the shore was the design, the cottages with their innocent and tranquil design, their tiny docks with the flagpole and the American flag floating against the white clouds in the blue sky, the little paths over the roots of the trees leading from camp to camp and the paths leading back to the outhouses and the can of lime for sprinkling, and at the souvenir counters at the store the miniature birch-bark canoes and the postcards that showed things looking a little better than they looked. This was the American family at play, escaping the city heat, wondering whether the newcomers in the camp at the head of the cove were "common" or "nice," wondering whether it was true that the people who drove up for Sunday dinner at the farmhouse were turned away because there wasn't enough chicken.

It seemed to me, as I kept remembering all this, that those 9 times and those summers had been infinitely precious and worth saving. There had been jollity and peace and goodness. The arriving (at the beginning of August) had been so big a business in itself, at the railway station the farm wagon drawn up, the first smell of the pine-laden air, the first glimpse of the smiling farmer, and the great importance of the trunks and your father's enormous authority in such matters, and the feel of the wagon under you for the long ten-mile haul, and at the top of the last long hill catching the first view of the lake after eleven months of not seeing this cherished body of water. The shouts and cries of the other campers when they saw you, and the trunks to be unpacked, to give up their rich burden. (Arriving was less exciting nowadays, when you sneaked up in your car and parked it under a tree near the camp and took out the bags and in five minutes it was all over, no fuss, no loud wonderful fuss about trunks.)

Peace and goodness and jollity. The only thing that was wrong 10 now, really, was the sound of the place, an unfamiliar nervous sound of the outboard motors. This was the note that jarred, the one thing that would sometimes break the illusion and set the years moving. In those other summertimes all motors were inboard; and when they were at a little distance, the noise they made was a sedative, an ingredient of summer sleep. They were one-cylinder and two-cylinder engines, and some were make-and-break and some were jump-spark, but they all made a sleepy sound across the lake. The one-lungers throbbed and fluttered, and the twin-cylinder ones purred and purred, and that was a quiet sound, too. But now the campers all had outboards. In the daytime, in the hot mornings, these motors made a petulant, irritable sound; at night, in the still evening when the afterglow lit the water, they whined about one's ears like mosquitoes. My boy loved our rented outboard, and his great desire was to achieve single-handed mastery over it, and authority, and he soon learned the trick of choking it a little (but not too much), and the adjustment of the needle valve. Watching him I would remember the things you could do with the old one-cylinder engine with the heavy flywheel, how you could have it eating out of your hand if you got really close to it spiritually. Motorboats in those days didn't have clutches, and you would make a landing by shutting off the motor at the proper time and coasting in with a dead rudder. But there was a way of reversing them, if you learned the trick, by cutting the switch and putting it on again exactly on the final dying revolution of the flywheel, so that it would kick back against compression and begin reversing. Approaching a dock in a strong following breeze, it was difficult to slow up sufficiently by the ordinary coasting method, and if a boy felt he had complete mastery over his motor, he was tempted to keep it running beyond its time and then reverse it a few feet from the dock. It took a cool nerve, because if you threw the switch a twentieth of a second too soon you would catch the flywheel when it still had speed enough to go up past center, and the boat would leap ahead, charging bull-fashion at the dock.

We had a good week at the camp. The bass were biting well   11
and the sun shone endlessly, day after day. We would be tired at night and lie down in the accumulated heat of the little bedrooms after the long hot day and the breeze would stir almost imperceptibly outside and the smell of the swamp drift in through the rusty screens. Sleep would come easily and in the morning the red squirrel would be on the roof, tapping out his gay routine. I kept remembering everything, lying in bed in the mornings—the small steamboat that had a long rounded stern like the lip of a Ubangi, and how quietly she ran on the moonlight sails, when the older boys played their mandolins and the girls sang and we ate doughnuts dipped in sugar, and how sweet the music was on the water in the shining night, and what it had felt like to think about girls then. After breakfast we would go up to the store and the things were in the same place—the minnows in a bottle, the plugs and spinners disarranged and pawed over by the youngsters from the boys' camp, the Fig Newtons and the Beeman's gum. Outside, the road was tarred and cars stood in front of the store. Inside, all was just as it had always been, except there was more Coca-Cola and not so much Moxie [1] and root beer and birch beer

[1] Brand name of an old-fashioned soft drink.

and sarsaparilla. We would walk out with the bottle of pop apiece and sometimes the pop would backfire up our noses and hurt. We explored the streams, quietly, where the turtles slid off logs and dug their way into the soft bottom; and we lay on the town wharf and fed worms to the tame bass. Everywhere we went I had trouble making out which was I, the one walking at my side, the one walking in my pants.

One afternoon while we were there at that lake a thunderstorm 12 came up. It was like the revival of an old melodrama that I had seen long ago with childish awe. The second-act climax of the drama of the electrical disturbance over a lake in America has not changed in any important respect. This was the big scene, still the big scene. The whole thing was so familiar, the first feeling of oppression and heat and a general air around camp of not wanting to go very far away. In midafternoon (it was all the same) a curious darkening of the sky, and a lull in everything that had made life tick; and then the way the boats suddenly swung the other way at their moorings with the coming of a breeze out of the new quarter, and the premonitory rumble. Then the kettle drum, then the snare, then the bass drum and cymbals, then crackling light against the dark, and the gods grinning and licking their chops in the hills. Afterward the calm, the rain steadily rustling in the calm lake, the return of light and hope and spirits, and the campers running out in joy and relief to go swimming in the rain, their bright cries perpetuating the deathless joke about how they were getting simply drenched, and the children screaming with delight at the new sensation of bathing in the rain, and the joke about getting drenched linking the generations in a strong indestructible chain. And the comedian who waded in carrying an umbrella.

When the others went swimming, my son said he was going in, 13 too. He pulled his dripping trunks from the line where they had hung all through the shower and wrung them out. Languidly, and with no thought of going in, I watched him, his hard little body, skinny and bare, saw him wince slightly as he pulled up around his vitals the small, soggy, icy garment. As he buckled the swollen belt, suddenly my groin felt the chill of death.

George Orwell
Politics and the English Language

Eric Arthur Blair (1903–1950, pseudonym George Orwell) was a British novelist and essayist born in Bengal, India. He was educated at Eton but, he said, "learned very little," returning to the East, where he served with the Indian Imperial Police in Burma from 1922 to 1927 and ruined his health. A dishwasher, a poor tutor, and an assistant in a London bookshop, Orwell finally began earning enough money from his writing to move to the country about 1935. He served briefly in the Spanish Civil War, was wounded, and afterwards settled in Hertfordshire, England, to raise hens and vegetables and write books. A brilliant political satirist, Orwell is best known for Animal Farm (1945) and Nineteen Eighty-Four (1949), an attack on political dictatorship. "Politics and the English Language" is perhaps the best essay in English on the social necessity of responsible writing.

Most people who bother with the matter at all would admit   1
that the English language is in a bad way, but it is generally
assumed that we cannot by conscious action do anything
about it. Our civilization is decadent and our language—so the
argument runs—must inevitably share in the general collapse.
It follows that any struggle against the abuse of language is a
sentimental archaism, like preferring candles to electric light
or hansom cabs to aeroplanes. Underneath this lies the half-
conscious belief that language is a natural growth and not an
instrument which we shape for our own purposes.

Now, it is clear that the decline of a language must ulti-   2
mately have political and economic causes: it is not due simply
to the bad influence of this or that individual writer. But an
effect can become a cause, reinforcing the original cause and
producing the same effect in an intensified form, and so on

375

indefinitely. A man may take to drink because he feels himself to be a failure, and then fail all the more completely because he drinks. It is rather the same thing that is happening to the English language. It becomes ugly and inaccurate because our thoughts are foolish, but the slovenliness of our language makes it easier for us to have foolish thoughts. The point is that the process is reversible. Modern English, especially written English, is full of bad habits which spread by imitation and which can be avoided if one is willing to take the necessary trouble. If one gets rid of these habits one can think more clearly, and to think clearly is a necessary first step towards political regeneration: so that the fight against bad English is not frivolous and is not the exclusive concern of professional writers. I will come back to this presently, and I hope that by that time the meaning of what I have said here will have become clearer. Meanwhile, here are five specimens of the English language as it is now habitually written.

These five passages have not been picked out because they are ³ especially bad—I could have quoted far worse if I had chosen—but because they illustrate various of the mental vices from which we now suffer. They are a little below the average, but are fairly representative samples. I number them so that I can refer back to them when necessary:

(1) I am not, indeed, sure whether it is not true to say that the Milton who once seemed not unlike a seventeenth-century Shelley had not become, out of an experience ever more bitter in each year, more alien [*sic*] to the founder of that Jesuit sect which nothing could induce him to tolerate.

Professor Harold Laski (Essay in *Freedom of Expression*)

. (2) Above all, we cannot play ducks and drakes with a native battery of idioms which prescribes such egregious collocations of vocables as the Basic *put up with* for *tolerate* or *put at a loss* for *bewilder*.

Professor Lancelot Hogben (*Interglossa*)

(3) On the one side we have the free personality: by definition it is not neurotic, for it has neither conflict nor dream. Its desires, such as they are, are transparent, for they are just what institutional approval keeps in the forefront of consciousness; another institutional pattern would alter their number and intensity; there is little in them that is natural, irreducible, or culturally dangerous. But *on the other side*, the social bond itself is nothing but the mutual

reflection of these self-secure integrities. Recall the definition of love. Is not this the very picture of a small academic? Where is there a place in this hall of mirrors for either personality or fraternity?

Essay on psychology in Politics (New York)

(4) All the 'best people' from the gentlemen's clubs, and all the frantic fascist captains, united in common hatred of Socialism and bestial horror of the rising tide of the mass revolutionary movement, have turned to acts of provocation, to foul incendiarism, to medieval legends of poisoned wells, to legalize their own destruction of proletarian organizations, and rouse the agitated petty-bourgeoisie to chauvinistic fervour on behalf of the fight against the revolutionary way out of the crisis.

Communist pamphlet

(5) If a new spirit *is* to be infused into this old country, there is one thorny and contentious reform which must be tackled, and that is the humanization and galvanization of the B.B.C. Timidity here will bespeak cancer and atrophy of the soul. The heart of Britain may be sound and of strong beat, for instance, but the British lion's roar at present is like that of Bottom in Shakespeare's *Midsummer Night's Dream*—as gentle as any sucking dove. A virile new Britain cannot continue indefinitely to be traduced in the eyes or rather ears, of the world by the effete languors of Langham Place, brazenly masquerading as 'standard English'. When the Voice of Britain is heard at nine o'clock, better far and infinitely less ludicrous to hear aitches honestly dropped than the present priggish, inflated, inhibited, school-ma'amish arch braying of blameless bashful mewing maidens!

Letter in Tribune

4

Each of these passages has faults of its own, but, quite apart from avoidable ugliness, two qualities are common to all of them. The first is staleness of imagery: the other is lack of precision. The writer either has a meaning and cannot express it, or he inadvertently says something else, or he is almost indifferent as to whether his words mean anything or not. This mixture of vagueness and sheer incompetence is the most marked characteristic of modern English prose, and especially of any kind of political writing. As soon as certain topics are raised, the concrete melts into the abstract and no one seems able to think of turns of speech that are not hackneyed: prose consists less and less of *words* chosen for the sake of their meaning, and more and more of *phrases* tacked together like the sections of a prefabricated hen-house. I list below, with notes and examples, various of the tricks by means of which the work of prose-construction is habitually dodged:

Dying Metaphors

A newly invented metaphor assists thought by evoking a visual [5] image, while on the other hand a metaphor which is technically "dead" (e.g. *iron resolution*) has in effect reverted to being an ordinary word and can generally be used without loss of vividness. But in between these two classes there is a huge dump of worn-out metaphors which have lost all evocative power and are merely used because they save people the trouble of inventing phrases for themselves. Examples are *Ring the changes on, take up the cudgels for, toe the line, ride roughshod over, stand shoulder to shoulder with, play into the hands of, no axe to grind, grist to the mill, fishing in troubled waters, on the order of the day, Achilles' heel, swan song, hotbed.* Many of these are used without knowledge of their meaning (what is a "rift", for instance?), and incompatible metaphors are frequently mixed, a sure sign that the writer is not interested in what he is saying. Some metaphors now current have been twisted out of their original meaning without those who use them even being aware of the fact. For example, *toe the line* is sometimes written *tow the line*. Another example is *the hammer and the anvil,* now always used with the implication that the anvil gets the worst of it. In real life it is always the anvil that breaks the hammer, never the other way about: a writer who stopped to think what he was saying would be aware of this, and would avoid perverting the original phrase.

Operators or Verbal False Limbs

These save the trouble of picking out appropriate verbs and [6] nouns, and at the same time pad each sentence with extra syllables which give it an appearance of symmetry. Characteristic phrases are: *render inoperative, militate against, make contact with, be subjected to, give rise to, give grounds for, have the effect of, play a leading part (role) in, make itself felt, take effect, exhibit a tendency to, serve the purpose of, etc., etc.* The keynote is the elimination of simple verbs. Instead of being a single word, such as *break, stop, spoil, mend, kill,* a verb becomes a *phrase,* made up of a noun or adjective tacked on to some general-purposes verb such as *prove, serve, form, play, render.* In addition, the passive voice is wherever possible used in preference to the active, and noun constructions are used instead of gerunds (*by examination of* instead of *by examining*). The range of verbs is further cut down by means of the *-ize* and *de-* formation, and the banal statements are given an appearance of profundity by means of the *not un-* formation. Simple conjunctions and prepositions are replaced by such phrases as *with respect to, having regard to, the fact that, by dint of, in view of, in the interests of, on the hypothesis that;* and the ends of sentences are saved from anticlimax by such. resounding commonplaces as *greatly to be desired, cannot be left out of account, a development to be expected in the near future, deserving of serious consideration, brought to a satisfactory conclusion,* and so on and so forth.

Pretentious Diction

Words like *phenomenon, element, individual* (as noun), *objec-* [7] *tive, categorical, effective, virtual, basic, primary, promote, constitute, exhibit, exploit, utilize, eliminate, liquidate,* are used to dress up simple statements and give an air of scientific impartiality to biased judgments. Adjectives like *epoch-making, epic, historic, unforgettable, triumphant, age-old, inevitable, inexorable, veritable,* are used to dignify the sordid processes of international politics, while writing that aims at glorifying war usually takes on an archaic colour, its characteristic words being: *realm, throne, chariot, mailed fist, trident, sword shield, buckler, banner, jackboot, clarion.* Foreign words and expressions such as *cul de sac, ancien régime, deus ex machina, mutatis mutandis, status quo, gleichschaltung, weltanschauung* are used to give an air of culture and elegance. Except for the useful abbreviations *i.e., e.g.,* and *etc.,* there is no real need for any of the hundreds of foreign phrases now current in English. Bad writers, and especially scientific, political and sociological writers, are nearly always haunted by the notion that Latin or Greek words are grander than Saxon ones, and unnecessary words like *expedite, ameliorate, predict, extraneous, deracinated, clandestine, subaqueous* and hundreds of others constantly gain ground from their Anglo-Saxon opposite numbers.[1] The jargon peculiar to Marxist writing (*hyena, hang-man, cannibal, petty bourgeois, these gentry, lacquey, flunkey, mad dog, White Guard,* etc.) consists largely of words and phrases translated from Russian, German or French; but the normal way of coining a new word is to use a Latin or Greek root with the appropriate affix and, where necessary, the *-ize* formation. It is often easier to make up words of this kind (*deregionalize, impermissible, extramarital, nonfragmentatory* and so forth) than to think up the English words that will cover one's meaning. The result, in general, is an increase in slovenliness and vagueness.

Meaningless Words

In certain kinds of writing, particularly in art criticism and liter- **8** ary criticism, it is normal to come across long passages which are almost completely lacking in meaning.[2] Words like *romantic, plastic, values, human, dead, sentimental, natural, vitality,* as used in art criticism, are strictly meaningless in the sense that they not only do not point to any discoverable object, but are hardly ever expected to do so by the reader. When one critic writes, "The outstanding feature of Mr. X's work is its living quality", while another writes, "The immediately striking thing about Mr. X's work is its peculiar deadness", the reader accepts this as a simple difference of opinion. If words like *black* and *white* were involved, instead of the jargon words *dead* and *living,* he would see at once that language was being used in an improper way. Many political words are similarly abused. The word *Fascism* has now no meaning except in so far as it signifies "something not desirable". The

---

[1] An interesting illustration of this is the way in which the English flower names which were in use till very recently are being ousted by Greek ones, *snapdragon* becoming *antirrhinum, forget-me-not* becoming *myosotis,* etc. It is hard to see any practical reason for this change of fashion: it is probably due to an instinctive turning-away from the more homely word and a vague feeling that the Greek word is scientific [Orwell's note].

[2] Example: "Comfort's catholicity of perception and image, strangely Whitmanesque in range, almost the exact opposite in aesthetic compulsion, continues to evoke that trembling atmospheric accumulative hinting at a cruel, an inexorably serene timelessness . . . Wrey Gardiner scores by aiming at simple bull's-eyes with precision. Only they are not so simple, and through this contented sadness runs more than the surface bittersweet of resignation" (*Poetry Quarterly*) [Orwell's note].

words *democracy, socialism, freedom, patriotic, realistic, justice,* have each of them several different meanings which cannot be reconciled with one another. In the case of a word like *democracy,* not only is there no agreed definition, but the attempt to make one is resisted from all sides. It is almost universally felt that when we call a country democratic we are praising it: consequently the defenders of every kind of régime claim that it is a democracy, and fear that they might have to stop using the word if it were tied down to any one meaning. Words of this kind are often used in a consciously dishonest way. That is, the person who uses them has his own private definition, but allows his hearer to think he means something quite different. Statements like *Marshal Pétain was a true patriot, The Soviet Press is the freest in the world, The Catholic Church is opposed to persecution,* are almost always made with intent to deceive. Other words used in variable meanings, in most cases more or less dishonestly, are: *class, totalitarian, science, progressive, reactionary, bourgeois, equality.*

Now that I have made this catalogue of swindles and perversions, let me give another example of the kind of writing that they lead to. This time it must of its nature be an imaginary one. I am going to translate a passage of good English into modern English of the worst sort. Here is a well-known verse from *Ecclesiastes*: 9

> I returned and saw under the sun, that the race is not to the swift, nor the battle to the strong, neither yet bread to the wise, nor yet riches to men of understanding, nor yet favour to men of skill; but time and chance happeneth to them all.

Here it is in modern English: 10

> Objective consideration of contemporary phenomena compels the conclusion that success or failure in competitive activities exhibits no tendency to be commensurate with innate capacity, but that a considerable element of the unpredictable must invariably be taken into account.

This is a parody, but not a very gross one. Exhibit (3), above, 11 for instance, contains several patches of the same kind of English. It will be seen that I have not made a full translation. The beginning and ending of the sentence follow the original meaning fairly closely, but in the middle the concrete illustrations—race, battle, bread—dissolve into the vague phrase "success or failure in competitive activities". This had to be so, because no modern writer of the kind I am discussing—no one capable of using phrases like "objective consideration of contemporary phenomena"—would ever tabulate his thoughts in that precise and detailed way. The whole tendency of modern prose is away from concreteness. Now analyse these two sentences a little more closely. The first contains forty-nine words but only sixty syllables, and all its words are those of everyday life. The second contains thirty-eight words of ninety syllables: eighteen of its words are from Latin roots, and one from Greek. The first sentence contains six vivid images, and only one phrase ("time and chance") that could be called vague. The second contains not a single fresh, arresting phrase, and in spite of its ninety syllables it gives only a shortened version of the meaning contained in the first. Yet without a doubt it is the second kind of sentence that is gaining ground in modern English. I do not want to exaggerate. This kind of writing is not yet universal, and outcrops of simplicity will occur here and there in the worst-written page. Still, if you or I were told to write a few lines on the uncertainty of human fortunes, we should probably come much nearer to my imaginary sentence than to the one from *Ecclesiastes*.

As I have tried to show, modern writing at its worst does not   12 consist in picking out words for the sake of their meaning and inventing images in order to make the meaning clearer. It consists in gumming together long strips of words which have already been set in order by someone else, and making the results presentable by sheer humbug. The attraction of this way of writing is that it is easy. It is easier—even quicker, once you have the habit—to say *In my opinion it is a not unjustifiable assumption that* than to say *I think*. If you use ready-made phrases, you not only don't have to hunt about for words; you also don't have to bother with the rhythms of your sentences, since these phrases are generally so arranged as to be more or less euphonious. When you are composing in a hurry—when you are dictating to a stenographer, for instance, or making a public speech—it is natural to fall into a pretentious, Latinized style. Tags like *a consideration which we should do well to bear in mind* or *a conclusion to which all of us would readily assent* will save many a sentence from coming down with a bump. By using stale metaphors, similes and idioms, you save much mental effort, at the cost of leaving your meaning vague, not only for your reader but for yourself. This is the significance of mixed metaphors. The sole aim of a metaphor is to call up a visual image. When these images clash—as in *The Fascist octopus has sung its swan song, the jack-boot is thrown into the melting pot*—it can be taken as certain that the writer is not seeing a mental image of the objects he is naming; in other words he is not really thinking. Look again at the examples I gave at the beginning of this essay. Professor Laski (1) uses five negatives in fifty-three words. One of these is superfluous, making nonsense of the whole passage, and in addition there is the slip *alien* for akin, making further nonsense, and several avoidable pieces of clumsiness which increase the general vagueness. Professor Hogben (2) plays ducks and drakes with a battery which is able to write prescriptions, and, while disapproving of the everyday phrase *put up with*, is unwilling to look *egregious* up in the dictionary and see what it means. (3), if one takes an uncharitable attitude towards it, is simply meaningless: probably one could work out its intended meaning by reading the whole of the article in which it occurs. In (4), the writer knows more or less what he wants to say, but an accumulation of stale phrases chokes him like tea leaves blocking a sink. In (5), words and meaning have almost parted company. People who write in this manner usually have a general emotional meaning—they dislike one thing and want to express solidarity with another—but they are not interested in the detail of what they are saying. A scrupulous writer, in every sentence that he writes, will ask himself at least four questions, thus: What am I trying to say? What words will express it? What image or idiom will make it clearer? Is this image fresh enough to have an effect? And he will probably ask himself two more: Could I put it more shortly? Have I said anything that is avoidably ugly? But you are not obliged to go to all this trouble. You can shirk it by simply throwing your mind open and letting the ready-made phrases come crowding in. They will construct your sentences for you—even think your thoughts for you, to a certain extent—and at need they will perform the important service of partially concealing your meaning even from yourself. It is at this point that the special connection between politics and the debasement of language becomes clear.

In our time it is broadly true that political writing is bad writing. 13 Where it is not true, it will generally be found that the writer is some kind of rebel, expressing his private opinions and not a "party line". Orthodoxy, of whatever colour, seems to demand a lifeless, imitative style. The political dialects to be found in pamphlets, leading articles, manifestos, White Papers and the speeches of under-secretaries do, of course, vary from party to party, but they are all alike in that one almost never finds in them a fresh, vivid, home-made turn of speech. When one watches some tired hack on the platform mechanically repeating the familiar phrases—*bestial atrocities, iron heel, bloodstained tyranny, free peoples of the world, stand shoulder to shoulder*—one often has a curious feeling that one is not watching a live human being but some kind of dummy: a feeling which suddenly becomes stronger at moments when the light catches the speaker's spectacles and turns them into blank discs which seem to have no eyes behind them. And this is not altogether fanciful. A speaker who uses that kind of phraseology has gone some distance towards turning himself into a machine. The appropriate noises are coming out of his larynx, but his brain is not involved as it would be if he were choosing his words for himself. If the speech he is making is one that he is accustomed to make over and over again, he may be almost unconscious of what he is saying, as one is when one utters the responses in church. And this reduced state of consciousness, if not indispensable, is at any rate favourable to political conformity.

In our time, political speech and writing are largely the defence   14
of the indefensible. Things like the continuance of British rule in India, the Russian purges and deportations, the dropping of the atom bombs on Japan, can indeed be defended, but only by arguments which are too brutal for most people to face, and which do not square with the professed aims of political parties. Thus political language has to consist largely of euphemism, question-begging and sheer cloudy vagueness. Defenceless villages are bombarded from the air, the inhabitants driven out into the countryside, the cattle machine-gunned, the huts set on fire with incendiary bullets: this is called *pacification*. Millions of peasants are robbed of their farms and sent trudging along the roads with no more than they can carry: this is called *transfer of population* or *rectification of frontiers*. People are imprisoned for years without trial, or shot in the back of the neck or sent to die of scurvy in Arctic lumber camps: this is called *elimination of unreliable elements*. Such phraseology is needed if one wants to name things without calling up mental pictures of them. Consider for instance some comfortable English professor defending Russian totalitarianism. He cannot say outright, "I believe in killing off your opponents when you can get good results by doing so". Probably, therefore, he will say something like this:

"While freely conceding that the Soviet régime exhibits certain   15 features which the humanitarian may be inclined to deplore, we must, I think, agree that a certain curtailment of the right to political opposition is an unavoidable concomitant of transitional periods, and that the rigours which the Russian people have been called upon to undergo have been amply justified in the sphere of concrete achievement."

The inflated style is itself a kind of euphemism. A mass of Latin 16
words falls upon the facts like soft snow, blurring the outlines and covering up all the details. The great enemy of clear language is insincerity. When there is a gap between one's real and one's declared aims, one turns as it were instinctively to long words and exhausted idioms, like a cuttlefish squirting out ink. In our age there is no such thing as "keeping out of politics". All issues are political issues, and politics itself is a mass of lies, evasions, folly, hatred and schizophrenia. When the general atmosphere is bad, language must suffer. I should expect to find—this is a guess which I have not sufficient knowledge to verify—that the German, Russian and Italian languages have all deteriorated in the last ten or fifteen years, as a result of dictatorship.

But if thought corrupts language, language can also corrupt 17
thought. A bad usage can spread by tradition and imitation, even among people who should and do know better. The debased language that I have been discussing is in some ways very convenient. Phrases like *a not unjustifiable assumption, leaves much to be desired, would serve no good purpose, a consideration which we should do well to bear in mind,* are a continuous temptation, a packet of aspirins always at one's elbow. Look back through this essay, and for certain you will find that I have again and again committed the very faults I am protesting against. By this morning's post I have received a pamphlet dealing with conditions in Germany. The author tells me that he "felt impelled" to write it. I open it at random, and here is almost the first sentence that I see: "(The Allies) have an opportunity not only of achieving a radical transformation of Germany's social and political structure in such a way as to avoid a nationalistic reaction in Germany itself, but at the same time of laying the foundations of a co-operative and unified Europe." You see, he "feels impelled" to write—feels, presumably, that he has something new to say—and yet his words, like cavalry horses answering the bugle, group themselves automatically into the familiar dreary pattern. This invasion of one's mind by ready-made phrases (*lay the foundations, achieve a radical*

transformation) can only be prevented if one is constantly on guard against them, and every such phrase anaesthetizes a portion of one's brain.

I said earlier that the decadence of our language is probably 18 curable. Those who deny this would argue, if they produced an argument at all, that language merely reflects existing social conditions, and that we cannot influence its development by any direct tinkering with words and constructions. So far as the general tone or spirit of a language goes, this may be true, but it is not true in detail. Silly words and expressions have often disappeared, not through any evolutionary process but owing to the conscious action of a minority. Two recent examples were *explore every avenue* and *leave no stone unturned*, which were killed by the jeers of a few journalists. There is a long list of flyblown metaphors which could similarly be got rid of if enough people would interest themselves in the job; and it should also be possible to laugh the *not un-* formation out of existence,[3] to reduce the amout of Latin and Greek in the average sentence, to drive out foreign phrases and strayed scientific words, and, in general, to make pretentiousness unfashionable. But all these are minor points. The defence of the English language implies more than this, and perhaps it is best to start by saying what it does *not* imply.

To begin with it has nothing to do with archaism, with the 19 salvaging of obsolete words and turns of speech, or with the setting up of a "standard English" which must never be departed from. On the contrary, it is especially concerned with the scrapping of every word or idiom which has outworn its usefulness. It has nothing to do with correct grammar and syntax, which are of no importance so long as one makes one's meaning clear, or with the avoidance of Americanisms, or with having what is called a "good prose style". On the other hand it is not concerned with fake simplicity and the attempt to make written English colloquial. Nor does it even imply in every case preferring the Saxon word to the Latin one, though it does imply using the fewest and shortest words that will cover one's meaning. What is above all needed is to

---

[3] One can cure oneself of the *not un-* formation by memorizing this sentence: A *not unblack dog was chasing a not unsmall rabbit across a not ungreen field* [Orwell's note].

let the meaning choose the word, and not the other way about. In prose, the worst thing one can do with words is to surrender to them. When you think of a concrete object, you think wordlessly, and then, if you want to describe the thing you have been visualizing you probably hunt about till you find the exact words that seem to fit. When you think of something abstract you are more inclined to use words from the start, and unless you make a conscious effort to prevent it, the existing dialect will come rushing in and do the job for you, at the expense of blurring or even changing your meaning. Probably it is better to put off using words as long as possible and get one's meaning as clear as one can through pictures or sensations. Afterwards one can choose—not simply *accept*—the phrases that will best cover the meaning, and then switch round and decide what impression one's words are likely to make on another person. This last effort of the mind cuts out all stale or mixed images, all prefabricated phrases, needless repetitions, and humbug and vagueness generally. But one can often be in doubt about the effect of a word or a phrase, and one needs rules that one can rely on when instinct fails. I think the following rules will cover most cases:

(i) Never use a metaphor, simile or other figure of speech which you are used to seeing in print.

(ii) Never use a long word where a short one will do.

(iii) If it is possible to cut a word out, always cut it out.

(iv) Never use the passive where you can use the active.

(v) Never use a foreign phrase, a scientific word or a jargon word if you can think of an everyday English equivalent.

(vi) Break any of these rules sooner than say anything outright barbarous.

These rules sound elementary, and so they are, but they demand a deep change of attitude in anyone who has grown used to writing in the style now fashionable. One could keep all of them and still write bad English, but one could not write the kind of stuff that I quoted in those five specimens at the beginning of this article.

I have not here been considering the literary use of language, [20] but merely language as an instrument for expressing and not for concealing or preventing thought. Stuart Chase and others have come near to claiming that all abstract words are meaningless, and have used this as a pretext for advocating a kind of political quietism. Since you don't know what Fascism is, how can you struggle against Fascism? One need not swallow such absurdities as this, but one ought to recognize that the present political chaos is connected with the decay of language, and that one can probably bring about some improvement by starting at the verbal end. If you simplify your English, you are freed from the worst follies of orthodoxy. You cannot speak any of the necessary dialects, and when you make a stupid remark its stupidity will be obvious, even to yourself. Political language—and with variations this is true of all political parties, from Conservatives to Anarchists—is designed to make lies sound truthful and murder respectable, and to give an appearance of solidity to pure wind. One cannot change this all in a moment, but one can at least change one's own habits, and from time to time one can even, if one jeers loudly enough, send some worn-out and useless phrase—some *jackboot, Achilles' heel, hotbed, melting pot, acid test, veritable inferno* or other lump of verbal refuse—into the dustbin where it belongs.

Mary E. Mebane

The Back of the Bus

Mary E. Mebane (pronounced "Mebban") was born in 1933 in the Wildwood community just outside Durham, North Carolina, a member of the last generation to endure legal segregation in the South. The daughter of a dirt farmer who sold junk to raise cash, she attended North Carolina College in Durham (graduating summa cum laude) and later the University of North Carolina at Chapel Hill (where she took the M.A. and Ph.D.). A frequent contributor to the OpEd Page of the New York Times, Mebane teaches at the University of Wisconsin—Milwaukee. "The Back of the Bus" (editor's title) is a complete chapter from her autobiography, Mary (1981), a book that tells how Mebane learned "what no one I knew had ever consciously explored: how to break out."

Historically, my lifetime is important because I was part [1] of the last generation born into a world of total legal segregation in the Southern United States. When the Supreme Court outlawed segregation in the public schools in 1954, I was twenty-one. When Congress passed the Civil Rights Act of 1964, permitting blacks free access to public places, I was thirty-one. The world I was born into had been segregated for a long time—so long, in fact, that I never met anyone who had lived during the time when restrictive laws were not in existence, although some people spoke of parents and others who had lived during the "free" time. As far as anyone knew, the laws as they then existed would stand forever. They were meant to—and did—create a world that fixed black people at the bottom of society in all aspects of human life. It was a world without options.

Most Americans have never had to live with terror. I had had   2
to live with it all my life—the psychological terror of segregation,
in which there was a special set of laws governing your movements. You violated them at your peril, for you knew that if you
broke one of them, knowingly or not, physical terror was just
around the corner, in the form of policemen and jails, and in some
cases and places white vigilante mobs formed for the exclusive
purpose of keeping blacks in line.

It was Saturday morning, like any Saturday morning in dozens   3
of Southern towns.

The town had a washed look. The street sweepers had been busy   4
since six o'clock. Now, at eight, they were still slowly moving
down the streets, white trucks with clouds of water coming from
underneath the swelled tubular sides. Unwary motorists sometimes
got a windowful of water as a truck passed by. As it moved on, it
left in its wake a clear stream running in the gutters or splashed on
the wheels of parked cars.

Homeowners, bent over industriously in the morning sun, were   5
out pushing lawn mowers. The sun was bright, but it wasn't too
hot. It was morning and it was May. Most of the mowers were glad
that it was finally getting warm enough to go outside.

Traffic was brisk. Country people were coming into town early   6
with their produce; clerks and service workers were getting to the
job before the stores opened at ten o'clock. Though the big stores
would not be open for another hour or so, the grocery stores,
banks, open-air markets, dinettes, were already open and filling
with staff and customers.

Everybody was moving toward the heart of Durham's down-   7
town, which waited to receive them rather complacently, little
knowing that in a decade the shopping centers far from the center
of downtown Durham would create a ghost town in the midst of
the busiest blocks on Main Street.

Some moved by car, and some moved by bus. The more affluent   8
used cars, leaving the buses mainly to the poor, black and white,
though there were some businesspeople who avoided the trouble of
trying to find a parking place downtown by riding the bus.

I didn't mind taking the bus on Saturday. It wasn't so crowded.   9
At night or on Saturday or Sunday was the best time. If there were
plenty of seats, the blacks didn't have to worry about being asked
to move so that a white person could sit down. And the knot of
hatred and fear didn't come into my stomach.

I knew the stop that was the safety point, both going and com- [10]
ing. Leaving town, it was the Little Five Points, about five or six
blocks north of the main downtown section. That was the last stop
at which four or five people might get on. After the stop, the driver
could sometimes pass two or three stops without taking on or
letting off a passenger. So the number of seats on the bus usually
remained constant on the trip from town to Braggtown. The nearer
the bus got to the end of the line, the more I relaxed. For if a white
passenger got on near the end of the line, often to catch the return
trip back and avoid having to stand in the sun at the bus stop until
the bus turned around, he or she would usually stand if there were
not seats in the white section, and the driver would say nothing,
knowing that the end of the line was near and that the standee
would get a seat in a few minutes.

On the trip to town, the Mangum Street A&P was the last point [11]
at which the driver picked up more passengers than he let off.
These people, though they were just a few blocks from the downtown section, preferred to ride the bus downtown. Those getting on
at the A&P were usually on their way to work at the Duke University Hospital—past the downtown section, through a residential
neighborhood, and then past the university, before they got to
Duke Hospital.

So whether the driver discharged more passengers than he took [12]
on near the A&P on Mangum was of great importance. For if he
took on more passengers than got off, it meant that some of the
newcomers would have to stand. And if they were white, the driver
was going to have to ask a black passenger to move so that a white
passenger could sit down. Most of the drivers had a rule of thumb,
though. By custom the seats behind the exit door had become "colored" seats, and no matter how many whites stood up, anyone
sitting behind the exit door knew that he or she wouldn't have to
move.

The disputed seat, though, was the one directly opposite the exit [13]
door. It was "no-man's-land." White people sat there, and black
people sat there. It all depended on whose section was fuller. If the
back section was full, the next black passenger who got on sat in
the no-man's-land seat; but if the white section filled up, a white
person would take the seat. Another thing about the white people:
they could sit anywhere they chose, even in the "colored" section.
Only the black passengers had to obey segregation laws.

On this Saturday morning Esther and I set out for town for our [14] music lesson. We were going on our weekly big adventure, all the way across town, through the white downtown, then across the railroad tracks, then through the "colored" downtown, a section of run-down dingy shops, through some fading high-class black neighborhoods, past North Carolina College, to Mrs. Shearin's house.

We walked the two miles from Wildwood to the bus line.   15
Though it was a warm day, in the early morning there was dew on the grass and the air still had the night's softness. So we walked along and talked and looked back constantly, hoping someone we knew would stop and pick us up.

I looked back furtively, for in one of the few instances that I   16
remembered my father criticizing me severely, it was for looking back. One day when I was walking from town he had passed in his old truck. I had been looking back and had seen him. "Don't look back," he had said. "People will think that you want them to pick you up." Though he said "people," I knew he meant men—not the men he knew, who lived in the black community, but the black men who were not part of the community, and all of the white men. To be picked up meant that something bad would happen to me. Still, two miles is a long walk and I occasionally joined Esther in looking back to see if anyone we knew was coming.

Esther and I got to the bus and sat on one of the long seats at the   17
back that faced each other. There were three such long seats—one on each side of the bus and a third long seat at the very back that faced the front. I liked to sit on a long seat facing the side because then I didn't have to look at the expressions on the faces of the whites when they put their tokens in and looked at the blacks sitting in the back of the bus. Often I studied my music, looking down and practicing the fingering. I looked up at each stop to see who was getting on and to check on the seating pattern. The seating pattern didn't really bother me that day until the bus started to get unusually full for a Saturday morning. I wondered what was happening, where all these people were coming from. They got on and got on until the white section was almost full and the black section was full.

There was a black man in a blue windbreaker and a gray pork-   18
pie hat sitting in no-man's-land, and my stomach tighened. I wondered what would happen. I had never been on a bus on which a

black person was asked to give a seat to a white person when there was no other seat empty. Usually, though, I had seen a black person automatically get up and move to an empty seat farther back. But this morning the only empty seat was beside a black person sitting in no-man's-land.

The bus stopped at Little Five Points and one black got off. A [19] young white man was getting on. I tensed. What would happen now? Would the driver ask the black man to get up and move to the empty seat farther back? The white man had a businessman's air about him: suit, shirt, tie, polished brown shoes. He saw the empty seat in the "colored' section and after just a little hesitation went to it, put his briefcase down, and sat with his feet crossed. I relaxed a little when the bus pulled off without the driver saying anything. Evidently he hadn't seen what had happened, or since he was just few stops from Main Street, he figured the mass exodus there would solve all the problems. Still, I was afraid of a scene.

The next stop was an open-air fruit stand just after Little Five [20] Points, and here another white man got on. Where would he sit? The only available seat was beside the black man. Would he stand the few stops to Main Street or would the driver make the black man move? The whole colored section tensed, but nobody said anything. I looked at Esther, who looked apprehensive. I looked at the other men and women, who studiously avoided my eyes and everybody else's as well, as they maintained a steady gaze at a far-distant land.

. Just one woman caught my eye; I had noticed her before, and I [21] had been ashamed of her. She was a stringy little black woman. She could have been forty; she could have been fifty. She looked as if she were a hard drinker. Flat black face with tight features. She was dressed with great insouciance in a tight boy's sweater with horizontal lines running across her flat chest. It pulled down over a nondescript skirt. Laced-up shoes, socks, and a head rag completed her outfit. She looked tense.

The white man who had just gotten on the bus walked to the [22] seat in no-man's-land and stood there. He wouldn't sit down, just stood there. Two adult males, living in the most highly industrialized, most technologically advanced nation in the world, a nation that had devastated two other industrial giants in World War II and had flirted with taking on China in Korea. Both these men, either of whom could have fought for the United States in Germany or Korea, faced each other in mutual rage and hostility. The white one wanted to sit down, but he was going to exert his authority and force the black one to get up first. I watched the driver in the rearview mirror. He was about the same age as the antagonists. The driver wasn't looking for trouble, either.

"Say there, buddy, how about moving back," the driver said, 23 meanwhile driving his bus just as fast as he could. The whole bus froze—whites at the front, blacks at the rear. They didn't want to believe what was happening was really happening.

The seated black man said nothing. The standing white man 24 said nothing.

"Say, buddy, did you hear me? What about moving on back." 25 The driver was scared to death. I could tell that.

"These is the niggers' seats!" the little lady in the strange outfit 26 started screaming. I jumped. I had to shift my attention from the driver to the frieze of the black man seated and white man standing to the articulate little woman who had joined in the fray.

"The government gave us these seats! These is the niggers' seats." 27 I was startled at her statement and her tone. "The president said that these are the niggers' seats!" I expected her to start fighting at any moment.

Evidently the bus driver did, too, because he was driving faster 28 and faster. I believe that he forgot he was driving a bus and wanted desperately to pull to the side of the street and get out and run.

"I'm going to take you down to the station, buddy," the driver 29 said.

The white man with the briefcase and the polished brown shoes 30 who had taken a seat in the "colored" section looked as though he might die of embarrassment at any moment.

As scared and upset as I was, I didn't miss a thing. 31

By that time we had come to the stop before Main Street, and 32 the black passenger rose to get off.

"'You're not getting off, buddy. I'm going to take you down- 33 town." The driver kept driving as he talked and seemed to be trying to get downtown as fast as he could.

"These are the niggers' seats! The government plainly said these 34 are the niggers' seats!" screamed the little woman in rage.

I was embarrassed at the use of the word "nigger" but I was proud of the lady. I was also proud of the man who wouldn't get up. [35]

The bus driver was afraid, trying to hold on to his job but plainly not willing to get into a row with the blacks. [36]

The bus seemed to be going a hundred miles an hour and everybody was anxious to get off, though only the lady and the driver were saying anything. [37]

The black man stood at the exit door; the driver drove right past the A&P stop. I was terrified. I was sure that the bus was going to the police station to put the black man in jail. The little woman had her hands on her hips and she never stopped yelling. The bus driver kept driving as fast as he could. [38]

Then, somewhere in the back of his mind, he decided to forget the whole thing. The next stop was Main Street, and when he got there, in what seemed to be a flash of lightning, he flung both doors open wide. He and his black antagonist looked at each other in the rearview mirror; in a second the windbreaker and porkpie hat were gone. The little woman was standing, preaching to the whole bus about the government's gift of these seats to the blacks; the man with the brown shoes practically fell out of the door in his hurry; and Esther and I followed the hurrying footsteps. [39]

We walked about three doors down the block, then caught a bus to the black neighborhood. Here we sat on one of the two long seats facing each other, directly behind the driver. It was the custom. Since this bus had a route from a black neighborhood to the downtown section and back, passing through no white residential areas, blacks could sit where they chose. One minute we had been on a bus in which violence was threatened over a seat near the exit door; the next minute we were sitting in the very front behind the driver. [40]

The people who devised this system thought that it was going to last forever. [41]

Joan Didion

Holy Water

Novelist Joan Didion, author of Play It As It Lays (1970) and A
Book of Common Prayer (1977) has emerged in recent years as one
of America's leading essayists. In Slouching Toward Bethlehem
(1968) and The White Album (1979), Didion probes our national
life, from the American family to the American freeway, recording
its impressions upon her own jangled nerves. A native of California
—she was born in Sacramento in 1934 and attended Berkeley—
Didion reveals in "Holy Water" what few outsiders realize: that
Eden on the West Coast would be a desert except for a precious
commodity artificially collected and precariously transported
through a network of channels, reservoirs, and human error. "Holy
Water" is reprinted from The White Album.

Some of us who live in arid parts of the world think about   1
water with a reverence others might find excessive. The water
I will draw tomorrow from my tap in Malibu is today crossing
the Mojave Desert from the Colorado River, and I like to think
about exactly where that water is. The water I will drink tonight in a restaurant in Hollywood is by now well down the
Los Angeles Aqueduct from the Owens River, and I also think
about exactly where that water is: I particularly like to imagine it as it cascades down the 45-degree stone steps that aerate
Owens water after its airless passage through the mountain
pipes and siphons. As it happens my own reverence for water
has always taken the form of this constant meditation upon
where the water is, of an obsessive interest not in the politics
of water but in the waterworks themselves, in the movement
of water through aqueducts and siphons and pumps and fore-
bays and afterbays and weirs and drains, in plumbing on the
grand scale. I know the data on water projects I will never see.

I know the difficulty Kaiser had closing the last two sluiceway gates on the Guri Dam in Venezuela. I keep watch on evaporation behind the Aswan in Egypt. I can put myself to sleep imagining the water dropping a thousand feet into the turbines at Churchill Falls in Labrador. If the Churchill Falls Project fails to materialize, I fall back on waterworks closer at hand—the tailrace at Hoover on the Colorado, the surge tank in the Tehachapi Mountains that receives California Aqueduct water pumped higher than water has ever been pumped before—and finally I replay a morning when I was seventeen years old and caught, in a military-surplus life raft, in the construction of the Nimbus Afterbay Dam on the American River near Sacramento. I remember that at the moment it happened I was trying to open a tin of anchovies with capers. I recall the raft spinning into the narrow chute through which the river had been temporarily diverted. I recall being deliriously happy.

I suppose it was partly the memory of that delirium that led me to visit, one summer morning in Sacramento, the Operations Control Center for the California State Water Project. Actually so much water is moved around California by so many different agencies that maybe only the movers themselves know on any given day whose water is where, but to get a general picture it is necessary only to remember that Los Angeles moves some of it, San Francisco moves some of it, the Bureau of Reclamation's Central Valley Project moves some of it and the California State Water Project moves most of the rest of it, moves a vast amount of it, moves more water farther than has ever been moved anywhere. They collect this water up in the granite keeps of the Sierra Nevada and they store roughly a trillion gallons of it behind the Oroville Dam and every morning, down at the Project's headquarters in Sacramento, they decide how much of their water they want to move the next day. They make this morning decision according to supply and demand, which is simple in theory but rather more complicated in practice. In theory each of the Project's five field divisions—the Oroville, the Delta, the San Luis, the San Joaquin and the Southern divisions—places a call to headquarters before nine A.M. and tells the dispatchers how much water is needed by its local water contractors, who have in turn based their morning estimates on orders from growers and other big users. A schedule is made. The gates open and close according to schedule. The water flows south and the deliveries are made.

In practice this requires prodigious coordination, precision, and   3
the best efforts of several human minds and that of a Univac 418.
In practice it might be necessary to hold large flows of water for
power production, or to flush out encroaching salinity in the Sac-
ramento-San Joaquin Delta, the most ecologically sensitive point
on the system. In practice a sudden rain might obviate the need for
a delivery when that delivery is already on its way. In practice
what is being delivered here is an enormous volume of water, not
quarts of milk or spools of thread, and it takes two days to move
such a delivery down through Oroville into the Delta, which is the
great pooling place for California water and has been for some
years alive with electronic sensors and telemetering equipment and
men blocking channels and diverting flows and shoveling fish away
from the pumps. It takes perhaps another six days to move this
same water down the California Aqueduct from the Delta to the
Tehachapi and put it over the hill to Southern California. "Putting
some over the hill" is what they say around the Project Operations
Control Center when they want to indicate that they are pumping
Aqueduct water from the floor of the San Joaquin Valley up and
over the Tehachapi Mountains. "Pulling it down" is what they say
when they want to indicate that they are lowering a water level
somewhere in the system. They can put some over the hill by
remote control from this room in Sacramento with its Univac and
its big board and its flashing lights. They can pull down a pool in
the San Joaquin by remote control from this room in Sacramento
with its locked doors and its ringing alarms and its constant print-
outs of data from sensors out there in the water itself. From this
room in Sacramento the whole system takes on the aspect of a
perfect three-billion-dollar hydraulic toy, and in certain ways it is.
"LET'S START DRAINING QUAIL AT 12:00" was the 10:51
A.M. entry on the electronically recorded communications log the
day I visited the Operations Control Center. "Quail" is a reservoir
in Los Angeles County with a gross capacity of 1,636,018,000
gallons. "OK" was the response recorded in the log. I knew at that
moment that I had missed the only vocation for which I had any
instinctive affinity: I wanted to drain Quail myself.

Not many people I know carry their end of the conversation   4
when I want to talk about water deliveries, even when I stress
that these deliveries affect their lives, indirectly, every day. "Indi-

rectly" is not quite enough for most people I know. This morning, however, several people I know were affected not "indirectly" but "directly" by the way the water moves. They had been in New Mexico shooting a picture, one sequence of which required a river deep enough to sink a truck, the kind with a cab and a trailer and fifty or sixty wheels. It so happened that no river near the New Mexico location was running that deep this year. The production was therefore moved today to Needles, California, where the Colorado River normally runs, depending upon releases from Davis Dam, eighteen to twenty-five feet deep. Now. Follow this closely: yesterday we had a freak tropical storm in Southern California, two inches of rain in a normally dry month, and because this rain flooded the fields and provided more irrigation than any grower could possibly want for several days, no water was ordered from Davis Dam.

No orders, no releases. 5

Supply and demand. 6

As a result the Colorado was running only seven feet deep past 7 Needles today, Sam Peckinpah's desire for eighteen feet of water in which to sink a truck not being the kind of demand anyone at Davis Dam is geared to meet. The production closed down for the weekend. Shooting will resume Tuesday, providing some grower orders water and the agencies controlling the Colorado release it. Meanwhile many gaffers, best boys, cameramen, assistant directors, script supervisors, stunt drivers and maybe even Sam Pekinpah are waiting out the weekend in Needles, where it is often 110 degrees at five P.M. and hard to get dinner after eight. This is a California parable, but a true one.

I have always wanted a swimming pool, and never had one. 8 When it became generally known a year or so ago that California was suffering severe drought, many people in water-rich parts of the country seemed obscurely gratified, and made frequent reference to Californians having to brick up their swimming pools. In fact a swimming pool requires, once it has been filled and the filter has begun its process of cleaning and recirculating the water, virtually no water, but the symbolic content of swimming pools has always been interesting: a pool is misapprehended as a trapping of affluence, real or pretended, and of a kind of hedonistic attention to the body. Actually a pool is, for many of us in the West, a symbol not of affluence but of order, of control over the uncontrollable. A pool is water, made available and useful, and is, as such, infinitely soothing to the western eye.

It is easy to forget that the only natural force over which we 9 have any control out here is water, and that only recently. In my memory California summers were characterized by the coughing in the pipes that meant the well was dry, and California winters by all-night watches on rivers about to crest, by sandbagging, by dynamite on the levees and flooding on the first floor. Even now the place is not all that hospitable to extensive settlement. As I write a fire has been burning out of control for two weeks in the ranges behind the Big Sur coast. Flash floods last night wiped out all major roads into Imperial County. I noticed this morning a hair-line crack in a living-room tile from last week's earthquake, a 4.4 I never felt. In the part of California where I now live aridity is the single most prominent feature of the climate, and I am not pleased to see, this year, cactus spreading wild to the sea. There will be days this winter when the humidity will drop to ten, seven, four. Tumbleweed will blow against my house and the sound of the rattlesnake will be duplicated a hundred times a day by dried bougainvillea drifting in my driveway. The apparent ease of California life is an illusion, and those who believe the illusion real live here in only the most temporary way. I know as well as the next person that there is considerable transcendent value in a river running wild and undammed, a river running free over granite, but I have also lived beneath such a river when it was running in flood, and gone without showers when it was running dry.

"The West begins," Bernard DeVoto wrote, "where the average 10 annual rainfall drops below twenty inches." This is maybe the best definition of the West I have ever read, and it goes a long way toward explaining my own passion for seeing the water under control, but many people I know persist in looking for psychoanalytical implications in this passion. As a matter of fact I have explored, in an amateur way, the more obvious of these implications, and come up with nothing interesting. A certain external reality remains, and resists interpretation. The West begins where the average annual rainfall drops below twenty inches. Water is important to people who do not have it, and the same is true of control. Some fifteen years ago I tore a poem by Karl Shapiro from a magazine and pinned it on my kitchen wall. This fragment of paper is now on the wall of a sixth kitchen, and crumbles a little whenever I touch it, but I keep it there for the last stanza, which has for me the power of a prayer:

> *It is raining in California, a straight rain*
> *Cleaning the heavy oranges on the bough,*
> *Filling the gardens till the gardens flow,*
> *Shining the olives, tiling the gleaming tile,*
> *Waxing the dark camellia leaves more green,*
> *Flooding the daylong valleys like the Nile.*

I thought of those lines almost constantly on the morning in Sacramento when I went to visit the California State Water Project Operations Control Center. If I had wanted to drain Quail at 10:51 that morning, I wanted, by early afternoon, to do a great deal more. I wanted to open and close the Clifton Court Forebay intake gate. I wanted to produce some power down at the San Luis Dam. I wanted to pick a pool at random on the Aqueduct and pull it down and then refill it, watching for the hydraulic jump. I wanted to put some water over the hill and I wanted to shut down all flow from the Aqueduct into the Bureau of Reclamation's Cross Valley Canal, just to see how long it would take somebody over at Reclamation to call up and complain. I stayed as long as I could and watched the system work on the big board with the lighted checkpoints. The Delta salinity report was coming in on one of the teletypes behind me. The Delta tidal report was coming in on another. The earthquake board, which has been desensitized to sound its alarm (a beeping tone for Southern California, a high-pitched tone for the north) only for those earthquakes which register at least 3.0 on the Richter Scale, was silent. I had no further business in this room and yet I wanted to stay the day. I wanted to be the one, that day, who was shining the olives, filling the gardens, and flooding the daylong valleys like the Nile. I want it still.

Carl Sagan
The Quest for
Extraterrestrial Intelligence

Winner of the Pulitzer Prize for Dragons of Eden (1977), Carl
Sagan is director of the Laboratory for Planetary Studies and
Duncan Professor of Astronomy at Cornell University. Sagan has
received medals from NASA for his contributions to the Mariner,
Viking, and Voyager expeditions to the planets, and he has
become a familiar face to viewers of PBS television as a result of
his popular "Cosmos" series. A New Yorker, born in 1933, Sagan
was trained in astronomy at the University of Chicago. He is a
former editor of Icarus, an international journal of solar system
studies, and the author of over four hundred scientific and popular
articles and more than a dozen books, including Intelligent Life in
the Universe (1963), The Cosmic Connection (1973), Murmurs of
Earth (1977), and Cosmos (1980). "The Quest for Extraterrestrial
Intelligence" is reprinted from Broca's Brain (1979), a collection of
essays on the romance of science.

> Now the Sirens have a still more fatal weapon than their
> song, namely their silence . . . Someone might possibly
> have escaped from their singing; but from their silence,
> certainly never.
>
> —FRANZ KAFKA
> *Parables*

Through all of our history we have pondered the stars and
mused whether humanity is unique or if, somewhere else in
the dark of the night sky, there are other beings who con-
template and wonder as we do, fellow thinkers in the cosmos.
Such beings might view themselves and the universe differently. Somewhere else there might be very exotic biologies and
technologies and societies. In a cosmic setting vast and old
beyond ordinary human understanding, we are a little lonely;
and we ponder the ultimate significance, if any, of our tiny

but exquisite blue planet. The search for extraterrestrial intelligence is the search for a generally acceptable cosmic context for the human species. In the deepest sense, the search for extraterrestrial intelligence is a search for ourselves.

In the last few years—in one-millionth the lifetime of our species on this planet—we have achieved an extraordinary technological capability which enables us to seek out unimaginably distant civilizations even if they are no more advanced than we. That capability is called radio astronomy and involves single radio telescopes, collections or arrays of radio telescopes, sensitive radio detectors, advanced computers for processing received data, and the imagination and skill of dedicated scientists. Radio astronomy has in the last decade opened a new window on the physical universe. It may also, if we are wise enough to make the effort, cast a profound light on the biological universe.

Some scientists working on the question of extraterrestrial intelligence, myself among them, have attempted to estimate the number of advanced technical civilizations—defined operationally as societies capable of radio astronomy—in the Milky Way Galaxy. Such estimates are little better than guesses. They require assigning numerical values to quantities such as the numbers and ages of stars; the abundance of planetary systems and the likelihood of the origin of life, which we know less well; and the probability of the evolution of intelligent life and the lifetime of technical civilizations, about which we know very little indeed.

When we do the arithmetic, the sorts of numbers we come up with are, characteristically, around a million technical civilizations. A million civilizations is a breathtakingly large number, and it is exhilarating to imagine the diversity, lifestyles and commerce of those million worlds. But the Milky Way Galaxy contains some 250 billion stars, and even with a million civilizations, less than one star in 200,000 would have a planet inhabited by an advanced civilization. Since we have little idea which stars are likely candidates, we will have to examine a very large number of them. Such considerations suggest that the quest for extraterrestrial intelligence may require a significant effort.

Despite claims about ancient astronauts and unidentified flying objects, there is no firm evidence for past visitations of the Earth by other civilizations. We are restricted to remote signaling and, of the long-distance techniques available to our technology, radio is by far the best. Radio telescopes are relatively inexpensive; radio signals travel at the speed of light, faster than which nothing can go; and the use of radio for communication is not a short-sighted or anthropocentric activity. Radio represents a large part of the electromagnetic spectrum, and any technical civilization anywhere in the Galaxy will have discovered radio early—just as in the last few centuries we have explored the entire electromagnetic spectrum from short gamma rays to very long radio waves. Advanced civilizations might very well use some other means of communication with their peers. But if they wish to communicate with backward or emerging civilizations, there are only a few obvious methods, the chief of which is radio.

The first serious attempt to listen for possible radio signals from other civilizations was carried out at the National Radio Astronomy Observatory in Greenbank, West Virginia, in 1959 and 1960. It was organized by Frank Drake, now at Cornell University, and was called Project Ozma, after the princess of the Land of Oz, a place very exotic, very distant and very difficult to reach. Drake examined two nearby stars, Epsilon Eridani and Tau Ceti, for a few weeks with negative results. Positive results would have been astonishing becaue as we have seen, even rather optimistic estimates of the number of technical civilizations in the Galaxy imply that several hundred thousand stars must be examined in order to achieve success by random stellar selection.   6

Since Project Ozma, there have been six or eight other such programs, all at a rather modest level, in the United States, Canada and the Soviet Union. All results have been negative. The total number of individual stars examined to date in this way is less than a thousand. We have performed something like one tenth of one percent of the required effort.   7

However, there are signs that much more serious efforts may be mustered in the reasonably near future. All the observing programs to date have involved quite tiny amounts of time on large telescopes, or when large amounts of time have been committed, only very small radio telescopes could be used. A comprehensive examination of the problem was recently made by a NASA committee chaired by Philip Morrison of the Massachusetts Institute of Technology. The committee identified a wide range of options, including new (and expensive) giant ground-based and spaceborne radio telescopes. It also pointed out that major progress can be   8 made at modest cost by the development of more sensitive radio receivers and of ingenious computerized data-processing systems. In the Soviet Union there is a state commission devoted to organizing a search for extraterrestrial intelligence, and the large RATAN-600 radio telescope in the Caucasus, recently completed, is devoted part-time to this effort. Hand in hand with the recent spectacular advances in radio technology, there has been a dramatic increase in the scientific and public respectability of the entire subject of extraterrestrial life. A clear sign of the new attitude is the Viking missions to Mars, which are to a significant extent dedicated to the search for life on another planet.

But along with the burgeoning dedication to a serious search, a slightly negative note has emerged which is nevertheless very interesting. A few scientists have lately asked a curious question: If extraterrestrial intelligence is abundant, why have we not already seen its manifestations? Think of the advances by our own technical civilization in the past ten thousand years and imagine such advances continued over millions or billions of years more. If only a tiny fraction of advanced civilizations are millions or billions of years more advanced than ours, why have they not produced artifacts, devices or even industrial pollution of such magnitude that we would have detected it? Why have they not restructured the entire Galaxy for their convenience?

Skeptics also ask why there is no clear evidence of extraterrestrial visits to Earth. We have already launched slow and modest interstellar spacecraft. A society more advanced than ours should be able to ply the spaces between the stars conveniently if not effortlessly. Over millions of years such societies should have established colonies, which might themselves launch interstellar expeditions. Why are they not here? The temptation is to deduce that there are at most a few advanced extraterrestrial civilizations —either because statistically we are one of the first technical civilizations to have emerged or because it is the fate of all such civilizations to destroy themselves before they are much further along than we.

It seems to me that such despair is quite premature. All such arguments depend on our correctly surmising the intentions of beings far more advanced than ourselves, and when examined more closely I think these arguments reveal a range of interesting human conceits. Why do we expect that it will be easy to recognize the manifestations of very advanced civilizations? Is our situation not closer to that of members of an isolated society in the Amazon basin, say, who lack the tools to detect the powerful international radio and television traffic that is all around them? Also, there is a wide range of incompletely understood phenomena in astronomy. Might the modulation of pulsars or the energy source of quasars, for example have a technological origin? Or perhaps there is a galactic ethic of noninterference with backward or emerging civilizations. Perhaps there is a waiting time before contact is considered appropriate, so as to give us a fair opportunity to destroy ourselves first, if we are so inclined. Perhaps all societies significantly more advanced than our own have achieved an effective personal immortality and lose the motivation for interstellar gallivanting, which may, for all we know, be a typical urge only of adolescent civilizations. Perhaps mature civilizations do not wish to pollute the cosmos. There is a very long list of such "perhapses," few of which we are in a position to evaluate with any degree of assurance.

The question of extraterrestrial civilizations seems to me entirely open. Personally, I think it far more difficult to understand a universe in which we are the only technological civilization, or one of a very few, than to conceive of a cosmos brimming over with intelligent life. Many aspects of the problem are, fortunately, amenable to experimental verification. We can search for planets of other stars, seek simple forms of life on such nearby planets as Mars, and perform more extensive laboratory studies on the chemistry of the origin of life. We can investigate more deeply the evolution of organisms and societies. The problem cries out for a long-term, open-minded, systematic search, with nature as the only arbiter of what is or is not likely.   [12]

If there are a million technical civilizations in the Milky Way   [13]
Galaxy, the average separation between civilizations is about 300 light-years. Since a light-year is the distance that light travels in one year (a little under 6 trillion miles), this implies that the one-way transit time for an interstellar communication from the nearest civilization is some 300 years. The time for a query and a response would be 600 years. This is the reason that interstellar dialogues are much less likely—particularly around the time of first contact—than interstellar monologues. At first sight, it seems remarkably selfless that a civilization might broadcast radio mes-

sages with no hope of knowing, at least in the immediate future, whether they have been received and what the response to them might be. But human beings often perform very similar actions as, for example, burying time capsules to be recovered by future generations, or even writing books, composing music and creating art intended for posterity. A civilization that had been aided by the receipt of such a message in its past might wish similarly to benefit other emerging technical societies.

For a radio search program to succeed, the Earth must be among [14] the intended beneficiaries. If the transmitting civilization were only slightly more advanced than we are, it would possess ample radio power for interstellar communication—so much, perhaps, that the broadcasting could be delegated to relatively small groups of radio hobbyists and partisans of primitive civilizations. If an entire planetary government or an alliance of worlds carried out the project, the broadcasters could transmit to a very large number of stars, so large that a message is likely to be beamed our way, even though there may be no reason to pay special attention to our region of the sky.

It is easy to see that communication is possible, even without [15] any previous agreement or contact between transmitting and receiving civilizations. There is no difficulty in envisioning an interstellar radio message that unambiguously arises from intelligent life. A modulated signal (beep, beep-beep, beep-beep-beep . . .) comprising the numbers 1, 2, 3, 5, 7, 11, 13, 17, 19, 23, 29, 31—the first dozen prime numbers—could have only a biological origin. No prior agreement between civilizations and no precautions against Earth chauvinism are required to make this clear.

Such a message would be an announcement, or beacon, signal, [16] indicating the presence of an advanced civilization but communicating very little about its nature. The beacon signal might also note a particular frequency where the main message is to be found, or might indicate that the principal message can be found at higher time resolution at the frequency of the beacon signal. The communication of quite complex information is not very difficult, even for civilizations with extremely different biologies and social conventions. Arithmetical statements can be transmitted, some true and some false, each followed by an appropriate coded word (in dahs and dits, for example), which would transmit the ideas of true and false, concepts that many people might guess would be extremely difficult to communicate in such a context.

But by far the most promising method is to send pictures. A [17]
repeated message that is the product of two prime numbers is
clearly to be decoded as a two-dimensional array, or raster—that
is, a picture. The product of three prime numbers might be a three-
dimensional still picture or one frame of a two-dimensional motion
picture. As an example of such a message, consider an array of
zeros and ones which could be long and short beeps or tones on
two adjacent frequencies, or tones of different amplitudes, or even
signals with different radio polarizations. In 1974 such a message
was transmitted to space from the 305-meter antenna at the
Arecibo Observatory in Puerto Rico, which Cornell University
runs for the National Science Foundation. The occasion was a
ceremony marking the resurfacing of the Arecibo dish, the largest
radio/radar telescope on the planet Earth. The signal was sent to a
collection of stars called M13, a globular cluster comprising about
a million separate suns which happened to be overhead at the time
of the ceremony. Since M13 is 24,000 light-years away, the message will take 24,000 years to arrive there. If any responsive creature is listening, it will be 48,000 years before we receive a reply.
The Arecibo message was clearly intended not as a serious attempt
at interstellar communication, but rather as an indication of the
remarkable advances in terrestrial radio technology.

The decoded message says something like this: "Here is how we [18]
count from one to ten. Here are the atomic numbers of five chemical elements—hydrogen, carbon, nitrogen, oxygen and phosphorus
—that we think are interesting or important. Here are some ways
to put these atoms together: the molecules adenine, thymine,
guanine and cytosine, and a chain composed of alternating sugars
and phosphates. These molecular building blocks are in turn put
together to form a long molecule of DNA comprising about four
billion links in the chain. The molecule is a double helix. In some
way this molecule is important for the clumsy-looking creature at
the center of the message. That creature is 14 radio wavelengths,
or about 176 centimeters, high. There are about four billion of
these creatures on the third planet from our star. There are nine
planets altogether—four little ones on the inside, four big ones
toward the outside and one little one at the extremity. This message is brought to you courtesy of a radio telescope 2,430 wavelengths, or 306 meters, in diameter. Yours truly."

With many similar pictorial messages, each consistent with and [19]
corroborating the others, it is very likely that almost unambiguous

interstellar radio communication could be achieved even between two civilizations that have never met. Our immediate objective is not to send such messages because we are very young and backward; we wish to listen.

The detection of intelligent radio signals from the depths of space would approach in an experimental and scientifically rigorous manner many of the most profound questions that have concerned scientists and philosophers since prehistoric times. Such a signal would indicate that the origin of life is not an extraordinary, difficult or unlikely event. It would imply that, given billions of years for natural selection, simple forms of life evolve generally into complex and intelligent forms, as on Earth; and that such intelligent forms commonly produce an advanced technology, as has also occurred here. But it is not likely that the transmissions we receive will be from a society at our own level of technological advance. A society only a little more backward than ours will not have radio astronomy at all. The most likely case is that the message will be from a civilization far in our technological future. Thus, even before we decode such a message, we will have gained an invaluable piece of knowledge: that it is possible to avoid the dangers of the period through which we are now passing. [20]

There are some who look on our global problems here on Earth —at our vast national antagonisms, our nuclear arsenals, our growing populations, the disparity between the poor and the affluent, shortages of food and resources, and our inadvertent alterations of the natural environment—and conclude that we live in a system that has suddenly become unstable, a system that is destined soon to collapse. There are others who believe that our problems are soluble, that humanity is still in its childhood, that one day soon we will grow up. The receipt of a single message from space would show that it is possible to live through such technological adolescence: the transmitting civilization, after all, has survived. Such knowledge, it seems to me, might be worth a great price. [21]

Another likely consequence of an interstellar message is a strengthening of the bonds that join all human and other beings on our planet. The sure lesson of evolution is that organisms elsewhere must have separate evolutionary pathways; that their chemistry and biology and very likely their social organizations will be profoundly dissimilar to anything on Earth. We may well be able to communicate with them because we share a common universe [22]

—because the laws of physics and chemistry and the regularities of astronomy are universal. But they may always be, in the deepest sense, different. And in the face of this difference, the animosities that divide the people's of the Earth may wither. The differences among human beings of separate races and nationalities, religions and sexes, are likely to be insignificant compared to the differences between all human and all extraterrestrial intelligent beings.

If the message comes by radio, both transmitting and receiving   23
civilizations will have in common at least a knowledge of radio-physics. The commonality of the physical sciences is the reason that many scientists expect the messages from extraterrestrial civilizations to be decodable—probably in a slow and halting manner, but unambiguously nevertheless. No one is wise enough to predict in detail what the consequences of such a decoding will be, because no one is wise enough to understand beforehand what the nature of the message will be. Since the transmission is likely to be from a civilization far in advance of our own, stunning insights are possible in the physical, biological and social sciences, in the novel perspective of a quite different kind of intelligence. But decoding will probably be a task of years and decades.

Some have worried that a message from an advanced society   24
might make us lose faith in our own, might deprive us of the initiative to make new discoveries if it seemed that others had made those discoveries already, or might have other negative consequences. This is rather like a student dropping out of school because his teachers and textbooks are more learned than he is. We are free to ignore an interstellar message if we find it offensive. If we choose not to respond, there is no way for the transmitting civilization to determine that its message was received and understood on the tiny distant planet Earth. The translation of a radio message from the depths of space, about which we can be as slow and cautious as we wish, seems to pose few dangers to mankind; instead, it holds the greatest promise of both practical and philosophical benefits.

In particular, it is possible that among the first contents of such   25
a message may be detailed prescriptions for the avoidance of technological disaster, for a passage through adolescence to maturity. Perhaps the transmissions from advanced civilizations will describe which pathways of cultural evolution are likely to lead to the stability and longevity of an intelligent species, and which

other paths lead to stagnation or degeneration or disaster. There is, of course, no guarantee that such would be the contents of an interstellar message, but it would be foolhardy to overlook the possibility. Perhaps there are straightforward solutions, still undiscovered on Earth, to problems of food shortages, population growth, energy supplies, dwindling resources, pollution and war.

While there will surely be differences among civilizations, there may well be laws of development of civilizations which cannot be glimpsed until information is available about the evolution of many civilizations. Because of our isolation from the rest of the cosmos, we have information on the evolution of only one civilization—our own. And the most important aspect of that evolution—the future—remains closed to us. Perhaps it is not likely, but it is certainly possible that the future of human civilization depends on the receipt and decoding of interstellar messages from extraterrestrial civilizations. 26

And what if we make a long-term, dedicated search for extraterrestrial intelligence and fail? Even then we surely will not have wasted our time. We will have developed an important technology, with applications to many other aspects of our own civilization. We will have added greatly to our knowledge of the physical universe. And we will have calibrated something of the importance and uniqueness of our species, our civilization and our planet. For if intelligent life is scarce or absent elsewhere, we will have learned something significant about the rarity and value of our culture and our biological patrimony, painstakingly extracted over 4.6 billion years of tortuous evolutionary history. Such a finding will stress, as perhaps nothing else can, our responsibilities to the dangers of our time: because the most likely explanation of negative results, after a comprehensive and resourceful search, is that societies commonly destroy themselves before they are advanced enough to establish a high-power radio-transmitting service. In an interesting sense, the organization of a search for interstellar radio messages, quite apart from the outcome, is likely to have a cohesive and constructive influence on the whole of the human predicament. 27

But we will not know the outcome of such a search, much less the contents of messages from interstellar civilizations, if we do not make a serious effort to listen for signals. It may be that civilizations are divided into two great classes: those that make such an effort, achieve contact and become new members of a 28 loosely tied federation of galactic communities, and those that cannot or choose not to make such an effort, or who lack the imagination to try, and who in consequence soon decay and vanish.

It is difficult to think of another enterprise within our capability [29] and at a relatively modest cost that holds as much promise for the future of humanity.

Glossary

ABSTRACT General, having to do with essences and ideas: Liberty, truth, and beauty are abstract concepts. Most writers depend upon abstractions to some degree; however, abstractions that are not fleshed out with vivid particulars are not likely to hold a reader's interest. See CONCRETE.

ALLUSION A passing reference, especially to a work of literature. When Lindsy Van Gelder in "The Great Person-Hole Cover Debate" (Chapter 10) puts forth a "modest proposal" for using words of feminine gender wherever English traditionally uses masculine words, she has in mind Jonathan Swift's essay by that title (reprinted in "Essays for Further Reading"). This single brief reference carries the weight of Swift's entire essay behind it. Van Gelder is humorously implying that her immodest proposal (from a traditional masculine point of view) is about as likely to be adopted by staunch anti-feminists as Swift's tongue-in-cheek proposal that Ireland eat its children as a ready food supply for a poor country. Allusions, therefore, are an efficient means of enlarging the scope and implications of a statement. They work best, of course, when they refer to works most readers are likely to know.

ANALOGY A comparison that reveals a primary object or event by likening it to a secondary one, often more familiar than the first. In expository writing, analogies are used as aids to explanation and as organizing devices. In a persuasive essay, the author may argue that what is true in one case is also true in the similar case that he is advancing. An argument "by analogy" is only as strong as the terms of the analogy are similar. For examples of analogies and a discussion of their kinship with metaphors, see the introduction to Chapter 7.

APPEAL TO EMOTION, TO ETHICS, and TO REASON *See* Modes of Persuasion.

413

ARGUMENTATION *See* Persuasion.

CAUSE AND EFFECT A strategy of exposition. Writing a cause and effect essay is much like constructing a persuasive argument; it is a form of reasoning that carries the reader step by step through a proof. Instead of "proving" the validity of the author's reasoning in order to move the reader to action, however, an essay in cause and effect is concerned with analyzing why an event occurred and with tracing its consequences. See the introduction to Chapter 4 for further discussion of this strategy.

CLASSIFICATION A strategy of exposition that places an object (or person) within a group of similar objects and then focuses on the characteristics distinguishing it from others in the group. Classification is a mode of organizing an essay as well as a means of obtaining knowledge. The introduction to Chapter 2 defines this strategy in detail.

CLICHÉ A tired expression that has lost its original power to surprise because of overuse: *We came in on a wing and a prayer; The quarterback turned the tables and saved the day.*

COMPARISON AND CONTRAST A strategy of expository writing that explores the similarities and differences between two persons, places, things, or ideas. It differs from description in that it makes statements or propositions about its subjects. The introduction to Chapter 6 defines this kind of expository essay in some detail.

CONCRETE Definite, particular, capable of being perceived directly. Opposed to *abstract. Rose, Mississippi, pinch* are more concrete words than *flower, river, touch.* Five-miles-per-hour is a more concrete idea than slowness. It is a good practice, as a rule, to make your essays as concrete as possible, even when you are writing on a general topic. For example, if you are defining an ideal wife or husband, cite specific wives or husbands you have known or heard about.

CONNOTATIONS The implied meanings of a word; its overtones and associations over and above its literal, dictionary meaning. The strict meaning of *home,* for example, is "the place where one lives"; but the word connotes comfort, security, and love. The first word in each of the following pairs is the more neutral word; the second carries richer connotations: *like/adore; clothes/garb; fast/fleet; shy/coy; stout/obese; move about/skulk; interested/obsessed.* See DENOTATION.

DEDUCTION A form of logical reasoning or explaining that proceeds from general premises to specific conclusions. For example, from the general premises that all men are mortal and that Socrates is a man, we can deduce that Socrates is mortal. See the introduction to Chapter 9 for more examples.

DEDUCTIVE *See* Deduction.

DEFINITION A basic strategy of expository writing. Definitions set forth
the essential meaning or properties of a thing or idea. "Extended"
definitions enlarge upon that basic meaning by analyzing the
qualities, recalling the history, explaining the purpose, or giving
synonyms of whatever is being defined. Extended definitions
often draw upon such other strategies of exposition as classification, comparison and contrast, and process analysis. See the introduction to Chapter 5 for a full treatment of definition.

DENOTATION The basic dictionary meaning of a word without any of
its associated meanings. The denotation of *home*, for example, is
simply "the place where one lives." *See* Connotations.

DESCRIPTION One of the four traditional modes of discourse. Description appeals to the senses: it tells how a person, place, thing, or
idea looks, feels, sounds, smells, or tastes. "Scientific" description
reports these qualities; "evocative" description recreates them.
See the introduction to Chapter 8 for an extended definition of
the descriptive mode.

DICTION Word choice. Mark Twain was talking about diction when
he said that the difference between the almost right word and
the right word is the difference "between the lightning bug and
the lightning." "Standard" diction is defined by dictionaries
and other authorities as the language that educated native speakers of English use in their formal writing. Some other *Levels of
Diction* are as follows; when you find one of these labels attached
to words or phrases in your dictionary, avoid them in your own
formal writing:
  Nonstandard: Words like *ain't* that would never be used by an
    educated speaker who was trying to impress a stranger.
  Informal (or *Colloquial*): The language of conversation among
    those who write standard edited English. *I am crazy about you,
    Virginia*, is informal rather than nonstandard.
  Slang: Either the figurative language of a specialized group
    (*moll, gat, heist*) or fashionable coined words (*boondoggle,
    weirdo*) and extended meanings (*dead soldier* for an empty
    bottle; *garbage* for nonsense). Slang words often pass quickly
    into standard English or just as quickly fade away.
  Obsolete: Terms like *pantaloons* and *palfrey* (saddle horse) that
    were once standard but are no longer used.
  Regional (or *Dialectal*): For example, *remuda*, meaning a herd
    of riding horses, is used only in the Southwest.

ETYMOLOGY A word history or the practice of tracing such histories.
The modern English word *march*, for example, is derived from
the French *marcher* ("to walk"), which in turn is derived from the
Latin word *marcus* ("a hammer"). The etymological definition

of *march* is thus "to walk with a measured tread, like the rhythmic pounding of a hammer." In most dictionaries, the derivation, or etymology, of a word is explained in parentheses or brackets before the first definition is given.

EXPOSITION One of the four modes of discourse. Expository writing is informative writing. It explains or gives directions. All the items in this glossary are written in the expository mode; and most of the practical prose that you write in the coming years will be— e.g., papers and examinations, job applications, business reports, insurance claims, your last will and testament. See the Introduction for a discussion of how exposition is related to the other modes of discourse.

EXPOSITORY *See* Exposition.

FIGURES OF SPEECH Colorful words and phrases used in a nonliteral sense. Some of the most common figures of speech are:

Simile: A stated comparison, usually with *like* or *as: He stood like a rock.*

Metaphor: A comparison that equates two objects without the use of a stated connecting word: *Throughout the battle, Sergeant Phillips was a rock.*

Metonymy: The use of one word or name in place of another commonly associated with it. *The White House* [for the president] *awarded the sergeant a medal.*

Personification: Assigning human traits to nonhuman objects: *The very walls have ears.*

Hyperbole: Conscious exaggeration: *The mountain reached to the sky.*

Understatement: The opposite of hyperbole, a conscious playing down: *After forty days of climbing the mountain, we felt that we had made a start.*

Rhetorical Question: A question to which the author either expects no answer or answers himself: *Why climb the mountain? Because it is there.*

HYPERBOLE Exaggeration. *See* Figures of Speech.

INDUCTION A form of logical reasoning or explaining that proceeds from specific examples to general principles. As a rule, an inductive argument is only as valid as its examples are representative. See the introduction to Chapter 9.

INDUCTIVE *See* Induction.

IRONY An ironic statement implies a way of looking at the subject that is different (not necessarily opposite) from the stated way. For example, when Russell Baker writes in "A Nice Place to Visit" (Chapter 6) that Toronto "seems hopelessly bogged down in civilization," what he implies is that New Yorkers define "civilization" in an uncivilized way. His apparent attack on Canadian manners is really a swipe at American ill-manneredness. We should be bogged down in such crudity, he is saying. Irony of situation, as opposed to *verbal* irony, occurs when events in real life or in a narrative turn out differently than the characters or people had expected. It was ironic that Hitler, with his dream of world domination, committed suicide in the end.

METAPHOR A direct comparison that identifies one thing with another. *See* Figures of Speech.

MODES OF DISCOURSE Means or forms of writing or speaking. The four traditional modes of discourse are Narration, Exposition, Description, and Persuasion. This book is organized around these four modes. Chapter 1 gives examples of narration. Exposition is explained in Chapters 2–7; description, in Chapter 8; and persuasion (and argumentation), in Chapters 9 and 10.

MODES OF PERSUASION There are three traditional modes (or means) of persuading an audience to action or belief: the appeal to reason, the appeal to emotion, and the appeal to ethics. When applying the first of these, a writer convinces the reader by the force of logic; he or she constructs an argument which the reader finds to be correct or valid. When appealing to emotion, the writer tries to excite in the reader the same emotions the writer felt upon first considering the proposition he or she is advancing or some other emotion that will dispose the reader to accept that proposition. The appeal to ethics is an appeal to the reader's sense of what constitutes upright behavior. The writer convinces the reader that the writer is a good person who deserves to be heeded because of his or her admirable character. See the introductions to Chapters 9 and 10 for detailed discussions of these three modes.

NARRATION One of the four traditional modes of discourse. An accounting of actions and events that have befallen someone or something. Because narration is essentially story-telling, it is the mode most often used in fiction; however, it is also an important element in nonfictional writing and speaking. The opening of Lincoln's Gettysburg Address, for example, is in the narrative mode: "Fourscore and seven years ago our fathers brought forth on this continent a new nation. . . ."

PERSON The aspect of grammar that describes the person speaking, spoken to, or spoken about in a sentence or paragraph. There are three persons: first (I or we), second (you), and third (he, she, it, and they). *See also* Point of View.

PERSONIFICATION Attributing human characteristics to the nonhuman. *See* Figures of Speech.

PERSUASION The art of moving an audience to action or belief. According to traditional definitions, a writer can persuade a reader in one of three ways: by appealing to his or her reason, emotions, or sense of ethics. (*See* Modes of Persuasion.) *Argumentation*, as the term is understood in this book, is the form of persuasion that emphasizes the first of these appeals. An argument may be more concerned with pursuing a line of reasoning or stating the issued raised by a problem than with inciting someone to action. Nevertheless, an argument must persuade us that what it says is not only true but worthwhile; it must move us to believe if not to act. For a full explanation of persuasion and argumentation, see the introductions to Chapters 9 and 10.

PERSUASIVE ARGUMENT *See* Persuasion.

PLOT An aspect of narrative. Plot is the sequence of events in a story. It therefore has to do with actions rather than ideas.

POINT OF VIEW The vantage from which a story is told or an account given. Point of view is often described according to the grammatical person of a narrative. An "I" narrative, for example, is told from the "first person" point of view. A narrative that refers to "he" or "she" is told from the "third person" point of view. If the speaker of a third-person narrative seems to know everything about his or her subject, including their thoughts, the point of view is also "omniscient"; if the speaker's knowledge is incomplete, the point of view is third-person "limited." Sometimes point of view is described simply by characterizing the speaker of an essay. David E. Dubber's "Crossing the Bar on a Fiberglas Pole," for example, is told from the point of view of a dedicated college athlete as he arches over the horizontal bar in a pole-vaulting competition.

PROCESS ANALYSIS A form of expository writing that breaks a process into its component operations or that gives directions. Most "How To" essays are essays in process analysis: how to grow cotton; how to operate a fork lift; how to avoid shark bite. Process analyses are usually divided into stages or steps arranged in chronological order. They differ from narratives in that they tell *how* something functions rather than *what* happens to something or someone. See the introduction to Chapter 3 for further discussion of this expository technique.

RHETORIC The art of using language effectively in speech and in writing. The term originally belonged to oratory, and it implies the presence of both a speaker (or writer) and a listener (or reader). This book is a collection of the rhetorical techniques and strategies that some successful writers have found helpful for communicating effectively with an audience.

RHETORICAL QUESTION A question that is really a statement. *See* Figures of Speech.

SATIRE A form of writing that attacks a person or practice in hopes of improving either. For example, in "A Modest Proposal" ("Essays For Further Reading"), Jonathan Swift satirizes the materialism that had reduced his native Ireland to extreme poverty. His intent was to point out the greed of even his poorest countrymen and thereby shame them all into looking out for the public welfare instead of exploiting the country's last resources. This desire to correct vices and follies distinguishes *satire* from *sarcasm*, which is intended primarily to wound. *See also* Irony.

SATIRIZE *See* Satire.

SIMILE A comparison that likens one thing to another. *See* Figures of Speech.

SLANG Popular language that often originates in the speech of a particular group or subculture. *See* Diction.

SYNTAX The interrelationship among words. In the sentence, *The police chased the woman who had beaten her dog,* the phrase *the woman who had beaten her dog* is the "direct object." This term describes the syntax of the phrase because it defines the function of the phrase within the context of the entire sentence. In a larger sense, syntax refers to the total network of relationships, including meanings, among words in a discourse.

TENSE The time aspect of verbs. In the sentence, *He took the money and ran,* the past-tense forms indicate that the taking and running occurred at an earlier time than the writer's telling about those actions. There are six basic tenses in English: past, present, future, and the perfect forms of these three: past perfect, present perfect, and future perfect. (Here "perfect" means completed. An action in the future perfect—*He will have left,* for example—will be completed in the future before another stated future action: *He will have left before the police arrive.*) In writing, it is a good idea not to switch tenses unnecessarily. If you start an essay in the past tense, stick to that tense unless the sense of your remarks requires a change: *He took the money, but the police will catch him.*

TONE An author's revealed attitude toward his subject or audience: sympathy, longing, amusement, shock, sarcasm—the range is endless. When analyzing the tone of a passage, consider what quality of voice you should assume for reading it aloud. Woody Allen's "Slang Origins" (Chapter 5), for example, should sound slightly high-pitched and nasal, like the words of an absent-minded pedant reading a lecture with a "dead pan" expression of the sort Allen himself often wears on the screen.

TOPIC SENTENCE The sentence in a paragraph that comes closest to stating the topic of the paragraph as a whole. The topic sentence is often the first sentence, but it may appear anywhere in the paragraph. Some paragraphs do not have clear-cut topic sentences, especially if they function chiefly to link preceding paragraphs with those to follow.

TRANSITION   The act of passing from one topic (or aspect of a topic) to another; the word, phrase, sentence, or paragraph that accomplishes such a passage. For an excellent example, see Alexander Petrunkevitch's "Intelligence vs. Instinct" in "Paragraphs for Analysis." Polished transitions are necessary if an essay is to be carefully organized and developed.

UNDERSTATEMENT   A verbal playing down or softening for humorous or ironic effect. See Figures of Speech.

Acknowledgments Continued